MAN OF NO PROPERTY

Mary

Man of No Property
An Autobiography (Volume Two)

C. S. Andrews

Our freedom must be had at all hazards. If the men of property will not help us they must fall; we will free ourselves by the aid of that large and respectable class of the community — the men of no property.

THEOBALD WOLFE TONE
Journal: March 1796

THE MERCIER PRESS
DUBLIN and CORK

The Mercier Press Limited, 4 Bridge Street, Cork
24 Lower Abbey Street, Dublin 1

First Published 1982

ISBN 0 85342 680 5

490395/920|AND

In Memory of Mary

The author and publishers would like to thank the *Irish Press* and the *Irish Times* for use of their photographs and Ruth Brandt for permission to use the drawing of Frederick Weckler.

Contents

Foreword

I have already written in *Dublin Made Me* an account of my childhood, boyhood and early manhood as recollected in my seventies. That account covered my memories almost to my twenty-third birthday.

In it I said my reactions to the events, people and incidents described were largely based on emotion and enthusiasm. I tried to recall these events and people as I saw them at the time. I did not always succeed in this as it was sometimes impossible to prevent my mature experience obtruding into the narrative. In these further recollections written in my late seventies, the weight of years compel me to write or comment on the experiences of my life as they are now imprinted on me.

I write largely from memory, as I did in my earlier book *Dublin Made Me*. I again disclaim any intention of writing an historical account of the period, even of those events in public life in which this time I played a significant role. To quote Montaigne: 'I desire therein to be viewed as I appear in mine own genuine, simple, and ordinary manner without study and artifice: for it is myself I paint. My defects are therein to be read to the life and my imperfections and my natural form as far as public reverence hath permitted me.'

I cannot pretend to have discarded my emotionalism — that is a part of my genetic inheritance — but I entered the period of my life with which this book begins with the emotionalism tempered by an acquired capacity to cast a cold eye on life, on death; but I did not pass by. I am conscious of the ineluctable frailty of the human condition. I am even more conscious of the impossibility of the interpretation of human motives. If I suggest in the narrative that men act thus and thus for this reason or that I do so in the awareness of being possibly quite wrong in my interpretation, but it is how these motives and actions appear to me now.

C. S. Andrews
7 October 1982

Acknowledgements

I wish to acknowledge the assistance I got from the semi-state companies with which I was associated in my working life: Bord Fáilte, the Electricity Supply Board, Bord na Móna, Córas Iompair Éireann, Radio Telefís Éireann, and the Institute of Public Administration. I am grateful to Alf Mac Lochlainn of the National Library who was always ready to help with information and comment and to my friend Brian Walsh who kindly read the completed draft and made many suggestions. My thanks are due to Mona Campbell who typed the manuscript. I am deeply indebted to Rev. P. Tuohy, who indexed the book. But above all, I am indebted to my friend and former colleague, C. B. Murphy, who edited the manuscript as it was being produced and without whose help I do not think the book would ever have been completed. Finally, I thank my wife Joyce whose wit and wisdom helped me over many of my periods of discouragement.

1

Aftermath of the Civil War

In the spring of 1924 I was released from internment where I had been held for a year since the end of the Civil War in what was then the Irish Free State. I was a little over twenty-two years of age.

I did not need to put pen to paper to list the assets and liabilities with which I faced the future. I am sure that I knew them. My greatest asset was my home and parents; my mother ran a creamery shop in Terenure over which we lived, my father had a small auctioneering business in Capel Street. They were prosperous businesses in a modest way. Whatever material success they attained my parents did not change their modest but very comfortable way of life. My brother, Patrick, had joined the Free State civil service while I was away from home. This fact had not been mentioned to me in my letters from home lest he be penalised because of my anti-government activites. His job added to the family income. Since he was my only and very much younger brother and we had no sister I was the only one to be provided for. As our parents' lives were totally devoted to the welfare of their two children I felt enveloped in a cocoon of security than which no one can have a greater asset.

I had what I think was a good if academically undistinguished secondary education, thanks to the Christian Brothers. They had encouraged in me a natural curiosity, a taste for literature and a deep interest in the history of Europe and Ireland. I was interested in the theatre and the theory of drama. I liked paintings. I was, for my age and circumstances, unusually well informed even though the only intellectual equipment with which I was endowed was an exceptionally good memory. I had attended university for two terms before my career there was interrupted by arrest and imprisonment by the British. Two terms were not very long but they were sufficient to give me a taste of the pleasures of university life though not a mature appreciation of the value of higher education. Not to have been to a university is often a source of regret, sometimes of very bitter regret, to those who have had very successful careers in business or politics or the public service.

Whatever one asserts about the use of force for political ends, its morality and stupidity, it is nevertheless true to say that, in the popular estimate of any nation, volunteer soldiers who have seen active service enjoy greater esteem than any other section of the community. I had fought in the Black and Tan War and in the Civil War. By the standards of most wars the amount of fighting I did was trivial but nonetheless it was enough to earn me the chrism of combat. I had travelled on foot through most of Leinster, Munster and three of the Ulster counties. I knew most of the leaders of the IRA and I had acquired friends all over the country through my travels and through my prison associations. I received gratefully the open handed hospitality of rural Ireland. It was unusual for someone so much a product of the pavement to have the good luck to have visited the homes of so many people outside his native environment. I was indifferent to possessions of any kind except books of which I had accumulated a small collection. I was ambitious to the extent that I did not want to form part of a congeries of clerks totting up columns of figures day in day out. Considering the low base line from which I was starting this aim did not seem unattainable even allowing for the unprivileged position in which we Republicans found ourselves at the end of the Civil War.

I was good at games, particularly at football, handball and swimming. I had played from time to time cricket, hockey and at one stage billiards and snooker. I was a good shot with a rifle but at targets only; I disliked killing wild things. I had fished in the Rivers Dodder and Liffey for trout with worms and flies; I did not regard fish as being in the same category as birds or animals.

Those were my assets. My principal liability was a feeling of self-consciousness — at times literally painful — arising from my ungainly build and unprepossessing facial appearance. From this flowed a compensating aggressiveness and self-assertiveness which antagonised many people. I held strong opinions on most topics of common interest at the time. I was intolerant of views with which I didn't agree. My opinions were rarely the subject of deep thought, but rather a reflection of my many and deep prejudices. I lacked the concentration necessary to be a student and an academic, which is what would have appealed to me temperamentally. I lacked the intellectual capacity to understand philosophy with which I would have liked to come to terms. I suffered from the very considerable disadvantage of never having been out of Ireland nor having met any foreigners, even Britishers, except in the army of occupation. Although even as a schoolboy I had a sceptical view of the more absurd practices and pieties of religion, I was uncomfortable about the break I had made with the church at the time of the virtual excommunication of Republicans by the hierarchy. It was a loss to me not to belong.

I was nearly totally ignorant of the usages of mixed society, despite the efforts of my mother to persuade me to attend dancing classes. At school, in the IRA and even in my short spell in the university I associated exclusively with boys and men. I was by nature impatient. I always wanted to pass on to the next thing to be done, with the result that I did nothing very thoroughly. I had difficulty in coping with even the few simple mechanical appliances that came my way. Mending a bicycle puncture sometimes resulted in my father having to buy me a new tube since as often as not the tube was ripped in my attempts to remove the tyre. I was so maladroit that my mother would not allow me to handle china. I had an unusual capacity for knocking things down. Photography and fretwork were the only hobbies I cultivated which required some measure of manual dexterity. Thus equipped I entered the world of the mid-twenties with no very clear idea of what I wanted to do to earn a living.

The defeat of the Republic had been a matter of great disappointment to me. As the climax of the Civil War was reached I had been close to the events associated with it. I saw all the devotion to the ideal of the Republic, supported by bravery, endurance and an indifference to self-interest, crumble through lack of political expertise. The leadership of the IRA (and of course its enthusiastic members like me) had become largely the victims of shibboleths of their own creation. They turned too late to de Valera, the one man who could have led them out of the political morass where they had got bogged down at the time of the 1922 Army Convention. Eventually he did succeed in using to advantage the stepping stones embedded in the Treaty settlement to open up the way for re-establishing the Republic. But from the time of his release in July 1924 until he came to power in the the Twenty-six counties there was a lapse of eight years. It seemed to me and my like an interminable period. Eaten up by bitterness and adhering to 'principle' — that fatuous word so all-pervasive and such a darkener of counsel in the story of the Republic — we wasted valuable years giving allegiance to an ineffective, and largely imaginary, underground government and army before de Valera and Seán Lemass broke with Sinn Féin and the Second Dáil to form Fianna Fáil.

During those eight years we saw the Free State administration entrenching itself and showing all signs of retaining power for ever. A mutiny in the army might have dislodged them but the government bought it off successfully. They had learned the truism that there are few problems that money will not solve. They accepted the theory that whatever economic prosperity the nation might achieve could only result from its capacity to sell our agricultural products in the British market; hence the catch cry: 'one more cow, one more sow, one more acre under the plough'. Our role in the world was to be an agricultural annex of Britain or, as some of them referred to it, the 'mainland'.

They had adopted without noticeable change the governmental institutions of Britain. The procedure in the Dáil and the processing of legislation were identical to those operating in the House of Commons, leaving aside a few details such as Black Rod. The Courts followed the same judicial practices, wigs and all. Poyning's Law was refurbished in the shape of an appeal to the Privy Council. The civil service as it existed before the Treaty had been kept undisturbed in structure and nearly intact in personnel.

Although the *Freeman's Journal* ceased publication at the end of 1924, to the satisfaction of us Republicans, the remaining Dublin dailies continued to publish the British Court Circular and as late as September 1927 the *Irish Independent* gave the Irish public the interesting information that: 'Queen Mary, who has been staying with Princess Mary and Viscount Lascelles at Goldsborough Hall since last Friday, leaves for Balmoral today. The Duke of York will leave Balmoral tomorrow when he will re-join the Duchess of York and Princess Elizabeth at Glamis Castle. The Duke and Duchess are expected to visit Edinburgh next Wednesday for the unveiling of the Scots-American War Memorial'. It also told us that 'Lord Decies is taking the waters at Vichy' — thus providing the Irish dimension.

Implicit in all this was the assumption that we were still part of the Empire. That, too, was the assumption clearly exemplified in the composition of the Senate. In fact not merely had the Free Staters adopted the British system of government but they accepted and proceeded to imitate the British social system having at its pinnacle a governor-general in lieu of a king and a senate in lieu of a house of lords. The first governor-general, Tim Healy, did not fill the role successfully. He was too old and too thoroughly despised and disliked by the mass of the people to be a centre of social attraction. Not even the most ambitious social climber would want to be 'received' by him. It was the common belief that the government had been persuaded by Lord Beaverbrook to appoint him. The vice-regal lodge was a generous reward for the man who had wrecked Parnell.

A fair argument in favour of the acceptance of the Treaty was that it would provide stepping stones to the Republic. When Michael Collins died that possibility was no longer realistic as those like Liam Tobin and Frank Thornton, his closest military collaborators found out to their cost. Tobin was relegated to the post of aide-de-camp to Tim Healy and Thornton was eased out of the army. Fortunately Thornton, unlike Tobin, had somewhere to go and he went.

The Senate consisted of sixty members, thirty of whom were to be nominated by the President of the Executive Council, W. T. Cosgrave. Cosgrave had been selected for the post for no better reason than that he was the senior survivor amongst the Free Staters of the old pre-Treaty cabinet. He had the additional cachet of having been 'out' in 1916. Cosgrave had been a publican and, like every successful Dublin publican, he had yearnings towards respectability. Ordinarily, however successful a publican had been, he could never have hoped for upper class social acceptance. But now he had arrived. Not merely was he accepted by what remained of the ascendancy but he became their well-respected patron. He had joined what Brendan Behan called 'the horse Protestants'. In his nominations to the Senate he stated without equivocation that the government 'stood absolutely on class'. His nominations, with few exceptions, consisted of members of the landed gentry or of wealthy unionists. It would have been difficult to imagine them using the stepping stones said to be embodied in the Free State charter to achieve a Republic.

The ethos of the Republican Movement before the Treaty had been egalitarian. We assumed that except for the usual tendency of tuppence-halfpenny to look down on tuppence the Irish nation in the mass was a classless society. There was no social immobility based on birth or inherited wealth. To us the make-up of the Senate was just one example of the extent the Free Staters were prepared to go to keep in step with the manners, customs and values of the British. Some of the senators were men of distinction by any standards; some had little to recommend them except wealth and the Protestant religion. Neither wealth nor religion seemed good reasons for their selection. It was wrong-headed policy to treat Protestant Irishmen differently from their fellow citizens in any circumstances. It was part of the Republican ethic that all Irishmen were equal and should be treated equally by the organs of state.

The senators, distinguished or not, had one thing in common: they were strong supporters of the Treaty and had a bitter hatred of us Republicans. The Clerk of the Senate, Donal O'Sullivan, a scholarly and priggish socialite, who refused to hang the ritual portrait of Collins in his home because Collins used bad language, wrote a well-researched history of the Senate disfigured by the partisanship of the time. Over the years Republicans of whatever kind have acquired the image of being anti-intellectual; they live, it is said, on their ignorant emotions. O'Sullivan's book, scholar though he was, is a clear statement of that point of view. As a nasty polemic directed against de Valera and all he stood for it encapsulated all the contempt for Republicans felt by him and his kind. It is not to be wondered at that Republicans were short on intellectualism since the bulk of the professional and literary class was solidly behind the Free State.

The Free Staters plunged deeper and deeper into the mire created by the Treaty. Having been out-manoeuvred by the British in the matter of the Boundary Commission they represented the betrayal as 'a damn good bargain'. Except for the damming of the Shannon and the foundation of the Electricity Supply Board — no small achievement it must be admitted — and a half-hearted attempt to start a sugar beet industry, they contributed nothing to the economic development of the country. An intense and expensive effort was made to revive the Irish language; through pedagogic inexperience the campaign had little success. It was dominated on the one hand by pedants and on the other by native speakers of rural origin and background. If in Ireland the word peasant could be used without offence the bulk of native speakers could be classified as peasants. They hardly provided the best foundation on which to base the revival of the language. Furthermore the revival effort relied too much on money and material rewards; dispensing money was not a good way to evoke patriotic enthusiasm. Nor was the effort assisted by us Republicans. As in every other project initiated by the Free Staters we opted out. Unfortunately we did nothing to promote the language ourselves. My belief is that from the time the Volunteers took the Oath of Allegiance to Dáil Éireann and became the IRA, interest in the language movement among Republicans began to decline. Certainly at the end of the Civil War it scarcely existed.

Economic depression had begun to take effect after the relative prosperity of the Great War years. What jobs the government could create, such as public works on roads and drainage schemes, went to demobilised soldiers and supporters of the Free State regime — not an unreasonable policy to be expected from the government. There was a mini-diaspora of Republicans; it is estimated that 100,000 emigrated between 1924 and 1927 — principally to the USA. It is probably from that nucleus, or their descendants, that succour has been coming to the Provos in our day.

Even though military activities had ceased the IRA organisation had not yet disintegrated and when they were released from jail many of the Army Executive went underground. On the political scene Sinn Féin — the political wing of the Republican party — continued to exist with some semblance of reality. It is true that the great Sinn Féin party taken over from Arthur Griffith had come apart after the Treaty and only a rump of the organisation remained faithful to the Republican cause, but it was a rump sufficiently strong to have ensured a surprising measure of success in the election of 1923. The party workers in that election were all older men — most of the younger members were in jail or on the run — but in the face of threats, harassments and actual physical assault, often by trigger-happy CID men, their efforts ensured that the ideals of the Republican movement did not go by default and were openly proclaimed.

Unfortunately, and contrary to what might have been expected, the return of the prisoners from the jails and internment camps did not accelerate the growth of the Republican Party, the nucleus of which had successfully survived the Civil War. In fact, there was a decline in numbers and financial resources. It became increasingly evident to the Republican leadership, and more evident to the rank and file members of the organisation, that there was no hope of attaining power and undoing the Treaty debacle while abstention from the Dáil was part of policy. In addition the Party made no effort to deal with the economic and social problems which at the time offered a fertile ground from which to draw mass support. Hence between 1924 and 1926 there was a general sense of depression among Republicans. In Dublin especially the problems of purely personal survival of those IRA men who did not emigrate left them with very little heart or enthusiasm for 'the cause'. The first evidence of a recognition of the realities came from Seán Lemass in the columns of *An Phoblacht*. He had stood as a candidate for a by-election in 1925. To everyone's surprise — that is to say to the surprise of all us Republicans — he was elected. We regarded the election as an event of no significance. We didn't dream that any consequence would flow from it nor, I think, did Seán Lemass. He was Minister for Defence in the Republican Dáil. He owed no allegiance to the Free State and, like the other members of Sinn Féin, he had no intention of taking his seat in the Dáil. In a series of articles published about this time he analysed the shortcomings of the party, the futility of pursuing its current policies and the need to concentrate on politically realisable objectives. The Lemass initiative, which later became known as the 'New Departure', caused a major furore in Sinn Féin circles. It also marked him out as a future leader and maker of party policy.

My immediate impulse following my release was to make contact with my friends. My most intimate friend, Hubert Earle, had been released from Gormanstown internment camp where he had spent nearly two years from the first week of the Civil War. My first visit was to him. I found him at eleven o'clock on a Saturday morning, unshaved and unwashed, sitting in his pyjamas playing the piano. He was in a state of depression. He had no welcome for me at all. He blamed me for persuading him to oppose the Treaty against his better judgment. At the best of times Earle was dyspeptic. To his dyspepsia had been added anxiety about the continuation of the County Council scholarship allowance which was helping to finance his university studies. He was not sure whether it would be paid or not, or if he would be able to complete his master's degree course in Chemistry.

He hoped that, having got his M.Sc., he would get a job as a junior chemist in the recently formed state laboratory. The stipulation that he would have to sign a form pledging allegiance to the Free State regime did not upset him at all. He had washed his hands of any kind of politics and had no aim beyond getting a job with a salary sufficient to support him. He once declared to me that if he got a job opening and shutting doors at £5 per week he would be satisfied; the odd thing about that statement was that he meant it. He dreaded responsibility of any kind.

My riposte to his 'door opening' pronouncement was to assert that if I was a member of a sodality I would prefer to be carrying the banner than walking in the ranks of the procession. Or if I was playing football I would prefer to be captain of the team rather than merely a right-half. It is a curious phenomenon of Irish life that, particularly in political circles, ambition is regarded as almost a dirty word. I think that if a politician is worth his salt he should be ambitious for advancement. In life there are the leaders and the led. I suppose it is a matter of temperament but to me to be the leader is much preferable to being the led.

In the IRA Company of which we were members during the Black and Tan War Earle could not be persuaded to take charge of a squad. He was a man of above average intelligence. As a chemist he had an unusual capacity to set up complicated apparatus for experimental work. Earle could easily have become a specialist in that field but he preferred the idea of opening and shutting doors. He got his M.Sc., and his job in the State Laboratory. Eventually, just before he reached the age of retirement, by the process of Buggin's Turn he became State Chemist. He was, I think, grateful that he did not have to carry the burden of the post too long.

I listened to his tirade against me and against all Republicans with amusement. I asked why, if he felt so badly about the Movement and if he thought that he had made such a mistake, he did not sign the form which would have secured his release from Gormanstown. He found it difficult to admit that he could not bring himself to 'let down his fellow prisoners', to some of whom he was very attached, particularly one Rosie Behan, who became notable in later life as the father of Brendan Behan the writer. Many years afterwards I was having a drink with Earle in a pub in Merrion Row when a big boisterous young man came in calling loudly for a large brandy and joshing the barman. Earle, who always found noise disagreeable, looked with distaste at the noisy one and to my surprise accosted him: 'Young man, are you by chance a son of Rosie Behan?' Brendan acknowledged his identity with some embarrassment and became even more disconcerted when Earle demanded: 'Will you for jaysus' sake keep your voice down; you're the dead spit of your father but you're no credit to him.'

When I felt Earle had purged his emotions sufficiently I persuaded him to shave, wash and dress himself and to come home with me to dinner. He was very welcome at our house and had already visited my parents since his release. We spent the rest of the afternoon, the evening and late into the night swapping experiences of the Civil War and the internment camps. He had no current contact or indeed information on up-to-date developments on either the IRA or Sinn Féin fronts. Nor had he much information about events in University College outside his own immediate interest. He went into the chemistry department in the mornings and worked very hard under Professor Hugh Ryan, one of the few of the staff of UCD who were Republican supporters. Earle's only diversion was singing in the choir of Rathfarnham church, which provided him with an opportunity to meet girls, of whose company he was very fond. Political attachment did not interfere with his pre-Treaty friendships. Earle also developed a taste for alcohol to which he always referred as C_2H_5OH. In his later years he used to cast scorn on the commonly held belief that one should not mix the barley with the grape, in the form of whiskey and wine, at the same drinking session. They were all C_2H_5OH to him.

In almost every respect Earle was different from me in his way of life and even in his physical appearance — I being tall and thin, he being low-sized and pudgy. Yet for years after the Civil War we spent most Saturday afternoons and evenings together, even after my marriage. We had virtually no interests in common. He read only the headlines of the newspapers. We had different tastes in books; he refused to read anything except 'whodunnits'. Our very close friendship has been a lifelong surprise to me. He was slightly older than I but much more intelligent. He had considerable musical talent and very deft hands. He presented himself very well. he had a beautiful speaking voice to which I attributed his success with women. While inclined to be irascible he was neither malicious nor offensive and he was always polite to older people. But apart from what girls he acquired from time to time he had no close friends except me. While he confided his problems to me and I could influence him in almost any way I wished, I could never take him seriously. Being a good raconteur he amused me with an endless supply of stories, mostly erotic, and tales of his amorous adventures, most of which I disbelieved.

Earle was not typical of the IRA man coming back from the wars. Generally they were not so detached from politics and the state of the country as he was nor did they feel so tolerant of the Free State and its cohorts. For my part, I would not associate with any active supporters of the government nor with anyone who was or had been in the Free State army or police force. Initially I made the mistake of thinking that everyone I met who had not taken the Republican side in the Civil War was personally hostile to me. It took me a while to realise that this was far from being the case. Most people I knew were glad to welcome us back into the community even though they might have disapproved of our beliefs and activities. The fact of having been active 'Irregulars' gave us a certain cachet among the public at large. They instinctively felt that we had staked our lives and our liberties on our beliefs.

Having dealt with Earle my next concern was to get in touch with the IRA which was still in existence though largely underground. Its headquarters was hunted for continuously by the CID and the Free State army. I had some difficulty in making a contact because locally, in Terenure and Rathfarnham, the organisation had fallen to pieces. Kenny, who was the kingpin of that area, had been forced to emigrate to England in search of work. My other principal contacts were missing: Ernie O'Malley, the hero of the Civil War, was still suffering from the effect of his war wounds and John Dowling, the director of organisation, had gone to join his brother in America for a long holiday. Finally I got in touch with my friend and schoolmate Frank Kerlin, the assistant director of intelligence. Kerlin was one of the few officers of the headquarters of the IRA who distinguished himself in the Civil War; in addition, he had escaped arrest. He took me to see Michael Carolan, the acting director of intelligence, who had his office in the house of the county librarian, Roisin Walsh, at Templeogue. I knew Carolan well — we had both taken part in the Mountjoy hunger strike in 1920. He was a Belfast man with a quiet, soft, cultured (and cultivated) voice, which makes even a Belfast accent attractive to Dubliners. Thanks to his hostess, who was a strong Republican, he had acquired the loan of the first edition of James Joyce's *Ulysses* published by the Shakespeare Press in Paris. He showed it to me with great enthusiasm, thumbing rapidly through the pages until reaching the famous Molly Bloom soliloquy on which he dwelt with shocked surprise which I knew he did not feel — nor did I. I had heard something of Joyce and had seen, rather than read, some discussion of *Ulysses* in the *New Statesman* but it had passed me by. The same could not be said of Molly Bloom. This was my first introduction to *Ulysses* which later became for me a source of entertainment and much enjoyable conversation with other Joyce enthusiasts over the years.

Kerlin and I discussed the political situation and agreed that there was no possibility of the IRA ever again becoming an effective military force. Nevertheless, the pretence went on. In July 1924 all the Civil War prisoners including de Valera had been released from jail and a full scale meeting of the IRA Executive, presided over by Dev, was held in August. The following extract from a report from the Chief-of-Staff, Frank Aiken, to the Executive gives a measure of the cloud-cuckoo land in which the leaders of the IRA appeared to be living in 1924 and which I, of course, inhabited as well:

Commission on Regulations and Organisation: For some time past GHQ staff has decided to get out a definite set of regulations regarding discipline and court-martials. A Commission has been appointed for that purpose, and will make recommendations to GHQ as soon as possible. A Commission on organisation could not have been set up to any purpose until after the Executive meeting. I suggest that this Executive should discuss the organisation of Army and say definitely whether name of unit and ranks of the officers commanding units are to be based on sizes of area or on numbers. For the work before us I believe they should be based on numbers as far as possible.

In the summer of 1924 the released IRA men were merely milling about wondering what to do next. Much of my time was spent renewing acquaintance with my family. I spent a couple of nights in Summerhill with my grandmother, making my peace with my Uncle Christy with whom I had quarrelled about the death of Michael Collins. By that time Christy had settled down, married and was rearing a family, still in Summerhill but living in premises across the street from my grandmother in number 'Forty-Two' where I had been born and spent the first nine years of my life. The dairy business had been transferred with him so that 'Forty-Two' was again a private house — really a lodging house — where my grandmother survived on the earnings of her Corinthian son, Simon, who spent all his time absorbed in horse racing and race meetings. I was delighted to see my grandmother, even though she constantly talked of death and of the wonderful reward she expected in heaven. If ever anyone had the death wish it was my grandmother. With her profound faith and considering the hardship she had endured in this life, I could well understand that anything she was likely to experience in the next would be an improvement. In the matter of religious practices — Masses, Communions, prayer, meditation and pious reading — nothing was omitted that would bring her esteem in the sight of God. On the purely human level she was kind to everyone, undertook every housekeeping task, cooking, cleaning, sewing, knitting from morning until night. She combined successfully the virtues of Martha and Mary.

She had a great welcome for me as had my reformed Uncle Christy and his new wife who was a cultivated woman. She was a dressmaker who had learned her trade in Paris. I visited the few friends I knew in the neighbourhood, including the Waldron family whom I always regarded as West British in the extreme. Waldron senior had been head porter in the Bank of Ireland. I met the only son, Leo, my contemporary and was almost incredulous to find that not merely had he served in the IRA but had been a member of the full-time Active Service Unit. He had taken a neutral stance in the Civil War, having joined the technical branch of the Department of Education. Curiously his parents had no idea of his sympathies or activities.

I made a trip by train down to Tullow to see Aunt Lily Murphy, my godmother, to whom I was devoted. Alas, I found that the economic circumstances of herself and her brother Patrick, for whom she kept house, had deteriorated. They had owned considerable house property but their only livelihood now was a small pub run by Patrick. My father always attributed their declining circumstances to their inordinate devotion to religion. Patrick's talents — he was a man of more than usual intelligence — were wasted in a bar room even if he had any interest in selling drink, which he had not. In his heart he felt that to be a publican was an unworthy occupation. He found it difficult to reconcile his conscience with the liquor trade. During the weekday evening services he turned the key in the bar door and went to church instead. As I knew from previous experience, the Rosary with innumerable little trimmings filled the half-hour immediately before bed time. Aunt Lily was just as devoted to spiritual matters as Patrick. Between them they seemed to be indifferent to the things of this world. If they had lived in India they would undoubtedly have been on the road with the begging bowl. Perhaps the customs of India do not admit of women with begging bowls but no doubt Aunt Lily would have found some alternative vocation directed towards the sal-

vation of her immortal soul. I spent a weekend with them conform-
ing to the customs of the house. I refrained from any comment on
the bishops' condemnation of those of us who had opposed the Free
State by force. The Civil War had caused Patrick and Lily deep distress; for them, who had an idealised image of Ireland as the most
Christian country in the world, fraternal strife was a disaster for
which prayer was the only remedy. Patrick and Lily Murphy were
happy people. They had all the material goods that they desired.
The expression 'consumer durable' had not then been invented but,
even if it had, it would have had no significance for them compared
with the consolations of religion which filled their lives.

2

A Circle of Friends

On returning from Tullow I had planned to go into UCD to arrange with Dr Coffey, the president, about resuming my studies — this time in agriculture — but this had to be deferred in response to a request from Carolan that I should check, in consultation with the local commanders, on the state of the IRA organisation in Counties Kildare and Meath. With some reluctance I agreed to the task. Having spent some days in Carbury with Tom Harris I was compelled to report that, so far as Kildare was concerned, the IRA was no longer viable nor was there any prospect of its revival. Michael Hilliard in Navan wasn't quite so pessimistic but his attitude was that of a young man who would never be prepared to accept defeat on any national issue; in fact the situation, as I saw it, was equally hopeless there. Having conveyed this information to headquarters I also made it known to Kerlin that I couldn't be relied upon to undertake any further missions of this kind. I had to take some steps to provide for my future and I felt that it did not lie in full membership of the IRA.

I did not resign from the IRA but I did not want to be asked to leave Dublin. I asked for and got indefinite leave. There was once a stage in my young life when I would have been prepared to spend all my time and energy in the role of a revolutionary but not any longer. Some months later I took on my last country assignment. The remains of the Republicans executed during the Civil War were handed back to their relations in October. The bodies of Liam Mellowes, Rory O'Connor, Dick Barrett and Joe McKelvey were taken to the Hardwicke Hall where they lay in state for a few days. It was noticeable that no massive crowds came to pay their last respects. With the current headquarters staff still on the run, there was a scarcity of senior IRA men available to represent GHQ at the funerals and I was asked by Carolan to stand in.

Following the ceremony at the Hardwicke Hall, Mellowes' coffin was brought to the Carmelite Church in Whitefriar Street where Mass was said before leaving for Wexford. Only a few of us followed the hearse bearing his remains to Castletown cemetery and only a few sympathisers came to the graveside for the burial. Someone said a decade of the Rosary and the mourners dispersed.

The proceedings were monitored by the CID and harassed by this show of force none of us were quite sure whether we might not be arrested or worse. The CID shot and killed John Hughes, a Republican mourner at a similar ceremony in Dundalk cemetery. We Republicans were completely at the mercy of the police. We were in fact outlaws.

But before that valediction to the IRA and while the arrangements for the resumption of my university studies were still in the air something occurred which affected my whole future life. Shortly after returning from visiting my relatives in Tullow, I was stopped on the street in Terenure by a stout, red-faced, heavy-jowled, elderly man whom I had never seen before. He asked if I was Todd Andrews. When I answered yes he said that he had heard a lot about me from some of his friends and he wondered what I was doing. I replied that I was thinking of studying for a degree in agriculture at UCD but had not fully made up my mind. At this stage he introduced himself as William O'Brien Hession and went on to say that he was in practice as a public auditor and accountant and would like to make a proposal that he thought would be of interest to me. We discussed the matter further that same evening at his home in Terenure when I learned something of his background. He was a Limerick man who had emigrated to South Africa after the Boer War and worked in the government service as an accountant until his retirement. Returning home after the First World War he had set up a practice as a public accountant in an office in O'Connell Street. He was a member of the Society of Incorporated Accountants. He questioned the wisdom of my seeking to obtain a qualification in agriculture, maintaining that there was no future in it unless there was a prospect of owning one's own farm and went on to suggest that I might take up accountancy. I told him that I had thought of that possibility but had abandoned the idea as it would involve payment of an apprenticeship fee of £200 and I was not prepared to ask my father for that not inconsiderable sum. He assured me that this was not an insurmountable obstacle. He would be prepared to give me my Articles of Apprenticeship together with £1 per week in pocket money if I agreed to work in his office. At the same time I would be free to study for a commerce degree at the university which would reduce my accountancy apprenticeship by two or three years. At the time it seemed a very attractive proposition and although I had no enthusiasm for a life spent poring over figures I thought that it might lead to a career less uncertain than the prospects offered by agriculture. I asked him for a day or two to think over his generous proposal. He agreed and then we went on to talk about the political situation. I left him refreshed, having listened to a tirade of abuse directed at the Free Staters collectively and individually which drew me sympathetically to him.

It transpired that one of the people who had spoken well of me to O'Brien Hession was a close friend of mine named Tom McMahon, a County Council engineer who had the distinction, amongst my friends, of having a job and a motor-car. Tom McMahon was still active in the IRA. He told me that O'Brien Hession was a very decent man who had supported the Republican movement both before and during the Civil War. McMahon was also able to give me some information about O'Brien Hession's auditing business which was not very large and which included Liam O'Doherty whom I knew slightly when he was O/C of the Fifth Battalion of the Dublin Brigade. I also consulted Dermot Lawlor with whose brother Fintan I had been very friendly at school. He had taken a B.Comm. degree at UCD and was working as an articled apprentice in an accountant's office. He advised me to accept O'Brien Hession's offer which, knowing the situation in the profession, he thought to be magnanimous.

Curiously, I did not discuss the proposal with my parents simply because I knew that they would agree to whatever course of action I chose to follow. Even my mother, now that I was home safely, was very proud of me; they felt that whatever I did was right. Before finally committing myself I discussed the position with Denis Coffey, the president of UCD, who gave me a very warm reception. He also felt that I would be well advised to take up O'Brien Hession's offer and was able to assure me that I would be credited with the first year's exam in commerce even though I had not done the course. This was early in June 1924. I had until October before my second year lectures in Commerce began.

I reported to O'Brien Hession's office and was introduced to Liam O'Doherty and the one other member of the staff, named McGrath. It was obvious from the start that O'Brien Hession was not a dynamic businessman. On his rare appearances at the office he made a habit of sucking peppermints in a futile attempt to stifle whiskey fumes. In practice McGrath and O'Doherty ran the business which consisted of one large and very valuable client and a number of small accounts. My worst fears were realised when I was handed sheets of figures to be checked. Boredom and terror at the prospect of a lifetime spent wrestling with figures took possession of me. Under Dermot Lawlor's tuition I had acquired some rudimentary knowledge of book-keeping and accountancy but I learned nothing of value in O'Brien Hession's office. My promised stipend of £1 a week was paid only sporadically; as often as not it was forgotten perhaps because of scarcity of funds. How McGrath and

O'Doherty fared in this respect I cannot say. Although I spent a lot of time talking to O'Doherty the discussion was always about political events in which we were equally interested and equally partisan. It became clear to me that my apprenticeship articles would not be forthcoming without exercising considerable pressure. This I was not prepared to do because within a few months I came to realise that auditing, which was the only career open to a professional accountant at that time, was not one I wished to follow. So when the College opened I bade adieu to O'Brien Hession and to the auditing profession. We parted on very good terms and continued to meet occasionally in the evenings getting off the tram in Terenure and walking home together, although for my part conversation was limited to listening to violent and mostly incoherent denunciation of W. T.Cosgrave, the head of the Free State government, for whom he had a special hatred.

In the meantime I had begun what proved to be the happiest period of my life. Most importantly for me, I met and made friends with women. I did not realise it at the time but, in fact, I had not had a normal adolescence. Amongst my multitudinous friends I had never known a girl who was more than a passing acquaintance. My boyhood and early manhood, spent as they were in all-male schools, football clubs and the IRA, had left me emotionally immature in the matter of inter-sex relations to an extent which would be incredible today but which was at that time the not uncommon experience of a man of nearly twenty-three years of age, as I was when I came home from the Civil War. On the other hand, I was far from ignorant of the argot of the physiology of sex. I knew all the slang words used to describe the human anatomy, male and female. I knew all the slang words used to describe the variations of the love-making process and the acrobatics of the marriage bed of which most Irish men and women, married or unmarried, had little practical knowledge. But I knew nothing about women beyond their home-making functions and their ability to provide some of the services required to support the IRA military operations. I knew from books the life stories of many women but they were fictional characters, the products of situations and environments remote from any which I was likely to experience. Among my fictional acquaintances were Maeve and Deirdre, Gráinne, Moll Flanders, Becky Sharp, Hedda Gebler, Anna Karenina, not to speak of Dido, Helen, Leda and the innumerable women and goddesses of the classical world whose adventures (mainly erotic) I was familiar with as a derivative of English poetry reading. But with all that literary information the feminine dimension in humanity was to me a closed book. Consequently when, in the process of picking up the threads of my life, I began to **meet** and get to know women as friends and companions, a new world was open to me. It was a world where my perceptions were sharpened, the range of my naturally curious mind extended and my social confidence marvellously improved.

In the aftermath of the Civil War we Republicans swarmed together. We had no social relations with anyone who had not been on our side, either as participants or active sympathisers, in opposition to the Treaty. We formed little coteries based on nothing more than good fellowship, a welcoming household, shared experiences, and a commonly-held Republican faith. These groups were far from being mutually exclusive but, as in any group, there were what might be called full or occasional members. I was associated with several of these groups but those with which I spent most of my leisure time tended to congregate at the home of the Lawlor family in Heytesbury Street and in a flat in Dawson Street occupied by a number of women who had been active in the Civil War.

The Lawlor family were committed Republicans. Their house in the Black and Tan days had been used as the office of the Department of Fisheries set up by Dáil Éireann. Bríd, the older of the two girls, had been a member of Cumann na mBan, and Fintan, the oldest of the boys, had been an active volunteer in the War of Independence and later in the Civil War up to the time of his arrest. He had been a classmate of mine at school and it was through him that I was introduced to the household. Fintan was one of those people who had a permanent inability to be on time. He lived literally next door to the school and yet never arrived either in the morning or in the afternoon until class had well begun. He had a remarkable mathematical talent. He had no difficulty in getting a scholarship to UCD and, at the time when I became a regular visitor to the house, had just obtained his B.Sc. degree and was studying for a master's degree in chemistry.

Men react differently to political imprisonment. For example, Earle was demoralised and expressed his frustration by pronouncing a curse on both their houses — Free State and Republican alike. Fintan also took jail badly and emerged with a total hatred of the Free State and all it stood for; anarchism would be a fair description of his beliefs to judge from his conversation. He was a little eccentric. Having discovered the newly developed attractions of radio broadcasting by use of the 'cat's whiskers', he took to staying up all night listening in to radio programmes as reception was better at night. As a result he found it difficult to concentrate on study and impossible to get up in the morning. Neither could he be relied upon to keep an appointment.

Mr and Mrs Lawlor were to me 'the salt of the earth' and the 'heart of the corn'. 'Old Mr Lawlor', as we always referred to him, was a bookbinder by trade and like so many of his kind was above average in intelligence. He had a passion for books. He had accumulated an astonishingly good collection by discriminate buying — at the cost of pennies — from the book barrows which, at that time, lined Aston's Quay and from Woods, the well-known second-hand bookshop in Aungier Street. He was a slightly built, greying man who spoke little and what little he said was plausible and worth listening to. But it was Mrs Lawlor who was the real manager and organiser of the family, working economic miracles with the earnings which at that time even so highly skilled a tradesman as a bookbinder could command. Both Bríd and Fintan had won university scholarships, as a little later did Dermot, and all completed their university studies with distinction. Bríd's degree was so good that she was offered a university teaching post but she elected to take an administrative job in Dublin Corporation which she won in open examination. At this time Dermot had just finished his Commerce degree and had begun his articles in chartered accountancy. Maureen, the youngest daughter, was a schoolgirl and there was a handicapped child. It was Mrs Lawlor who saw to it that neither her own nor her husband's personal comfort and convenience would stand in the way of what was referred to in those days as 'the betterment of the children'. She must have had her share of stress and anxiety but never showed it. To me she had the appearance of an old woman but she was always smiling and had a great natural warmth. She would never let me leave the house, however late it was, without a cup of tea, bread and butter and cake. She was always concerned with the welfare of her friends and their families. She was one of those people who had the capacity to make one feel better merely through meeting her and I met her often. I developed a deep affection for her and will remember her kindness to me always. It was families of the stamp of the Lawlors — the educated tradesmen — who formed the nucleus of the nationalist movement in Dublin which, in successive generations, came out in support of Tone, Emmet, the Young Irelanders, the Fenians and the men of 1916. Moral integrity was their great characteristic.

The other habitués of the Lawlor household were all school friends and were all at this time at university together. They all, except me, had university scholarships. We knew one another intimately and also each other's families. Besides the Lawlor brothers and myself, the regular members of the group were Danny Mulhall, Dermot McCarthy, Jack Lennon, Bert Earle and Kevin McHenry. Sometimes we were joined by Frank Kerlin, by far the brainiest of the lot, who became the youngest TD in Dáil Éireann; he died young to the great loss of the nation.

We were the children of unimportant people — the men of no property of whom Wolfe Tone spoke — who had no ambition beyond rearing their families to be educated and decent citizens. McCarthy, Dermot Lawlor and I graduated in commerce; Earle, Lennon, Fintan Lawlor and Mulhall in chemistry; McHenry in engineering. With the exception of McCarthy, who set up as a public accountant and Kerlin, whose people had a small wallpaper business, we all entered the public service.

We were typical products of University College but if we ever thought of any institution as our Alma Mater it would have been Synge Street CBS. We tended to regard UCD as a sort of high grade technical school. The Newman idea of a university as a factor in our lives and as a formative influence in shaping the national ethos was remote from our thinking. We knew nothing of Newman or of his historic contribution to higher education in Ireland which had resulted, after various mutations, in the establishment of the National University a mere twelve years before. We could not then foresee the massive and popular expansion in university education which has since taken place or the vital role which UCD and its sister colleges were to play in the production of the adminstrators and technocrats, scholars and scientists who have provided the mainspring of our national advancement.

We were not careerists. Our aim was to secure employment but we were not particularly ambitious or selective as to the nature of the job. We were lucky to be able to look ahead to a reasonable prospect of employment because so many Republican followers found it impossible to get work and many, if they were to eat, were forced to emigrate. We all, except Dermot McCarthy, finished our careers as state pensioners or in the state service. Earle became Chief State Chemist. Jack Lennon, who was the most distinguished among us academically having taken a doctorate at Oxford, was Director of Industrial Research during the Emergency and afterwards Director of the Patents Office. Fintan Lawlor was a senior member of the Institute for Industrial Research and Standards. Kevin McHenry was Assistant Chief Engineer of the Department of Posts and Telegraphs and his immediate superior was Brendan Mangan who, while not a member of our group, had been our classmate and close friend. Dermot Lawlor succeeded me as Managing Director of Bord na Móna when I became Chairman of CIE. Danny Mulhall, whom we all loved, was the least fortunate among us. Family circumstances compelled him to leave the university and seek work as a docker in Liverpool. Happily the situation improved

to the extent that he was able to return to Ireland to complete his
university studies and take his degree. When Fianna Fáil came into
power he entered the army as head of their newly formed Chemical
Corps. He died young.

We were a doubly bonded group. We had been close to one
another from early boyhood. We were dyed-in-the-wool Republicans. We held strongly to the social ethos of Republicanism in that,
with one exception, we were puritanical in outlook and behaviour.
We didn't drink. We respected women and, except for the amorous
Earle, knew nothing about them. We disapproved of any kind of
ostentation. We disapproved of the wearing of formal clothes —
tuxedos, evening or morning dress and above all silk hats. We disapproved of horse racing and everything and everyone associated
with it. We disapproved of any form of gambling. We disapproved
of golf and tennis and the plus-fours and white flannels that went
with them. We disapproved of anyone who took an interest in food.
We ate our meals in the same spirit of detachment with which we
dressed or shaved each day. Eating was accepted as an inescapable
part of the act of living but served no other purpose. We disapproved of elaborate wedding ceremonies requiring bouquets and
buttonholes, red carpets and train bearers. We disapproved of
women 'making up' or wearing jewellery. It might well be asked in
what areas our interests lay having excluded so many components
of the good life. The answer would be politics in its broadest sense.
We talked about the incidents in which we had been involved during the Black and Tan War and during the Civil War; of ambushes,
of escapes, of hunger strikes, of the internment camps and jails; of
the personalities that had come our way over these years and of
losses that had affected us intimately. We often spoke of Bobby
Bonfield who had been a popular and highly regarded member of
our class at school and had been murdered by some of W. T.
Cosgrave's bodyguard during the Civil War. Bobby had a peculiar
talent; he could imitate anyone's handwriting to perfection. If a
parent's letter had to be produced to excuse an absence from
school, Bobby could always oblige. We also talked about Paddy
Mannion, another friend and classmate of our early years, who had
left school when he was fifteen. He had been shot out of hand at
Baggot Street Bridge by a Free State murder gang. Bonfield had
been an only son. Mannion had been an only child. These deaths
were typical tragedies of the Civil War which were impossible for us
to forget.

Our political arguments were not directed to establishing the
truth; we merely asserted our very badly informed views in a loud
voice. Communism and the Russian revolution though seldom

mentioned were subjects which provoked particularly violent shouting matches. We were in the happy position that nothing we said
could insult or give mutual offence. Nor could we indulge in any
pretentions even if we wanted to. We knew each other's oddities
and abilities — physical and intellectual. We regarded ourselves as
of no particular importance in the community, nor ever likely to be.

Apart from me, none of the group were theatre-goers and none
except myself and Earle (when I bullied him into playing) had much
interest in football or indeed in any other game. We had a common,
if unusual, interest in that we were all Francophiles and looked
towards the day when we could afford to visit France. We read a lot
and argued about the latest literary discovery. Sometimes we
played cards — twenty-five, solo or Bridge —for very small stakes
visiting each other's homes ostensibly for this purpose but really for
the elaborate 'spreads' which our mothers supplied on these occasions including a variety of sandwiches, sausage rolls, apple tarts,
sponge cakes and trifles. I loathed card sessions, particularly
Bridge, and avoided them as much as possible.

At the long Easter and Whit weekends it was our practice to go
on what are now called hiking trips. On the Friday evening preceding the holiday we started from my home in Terenure and walked to
Enniskerry spending the night in the local hotel. Next morning we
got up early and set off to climb Djouce Mountain descending into
the valley of the Inchivore river which connects Lough Tay and
Lough Dan. The second night was spent at Doyle's farmhouse at
Lough Dan and the next day we crossed over to Glenmalure and on
to Roundwood where we usually stayed overnight before returning
home.

The members of this group maintained a close relationship
throughout their lives and were amused to observe each other's
changing values and standards. Within ten years we had all played
golf and tennis with varying success. We had worn black ties and
even white ties. We had joined Bridge clubs. We had sampled
alcohol and eaten out in restaurants. Some of us had developed
views on wine and how to cook steak. We had even modified our
views on cosmetics and women's dress. We had visited France.
Most of us had married. Our surrender to the bourgeois way of life
might be measured by the readiness of our acceptance of its
trappings, although I think the pejorative use of the word
'bourgeois' applies to a frame of mind rather than a style of living.

Gambling and race meetings were still taboo. Plus-fours had
gone out of fashion and I hardly think that any of us ever fell to the
level of the top hat — the nadir, in Republican eyes, of sartorial
affectation. In fairness it should be said that none of us ever got

grandiose notions about ourselves or about our families and, since we had no income apart from our salaries, none of us ever became rich and were thus relieved of the temptation to indulge in any form of ostentation. We were not status seekers in the social sense and 'status symbols' would have been meaningless to us even if the term had been invented at the time.

I think I was the first to break our self-imposed taboo on bourgeois pastimes. Jack McHenry, a slightly older family and school friend, who afterwards became President of University College, Cork, had come home for the summer holidays from Cambridge where he was studying for a post-graduate degree in physics. For want of something better to do, Jack suggested that we should play tennis on a disused back court in the college sports grounds. I had never played tennis so Jack undertook to teach me. I got interested in the game and we played for hours on end with the result that I became quite adept. I had a natural aptitude for all ball games and tennis suited me because of my height, quick eye reaction and the fact that, played at our level, it did not require much stamina.

We joined the University tennis club which meant that we had to wear white flannels. It was my first sartorial compromise with bourgeois values. I was not a very welcome addition to the club. The women members, especially the products of expensive convents, had 'notions'; they had begun to read Emily Post. A match had been arranged with University College, Galway, for which a team consisting of six men and six women was selected to play. The match was to take place in Galway and a whole series of entertainments had been arranged by Martin Mór McDonogh, the Cumann na nGaedheal TD and a big figure in Galway, in connection with the event. Donny Coyle, my classmate at school and future brother-in-law, had been pressing me for some time to visit him in Galway and had undertaken to show me around Connemara which was still unknown country to me.

As the standard of University tennis was low, I saw a chance of getting a free ticket to Galway if only I could make the team. According to the club rules, any member was entitled to challenge the number six player for his place on the team and I decided to do so. My opponent was Tommy Connolly, now one of our great constitutional lawyers, whom I succeeded in beating in the challenge game. The lady captain of the club, a snob of the highest order, who regarded me as a barbarous gunman, was deeply shocked at the prospect of my inclusion in the team, but was forced to accept the situation. She was even more shocked to discover at our first meal in the Great Southern Hotel that when eating hors d'oeuvres — incidentally the first time I had tasted this dish — I used a knife and fork instead of the bread and fork favoured in polite circles.

Apart from playing and losing a few tennis matches, I spent the few days in Galway touring Connemara with Donny Coyle. Even though I had seen similar conditions in Donegal and West Cork, the barren wasteland of Connemara, set against magnificent scenery of mountains and sea, was a revelation to me. I was glad that Tommy Connolly, whom I replaced on the team, came with the other players to Galway. Over the years I got to know him well. He was one of the brightest minds produced by UCD as well as the kindest and most entertaining of men.

Even more important for me than the predominantly male company which congregated at Lawlor's was a group of women I met and became friendly with. From time to time I dropped into the headquarters of Sinn Féin in Suffolk Street to meet old friends and exchange gossip about the movement and state of the party. Among them was Kathleen McLoughlin, a woman I had known slightly during the Truce when she worked on Emmet Dalton's staff in the liaison office in the Gresham Hotel. She was a native of Donegal and during the Civil War she had worked with a group of Cork IRA men who had been sent to Donegal to stiffen local resistance. When the Cork men were withdrawn, Kathleen and a companion, Roisin O'Doherty, a member of the well-known Derry Republican family, had come with them. They had to walk almost all the way from Donegal and on their arrival in Dublin were in a state of physical collapse. Following our meeting in Suffolk Street Kathleen invited me to tea at her flat and in time I became a frequent visitor. Never having been in a flat before I was surprised at first to find that it was so large. It was shared by Kathleen's friend, Roisin O'Doherty, and several other women among whom Mary McCarthy, who came from West Cork and was a lecturer in Irish in UCD, was the principal tenant.

Mary McCarthy was a woman in her late twenties slightly above average height with a beautifully modelled face and dark hair. She had very pale skin and wore no make-up, not even lipstick. She dressed expensively but rather severely. I recognised the quality of her clothes because, even if I knew nothing about women, as a result of my mother's preoccupation with fashion, I could not help observing and knowing something about women's dress. In my old age I still retain this minor accomplishment. Mary McCarthy spoke with a very pronounced West Cork accent — the softest voice I ever heard. Her personality induced confidences to which she listened with sympathetic understanding. Because I confused mathematical ability with intelligence, and because most of my classmates were good, some indeed brilliant, at mathematics the fact that I was by contrast innumerate had left me with a sense of intellectual inadequacy. Mary, drawing on her educational background, convinced me that there were many manifestations of intelligence apart from mathematical virtuosity. She also very flatteringly convinced me that my own low estimate of myself was not shared by the people who knew me in the movement. She was deeply interested in the Irish language and literature. When Daniel Corkery's *The Hidden Ireland* was published in 1925, she read it with enthusiasm and lent it to me. The book failed to impress me to anything like the same extent. While I was convinced of the necessity of saving the language I was rather more critical and sceptical of the virtues and achievements of Gaelic Ireland than was she or Daniel Corkery.

Although she was some years older than I was, I established an immediate rapport with Mary McCarthy. It was in no sense a *coup de foudre* but her personality had something of the same effect on me as that of another woman — Eileen O'Sullivan, afterwards wife of Donal O'Callaghan who succeeded Terence MacSwiney as Lord Mayor of Cork — whom I had encountered in the course of a long and arduous cross-country trek to join Liam Lynch, whose adjutant I was, in West Cork.

Mary, Kathleen and Roisin formed the hard core of the flat dwellers of 21 Dawson Street, although from time to time there were others who took up residence there for longer or shorter spells. Notable among them were Kid Bulfin, a daughter of William Bulfin who wrote the popular book *Rambles in Eirinn,* and a woman from Belfast named Daisy MacMackin. Daisy MacMackin was a woman of exceptional intelligence. She was petite, with striking red hair and a beautiful speaking voice. She came from a working-class family and had put herself through Queen's University by scholarship. Irish and French were her main subjects. She won a travelling scholarship to the Sorbonne and specialised in phonetics. Having developed an interest in Russian she went to Moscow where she met and married an expatriate Irishman named Breslin. She came back to Ireland to have her baby but failed to get permission to return to Russia and her husband was not allowed to leave the country. She set up as a tutor giving 'grinds' to students of the Russian language and joined the staff of Trinity College, Dublin, as a lecturer in Russian. Her intelligence and scholarship were entirely subordinated to an immense compassion for all who were poor or lonely or sick or in any way under-privileged. All the energy which might have produced a great academic career was spent in helping the lame, the halt and the blind and working to create a society which would willingly accept its obligations to the disadvantaged and to those constitutionally unable to cope with day-to-day living.

Her heart was bigger than her great intelligence.

Besides myself, several other old IRA men were habitués of the flat. Some of these men were partly on the run; despite the amnesty of September 1924, they were always liable to be re-arrested and so kept out of sight as much as possible. The regular visitors included Patrick Murray, who had been our O/C in England during the Civil War, Andy Cooney who appeared to face certain execution having taken responsibility for an attempted breakout from Mountjoy when several Free State soldiers were killed, Seán MacBride who had escaped from jail, Tom McMahon the O/C Engineers, Dublin Brigade, and George Plunkett, the eldest surviving son of Count Plunkett.

Among the occasional visitors to the flat were Seán Russell who deserves special mention because of his leading part in subsequent events of national concern. At this time he held the rank of director of munitions in the IRA. In appearance he was a curiously built man. Everything about him seemed to be square, his face, head, shoulders and hips. He reminded me of a character out of *Rossum's Universal Robots*. Even his entrance to a room was strangely theatrical. The door was very slowly pushed open and he paused on the threshold before gradually advancing into the centre of the room. He had a fixed smile which seemed to signify that he took for granted how glad everybody in the room must be to see him. He stood apart making enigmatic, unintelligible remarks. My immediate impulse was to shout to him 'For God's sake sit down and say something'. I concluded that, in fact, he had nothing to say. When, years later, he appeared as a major figure on the national scene I found it impossible to fathom how such an indifferent personality could command the respect, let alone the obedience, of any body of Irishmen. Even less easy was it to understand how a combination of men of the quality of Russell, George Plunkett and J. L. O'Donovan — all of whom I knew well, Plunkett and O'Donovan intimately — could have deceived themselves into believing, despite their lack of physical and intellectual resources, in the possibility of bringing England to her knees by declaring war on her and organising the inept bombing campaign of 1938.

There were three words which were always virtually taboo in Republican circles — peasant, bourgeois and intellectual. Theoretically we have no peasants in Ireland. No Republican would admit to being a bourgeois. Intellectual was a particularly pejorative term because it suggested falsity and pretentiousness. In fact all the women in the flat were intellectuals. They were all well read and were at home in one or other of the continental languages. They all knew Irish history well and were familiar with world history. Kid

Bulfin, who was the youngest and most sophisticated of them, had read unusually extensively. She was a typical woman of the Twenties, elegant, smoking cigarettes through a very long holder, short skirted and not sparing decolletage. It was she who introduced me to Aldous Huxley, who was just then causing much literary excitement with the publication of *Crome Yellow.* Kathleen McLoughlin, who had a degree in German, introduced me to Thomas Mann with *Buddenbrooks,* and Daisy MacMackin introduced me to Mauriac and to the poetry of Victor Hugo and Ronsard. They were all interested in the theatre and, though not dedicated attenders to the extent that I was, they had seen much of the Abbey repertoire and later the principal plays at the Gate. They had all participated in one way or another on the Republican side of the Civil War and were acquainted with most of the prominent IRA men and political personalities connected with the movement.

On reflection it does seem strange that in such a closely knit group, such as the men and women who frequented 21 Dawson Street, the issue of what would now be called Women's Liberation never arose. I regarded Mary McCarthy and her friends as being more sensitive, more understanding and generally better informed than I was. I found their company preferable to that of the men I knew and with whom I associated. They were, of course women of a quality above the average. All my life I continued to regard female companionship of that calibre as being more satisfying than the male. It has also been my experience that, allowing for their physical limitations, there is no job which women cannot perform as efficiently as men. I am only too well aware, indeed, that the great services which women gave to the Republican movement were never fully recognised nor were their capacities fully utilised. I know that my attitude in the matter was exceptional.

As well as the regular visitors to the flat many IRA men, still more or less on the run, dropped in for an occasional chat. George Gilmore, who became a founder of 'Saor Éire', Moss Twomey and Seán Hyde from Cork, Paddy Lacken, Seán Hayes and Bill Quirke from Tipperary were frequently to be met there. The conversation which ranged through books, the theatre, politics and religion was always stimulating and to me of unfailing interest. So constant and generous was the hospitality extended to us (in my case it included a full meal two or three evenings a week) that I became guilty about our failure to return it. Our hosts were, of course, all earning money whereas none of their visitors, apart from Tom McMahon, were making a penny. Nevertheless any of us could have raised sufficient cash to take them out occasionally to tea or for a show. That we never attempted to do so was a measure of our lack of *savoir vivre* and in my case due certainly to mere shyness.

It was remarkable that in spite of the warm and affectionate relationship which we established with these women, and I was particularly close to Mary McCarthy, none of us at the time except Seán MacBride developed any sentimental relationships. Seán MacBride and Kid Bulfin fell in love with one another and got married. It was unthinkable that we should make physical advances to the women. If we thought of the subject at all we assumed that they would be outraged and that we would be humiliated. It never occurred to us that perhaps the women were not all that gratified by our chivalry or that our forbearance might be interpreted as indifference to their feminine charms. If there was anything in this supposition the error was rectified several years later when the group had gone their different ways. Mary McCarthy married George Plunkett (I was her sponsor at the wedding). Roisin O'Doherty married Patrick Murray and Kathleen McLoughlin married Moss Twomey. Our forbearance was a manifestation of the puritanism which infested the Republican movement. Puritanism was not an attribute characteristic of Irish men or women but the legend of the Fianna with its high ideals — 'truth on our lips, purity in our hearts and strength in our arms' — had permeated, through the activities of the Gaelic League and the teachings of Patrick Pearse, the Volunteers of 1916 and after. In our case the Christian Brothers had reinforced the process. The sex education inflicted on us was one that took much of the joy out of living. It was an education which encouraged repression of natural instincts which, if we had not been emotionally purged by involvement in the national struggle, could have produced serious neurotic disorder.

One afternoon my mother announced that there were two ladies at the hall door who wanted to see me. They were Kathleen McLoughlin and Daisy MacMackin who had come out from town to inform me that Seán MacBride and Kid Bulfin were to be married at University Church the following morning and that a party had been arranged for eight o'clock to celebrate the event at the flat. The announcement of the wedding had come as a great surprise. It was known, of course, that Kid and Seán were, in the parlance of the time, 'doing a line' but that any of us would marry at that stage in our lives was never envisaged. The near inevitability of marriage for all of us sooner or later was never really considered.

Embarrassment and shyness prevented me from inviting the women into the house. I could not bring myself to admit openly to the existence of women friends for fear of my parents' disapproval. To my surprise this breach of hospitality provoked a lecture from my mother. What, she wanted to know, would the visitors think of us for not offering them even a cup of tea after they had gone to the trouble of coming all the way out from the city with the news? My mother, who had been born and bred in Summerhill in the centre of the city, still regarded the suburb of Terenure as in the deep country although we had lived there for most of fifteen years. Had I not been so inhibited by the constraints of my Christian Brothers' education I should have recognised that my parents were most anxious that I would have normal friendly associations with women realising, as they did, the social and psychological, not to say physical deprivations resulting from the absence of such relationships. It took me a long time to comprehend how understanding and liberal in outlook my parents were.

The party in the flat was a great success. The women had prepared a fine array of sandwiches, had baked and bought cakes and, this being a special occasion, had got in a few bottles of red wine. I think Seán MacBride brought the wine so it must have been of good quality. I had tasted alcoholic drink only once before. While on the run in Tipperary I drank several glasses of strong cider without realising that it was highly alcoholic. When I complained of feeling unwell it took a doctor to persuade me that I was, in fact, tipsy. The two glasses of wine which I drank at the party had no effect on me at all. I did not specially like the taste but neither did it upset me. The party broke up at about 2 a.m. and I prepared to walk home to Terenure. Tom McMahon who owned the only car among us — it was a bull-nosed Morris — had undertaken to drive MacBride and his best man, Tom Daly, a very well-known IRA man from Kerry, to a safe house in Sandymount where they were staying overnight. The walk to Terenure presented no difficulty to me. I made the journey to and from Dawson Street several times a week. It occurred to me however that my parents might decide to await my return before retiring for the night and would possibly get the smell of wine from my breath. My mother had a horror of drink and my father, at any time a moderate drinker, had become a teetotaller as an example to my brother and me. I asked MacBride if I could spend the night with him on the pretext that I was too tired to walk home. He agreed and the three of us, he, Tom Daly and I, shared a very large bed in his lodgings. Tony Woods, a close friend of ours who was running his father's garage, had been asked by MacBride to call with a car the following morning to take him to University Church. MacBride and Woods had spent nearly two years together in Mountjoy jail where practical jokes were one of the prisoners' major pastimes. Woods was convinced that the invitation to act as chauffeur at MacBride's wedding was yet another practical joke and failed to turn up. At that time neither telephones nor taxis were readily available with the result that we arrived at the church three-quarters of an hour late having hitched a lift. Kid Bulfin, the bride, was waiting completely unperturbed by the delay.

After the marriage, they went to live in Roebuck House — the home of Seán's mother, Madame Maud Gonne MacBride. Despite difference of age, my knees always trembled on meeting her. She always imparted to me a sense of welcome and, though I must have been of little significance to her, a feeling that I counted for something. All the stories that have been told of her beauty, charm and goodness were authentic as far I was concerned.

3

UCD in the Twenties

When I returned to college there were three objectives uppermost in my mind. I had never studied seriously before and was now determined to work hard to get my degree. I intended to do my share in whatever efforts might be made to rebuild the Republic. As playing soccer had always meant a lot to me, both as a pastime and a source of congenial friendship, I naturally rejoined the college soccer club. But the most important consequence of my return to college was one which I could not then foresee. It brought me into contact with the woman who was to become the most important factor in my life.

The commerce degree at that time had the lowest standing in Academe, below even the B.A. pass degree in Trinity College which had an exceptionally poor reputation. I remember meeting a Trinity student friend of mine, who was preparing for his final B.A. examination, in St Stephen's Green one day. The book he was reading was Lamb's *Tales from Shakespeare*. It transpired that *Macbeth* was on the course and he was making a last minute effort to master the subject matter of the play.

I got and read the syllabus of the course 'leading to a degree in commerce' and found it unexpectedly interesting and revealing. Accountancy was an important feature of the course but I saw little difficulty in coping with that thanks to Dermot Lawlor's tuition and my brief experience in O'Brien Hession's office. What really surprised and interested me was the scope given to political economy and to national economics. Neither I nor any of my friends had any knowledge of economics apart from a vague acceptance of Arthur Griffith's doctrine of national self-sufficiency without any real grasp of its implications. I welcomed this opportunity to get to closer grips with the subject. Indeed looking through the commerce curriculum as a whole, I was impressed by the range of subjects covered and was a little mystified as to why so comprehensive a course should produce a degree which was generally held in such low esteem. It seemed to me that anyone who fully absorbed the contents of the course would be reasonably well informed in economic affairs as well as in business management and organisation.

Charles Oldham was the professor of national economics. He was something of a *rara avis* in the college, a Protestant home ruler. He was the founder in 1885 of the Contemporary Club which met weekly in Lincoln Chambers to debate any subject of interest to the members. John O'Leary, W. B. Yeats and George Russell were early members and from time to time nearly everyone involved in the literary renaissance was associated with it. The characteristic of the club was freedom of thought and freedom of expression. It survived into the 1940s when it was finally extinguished by the zealots of censorship, religious triumphalism and the dominance of materialism in the national ethos.

In appearance Oldham was a wiry old man with a rugged face and closely cropped white hair with which he was well endowed even in his late sixties. He had an uncommonly loud, harsh voice which had the effect of unintentionally intimidating his classes. His accent was unmistakably Dublin but of a kind peculiar to well educated Protestants and to Catholics of second generation affluence. It is the accent which might give substance to the claim that we speak good English, if not the best in the world. Home ruler though he was, Oldham saw no economic future for Ireland except as an appendage of England. I recall a lecture in which he lamented the stoppage of emigration caused by the Great War. The events of 1916 and after were caused, in his view, by this curb on population movement in that it forced the young men, for want of something better to do, to take to the barricades. Feeling this to be a rather simplistic explanation of the rise of the Volunteer movement I stood up in class and said so. Oldham was neither abashed nor annoyed by my interruption. He heard me out and proceeded in his raucous voice and painfully humourless manner to defend his argument with a wealth of statistics. He died at the end of the 1925 university year and was succeeded by George O'Brien. The contents of O'Brien's lectures were no more inspiring than Oldham's but they differed in the manner of delivery. O'Brien had a soft, pleasant voice and his accent was the carefully imitated version of that of an English public school. A French critic said that 'style is the man'; in Dublin accent is the man. O'Brien's accent betrayed his Irish origin. His father owned a well-known hotel in Dublin much, it might be said, to O'Brien's regret; he would have preferred to have come from the landed gentry. His aspirations were reflected in his lectures. He did not regard himself as a Castle Catholic; he thought of himself as belonging to the remnants of the Castle Establishment.

Father Tom Finlay was professor of political economy. He was a priest who established his apostolate among that section of the ascendancy really concerned with improving the lot of the Irish peasant, although that word was not often used. Sir Horace Plunkett was his guru and the co-operative movement was the vineyard in which he laboured. We take strong exception to the Punch cartoon of the Irishman with the long upperlip but the truth is that this feature is very common among us and it applied particularly to Father Finlay. There is nothing discreditable about a long upperlip except for its association with the Punch cartoon. Father Finlay was an old man who spoke with an old man's voice and it was difficult to follow his lectures. But that was not really necessary because he lectured straight from the textbook — Gide's *Principles of Political Economy*. Indeed attendance at his lectures could have been dispensed with altogether except to discover, for examination purposes, whatever topic interested him particularly. His current fixation, as I recall it, was the rate of exchange as illustrated by the comparative values of the franc and the pound sterling which depended on the price of a pennyweight of gold. He felt clearly no obligation to keep abreast of developments in economic theory. The name of Keynes was never mentioned even though the *Economic Consequences of the Peace* had been long since published. The first edition of Gide's textbook came out in 1889 and the version we were using had been published before the 1914 War after which economics were never the same again.

Professor Shields who taught the commerce subjects was the keystone of the department. When Oldham died he became dean of the faculty and held the post for the remaining thirty-six years of his academic life. His appointment came as a surprise to everyone; it could have happened only because Father Finlay was too old and George O'Brien too young. Shields had an unfortunate personality. At this time he was in his middle forties, a man of medium height, regular features and grey hair. His most noticeable feature was the colour of his face which was matt grey. It was probably this, combined with his rather weak blue eyes, which produced an impression of lifelessness. He was indifferent to his sartorial appearance and did not enhance his personality by speaking through closed teeth producing a faint hiss. He never smiled and had not a suspicion of humour. In short he lacked charm.

On paper Shields had everything. A doctorate in economics from London University was no mean accomplishment. He had written two well regarded books *The Evolution of Industrial Organisation* and *The Labour Contract*. He worked extremely hard, never missed a lecture, was always on time. He made himself readily available to give counsel; his students were encouraged to seek his advice though, in fact, few did. He kept detailed records of every man and woman who graduated in commerce, followed their subsequent careers and helped them to get employment where possible. Despite his dessicated appearance, he was at one time president of the college hurling and Gaelic football club. He was an alderman of Dublin Corporation during the 'Troubles' — on what party ticket is uncertain but it was hardly Sinn Féin. As a Catholic activist he devoted much of his time to the John Bosco Boys' Club, which he founded, and to the Society of St Vincent de Paul.

With this range of activities and interests Shields might well have been expected to become a major force in the college or at least to command the respect of his own faculty and induce some enthusiasm in his students. Unfortunately he not only lacked charm but exuded a withering dullness. His colleagues despised him, perhaps because he was excessively virtuous — Aristides the Just! His students regarded him as a figure of fun though not without a certain amount of affection. He enjoyed the accolade of a nickname — everyone knew him as 'Barney' Shields. It was a pity that he so conspicuously lacked the spark. With so much to give and such willingness to give it, he could have made the faculty a fruitful and respected training ground for administrators and managers such as it became in later years.

Shields' lectures were boring though not to the same extent as his colleagues' in economics who made no attempt to hold class interest. Shields commanded attention, though in rather an odd way. He read his lecture at dictation speed directly from his book *The Evolution of Industrial Organisation* and the students were expected to take down the contents verbatim. It reminded me of the dictation classes of my early school days. The boredom induced by this procedure was more than I could stand and as Shields walked round the hall to check that everyone was recording him properly I asked to be excused on the pretext that a wrist wound had impaired my writing powers. Instead of suggesting, as one might have expected, that I should get a copy of the textbook, Shields advised me to borrow the lecture notes of someone who had done the course previously — proof, if it was needed, that the contents never varied from year to year.

Shields supplied us with long supplementary reading lists. So many books were recommended that I decided to join the library of the Royal Dublin Society. I confess that my borrowings from the library included much which was irrelevant to the commerce course but I did read some books which, if of little practical value, gave me an insight into the complexities of business management, industrial relations, trade unionism and statistical theory and the bearing these subjects could have on people's lives. As I was always interested in the history of revolutions, I also read widely on the subject of Lenin, Kerensky and the October Revolution in Russia.

By the time I had spent one year under the ferrule of Father Finlay, one under George O'Brien and two under Professor Shields I understood why commerce was derisively known as the 'Dud's Degree'.

The curriculum included lectures in commercial law which were given by Professor Arthur Clery. It was apparent that, though commercial law formed part of the course, it was not to be taken seriously. The number of lectures was few and from the start Arthur Clery gave his students to understand that there would be no penalty for non-attendance and nobody would be failed in their final examination. He had the reputation of never awarding less than 80% of the top marks in this subject.

I had known Arthur Clery since my earlier short spell in UCD. He was a frequent visitor to the sports ground in Terenure, where much of my time was spent, and he amused himself by knocking around a hurling or tennis ball. He took an interest in the athletic club but his real sporting passion was rowing. As there were no rowing facilities in the college, he tried to persuade the students to join the Dolphin Club at Ringsend but without much success. I went there once or twice to humour him but found that rowing was not my sport as I had neither the heart nor the stamina.

Arthur Clery was a Dublin man and the son of a not very successful lawyer. He was educated at the Catholic University School and at Clongowes Wood, attended the old Royal University in St Stephen's Green and became a barrister. His income was meagre even though supplemented by journalism and he was glad to accept the Chair of the Law of Property and the Law of Contracts in UCD. In 1924 he would have been in the middle forties with a close resemblance to Humpty Dumpty in appearance. A man of average height he had a very large head and a truly enormous belly. It was odd that a man of such unsuitable physical build should actually engage in rowing or athletics of any kind. He had a pleasant smile for everyone but rarely a greeting and had a habit of humming softly to himself. He spoke quietly, almost in a whisper, though I have been told that on a political platform he could shout as loudly as the next. He loved dancing and frequented the student 'hops' in the Aula Maxima, mainly as master of ceremonies it must be admitted. He persuaded me to attend one of these 'hops' but I declined his offer of an introduction to a girl who, he said, could dance on a sixpence. There was a strong streak of class consciousness in him. He remarked to me once when a woman student was acting a bit boisterously at a dance that she was behaving 'like a shopgirl'. He was a bachelor who enjoyed the company of women only if they were in a group. He had an astringent tongue. Of a fellow student, who in an American university would have been rated as the man most likely to succeed, he said to me: 'Andrews, there are two kinds of men; one who present their worst characteristics to the world and the other who present their best. He (nodding towards the man in question) is of the latter class. Beware of him.' Many years afterwards I had good reason to recall this warning.

Arthur Clery was a Gaeilgeoir. He spent many summers learning Irish in Ballingeary but never succeeded in speaking it well. He had ambitions to become a singer and had his voice trained but it was too loud for the drawing room and not good enough for the concert platform. His separatist convictions developed only with the outbreak of the First World War. When Redmond advised the Irish nationalists to join the British forces, he reacted almost violently and became an implacable supporter of Sinn Féin. Despite his Republican ideology, he was nostalgic for the old Gaelic aristocracy. He believed that his family were in the same line of descent as the Miss Clary whom Napoleon is alleged to have courted but who married Marshal Bernadotte and lived to become Queen of Sweden.

Having served as a judge in the Republican courts he was entitled to a pension under the Free State regime but refused to accept it and also refused to pay income tax. He became chairman of the college Republican Club and I saw a good deal of him in that capacity. He was always very kind to me and from time to time I was invited to tea at his lodgings. I was often pressed into accompanying him on walks around the sports ground in Terenure. It was difficult to sustain a conversation with him because of his habit of persistently lapsing into humming tunes. In the course of one of these peregrinations he suddenly broke our silence and said quite out of the blue: 'Andrews, do you know you saved my life?' Of course I had no idea to what he was referring and in my astonishment pressed hard for an explanation but he refused to be drawn on the subject.

Arthur Clery had travelled widely in Europe. Abroad he never spoke English if it could be avoided; he distrusted England and English people. When I was preparing for my first visit to the continent in 1927 he proffered me some advice about travelling abroad. He strongly urged me to read in advance whatever literature was obtainable about the destinations I planned to visit. This proved to be a most valuable piece of advice and one that I have always been at pains to follow. Life has provided me with exceptionally generous opportunities for foreign travel and I have always found it an advantage to form a clear concept of what was to be seen and what, in particular, I wanted to see. Being briefed in advance about the subject of the visit has added immeasurably to my pleasure. Arthur Clery had developed other travel theories not so universally applicable. He insisted, for example, that one should never travel in groups of three. Parties of two, four or more were admissible but in the case of a trio two people were always liable to over-rule the wishes of the third resulting in bad feelings all round. Arthur Clery died in 1932, a sad unfulfilled man. At least he had the satisfaction of seeing the downfall of Cumann na nGaedheal whom he strongly felt to have betrayed the nation. He had contributed much in an unacademic way to my education.

Lectures finished at 1 p.m. except on two days a week when there was also an afternoon class so that I had plenty of leisure time. More so indeed than most other students because, due possibly to some physiological quirk, I had long since acquired the habit of awakening at 6 a.m. The interval between waking and breakfast I filled in with reading and since I also read in bed at night before going to sleep I consumed a large amount of printed matter. Reading has always been an addiction with me; I could not sit alone for any length of time, no matter what the circumstances, without some sort of reading material to occupy my attention. I read unselectively without any real discrimination between different authors and subjects but merely to satisfy an unceasing curiosity about all human activities. If I had any dominant taste in books, it was in the field of history and biography. I gained another advantage from these early morning hours wrested from unconsciousness in that I was never pressed for time. As a compensation, for me a short afternoon nap has always been necessary to recharge the batteries and this has also become a practice of a lifetime.

I was a mature student; most of my classmates would have been four or five years my junior. I had no interest in normal student activities or in college politics. The soccer club, which I rejoined, had grown little since my previous links with it in 1919. It was being run, very much as a one-man business, by an old friend of mine, Joe McGilligan, who was then finishing his medical course. Two other students from the medical school, Paddy Drury Byrne and Matt Peppard, and a dental student named Paddy O'Brien, also survived from the 1919 era. The club had an unexpectedly large intake in 1924; it included two first year students who became lifelong friends of mine — Jerry Dempsey, afterwards chief executive of Aer Lingus, and Mick Finnegan who did pioneering work as an engineer in Bord na Móna. Despite this, the club was having difficulty in fielding a first eleven each week to take its place in the Leinster League.

We played a match, at home or away, each Saturday and on most Wednesday afternoons held field training sessions in the college sports ground at Terenure. Training was not taken seriously — it merely consisted in kicking a ball around — and it is not surprising that few of our matches were won. Nevertheless we formed a very closely knit group and remained so long after we left college. I captained the club in 1926 when we won our only trophy, the Collingwood Cup, against Queen's University, Belfast.

As a young man I enjoyed many games but became passionately devoted to soccer. In all modesty I could claim to be a better than average amateur player and might possibly have emulated my brother Patrick's achievement in reaching international ranks were it not for one fatal flaw — a lack of stamina. This never took from my enjoyment as a player or, when I was too old to be actively involved, as a supporter and devotee of the game. Dalymount Park became my spiritual home and Bohemians my heroes. Soccer is about the only physical activity in which I gained any degree of expertise. One of my more amusing fantasies is that of becoming a professional club manager and I sometimes think that I could have had a successful career in that risky occupation. I follow the fortunes of the club managers in England and other soccer playing countries with special interest.

Apart from the pleasure of the game, I got abiding satisfaction from the camaraderie of the club. Being the smallest club in the college we literally huddled together to preserve our identity and cultivate our common interest. After graduation the members dispersed throughout the world but for those of us still living in Dublin the bonds forged in those engaging years still remain intact. My only other college involvement was in the athletic union for which I was induced to act as secretary. The union consisted of representatives of the various sports clubs and was intended to co-ordinate their activities. Because the college grants were small and members' subscriptions even smaller and less predictable, individual clubs occasionally got into financial difficulties and my help was invoked to straighten out their accounts. It was not a very onerous post.

My interest in the theatre was as keen as ever and since my return from the wars I had paid quite a few visits to the Abbey mostly in the company of two old IRA friends — the brothers Ben and Gus Carty. Both became doctors and Ben became our family doctor. It was surprising to observe the transformation which had taken place in the Civil War audience. The house was invariably packed from pit to gallery. I remember having to wait a full week for tickets for the first showing of T. C. Murray's *Autumn Fire*. The emergence of O'Casey as a playwright had aroused much theatrical excitement. His first two plays *The Shadow of a Gunman* and *Juno and the Paycock* had captured the imagination of middle-class Dublin. Joxer's accent confirmed them in their sense of superiority; they enjoyed having something to look down on.

I found time to renew my friendship with Jack Plunkett with whom I had shared a billet during our internment in Newbridge. The Plunketts lived in a big house in Ballsbridge which contained an enormous garage where Jack pursued his hobby (he had no need to earn a living) of tinkering with motor-car engines. I did not know or indeed care what Jack was trying to do with the half a dozen cars and motor bikes which always lay about in various states of disassembly. But I enjoyed our discussions on political and occasionally on religious matters. There was an additional bonus to be derived from these visits to the Plunkett household. Several times I had the good fortune to be invited by Jack's father, Count Plunkett, to inspect his library which was housed in a converted coach house. I never got an opportunity to examine the shelves in detail because my attention invariably focused on his splendid collection of books on the art of the Italian renaissance. The collection contained reproductions of many of the great painters of Venice, Florence and Sienna and under the Count's guidance I was introduced to their work. His *tour d' horizon* was garnished with much entertaining comment on the lives and times of these great artists which is still vivid in my mind. To have had lessons in art history from a master such as Count Plunkett does not fall to the lot of many. Fortunately I have been given the opportunity to build on this foundation by frequenting in the course of my life many of the great galleries of Europe and America and have, I hope, made some progress in art appreciation, though at an amateurish level.

Count Plunkett had some useful hints to offer on the subject of gallery-going. A visit should never last more than two hours because from that point onwards concentration flags. Since it is futile to attempt to digest the contents of an important gallery in the time available to a tourist the best course is to select from the catalogue the items particularly worth seeing and ignore the rest. I have always followed the Count's advice to my advantage.

My life was already well supplied with interests when I met Mary Coyle in the front hall of the college in the autumn of 1925. As a schoolboy I had been on intimate terms with her brothers, Donny and Hugh. At weekends we used to go on cycling trips together around County Dublin returning to the Coyle's house in Mespil Road for tea. Under their mother's influence the boys became interested in the Abbey Theatre. They, in turn, introduced me to the

Abbey and until we left school we went there often on Saturday nights. The first of the Abbey productions I can recall — this was before the 1914 War — were *The Rising of the Moon* and *The Workhouse Ward* by Lady Gregory. Since that time until my retirement from theatre-going some years ago there was little of the regular Abbey repertoire that I had not seen. The same would probably be true of the principal productions of the Gate, the Peacock, the Lyric and the Drama League as well as the many little theatres which have mushroomed sporadically in Dublin. Interest in the theatre was only the first piece of good fortune that I derived from the Coyle family.

On visits to the Coyle household with Donny and Hugh I had met their five sisters of whom Mary was the eldest. I had never taken much notice of any of the girls (and they even less of me) until one particular Sunday in 1917 when I overheard Mary saying to a visiting cousin, Mary Nolan: 'I think we should go to the Abbey this evening to hear G.K.C.' I was genuinely surprised that a girl should speak so familiarly of Chesterton. My own knowledge of him was limited to the fact that he was an important literary figure of the time. I cannot explain the effect of Mary's remark except to say my attention was drawn to her in some magnetic way and I ceased then and there to look on her as the sister of my friends. She was, in fact, a very beautiful girl and from that moment she became, and continued to be for many years, the principal focus of my secret daydreaming — *la belle dame lointaine.*

Her father died soon afterwards and instead of going to university as planned she entered the (at that time British) civil service. Being posted to London she disappeared temporarily from my life and did not return to Dublin until 1920 to take up a post as 'lady clerk' in Guinness' brewery. Having left school I lost touch with the Coyle brothers; they went into the family tea importing business whereas I was deeply preoccupied with the IRA.

I did not see Mary again until one evening well after the Civil War when she dropped into the communal flat at 21 Dawson Street. Knowing that she had been a member of Cumann na mBan and at one time a close friend of Kevin Barry's family, I was not surprised to find her in this company. Our meeting was warm and affectionate as befitted old acquaintances who had not seen each other for a long time and had much news to exchange. By this time she had left Guinness' and was working in the family tea business. She stayed at the flat only for a short time but long enough to revive my interest and reinforce my image of her as the most beautiful woman I had ever seen. She was a little above average height with a glorious head of golden hair which emphasised the beauty of great brown eyes set widely apart. She carried herself with a striking dignity. It must have been of such a woman that Yeats wrote:

> A woman of such shining loveliness
> That men cut corn at midnight by a tress
> A little golden tress.

When we met again in the front hall of Earlsfort Terrace at the beginning of my final year at college my heart gave the conventional jump. It transpired that the Coyle firm had agreed to give her time off to attend university and like myself she was studying for a degree in commerce. From then on I was constantly on the look-out for her in the intervals between lectures but, since I was a year ahead and the timetables did not coincide, there was much frustration and disappointment before my search was finally successful. By that time I had summoned sufficient courage to recall the incident of G.K.C. and the Abbey when I had become conscious for the first time of her existence. This gave me an opportunity to mention that a new play *The White Blackbird* by Lennox Robinson — had been put on at the Abbey and to suggest very tentatively that she might like to go along with me. To my surprise the invitation was readily accepted. That was the beginning of an association which lasted until her death forty-one years later. My recollection of the play is that it was thoroughly boring but this did not matter. My mind was concentrated more on Mary than on the stage.

Mary and I had many interests in common. She was a member of the executive of Cumann na mBan and a committed Republican. During the Black and Tan period she had served as a dispatch carrier for Dick Mulcahy, the IRA Chief-of-Staff, but she was violently opposed to the Treaty. She had been arrested twice; the first time at her home when she escaped by jumping through a window. The second arrest cost her a year in Kilmainham jail and a 14-day hunger strike. The management of Guinness' where she was working at the time became aware of her Republican connection. She was not exactly dismissed but it was suggested that she should either resign or give up her militant activities which were considered to be both unladylike and unsuitable for a Guinness employee. Being only too willing to escape from what she regarded as the soul-destroying paternalism of the firm she gladly resigned. The hierarchical staff structure and the anti-social attitudes which permeated the place were offensive to her. Like so many Cumann na mBan members she was a socialist and an egalitarian. Whoever knocked at her door, rich or poor, *íseal no uasal,* was received with exactly the same degree of courtesy. She admired and supported the efforts of Big Jim Larkin to create a measure of social justice.

But her real idol was Terence MacSwiney whose *Principles of Freedom* had become her bedside book and had a great influence on her politically. She knew and liked Countess Markievicz whose socialism, I believe, encouraged the members of Cumann na mBan in their left-wing propensities.

Mary was as much a book addict as myself and a subscription to the Times Lending Library in Switzer's enabled her to keep fairly up-to-date with her reading. I, for my part, had access to the resources of the RDS library. As we both read extensively we found in books almost unlimited material for conversation. Moving as we did exclusively in Republican circles there was no occasion to indulge in social gossip because, in our estimation, all Republicans lived conspicuously virtuous lives free from the taint of scandal and proof against character assassination. This may sound like a naïve, self-righteous statement but it is true. We looked with contempt on our Free State opponents who, with the pretentions of the *nouveau riche,* had adopted a life style of which dinner parties, card parties, garden parties, dances and, of course, horse racing became the favourite ingredients. Many of them to our satisfaction succumbed to debt, drink and fornication. That too sounds priggish but it also is true. As a generality it might be said that those who took the Republican side in the Civil War were more idealistic and less concerned with *la dolce vita* than their Free State counterparts.

Among the Cumann women fashionable clothes were despised. Any form of personal embellishment was avoided. Make-up was not commonly used by Irish women in those days but it was unknown among the Cumann na mBan. When I got on familiar terms with Mary I often hinted in vain that a new hat might be exchanged with advantage for the soft felt amorphous thing she insisted on wearing. She would have looked sensational with no hat at all so strikingly lovely was her hair but for a woman to appear hatless in public at that time would, in itself, have caused a sensation. Apart from any question of propriety, however, Mary did not require make-up to emphasise her beauty.

Mary had strong views about the equality of the sexes though she would hardly have subscribed to the more extreme expressions of today's women's liberation movement. In this respect also there was no divergence between us because even then I had begun to recognise that, in all things except physical aptitudes, women were equal to men and sometimes superior in intelligence, intuition and sensitivity. But I might add an observation, based on the experience of a lifetime, that silly men of whom there are plenty are rarely quite so silly as silly women of whom there are plenty too.

The company of women is an essential element in my concept of *joie de vivre*. To understand how indispensable it can be, one has only to attend a stag party or club dinner where the absence of women is made endurable only by an abundance of alcohol.

Mary was a religious woman but it was religion rationally conditioned. On being released from jail she resumed attendance at Mass and the sacraments thanks to the facilities provided for Republican activists by the Carmelite Fathers in Whitefriar Street. Eleven o'clock Mass at Whitefriar Street became a rendezvous for the graduates of the Free State prisons many of whom congregated outside the church till Mass was over to meet old friends. In contrast to her religious convictions she was, and remained throughout her life, anti-clerical in the sense that she believed in the complete separation of church and state. She was an Erastian though unaware of it at the time.

Mary loved flowers, especially wild flowers, and having been an all-Ireland medallist in botany at school she was well informed on their names and habits. During the summer when we picnicked together on Sundays at Glenasmole, Howth, Killiney and Powerscourt, all of them places easily reachable by bus, her botanical knowledge enhanced the pleasure of these expeditions. Like myself she was a Francophile but thanks to her mother, who spoke French very well, Mary's knowledge of the language was much better than mine.

My meeting with Mary Coyle coincided with a period when I was quickly developing in emotional and intellectual maturity. I was happy and carefree with nothing to regret in my past and no concern for the future. Every morning I woke up in anticipation of another day to be enjoyed. Any income I had was received from my parents but my needs were little. Apart from college fees, I needed money only for cigarettes and tramfares, cheap seats at the theatre and cinema and an occasional book. Neither I nor my friends suffered from *angst* or any form of psychological stress. We 'identified' with nothing nor were we 'committed' to anything except our Republican convictions. We were uncomplicated. We did not examine our psyches. We envied no one, had no social aspirations to be other than what Providence made us, were content with the warmth of our present associations and friendships. We held ourselves apart from the Free State regime with all its works and pomps, that is to the extent to which the petty harassments of the authorities — in particular the attentions of the CID — permitted us to do so. They were still unwilling to let us forget that we had lost the war.

4

The Republican Club

Ernie O'Malley and Andy Cooney, recognised heroes of the Civil War, had come back to college to resume their medical studies and formed the core of a small Republican group of which I was one. It only required a casual survey of political opinion to show that Republicanism enjoyed only vestigial support among the college staff. With the exception of Professors Hugh Ryan and Arthur Clery, all the senior teaching staff were known to be associated with Cumann na nGaedheal. Indeed some of the staff were virulently anti-Republican and we believed that the attack on the Four Courts and the savagery subsequently displayed by the Free State government in the conduct of the war was mainly inspired by luminaries of the college. Among the relatively few students with Republican sympathies were two who achieved prominence in later life, Tadgh Forbes at the Bar and Frank Ryan for his association with Saor Éire and subsequent service in the Spanish Civil War. At this time they were rival candidates for the post of *Reactaire* in An Cumann Gaedhlach and were more interested in the politics of the Society than in national or international issues. Persuaded by Andy Cooney I succeeded in putting an end to the feud so that our efforts could be concentrated on the formation of an organisation to revive Republicanism in the college.

We took counsel with Phyllis Ryan who was finishing some post-graduate work in the chemistry department and was about to set up professionally as a public analyst. She was a member of a famous Republican family which had split, as so many families did, on the issue of the Treaty. Later she married Seán T. Ó Ceallaigh who became the President of Ireland. She knew every Republican graduate in the city and was in a position to enlist support for our proposal. We came to the conclusion that the formation of a Sinn Féin Cumann would not be a practicality in the college and that a loose type of organisation which would bring together students and graduates of Republican sympathies would serve our purpose best. This was the origin of the UCD Republican Club.

It has often been alleged that the UCD authorities refused to recognise the club as a college society or allow it to meet on the college premises but this was not the case. We never sought the status of a college society nor would it have been appropriate considering the nature of the organisation. It was not an exclusively student body; many of the members were graduates and notable people at that. The chairman of the club was Arthur Clery, the secretary and treasurer was Conor Maguire (known as Alec). Mrs Hanna Sheehy Skeffington was one of the most active members. I served in the capacity of general factotum.

The club's first meeting was held, thanks to Countess Plunkett, in her house in Elgin Road. It took the form of a tea party and some of us felt rather overwhelmed by the appurtenances of her drawing room and the quality of the china. The Countess was regarded as a rather eccentric old lady partly because she went around on a tricycle and also because she frequently attended in person to the repairs of her considerable house-property, arriving to the dismay of the tenants complete with trowel and mortar. I got to know her well and found her a kind and humorous woman who could laugh at her own oddities.

At that time the National University and Trinity College were each allotted three parliamentary seats. The foremost objective of the club was to ensure that, in the event of a Dáil election, candidates would be put forward representing Republican policy and would get the fullest possible support from the university electorate. Our activities were mainly directed to raising money for the election fund and for Republican charities. We held dances and whist drives in various halls throughout the city — Woolworth's café in Grafton Street, the Court Laundry Hall in Hatch Street and Mills Hall in Merrion Row. But the high point of our existence was the organisation of the famous public debate between Seán O'Casey and Mrs Sheehy Skeffington in the aftermath of the riot which disrupted the original production of The Plough and the Stars at the Abbey Theatre.

I had met Seán O'Casey once before. A woman graduate whom I knew had invited O'Casey to look around the college building in Earlsfort Terrace and she asked me to accompany them. She was a woman I did not particularly like but as she came from a good Republican family it was difficult to refuse. At this time she was stage-struck and was playing walk-on parts at the Abbey where O'Casey apparently took a liking to her. We walked together up and down the long, bare, shabby corridors of the college, looked into the council chamber and the empty lecture rooms. There was nothing one could exhibit with any sense of pride. The building was of no architectural interest and as the college was always pressed for funds it was indifferently maintained. This did not seem to bother O'Casey who was much more interested in the lady than in sight-seeing. She took on the patronising air of one introducing a member of the working class to a seat of learning. He, in turn, seemed quite willing to be patronised. It was never quite clear what purpose my presence was supposed to serve because I contributed nothing to the occasion nor did I derive any satisfaction from making O'Casey's acquaintance. To me he was an unimpressive little man and I found his constant references to his impoverished background and deprived upbringing in the slums of Dublin a source of irritation. I was unaware of his connections with the Citizens' Army and the 1916 Rising and indeed knew nothing about him at that time except that he had written two very successful Abbey plays.

Mary and I got tickets for the opening night of *The Plough and the Stars*. Like many others Mary took exception to the part of the prostitute, Rosie Redmond, and to the carrying of the Tricolour into the pub. I found nothing objectionable in the play though I thought that it fell below the high dramatic standard of *Juno*. During the next few days Mary was completely incommunicado and I was unable to contact her on the telephone at her work nor was she at home when I called. Then came the news of the violent demonstration in the theatre which disrupted the play on its fourth performance and made big newspaper headlines. We were told how Ria Mooney and Sheelagh Richards, who played Rosie Redmond and Nora Clitheroe respectively, had been pulled off the stage and how Yeats had his big moment castigating the audience for disgracing themselves again and assuring the world that this was the apotheosis of O'Casey. I was unaware of Mary's involvement in the affair until she telephoned me the following day and described, in a state of great excitement, how Sheila Humphries, Bride O'Mullane, herself and several other Cumann na mBan members had organised the protest and recounted the exchanges which had taken place between the demonstrators and the cast. They had not heard Yeats' speech having been ejected from the house by the CID, one of whom knew Mary of old and was especially rough with her. My own feeling was that opposition to the play in the form of physical violence was foolish and unwarranted.

The controversy went on for weeks. Hanna Sheehy Skeffington, who had spoken from the gallery in protest against the play but had not otherwise taken part in the demonstration, recalled the *Playboy* riots of 1907 and the public debate which Yeats had organised in defence of the *Playboy* and the freedom of the theatre. She invited O'Casey to take part in a similar debate to be held under the auspices of the UCD Republican Club at which he would be given the opportunity to justify his artistic beliefs and reply to adverse criticism. Rather to our surprise the invitation was accepted and the meeting was arranged for Mills Hall.

Mrs Skeffington, supported by Eileen McCarville, a lecturer in English at UCD and a well-known and active Republican, presented the case for the prosecution while Gabriel Fallon, the Abbey actor, and Lyle Donaghy, a lawyer and author, acted as spokesmen for O'Casey. O'Casey himself spoke very effectively in defence of the play and his theatrical philosophy and his case got a good hearing. The one violent attack on O'Casey, which came from a National School teacher whom I knew slightly, was received with evident disapproval. O'Casey emerged well from the ordeal and to my eyes seemed quite pleased with the outcome. Shortly afterwards he left for London, not because, as the popular legend has it, of his frustration at the bigotry, narrow mindedness and censoriousness of Dublin but because he had been invited to attend the London production of *Juno and the Paycock*. As he himself said, he was lionised there and enjoyed the experience so much that he never came back.

In our brief encounter I recognised the early symptoms of addiction to lionisation. I saw several of his later plays — *The Silver Tassie, Red Roses for Me, Cock-a-doodle-dandy, The Bishop's Bonfire*. They were, to a mere member of the paying audience, poor value for money. I always felt that O'Casey, deprived of the expert theatrical guidance of Lennox Robinson, had gone adrift. His autobiographical works, or such of them as I managed to wade through, left me with an impression of total affectation — a prolonged whine from a *béal bocht*. But it cannot be denied that *Juno and the Paycock* is a great play by any standard and for this, if for nothing else, O'Casey will be remembered with respect.

Of the many public figures whom I met through my connection with the Republican Club the one I remember with most admiration and affection is Mrs Sheehy Skeffington. To me at the time she seemed to be well on in years but I have never met anyone, woman or man, who combined to the same degree clarity of mind and singleness of purpose. She was also a person of great courtesy and showed much kindness to me. Her forthright manner and impatience with humbug appealed to me as most endearing characteristics. I recall that she had no great liking for Dev; in her estimation he was anti-feminist.

My work in the Republican Club also brought me into contact with Sinn Féin headquarters staff then located in Suffolk Street and with the principal actors in the drama of the shattered Republic. Some, like Bob Brennan, I already knew; he was a journalist who became organiser-in-chief of the *Irish Press* and its first general manager, and later on Irish ambassador in the USA during the Second World War. But in the mid-twenties responsibilities of this magnitude had not entered his mind. Like others who depended for their livelihood on the Sinn Féin organisation he and his family lived on very short commons. We sometimes had coffee together in Roberts' cafe in Suffolk Street and it was on one of these occasions that I got from Bob, who reflected the common feeling that the organisation was threshing about aimlessly, a hint of the possibility of a change in policy which resulted in the formation of Fianna Fáil.

The misgivings about the state of the organisation and its future were also manifest in the columns of *An Phoblacht* — the party organ — which was edited by P. J. Ruttledge. Ruttledge, a solicitor from Mayo, had an exceptional 'record' in both the pre-Truce IRA and in the Civil War. He was a highly cultivated man with a very acute mind and was regarded, with Seán Lemass and Dr James Ryan, as one of Dev's principal political advisers to the extent that Dev ever needed or took advice. Lemass was, like myself, a frequent caller at Suffolk Street on party business. I had, of course, known him since the Civil War and recently we had served together on a committee set up to reorganise the IRA which, however, did not survive its first meeting. Later on in life my activities in the public service brought me into close contact with Lemass, the begetter of so many semi-state bodies, but we were never very much in rapport. Apart from political affiliations we had no common interests.

I got to know Frank Gallagher who had edited *The Bulletin,* the principal propaganda instrument of the Republican movement during the War of Independence. Our first meeting was in Mountjoy where we were on hunger strike together in 1920. When I met him again after the Civil War he was writing a book which, in my view, best captures the spirit of that historic period — *The Four Glorious Years.* Frank's morale never failed despite our defeat in the Civil War and his long imprisonment; he always exuded buoyancy and optimism. He became the first editor of the *Irish Press* and was in charge of the Government Information Bureau during the critical years of the Second World War.

Among the Suffolk Street entourage the central personality was, of course, Dev himself. To me he was a truly Olympian figure, remote and self-contained but also good humoured and affable. Diffidence prevented me from intruding on him unduly and any conversation I had with him was casual small talk. A tall man himself, he often joked with me about my height. I had first met him while engaged in target practice with Seán MacBride and Ernie O'Malley in the Rocky Valley in the early days of the Four Courts occupation. Due to some curious transposition of memory Dev insisted that our first meeting took place somewhere in the Comeragh Mountains during the Civil War and nothing I said then or later could persuade him otherwise.

I became very friendly with Joseph Connolly. He was a northern businessman, one of the few who continued actively to support Sinn Féin after the Civil War. Of all my acquaintances in Republican circles he was the only one who showed any concern for economic policy. I actually heard him discussing the democratic programme of the First Dáil which had been long since forgotten by even the most radical among us. I found his company all the more interesting because of my own late introduction to economics. He was, of course, much older than I, a very intense and humourless little man. He subsequently became a Senator, the first to hold Cabinet rank.

It is true to say that until the split in Sinn Féin which led to the formation of Fianna Fáil not the slightest interest in social problems, such as housing, public health or unemployment, was evident in the Republican movement. It was totally preoccupied with the question of political autonomy on the naïve assumption that the solution of this issue would automatically resolve all other national problems. It was this neglect of matters of immediate practical concern together with the constraints of the abstentionist policy (making it impossible for Sinn Féin deputies to function as public representatives should in dealing with constituency problems) that caused the decline in popular support for the party. It became standard Republican practice to ignore the workings of the Dáil and stand aside from the governmental process generally. The mood of Republicanism was entirely introverted, constantly nursing its hate for the Free State administration and its agencies, the army, the police and the civil service. We had neither social nor political intercourse with them. Old friends and comrades from the pre-Treaty days were ostracised. Coming home in a tram one evening I was met by a Dáil deputy with whom I had been on very friendly terms in the British internment camp in the Curragh and who subsequently supported the Treaty. He approached me with an outstretched hand and a beaming smile saying, 'How are you Christy?' (Todd had not yet become my universal sobriquet). I told him to f— off. I wasn't going to shake hands with a Free State murderer. His embarrassment and humiliation shocked me. I immediately regretted my uncouth behaviour and indeed all my life the incident has weighed on my conscience. My reaction was all too typical of our attitude to the institutions and servants of the state though personal encounters of this unfortunate kind were usually avoided by looking the other way in the street. Of course all the bitterness was not on our side; the Staters also had their share of zealots.

My determination not to allow my studies to be interrupted by further interludes in jail was almost thwarted by an episode in which I had no wish to participate. On 11 November every year a public procession and memorial service was held in Dublin to commemorate the Irishmen who died in the First World War. I had always been of the opinion that these men had gone to war and sacrificed their lives in the same spirit of idealism that motivated the Volunteers killed at home from 1916 onwards. I believed that they had been misled into joining the British forces by leaders who had been seduced, not by bribery, but by the lifestyle and perceptions of the upperclass British with whom they associated. It seemed reasonable to me that the O's and the Mac's of Menin Gate and those who populated the war cemeteries of Europe should be remembered at home. But I did not think it reasonable that these commemorations should be transformed by the loyalists of Dublin, headed by the British Legion, into demonstrations of allegiance to 'King and Country' which is exactly what they had become.

The 1924 'Poppy Day' ceremony had been held in College Green and had provoked a violent Republican reaction. I had done my share of the brawling. When arrangements were being made for the 1925 function the police, through some aberration, directed the organisers to transfer the venue to the south end of St Stephen's Green at the junction of Leeson Street and Earlsfort Terrace. No location could have been more provocative. For a week beforehand the chemical laboratories of UCD were turned over to the manufacture of 'offensive missiles'. When on the memorial day several thousand British Legion supporters congregated at the assembly point preparations had been fully made to create disruption. Several hundred students infiltrated the crowd and when the order was given for the traditional two minutes' silence smoke and stink bombs exploded in all directions. Mutual abuse and poppy snatching led to scuffles and fistfights until eventually the students withdrew inside the college gates which were then closed by the porters. It was no part of my scheme of things to get involved in further street brawling and in joining the crowd milling around Earlsfort Terrace, I had merely intended to watch the fun. But as we moved back into the college I came face to face with a British Legionary demonstrator brandishing a revolver. I grappled with him instinctively and using the punch favoured by Dublin corner-boys, known as the Ringsend uppercut, forced him to drop the revolver — a ·38 Webley — which I brought back to the college in triumph. But my feeling of elation did not last long. I had just succeeded in dumping the gun when the president, Dr Coffey, approached me and to my genuine dismay said: 'Andrews, will you take your men away; you have done enough.' I tried to explain truthfully but unsuccessfully that they were not 'my men'. On returning to the college forecourt I found that the demonstrators had dispersed and all that remained was a squad of CID men drawn up outside the gates who, immediately on spotting me, shouted, 'That's him!' It was only then I realised that the man I had disarmed was not a member of the British Legion but of the CID and that they were now determined to get their hands both on me and the missing gun. I was far from well disposed to returning the gun to what was to me a gang of police thugs; on the other hand I had no wish to go on the run or risk the possibility of six months in jail. At that stage, Joe McGilligan, my friend and fellow soccer player, came to the rescue. His brother was the Minister for Industry and Commerce, Patrick McGilligan, who was then high in the public estimation being the political sponsor of the Shannon Scheme. Joe opened negotiations with the CID squad who were prepared to listen to him respectfully as befitted his relationship with a Government Minister. They had already arrested three of the students who were being held outside the gates awaiting a police van to convey them to the Bridewell. Joe undertook to have the gun returned provided the prisoners were released and the whole incident regarded as closed. The CID men readily agreed to this compromise. To have to admit openly in court to being disarmed by a civilian would reflect no credit on them. Moreover they probably had no wish to advertise the fact that their presence on the scene was for the purpose of protecting a pro-British demonstration with which they had little sympathy. Honour was satisfied all round. The three students who had been arrested were Seán Lavin, the Olympic runner, Tom O'Rourke, who became one of the great teachers of Irish and English at Synge Street CBS and Frank Ryan who gained on this occasion his first experience of street brawling in which he later became adept.

De Valera withdrew from Sinn Féin in 1926 and in May the first meeting of Fianna Fáil was held in the La Scala picture house. I was an enthusiastic supporter of what was known as the 'New Departure', as indeed were nearly all members of the Republican Club, the Plunketts in my circle being notable exceptions. Mary like most of her colleagues on the executive of Cumann na mBan was strongly opposed to the 'New Departure'. So strong were her feelings on the subject and so intense were our arguments that for a while it appeared that our personal relationship would be irrevocably damaged. But that did not happen. However, even to please me she could not be persuaded to come with me to the momentous meeting in the La Scala picture house where Dev launched Fianna Fáil in an atmosphere of delirious enthusiasm. Republican morale was restored.

I thought that Mary's stand was due more to her feminist principles than to her political convictions. She regarded Dev, and even more so Frank Aiken, as what nowadays would be called sexists; in this opinion I don't think she was far wrong. Had she known Seán Lemass, her misgivings about the attitude of the Fianna Fáil leadership to women's status would have been reinforced. Dev always commanded the devoted service of women but I believed, and when I got to know him well I told him so, that he never gave women sufficient recognition for their dedication. I had particularly in mind Dorothy Macardle whose monumental work *The Irish Republic* provided his historical vindication. But there were others who got just as little appreciation. We all felt, even if we didn't say it, that he imposed to an unacceptable extent on the devotion of his two private secretaries, Kathleen O'Connell and Marie O'Kelly.

The split from Sinn Féin caused very little break in personal relations between the supporters and opponents of Dev and the 'New Departure' so that, when the Dáil was dissolved and the general election was announced for June 1927 we in the Republican Club had the undivided support of all shades of Republicanism — Fianna Fáil, Sinn Féin, IRA and Cumann na mBan. The fact that the Republican Club had not been constituted as a Sinn Féin Cumann made it possible to present an unbroken Republican front in the university election and we were also fortunate that, although he did not favour the 'New Departure', Professor Arthur Clery agreed to stand as an Independent Republican. With most unexpected massive and enthusiastic support he was elected. No one was as surprised as Arthur Clery; he believed that no one loved him.

Our satisfaction in Arthur Clery's victory was increased because he took over Eoin MacNeill's Dáil seat. MacNeill's failure was received with dismay by the UCD clique who, I think, had been largely responsible for triggering off the Civil War. And I think that Eoin MacNeill had a particularly unfortunate influence on the events that followed. He had been a virulent supporter of the Treaty and was held by us to be the principal culprit of the Boundary Commission debacle. The fact is that MacNeill was unfit for and should never have participated in party politics. Having served his purpose as a figurehead in founding the Volunteers he should have retired to Academe and enhanced his reputation as a great scholar. He would have reflected credit on himself and the nation. As a politican he did neither. He was the first in a long series of Irish academics who ventured into politics and whose political careers ended in discredited failure.

Apart from my activities in the UCD Republican Club, I put a lot of effort into persuading my old IRA friends to give their support to Fianna Fáil. I recall taking Seán MacEntee to meet a group of three ex-IRA men and four ex-Cumann na mBan women in Rathfarnham for a discussion on the subject. We met on a wet winter's evening in a hut built on what was known as the Strand. The only light available was an oil lamp; we had no heat and there were several leaks in the roof — a most depressing scene for a political debate. Matters were not improved by the attitude of a couple of the women who kept insisting that in addition to 'letting down' the Republic it was wrong 'in principle' to deal with Free State murderers. These assertions were repeated like the *deilín* of an Irish jig.

The meeting in Rathfarnham had a disproportionate effect on my attitude to politics. It confirmed me in my antipathy to seeking elective office. Temperamentally I could not pay the price of solicitation and compromise which that role requires. I came away exhausted, but not so MacEntee. He listened with great patience and politeness to arguments which must have sounded as painful and frustrating to him as to me. Courtesy was one of MacEntee's strengths as a politician. He was something of a paradox and quite untypical of his senior colleagues in the Fianna Fáil party. He liked the 'good life', as it would now be called, in the sense that he enjoyed *recherché* food and was a connoisseur of good wine. He cultivated a certain style of living and liked to entertain. He was a very good-looking man and enhanced his good looks by rather dandified dress. On the other hand of all the men who held ministerial office almost permanently while Fianna Fáil was in power, he was the most accessible to the humblest IRA man and would go to endless trouble to help them to get employment or with any similar problem. There are a great many old IRA men in the country who avoided emigration thanks to the exertions of Seán MacEntee. He was also a very brave man: he was caught tunnelling not out of but into Mountjoy Jail in an attempt to mount a rescue.

Despite all these distractions, I succeeded in keeping abreast of my studies. I never missed a lecture, annotated them carefully and read beyond the call of duty. As the final examination approached I felt confident of doing well. As part of the examination we were required to write and submit an essay dealing with the nationalisation of railways. I set about this task with genuine interest though naturally without a thought as to my future association with the railway business. I went to a lot of trouble to research the subject. The principle of nationalisation was the matter chiefly at issue and my main source book was *The Case for Nationalisation* by A. Emil Davies. My personal attachment to socialism, such as it was, stemmed largely from dislike of the British capitalist system and my emotional sympathy with the objectives of the Bolshevik revolution.

I opened my essay with quotations from the Communist Manifesto. The Communist Manifesto is at any time heady stuff. It advocates, among other things, 'the forcible overthrow of the whole extant social order', 'the expropriation of landed property', 'the abolition of the right of inheritance' and 'the acquisition by the State of all means of transport'. I had given really no serious thought to these matters but to me for whom the political institutions of the Free State were completely discredited they sounded like a revelation. In any event the proposal to nationalise transport was relevant to the subject of my essay. I sought the advice of Ronnie Mortished, the Assistant Secretary of the Irish Labour Party, who was very helpful and offered some useful suggestions. He was also good enough to read the finished text and approve its contents generally before it was submitted.

Unfortunately my treatment of the subject did not appeal to Professor Shields and his fellow examiners. I did not have the wit to realise that the rhetoric of the Communist Manifesto was not merely a challenge but a deep affront to Shields' social philosophy. His thinking was conditioned by the Syllabus of Errors in which Pius X condemned the exponents of modernism, socialism and even liberalism. Recent events had reinforced his extreme conservatism. The general strike in England had taken place some months earlier and even though it had quickly collapsed resistance by the coal miners continued. Social unrest on this scale was a shattering experience for Shields and his like; the objectives of the Communist Manifesto appeared to have come dangerously close to realisation in Britain and rather too near home for comfort.

A few days before the results of the examination were announced, Shields drew me aside in the corridor and, in words of sorrow rather than of anger, took me to task about the shortcomings of my essay. He assured me that I had done very well in the set papers but owing to my poor showing in the essay section — 'the worst in the class,' he said — all I could expect was to be awarded a second-class honours degree. I was bitterly disappointed and could hardly resist the temptation to tell him what to do with his degree. I had studied hard and knew that I must have got high marks in the commerce subjects as well as in economics and accountancy. Considering the effort I had put into its composition and the fact that it had Mortished's approval I could not understand why my essay should have fared so badly, unless as a result of unfair and uncritical judgment. I still think so to this day. However, I gained one incidental bonus from the whole sorry affair. It consolidated my incipient interest in socialism and, in particular, in the events and personalities of the Russian socialist experience. I even tried to read *Das Kapital* but never succeeded in getting beyond the first twenty pages.

Some notion of the extent of 'Barney' Shields' innocent but essential goodness is shown by an incident which took place many years later. He got the idea of inviting a group of what he regarded as his more successful students to high tea at Jury's Hotel. The meal consisted of bacon, eggs and sausages but the *pièce de resistance* was a large box of sweets which was placed open in the centre of the table. The guests numbered about a dozen top managers including Jerry Dempsey, General Manager of Aer Lingus and James Beddy, Managing Director of the Industrial Credit Corporation, as well as half a dozen senior chartered accountants. At the time I was Chairman of CIE. Clearly the box of sweets was intended as a special treat for the occasion; they were a substitute for drink, of which not a drop was offered. We could hardly believe our eyes.

I never got over the disappointment of the second-class degree. Even three Honorary Degrees and about twenty years membership of the Senate of the National University were no compensation for this debacle.

5

Tourism — the Early Days

During the summer and early autumn of 1926 I enjoyed life to the full. Mary and I met almost every evening. We went to the theatre once a week, often had tea together in the Grafton picture house café followed by a film in one or other of the many city cinemas, attended whist drives organised to raise money for political causes, or occasional 'hops' (student dances) in '86', as the Convocation Hall of University College in St Stephen's Green was universally known. I played a soccer match for the college team every Saturday and trained occasionally on Wednesday afternoons. My mornings were spent in the college gossiping about the political happenings of the day, picking teams for the soccer club and dealing with the affairs of the Athletic Union.

But the time had come for me to earn my living. I had no clear idea how to set about getting a job or indeed what kind of job I wanted. I did have very definite ideas about the kind of job I did not want. Clerical work in any shape or form was distasteful to me nor, after my unfortunate experience in O'Brien Hession's office, had I any interest in professional accountancy. The declaration of loyalty to the Free State required from all its employees meant, in effect, that I was barred from the entire public service. At the time this seemed part of a deliberate policy of penalising Republicans for their part in the Civil War; in retrospect it could hardly be regarded as an unreasonable requirement. On the whole the government's attitude in this respect was less vindictive than might have been expected. Apart from a few ministers with extremist propensities, government policy seemed to be aimed at reducing political tension and inducing the Republican opposition to participate in the normal political processes, on their terms no doubt, or else to leave the country. This relative liberality of spirit did not apply to the special branch of the police force, known as the 'Criminal Investigation Department', or to sections of the army who continued to harass Republicans disgracefully.

University degrees, except in the case of the professions, had little value in the job market. Due to the activities of the ESB, electrical engineers, for example, were assured of employment and the local authority services provided openings for civil engineers though often in roles well below what their training and capacity warranted. Many of the medical graduates had to emigrate in search of employment. Apart from institutions such as the State Laboratory there were few opportunities for chemists or physicists and most science graduates were forced to turn to teaching. For arts and commerce gratuates, teaching in secondary and technical schools was virtually the only source of employment apart from clerical or administrative posts in the public service which were, of course, effectively closed to Republicans.

My first effort at job finding was farcical. I was invited by Dr Henry Kennedy who was Secretary of the White Cross, a non-political organisaton set up to help Volunteers and their families during the Black and Tan War, to apply for a vacancy in a meat packing firm owned by Sir John Keane. I knew Dr Kennedy slightly but at that time I did not foresee that his invitation to apply for the job was to be the beginning of an intense and unfortunate relationship between us. I had no idea as to the precise nature of the job but I had some previous knowledge of Sir John Keane and of the fact that he owned a bacon factory in Cappoquin dating back to my visit to the Araglin area as adjutant to Liam Lynch, the chief-of-staff of the IRA, in 1922. The IRA had requisitioned a lorry-load of bacon from the factory and had distributed it to the people of the locality who were sheltering men on the run. Passing through Araglin with Liam Lynch's party we were agreeably surprised to be served rashers for breakfast and bacon and cabbage for dinner supplied, we were told, with the compliments of Sir John Keane.

I was summoned for an interview with Sir John Keane at the Kildare Street Club. I had been in the Kildare Street Club once before when it was occupied by the IRA for a time before the Civil War but I was curious to see it again in its normal role. As it happened, the opportunity never arose because the interview took place on the steps at the entrance of the building and was in every respect a most perfunctory one. Needless to say I failed to get the job. I was deeply resentful of Sir John Keane's cavalier behaviour but was consoled by the memory of how the decent people of Araglin, not to mention Liam Lynch and myself, had eaten well for once at his expense.

I was determined not to emigrate nor was I prepared to settle for a 'life of quiet desperation'. I began to read the 'Situations Vacant' columns in the newspapers. The first advertisement which attracted my notice was one to the effect that the Irish Tourist Association had a vacancy for an organiser at £4 per week. I had never heard of the Irish Tourist Association and knew nothing of its work. My only previous acquaintance with tourism was a jocular reference to the fact that it was the principal *industry* of Switzerland. I assumed that it must have some connection with the hotel business and, in particular, with hotels in such places as Dublin or Killarney which catered for rich English visitors and where Irish men and women were employed to provide the menial rather than the managerial services. However, the word 'organiser' impressed me partly because I was conscious of my own organising ability in any field and partly because it suggested something more to my taste than mere clerical employment.

The accepted wisdom of job hunting in Ireland in those days was that it depended heavily on 'influence' and I followed the conventional route. I decided to approach Seamus Moore, a friend of mine who was Secretary of the Motor Traders' Association and had been elected a TD for Wicklow. I hot-footed down to Beechmount Avenue in Ranelagh where Moore lived with the advertisement in my pocket. Unaccustomed to callers at this early hour he was still at his breakfast and rather grumpy at this unexpected intrusion.

Seamus was a square block of a man with an unusually large head. Although he spoke with rather disconcerting gravity he gave the impression of having difficulty in suppressing a violent temper. In reply to my enquiry he admitted, rather reluctantly, to a slight acquaintance with the Secretary of the Irish Tourist Association, Jack O'Brien. Rather to his annoyance I pressed him to make contact straightaway with O'Brien, enquire about my prospects of obtaining the job and at least arrange an interview. It was now getting on for 9.30 a.m. and I suggested to Seamus that he should call on O'Brien on his way into work so that no time would be lost in staking my claim. After many protests about the inconvenience of the hour and pressure of work he agreed to do so.

I believed that the early bird catches the worm and by custom I had always been an early bird. I was also convinced that if there was something to be done it was better that it be done quickly. However Seamus Moore's intervention produced results more promptly than could have been expected. At about 5.30 p.m. that same evening he called at my house with the news that O'Brien was willing to see me about employment in the Tourist Association. O'Brien turned out to be an ex-IRA man from Ballyporeen whom I had met in the course of my travels with Liam Lynch during the Civil War and who had been one of a party that escorted us through Glennaconna to Araglin. We had also been fellow students at UCD but as he had been a clerical student he was necessarily anonymous. Moore was almost as surprised as I at the satisfactory outcome of his mission and I seemed to have risen even higher in his estimation as a result of the success of my steam-rolling tactics.

O'Brien's office was in Westland Row and I was on the doorstep at ten o'clock on the morning following Seamus Moore's initiative. In 1926 the offices of the largest organisations in the country were of the most spartan kind. In the civil service itself only officers of the highest grades were entitled to a carpet — and then a mere strip — on the floor. Rooms in civil service offices to which the public had access were notoriously untidy and ill-equipped and the state of the lavatories was deplorable. Even knowing all this, I was not prepared for the austere conditions prevailing in the head office (there were no branch offices) of the ITA. It was situated in the basement of Westland Row railway station which had been leased to the ITA at a peppercorn rent. O'Brien shared a room with a secretary and there was one other larger room in which the rest of the staff were housed. The lavatory was in a small yard outside.

O'Brien welcomed me warmly and we spent some time recalling our previous meetings, reminiscing on the Civil War and discussing the new departure in the Republican movement brought about by the formation of the Fianna Fáil party. O'Brien had a clearer recollection of me than I had of him though he was a man of unusual appearance, black-haired and black-visaged with an eagle's nose. He struck me as a man of strong personality with considerable nervous energy. He was of middle height and a year or two older than I. I liked him from the first and felt that he was a man with whom, given the opportunity, I could work harmoniously.

O'Brien gave me a brief rundown on the origin and aims of the ITA. He felt that the post of organiser was not one for which I was really suitable as it called for the training and temperament of a commercial traveller and he doubted that I had either. There was, however, a vacancy on the staff for an accountant which he would be glad to offer me. The work involved was minimal at the moment but with the growth of the organisation a proper accounts system was required. He himself had been keeping the books up to then but was anxious to concentrate on other activities such as the publication of a new travel magazine, the production of guides to holiday resorts and a drive for increased income for the Association. The salary for the post of accountant had been fixed at £3 per week by the board.

O'Brien's account of the work and objectives of the ITA did nothing to increase my respect for the tourist business which I still conceived as one operating for the benefit of foreign visitors rather than for its native Irish employees. At that time tourism was very much in its infancy and its commercial possibilities were still unexplored. I did not appreciate its value as an invisible export or its potential contribution to the national economy. I wanted a job but not one valued at £3 per week and I told O'Brien that I could not

accept it at this figure. He sympathised with my reaction and undertook to get the salary increased to £4 per week at the next board
meeting in three weeks' time. I agreed to this arrangement and duly
reported for work on the following Monday.

While glad to get a job I felt no pride or satisfaction in working in
tourist development. I thought it a shoddy business and more
associated with national mendicity than with legitimate industry.
The staff of the Association at the time of my arrival was four in all.
O'Brien's secretary was Kitty Egan, a good-looking fair-haired
young woman in her early twenties. His second-in-command was
David Barry, an old IRA man from north Cork, in whose family
house I had slept during my trek from Araglin to Ballingeary in
1922. His function was to enlist the moral and financial support of
the hotels and travel agencies and, in particular, to persuade the
local authorities to contribute to the funds of the Association by
striking a rate for the promotion of tourism in their areas. The third
member of the team was Seán Fitzpatrick, a former adjutant of the
Third Tipperary Brigade. He had worked in the printing trade and
now acted as a general office factotum. The staff might well have
formed the nucleus of a cumann of the newly-established Fianna
Fáil party because all four were enthusiastic supporters of de
Valera although I was the only active member of the party. We
were, of course, all on Christian name terms — Jack, Dave, Seán
and Todd. We had many shared experiences and memories and
while O'Brien was unquestionably the boss he behaved, in his
personal relations, as *primus inter pares*.

My first task as an employed man was unusual. Following the
collapse of the general strike in England the miners' strike continued and there was an acute shortage of coal. The basement office
occupied by the ITA was particularly chilly but there was an ample
supply of old railway sleepers in a shed adjoining the building.
Barry, Fitzpatrick and I spent most of our mornings chopping up
railway sleepers for firing.

Barry and Fitzpatrick were very different from O'Brien in
character and motivation. Barry's only ambition was to marry the
girl to whom he was engaged. Fitzpatrick's aspirations were limited
to earning a modest living. He was typical of many men who had
carried military responsibility during the War of Independence.
They had exercised a degree of authority. Among their neighbours
and peer group they had gained a position of prestige. With the end
of the fighting their level of psychological satisfaction had been
fully achieved. They resembled the footballer whose life is spent
recalling the goal he scored to bring victory to his team in the cup
final; it was a day of glory which could never be repeated. Their

moments of distinction might be revived briefly as they took their places in the commemoration parades but, willy nilly in most cases, they settled for a quiet and untroubled life. Most men live such a life hoping to find compensation for the lack of personal satisfaction in the achievements of their children. They are frequently disappointed.

When I got down to real work I found that, apart from a certain disorder in the record system, which could be quickly cleared up, the accountancy skills required to keep track of the financial affairs of the ITA were meagre. I had got the income and expenditure figures sorted out in time to present a financial statement to the board meeting at which my salary was to be reviewed. On the evening of the meeting I asked O'Brien if approval had been granted for the promised increase. He explained, with deep apologies, that the agenda had been so protracted that the item dealing with my salary had not been reached but that I could rest assured that the matter would be put right at the next meeting in a month's time.

While I found it agreeable to work with O'Brien and his colleagues I had seen or learned nothing about tourism to disabuse my mind of the idea that I was working in a less than reputable field. Nor had I any faith in the future of the Association or per consequence of my own career prospects. In the circumstances I had little hesitation in making known to O'Brien that I was not prepared to continue working on the present basis but if and when he had arranged to pay me on the terms originally agreed I would come back to the job if still free to do so. I went home and had little difficulty in putting the ITA out of my mind nor did I expect to hear from it again. I had no difficulty also in resuming my previous leisurely activities loafing around college in the mornings and enjoying Mary's company in the evenings. Visits to the theatre or cinema or the friendly flat in Dawson Street occupied my time most pleasantly. My parents continued to supply what money I wanted and Mary had a small salary from her part-time work in the family business. By this time we were so closely involved with each other that any money we had was shared unquestioningly; masculine pride nor female demureness no longer affected our relationship.

I was enjoying this unprofitably agreeable existence without much thought for tomorrow when, to my surprise, a letter arrived from O'Brien formally appointing me Accountant to the Irish Tourist Association at £4 per week. I cannot say that the news gladdened my heart but a weekly salary of £4 was not bad for those days and even though I had no enthusiasm for what I really felt to be a demeaning occupation there was nothing better on offer.

I lost nothing in prestige by coming back. It was clear that

O'Brien had missed me more than I missed the £4 per week which, because it was paid montly, was referred to as a salary rather than a wage. Trivial as the distinction was it had a psychological importance. Fitzpatrick was paid £5 per week, Barry £6 and O'Brien earned the princely sum of £400 per annum. The secretary/typist was paid £2.10s per week. There were no deductions for social welfare contributions or superannuation. A further, if minor, advantage was that one was not required to sign an attendance book. My duties as accountant were even less onerous than I had expected. The total annual income of the ITA in 1926 was not much more than £10,000. About one third of this was derived from the local authorities and most of the balance was provided by subscriptions from the railway and shipping companies and about two hundred private members who were mainly hotel owners. A very small amount came from advertisements in the *Irish Travel* magazine which O'Brien had just started.

The Association had a board, or executive committee, which met monthly to deal with policy or other major matters. It consisted of what was commonly referred to as men of substance who were connected in some way with the tourist business. They were all strong supporters of the Free State regime and some were active politically. Having regard to the political climate of the time I thought that O'Brien showed great loyalty and courage in surrounding himself with a coven of ex-IRA men who had opposed the government in arms even though, with the exception of myself and that only in a political sense, they were no longer involved in the resistance movement. Certainly the political associations of the staff were never questioned by the board. This may have been due to the fact that the ITA as an organisation was insignificant nationally or, more probably, to the government's anxiety to diffuse the causes of opposition and encourage Republicans to return to normality.

When I joined the ITA the president was J. C. Foley, a Corkman who owned the Victoria Hotel among many other business interests. He was an intimate friend and supporter of President W. T. Cosgrave who had appointed him also a member of the Electricity Supply Board. The other members of the ITA board included, as far as I can recall, the general managers of the Great Southern Railway and of the Burns and Laird Line and two western hoteliers, Joseph Mongan of Carna and Edward Sweeney of Oughterard. I was far too junior at the time to have contact with any of these people though I had the ill-luck to encounter Mongan in later years when both of us were acting in different capacities. The ITA received no government subvention nor did the government have a nominee on the board. The board members were unpaid but nevertheless gave the Association as much dedication and service as the board of any of the semi-state companies with which I came to be associated.

The ITA was initiated in 1924 by J. C. Foley through the amalgamation of two other tourist organisations known as the 'Tourist Organisation Society' and the 'West of Ireland Tourist Development Association' which had become inactive and existed only in name. Foley, who was a friend of the O'Brien family, had O'Brien appointed to carry out the amalgamation. The new body was named the 'Irish Tourist Association' and O'Brien became its secretary. O'Brien with whom I became very friendly and who remained a friend until his comparatively early death told me that when he secured this appointment he was desperate for work. The small family business in Ballyporeen was incapable of supporting himself and his brothers and sisters and he was glad to accept whatever job was offered. At that time he knew as little about tourism as I did when I joined the ITA but with one great difference. From the very beginning he was attracted by the possibilities of the holiday business. With the encouragement of J. C. Foley he set about learning how the business had been developed abroad studying tourist literature and brochures produced in France, Switzerland and England. A personal visit to these countries to examine methods of tourist promotion on the spot would have been regarded in the circumstances of the time as a needless extravagance. Being a man of imagination O'Brien began to formulate plans and schemes to make Ireland a place where visitors would come to fish, hunt, motor or merely rest in naturally beautiful surroundings. I cannot say whether this vision was inspired to any extent by the popular author, Robert Hugh Benson, who at one time suggested that Ireland would fulfil its destiny by becoming a spiritual retreat house, a sort of monastery, for a Europe distressed and distracted by the pressures of everyday living.

O'Brien had ideas for improving hotel facilities, training hotel staffs, establishing schools of catering and providing resort amenities. He believed it should be the function of government to initiate and support these schemes even to the extent of building and managing hotels. As early as 1926 he had formed a clear concept of the pattern along which the development of the national tourist industry was to be subsequently organised. He had no doubt that this concept would be realised and so indeed it was but he paid a high price in his official life for its success.

O'Brien expounded with fervour on his vision of Ireland as the holidaymaker's Utopia. I listened and commented with amused scepticism. I believed neither in the possibility nor desirability of an

Ireland swarming with tourists. I could not rid my mind of the notion that Ireland's role in tourism lay in the supply of still more jarveys, gillies, waiters and chambermaids. Never during the years I spent working in the congenial company of O'Brien and his colleagues did I succeed in overcoming this association of ideas.

The physical working conditions in the basement at Westland Row made it impossible to establish a normal office system and routine. It was with relief we learned that arrangements had been made to move to new premises in Lower O'Connell Street where O'Brien and the board, with faith in the future, had succeeded in getting a suite of offices just vacated by the US consulate. The office space was more than adequate. O'Brien set up a proper board room which he himself occupied. Fitzpatrick and Barry shared a room as Barry's job involved him in much travel around the country. There was an enquiry desk where personal callers were dealt with by Fitzpatrick or Miss Egan.

I had an office to myself and found enough spare time on my hands to take on the editing and production of *Irish Travel*. Much of O'Brien's time was devoted to issuing appeals for funds and corresponding with people who might be in a position to further the interests of the Association. His persistence, energy and enthusiasm met with increasing success. Quite substantial subscriptions were received from the banks and commercial firms such as Guinness. Gradually the number of local authorities contributing to the ITA funds as well as the value of their contributions increased. In due course the work of the ITA came to be accepted as an important element in the national economy.

One of the major difficulties encountered initially by some great semi-state organisations was that of gaining public acceptance. The ESB in its early days became a target for much opposition in political and commercial circles as did Bord na Móna in the years which preceded the fuel emergency caused by the Second World War. Aer Lingus was almost strangled at birth because of its inability to generate public confidence and support.

I got a measure of satisfaction from the job of editing *Irish Travel* as well as some useful experience. My contacts with Alex Thom, the printers, gave me a passing acquaintance with the printing business in such matters as page layout, type faces and sizes, paper qualities, proof correction and photographic block making. In the course of a visit to the Photo Engraving Company I was walking one day along Abbey Street when I was accosted by two men brandishing revolvers and ordered to get into a car which had stopped by the pavement. In response to my protests they identified themselves as CID men and announced that I was being taken into custody without being given any explanation. I was taken to the Bridewell and placed immediately in a cell, uncharged and apparently without any reference to the regular police on duty there. It was then around midday and although I kept ringing the bell and banging the door my existence was completely ignored until a friendly policeman arrived with a mug of tea and a hunk of bread and margarine about three hours later. About 6 p.m. I was released and told that I could go home but was offered no reason for my detention.

Several times during the next few months I was again taken into custody by the CID while going around town on the Tourist Association's business. Usually I was picked up in the forenoon or early afternoon and detained in the Bridewell until after office hours. On one occasion I was arrested while visiting some friends in their home and detained, with another visitor who had been arrested for good measure, until the last tram had left the city so that we were forced to walk home. It was impossible to hold down a job while subject to this kind of harassment. O'Brien reported the matter to the board and one of the members, Senator P. W. Kenny from Waterford, undertook to raise the case with the President, W. T. Cosgrave, with whom he was friendly. His representations were successful and my persecution ceased. But it did not cease in many other cases and numbers of Republicans were constantly victimised by this tactic. By any standard the CID was composed of a pretty low form of humanity. Their behaviour was not the result of any government instruction; their aim was to exercise petty power and petty revenge.

As the financial position of the ITA improved O'Brien decided to undertake new projects. These included the production of travel brochures and local guide books and this work was assigned to me. I was also authorised to employ an assistant and having spoken to O'Brien I appointed Frank Ryan who later became a folk hero of left-wing Republicanism in Ireland and famous for his involvement in the Spanish Civil War. I had met Frank Ryan originally in UCD after the end of the Civil War and got to know him well as a member of the Republican Club. I had enlisted his help in the first of the two general elections of 1927 when we were running Professor Arthur Clery as a Fianna Fáil and, of course, abstentionist candidate. Frank played a very active part in the campaign. However, it was not until 1929 that he achieved real public notoriety as a protester against the British Legion Armistice Day celebrations and also from his connection with the Bass Company boycott organised by the IRA.

. He was working with me for some time before I became aware that Frank Ryan was an active IRA member. I warned him that the

ITA office should not be used as a repository for IRA documents as it would be an embarrassment for both O'Brien and myself if the organisation was found to be used in any way as a cover for IRA activities. Unfortunately my warning was disregarded. One day a senior CID officer named Peter Ennis with two of his aides entered the office, went straight to Frank Ryan's desk and unearthed a file of IRA documents. I was summoned to inspect the cache which Ryan admitted to be his property. Ennis and his party left having taken possession of the papers but to my surprise and relief without arresting either or both of us.

I remonstrated (and not in mild language) with Frank about his foolish behaviour and the difficulties it was likely to create for his colleagues in the Association. He was very contrite but had not much opportunity to apologise because the CID party came back within the hour with instructions to charge him with the possession of illegal documents. Ennis asked me to confirm that I had witnessed their discovery but I denied all knowledge of it. He went on to point out that I must have clearly overheard Frank's admission to ownership of the documents but this I also denied. In reply to his angry and persistent questioning I explained that from time to time I lost my sight and hearing and that I must have been blind and deaf during the raid and the subsequent interrogation. Ennis' response was to call me a rude name. Frank was placed under arrest and held overnight in Pearse Street barracks but to his surprise was released early next day without being charged or ill-treated in any way. He left the ITA of his own volition shortly after this incident and I saw him only occasionally thereafter.

Frank Ryan was uncharacteristic of the old IRA men of my vintage. He was too young to have taken part in the Black and Tan struggle and had been only peripherally involved in the Civil War. At college he was much more interested in the *Athbheocaint* (Irish language revival) than in politics. He was very socially inclined. He was prominent in a group of Gaeilgeoirí whose Sundays were spent attending *Aeraíochtí*, rambling through the countryside and winding up in the homes of the members who lived in Dublin. He enjoyed a pint and many of his evenings were spent drinking with two particularly close companions, both of them bright students as was Frank himself. One of them, a linguist of unusual facility, followed a diplomatic career rising to the rank of ambassador; the other man reached the top echelons of the public service.

Frank Ryan was always penniless. If he had money he always found a friend who had less. If he borrowed money it was certainly to help out someone in difficulty or to buy someone a meal. He was also susceptible to girls. One serious emotional setback seemed to have a disproportionate effect on him. It is not sensible to interpret any man's motivation but, for what it is worth, I believe that this sentimental reverse had the effect of driving Frank Ryan into extremist politics. I find it difficult to believe that he had any deeply felt politico-economic convictions. He could never be persuaded of the fundamental characteristic of sentimental love between men and women — it never lasts.

The text for the series of local tourist brochures and guide books was written jointly by Frank Ryan and myself although Frank's main pre-occupation was with the production of an omnibus *Guide to Ireland*. The cost of these publications was financed from paid advertisements usually extracted from hotels, pubs and local business firms by a mild form of blackmail. The advertising revenue necessary to meet the cost of the *Irish Travel* magazine required greater effort and I got O'Brien's permission to employ two canvassers on a commission basis. Two well known senior Republicans who, having no other income, and glad to earn a living on almost any terms, were hired for the job. For them it was a humiliating experience and it was no less embarrassing for me to ask them to undertake such soul-destroying work. The most distasteful aspect of our relationshp was the checking of payment claims since conflict inevitably arises between employer and employee where people are working on commission. In the end we had to fall back on the established advertising agencies to sell advertising space. My dealings with advertising agencies produced in me a distaste for the profession (if it can be dignified by the word) which has never been eradicated. I still regard it as a pernicious manifestation of the capitalist system. I believe it has been the creator of unreasonable expectations, popular discontent, and envy and unhappiness in our society.

The ITA continued to prosper thanks to Jack O'Brien. The annual general meeting provided an occasion for the hoteliers of Ireland and other interests connected with tourism to stage a trade convention. Several hundred delegates gathered each spring in the Aberdeen Hall of the Gresham Hotel to hear O'Brien present his annual report followed by a lunch and innumerable speeches. O'Brien made sure that the contents of the report were well publicised in the national press and that the speeches of the delegates were reported in the appropriate local newspapers. On the day of the meeting the Dublin and Cork evening papers came out with banner headlines proclaiming 'Ireland's Tourist Industry worth £1 million'. I used to tease O'Brien by enquiring why he selected so modest a figure. Why not put it at £2 million or £5 million (or indeed any other value) since whatever figure he hit on could not possibly be contradicted? At one time I toyed with the idea of doing an M.Econ. degree on tourism and went so far as to discuss the possibility with Professor Shields. He dissuaded me from pursuing the subject on the grounds that there were no reliable statistics on which a proper study could be based. I accepted his judgment with relief though also with the feeling that I had at least made some effort to achieve job satisfaction.

I left the ITA late in 1930 with no regrets apart from the loss of a group of congenial colleagues. I remained socially close to O'Brien for the rest of his life. I did him a disservice but with the best of intentions. I suggested to Seán Lemass that he should be appointed to a committee organised to raise funds on behalf of Fianna Fáil. This committee became the nucleus from which was developed the famous or infamous (depending on one's point of view) Taca of later years.

O'Brien, for no reason apparent to me, established a close rapport with Seán Lemass who did not easily take to people and as time went on he developed what was an even stranger friendship with Leydon, the secretary of the Department of Industry and Commerce. Why the rigid, puritanical Leydon should have taken to the gay, extroverted O'Brien is still a mystery to me.

Lemass and Leydon gave O'Brien and his associates in the tourist business every encouragement to expand their activities. This support culminated in the establishment of the Tourist Board which was given a very wide mandate including powers to own property and to build and manage hotels. Unfortunately the Board had neither the organisation nor adequately trained staff to handle such undertakings. Worse still, O'Brien, on whom the success of this ambitious and in my opinion imaginative scheme rested, had got himself into difficulties. He acquired what William James called 'the moral flabbiness born of the exclusive worship of the bitch goddess success'. He developed a way of life which was alien to his upbringing and real sentiments. He created many powerful enemies and would have fared better, both as a man and a public servant, without some of the friends he made on the fund-raising committee. Too often he met these friends in the bar lounges of Dublin hotels. They were glad to use him as a link with the centres of political power. They were businessmen and wealthy; he was a public official depending on an inadequate salary. They despised him because he was unable to invest in personal property and works of art. In this circle he was treated as something of a court jester. Perhaps carried away by a sense of importance and undoubted political influence he became brash and unpopular. His property deals on behalf of the Tourist Board became, unjustifiably, the target of political criticism. He publicly insulted the owner and editor of a provincial newspaper who thereafter, for months on end, pursued O'Brien's activities with vengeful and malicious comment. He always referred to O'Brien as 'J. P. O'Brien B.A. (Pass)'. The repetition of this sobriquet, which at first only raised smiles, finally succeeded in wrecking O'Brien's self-confidence by making him the subject of national ridicule.

He also alienated Smyllie, the editor of the influential *Irish Times* who retaliated by his interpretation of the term 'luxury' which O'Brien had used in a reference to the future development of Irish hotels. Smyllie insisted that to talk of 'luxury' hotels in the Irish context was senseless and ridiculous and suggested that O'Brien was suffering from *folie de grandeur* or some such aberration. The antagonism of the *Irish Times* contributed to the diminution of O'Brien's self-esteem.

At the beginning of my working life, O'Brien's fate taught me, amongst other things, to be circumspect in my dealings with journalists. In Gaelic Ireland all classes found it inexpedient to offend the bards. The journalists of our day have inherited that aspect of the bardic tradition. They have the power to make or break people the colour of whose eyes they dislike. At one time, only the Church and the press were immune from public criticism. Nowadays only the press has such immunity.

Public figures never dare to say openly what they really feel about the activities of journalists. Conflict with the government or even with the law about news reporting is met with protests about curtailment of the freedom of the press. But 'the press' is not an inanimate printing machine; it consists of people mostly acting anonymously. Correspondence from the public submitted for publication must bear the writer's name and address and if the editor disapproves of any particular expresson of opinion he can refuse to publish it; it is in effect censored.

Every editor will maintain that he has editorial freedom and this of course is true so long as his views do not conflict with those of the newspaper proprietors. Where disagreement occurs, it is likely that the proprietor's view will prevail. In fact, when we talk about the freedom of the press we are talking about the freedom to express unhindered the views of the owners of newspapers.

When the coalition government came to power in 1948, O'Brien's career was ended. He was not re-appointed to the Tourist Board. He was cast out without pension or gratuity and lived out his life in poverty. His friends in the Fianna Fáil businessmen's committee extended no helping hand. With all his faults, O'Brian could claim credit for bringing the tourist industry from small beginnings to the important national status which it enjoys today. He did the country a great service but was repaid by being made the victim of the most dispicable act of political vengeance which took place in my official lifetime. But I had long since left the Tourist Board when all this happened.

6

Marriage

My years in the Irish Tourist Association, while not providing much job satisfaction, were years of continuing expansion of my horizons. It was then that I realised a long felt wish to visit France. With the Lawlor brothers, Dermot and Fintan, I arranged to spend three weeks in France in July 1927. As it happened, the Lawlors left ahead of me on a Saturday and I was to follow on the Monday. I am not quite clear why we made this arrangement but I remember the circumstances well because on the Sunday morning Kevin O'Higgins, the Minister for Home Affairs, was assassinated. Although I had ceased to be a member of the IRA I, in common with all Republicans, held my breath expecting to be rounded up by the authorities. Indeed some were but not on such an extensive scale as was anticipated. Happily, I got away on my holiday as planned. Travelling by way of London I arrived at the Gare du Nord to find, to my disappointment, that the Lawlors were not there to meet me and I was even more disappointed on reaching the sleazy hotel in which we had booked rooms in the Rue Tronchet behind the Madeleine that they had gone out for the evening. Having registered and got my room I decided to take a walk around the block to pass the time. On leaving the hotel I was propositioned by a prostitute and continued to be similarly accosted at every few yards. I was really frightened that I might lose my money if not my virtue although my mother had sewn a false pocket into my jacket to carry my traveller's cheques and passport in safety. Such was my confidence in the French!

I got back to the hotel as quickly as possible to await the return of the Lawlors. It transpired that Fintan had mastered the intricacies of the Paris Metro. He knew the name of every important station on the system and how to get from one tourist attraction to the next so that when we set off next day to see the sights we had very cheap, efficient and speedy transport at our disposal. We never used a bus or a taxi so a large part of our holiday was spent underground seeing Paris only in selected spots. We achieved what seems to be an impossible feat; in the course of the whole visit we never saw the Eiffel Tower. Nevertheless we saw a lot and learned a great deal about the French way of life. Discovering that the standards of behaviour of what we considered to be the most highly civilised country in

Europe were very different from those prevailing at home was in itself a not inconsiderable gain to our education.

Apart from the superabundance of prostitutes, who at that time had largely left the streets of Dublin in the wake of the British army, we were surprised and a little dismayed to see women heavily made up with rouge and powder and eye shadow and even applying these preparations openly in the cafés and shops. Couples suddenly stopping in the street and falling into an embrace or kissing open-mouthedly in cafés was a startling and, of course, interesting experience. We were quite shocked to observe the urinating habits of men who relieved themselves without embarrassment against the nearest wall. But what really took our fancy was to see a man entering one of the cylindrical pavement lavatories called *vespasiennes* holding the hand of his waiting female companion while he pissed.

All three of us had a fair smattering of French. With a little aid from a pocket dictionary we had no difficulty in reading advertisements, public notices and the newspapers which were important to us who were hungry for news from home where we assumed the political situation was critical. We could also read *La Vie Parisienne* and *Paris Plaisirs,* which would be described in Ireland as smutty magazines. Using the Metro we found no problem in getting around the city and saw all the mandatory sights (except the Eiffel Tower) including Notre Dame, Sainte Chapelle, Les Invalides and the Conciergerie. We paid several visits to the Louvre where, of course, the Victory of Samothrace, the Venus de Milo and the Mona Lisa were the principal focus of our interest.

Our successful incursions into French culture and history were not matched by our experiments in French cuisine. Restaurant meals were cheap by the standards of Irish restaurants of the time; even with little experience of eating out at home we knew that. But we had no idea of how to spend money and were in constant fear of being cheated. We sought out the cheapest eating places and, having walked several streets and examined a dozen price menus posted outside the restaurants, we usually wound up at a *prix-fixe* establishment and settled for a meal consisting of soup, steak and chips and pastry or confiture. If we couldn't find a *prix-fixe* we judged the likely cost of the meal by the price of the soup or by whether the tables were served by waiters or waitresses; service by waitress was always cheaper. A further indication of the price was whether the tables were covered with linen or oil cloth. By the time we sat down to eat we were usually exhausted though, in search of variety, we often moved to some other café for our coffee. We visited Place Pigalle and went to see, rather than hear, Mistinguette singing at the Folies Bergères. The topless chorus was a novelty to us. It was the first time I saw a woman's breast fully exposed and contrary to what I expected (and I suppose hoped for) it gave me no thrill. I was not by nature a voyeur. We visited Montparnasse and drank coffee at the famous Rotonde restaurant; indeed much of our time was spent sitting on the terrace of the innumerable cafés drinking citronade partly because we were teetotallers and partly because it was cheaper than coffee. By this time we had seen enough of Paris and felt like exploring some of provincial France. I always had a hankering to visit Tours because I had heard Touraine described as the Garden of France and I remembered too that Tours was the scene of one of Creasy's *Decisive Battles of the World* where in the eighth century the Frankish king, Charles Martel, halted and turned back the Islamic invaders. We had also read of the castles built along the Loire and they seemed very romantic in our imagination. The chances of getting some swimming in the Loire was an added attraction.

We went down by train from Paris to Tours and on the way experienced an exhibition of French mores to be remembered and contrasted with our home customs. There were only two other passengers in the carriage, a young man and a young woman travelling separately. After a while the young man started to make advances to the woman which she apparently resented. Bursting with chivalry we consulted amongst ourselves (in Irish) as to whether or not to defend the young woman's honour. Fortunately we decided not to intervene because within half an hour the two were locked in one another's arms and were still there when we got off the train at Tours.

We planned to walk along the Loire from Tours to Chinon exploring the châteaux on the way but only got as far as Azay-le-Rideau having visited the castle at Langeais. At Azay-le-Rideau our feet gave out and having visited the local château we decided to stay there overnight and retrace our steps to Tours. Azay-le-Rideau is imprinted on my memory because my gastronomic education was broadened by seeing and eating French beans there for the first time. Embarking on a walking tour in that lovely countryside with its delightfully soft but sunny climate was a foolish idea. It was much too flat for enjoyable walking. Cycling would have been a better alternative but we didn't know that bicycles could be hired. In this, as in other respects, ignorance was our undoing. Nor did we get any swimming; the Loire was much too fast-flowing for us.

We returned to Paris for the final days of our holidays but before leaving for home we decided to expand our knowledge of *la vie française* by sampling champagne of which we had heard so much but were never likely to encounter at home. We bought a bottle of the cheapest champagne available, took it to our room and having locked the door we drank it from the mugs provided for tooth brushes. Being teetotallers and knowing its reputation we expected that the champagne would cause us to lose self-control and expose us to the solicitations of the prostitutes; hence the locked door. Having finished the bottle we waited for the effects of our debauch to develop but, of course, nothing happened. Our individual alcoholic intake was negligible; the quality of the champagne must have been sheer dregs but we had not drunk enough of it to get sick.

Despite Arthur Clery's advice against holidaying abroad in a party of three we had no problems on that score and arrived home as friendly as usual. In our view at the time the trip had been a wonderful success. Happily we had not been robbed or cheated nor had we at any time experienced that worry common to holidaymakers of running out of money. In fact we spent very much less than we could easily have afforded. My father had given me £25 for holiday expenses and I had £10 of my own but, when we got back to Dublin, I still had £15 intact. We did not know how to spend money for the simple reason that we had no practice in the art. Our frugality was due to ignorance just as shyness prevented us from talking, despite our fair competence in French, other than to waiters and railway porters. We did not take advantage of the very active tourist bureau at Tours which, had we known it, could have helped us to get so much more enjoyment from our visit. We were literally innocents abroad. We had neither *savoir faire* nor *savoir vivre* — we just lacked 'savvy'.

I was reminded of just how unsophisticated we were when, some forty years later I joined a group at a reception in Dublin Castle and overheard a man in his early twenties mention something about 'when I was in Moscow'. I had already paid two visits to Russia at a time when very few Irish people had done so and being somewhat surprised that so young a man should have been so adventurous, I said to him, 'What on earth were you doing in Moscow?' I felt very much 'put down' when he replied, 'A few of us were en route to Nepal and we went via Moscow.' It transpired that he was one of a group of UCD students going to Nepal on holiday. The incident seemed to me to exemplify the extraordinary change in our relations with the outside world which had taken place in Ireland in forty years. Our holiday in 1927, tentative and poorly organised as it seems in retrospect, was as much an adventure to us and gave us as much satisfaction as our successors in a later generation got from their travels to Nepal.

Back in Dublin, we found the political scene in a state of crisis following the assassination of O'Higgins. Republicans believed that the killing had been carried out by disgruntled members or ex-members of the Free State army or Garda Síochána. It is now more commonly accepted that a small group of dissident IRA men were responsible. It would be hypocritical to pretend that the death of O'Higgins caused a tear to be shed by any Republicans; nor were many shed by the general public and few by his colleagues. He was not a well-liked man.

The assassination was worse than a crime, it was a mistake. Fortunately, Dev was there to defuse the tension by denouncing the deed and fortunately for Fianna Fáil, the government reacted so savagely by introducing draconian legislation, that not merely Republicans but the general public took alarm at the possibility of the resumption of armed conflict. The severity of the measure was the cause of accelerated emigration by Republicans. The Free Staters next proceeded to strengthen their position by altering the electoral laws. Henceforward parliamentary candidates would have to undertake on nomination that they would take the oath of allegiance if elected. In effect, Dev and Fianna Fáil were given the option of entering the Dáil or being excluded from the political process, in which case the only course open to Republicans to achieve their aims would have been through militant action. Had Dev in his wisdom not accepted the lesser of two evils by entering the Dáil, oath or no oath, there would undoubtedly have been, sooner rather than later, a resort to arms if only in protest against the constant harassment to which Republicans were exposed for no reason except that they were opposed to the Free State.

The advent of Fianna Fáil to the Dáil in August 1927 meant that Cumann na nGaedheal, the government party, no longer had a clear majority. They escaped defeat on a vote of confidence thanks to a wayward independent deputy named John Jinks whose default was engineered by Bertie Smyllie, the editor of the *Irish Times,* and a Major Bryan Cooper, two 'characters' who might well have walked out of the pages of Charles Lever. Safely secluded in a pub Jinks was plied with drink till he was incapable of attending the vital Dáil session. The prank was in character with the tradition of the squireens of the west of Ireland to which tradition the two 'boyos' belonged. The government could not hope to survive on a basis of a drunken escapade so they dissolved the Dáil.

We had the problem in the University Republican Club of getting a candidate to stand for election since Arthur Clery would not accept a Republican nomination nor would he agree to take his seat in the Dáil even if he was elected. The fortunes of Fianna Fáil were not at that time so bright as to attract a queue of candidates. I spent many hours trying to persuade Arthur Clery to reconsider his decision but he regarded himself as oath-bound to the Republic. He urged me to try Conor Maguire, a young practising barrister who was secretary and treasurer of the club, which I did. Conor (or Alec as we called him) was equally reluctant to stand and when I made this known to Clery he told me to go back to Maguire. 'Offer him the crown a second time. Press him. He is an ambitious young man. Paint the picture of the future attorney-general. If you persist he won't refuse.' Clery's prediction was right. Conor didn't refuse a second time though his acceptance was reluctant. Having signed the necessary papers he departed for a holiday in Switzerland.

To my dismay a letter arrived to say he had changed his mind and requesting me to withdraw his nomination. He enclosed a cheque book and some papers in connection with the Republican Club. I hot-footed down to Seán Lemass who was now in personal command of the Fianna Fáil offices temporarily situated in Lower O'Connell Street. I told Seán the bad news and asked what he thought should be done to secure another candidate in the time available since there was less than a week to spare before nominations closed. Lemass was at his best. Looking coldly at me he enquired, 'Why do you have to ask me what you'll do?'

'But Maguire doesn't want to stand,' I said.

'Have you anyone else?' asked Lemass.

'No,' said I.

'Well!' said Lemass.

'Well?' I asked.

'Don't be an idiot. Put in Maguire's papers. If he's elected he can resign, but he won't,' commented Lemass.

That was the first direction I got from Lemass; its decisiveness was typical of him. We put in the papers. Conor barely missed being elected. But overall Fianna Fáil did surprisingly well in the election. We won fifty-two seats against Cumann na nGaedheal's sixty-two. The tide was turning. We faced the political future with rising enthusiasm.

With the elections over, Mary and I resumed our very agreeable routine combining the theatre, the pictures and picnics at weekends. We were regular visitors to The Studio, a Bohemian-style cabaret which Madame Bannard Cogley, with the aid of the painters Maurice McGonigal and Harry Kernoff, had established in a hall near the high school in Harcourt Street. We had been introduced to The Studio by McGonigal who was an old school and IRA friend of mine. Madame Cogley was a Frenchwoman married to a journalist, Fred Cogley, whom I knew from our jail days together. She was a petite woman of great vivacity and a charm which was enhanced by her heavily accented English. She endowed her cabaret with a distinctive French atmosphere. Her principal aide was Harry Kernoff. Kernoff was Jewish and eschewed regular occupation. He regarded it as the duty of his family to support him, which they did and necessarily so because, while Kernoff worked hard at his painting and woodcuts, he had no idea of how to merchandise them. Kernoff would have been a boon companion for Little Billie and Trilby's other friends.

But for a man and a woman in the situation Mary and I found ourselves, picture houses, theatres, cabarets or the Hill of Howth or Powerscourt Demesne or Glenasmole did not fulfil all our needs. We wanted to be alone but there was nowhere we could be alone. At that time attaining privacy was a common problem for courting couples; hence the popularity of the cinema. The Coyle house on Mespil Road was big but so was the family — besides Mary there were four girls and three boys as well as Mrs Coyle. All our friends — mine being exclusively amongst Republicans — assumed that we were engaged and would be married one day. Mary and I, although working on the same assumption, never discussed the question; marriage on my job prospects was too remote a possibility and we followed the principle of *carpe diem*. I called to the Coyle house fairly often but never stayed too long. Some extraordinary inbuilt shyness or diffidence prevented me from mentioning Mary to my parents nor did I have the nerve to ask my mother if I could bring her to dinner or tea. It never occurred to me that they might have sensed our relationship; if they were aware of it there was so little communication between us that it was never even hinted at. Even in the perspective of the years I cannot think how I could have misjudged so badly my parents' intelligence and understanding.

Mary and I had another problem. The first time I presented myself to the Coyle household in the role of suitor Mrs Coyle, who opened the door to me and knew me well, explained that the 'boys', that is Mary's brothers, Hugh and Donny were away and would not be home until the weekend. It never occurred to her that my interest was in Mary. Mary who had invited me to tea had been delayed on her way from the office but just arrived in time to save me the embarrassment of explaining the true purpose of my visit. Mrs Coyle, who was a widow, was a highly educated woman. She came from the kind of wealthy Limerick merchant families who are featured in Kate O'Brien's novels. She was one of the first women students in the old Royal University. She was, like Mary, an admirer of Jim Larkin. She was a feminist who knew and admired Hanna Sheehy Skeffington. She was a Republican supporter and allowed her home to be used as a 'safe' house during the Civil War while Mary was in jail. But she was also a mother and could scarcely be expected to be overjoyed at the prospect of her very beautiful daughter becoming involved with a man having so little worldly prospects. If she felt that way she never showed it to me. She was essentially liberal and intelligent enough to know that Mary was unlikely to be weaned from me by any form of outside interference. The senior branch of the family did not take that rational view. Mary's Uncle Hugh was head of the firm of Coyle Ltd, Tea Merchants, and his only son, David, had married into the family of Cantwell & Co., Wine Merchants. Both businesses were, at the time, prosperous; the Coyles and the Cantwells had risen in the world. Although the Hugh Coyles were declared Nationalists and had supported the Sinn Féin in pre-Treaty days they had now become part of the new bourgeoisie who were fervent supporters of the Free State and of its worst features. Like all people of their stripe they regarded de Valera as vainglorious and his IRA followers as *canaille*. Mary must be saved from a fate which they regarded as nearly as bad as death.

Mrs Cantwell, David Coyle's mother-in-law, took a hand in the play. She was a big-boned, good humoured, *grámhar,* kind-hearted woman who, I remember, dressed very well. Unfortunately she was a particularly silly woman and not noticeably literate. Between them all, new clothes were bought for Mary and she was taken on holidays to expensive resort hotels where she might meet men more suitable than I. Formal dinner parties were arranged for her where the principal course was eligible bachelors. I cannot say I was very pleased with these activities. I resented them although deriving some amusement from Mary's blow by blow account of the performance of the different actors in a drama in which I too was a performer; I was indeed the villain of the piece.

My resentment was assuaged and my sense of irony gratified when Mary solved the problem of our being alone and at the same time out of the cold. She had the key to the premises of Coyle Ltd in Abbey Street and in her Uncle Hugh's well-appointed inner office with its great leather chairs, an electric fire and appropriately the appurtenances of tea-making, we spent many comfortable evenings fortified by cold roast pork or ham, cakes from Roberts café and once even dressed crab. The crab was unfortunately tainted and we both suffered a minor attack of food poisoning. The real *bonne bouche* of our private parties lay in reflecting on the sense of outraged respectability which the senior members of the house of Coyle Ltd, Tea Merchants, and their allies would experience if it became known that Mary and I were using the innermost sanctum of the tribe as a lovers' rendezvous.

The year 1928 was half way through when our affaire took an

upturn. Fitzpatrick, Barry and I each had our salaries increased by £52 per annum. This increase had been expected but I got a welcome surprise when O'Brien's own salary came up for review three months later. A director whom I had never even seen insisted on my salary being increased by the same amount again so that I now had £312 per annum. The director — I think it was Baird of the London, Midland and Scottish Railways — pointed out that my performance was such that the Association should endeavour to retain my services. In principle his attitude was right but in the temper of the times the idea of obtaining a salary increase without asking was unusual.

About the same time Mary graduated with an honours B.Comm. degree and won the prize of £100 which was being offered for distinction that year. To celebrate the occasion we decided to visit Jammets, the most famous and most expensive restaurant in the city. It was an adventure even for Mary who had much greater aplomb than I. A waiter in tails presented us with a formidable menu in French and the prices listed for the different dishes, most of which we had never heard, seemed to be out of all reason. We did our best at choosing a meal on the basis of price rather than of taste. We did not want to leave the waiter under the impression that we were unaccustomed to the grandeur of Jammets, although when the bill was paid and we got outside we asked one another why the hell we should be concerned at the waiter's opinion of us particularly as he made a mistake in totting up the bill which Mary had no diffidence in correcting. It was a minor experience and it was an accumulation of minor experiences rather than any great upheaval that shaped our lives together. Mary decided to quit Coyle Ltd and succeeded in getting a part-time post in the Technical School in Parnell Square teaching English and Mathematics (then described as sums) which she valued at about £100-£150 per annum. Now clearly marriage was possible with a joint income in the region of £400 or £450. Neither of us had more than a few pounds saved even allowing for Mary's prize money but we decided to look for a flat to rent. We also decided to tell Mary's mother and my parents.

I found it extremely difficult to bring myself to inform my father of my decision to get married. My reluctance to admit openly that I was courting a girl or even that I had women friends can only be explained by the vestiges of Victorian morality which still stank in the 1920s. Many men never married because they couldn't bring themselves to tell their mothers. At that time, and indeed much later, it was quite common to define a 'good living' young man as one who didn't smoke, drink or go out with women. Usually it was added that he was a daily communicant. Women were put in the same undesirable category of indulgence as cigarettes or beer. When I did finally apprise my father of the situation between Mary and myself he merely grunted and asked if I had spoken to my mother. My mother was in the kitchen when I broke the news to her. She put on her Mona Lisa smile and asked if I really thought I was surprising her and my father by planning to get married. Without preliminaries she told me that they had plans for me; that they had decided to give me £600 to build or buy a house and that they would also furnish a bedroom as a wedding present for us. She went on to say that if we chose to build a house a grant of £150 would be available from the County Council. I was dumbfounded by my parents' reaction. It never occurred to me that they could have saved such a large sum of money because my father had been in trouble with income tax arrears arising from the old Dáil instruction not to pay tax. My mother reproached me for not having brought Mary to meet them and it was agreed that she should be asked to dinner on the following Sunday.

Mary told me that her mother took the news very well; she was no more surprised than my parents. She felt that Mary should get an engagement ring and announce our engagement in the *Irish Times*. We refused outright to announce our engagement formally. We had not intended to bother with a ring partly because of the expense but mainly because of its bourgeois connotations. However, to please Mrs Coyle I asked my father to buy me the cheapest ring that would be tolerably acceptable. He got one for £10 — not a very good one — and he insisted on making a present of it to Mary. Mary believed that Mrs Coyle was uneasy about having to explain me away to her circle of old ladies. Hugh Coyle, the old man of the tribe, thought Mary was foolish and wondered what we would live on, 'Tourist Associations come and go'. Donny and Hugh, Mary's brothers, were my allies in the two families. Anyway they had no warm regard for their uncle Hugh. He had insisted on conscripting them into the family business when they both wanted to go to university.

Mary's first dinner with my parents went as well as we hoped. My father, in particular, formed an immediate rapport with her. My mother gave her prospective daughter-in-law as cordial a welcome as she was capable of. My brother being involved in some football match did not put in an appearance.

When it came to finding a place to live Mary and I had different ideas. I preferred somewhere near to the city centre while Mary wanted to get away from it as far as possible. She protested that she would live in a caravan rather than in the city and really meant it. Finally we located a suitable site in Dundrum on the property of

Michael Doyle, the father of the future hotel magnate, Vincent Doyle. It was the first housing site to be developed in that area and we were the first immigrants into what has since become a conurbation. Though we subsequently changed houses twice we never left Dundrum parish. All our five children were born there. The months before we were married were fully occupied by supervising the building and furnishing of our home. There was also the dreaded ordeal of being produced for inspection by Mrs Coyle's contemporaries at specially organised Bridge parties. Never again did I want to see a Bridge table.

We were married at six o'clock in the morning at Haddington Road church with the minimum of ceremony. I went to Confession and Communion for the first time since the Civil War when the bishops had denied the sacraments to us Republicans. I wore my best suit and persuaded Mary to get a new coat, hat and skirt for the occasion. She was totally indifferent to clothes and could afford to be; if she wore hand-me-downs she would still cause people to look at her admiringly. We invited no guests to the church and the wedding breakfast was eaten at Mary's home in Mespil Road, prepared by Mary's sisters. The only people present were Mrs Coyle, Mary's brothers and sisters, my brother who had been my best man and my parents. There was a bottle of champagne on the table but it wasn't opened. No one wanted to drink.

In those days it was impossible to reach the continent without passing through England. If there is one benefit more than another that the aeroplane has conferred on us it is the freedom to travel almost anywhere in the world without a compulsory stop-over in England. Mary felt that plans for our honeymoon itinerary should be postponed until our arrival in London. Mary knew London well and a two-day stay was as much as she could tolerate. We spent these two days visiting the zoo which was of special interest to me, the Tower, the Egyptian room in the National Museum and some pictures in the National Gallery. We ate in Soho, averting our eyes from the naughty posters which were displayed everywhere and which we pretended not to have noticed — even in these circumstances we preserved our modesty. Mary decided that we should move on to Paris. We found Paris in the grip of a heat wave and as both of us had been there before and had seen the sights we saw no point in making a long stay. With the help of the tourist bureau of the French Railways we discovered St Aubin-sur-Mer, a small seaside resort about the size of Rush in County Dublin, twelve miles from Caen with which it was connected by a narrow-gauge railway. It was just the kind of place we were looking for. Our hotel was clean and cheap. Meals cost very little, the bathing facilities, particularly from a little harbour, were good while the weather could not have been more agreeable. We hired bicycles (at first a tandem with which we couldn't cope) and visited Bayeaux to see the tapestry and Caen to see the famous twin churches. We discovered Camembert cheese — another minor experience. Our holiday could not have been more enjoyable and while we did not follow the penurious way of life that distinguished my first visit to France it did not work out to be very expensive.

My father met us at Westland Row Station with the Terenure village taxi driven by Pat Brien who had transported the guns used by my Company when the Dublin Brigade IRA wiped out the British intelligence network on Bloody Sunday. My mother had one of her very large meals waiting to be placed on the table. It was late when we were ready to leave for our new home so I suggested that we should stay with my parents overnight. My father was enthusiastic but my mother less so and after a while she called me aside to assure me that we were very welcome to stay but she would advise against it. She felt that as Mary and I were embarking on a new life it would be proper to do so from the word go. She told me that during our absence everything in the house had been made ready for our return — linen laid out, beds made up and fires set in the sitting-room and kitchen stove. She had prepared a parcel of food-stuffs to take with us — refrigerators were not commonly available in those days. I was very touched no less by her wisdom than by her thoughtfulness. For the first time in years I kissed her affectionately. All my life I had underestimated my mother. I admired her much less than I did my father to whom I was deeply devoted.

I suppose nobody could have made a more propitious start in married life than did Mary and I. We had everything a young couple in our circumstances could want both in human and material terms. We had gone a good way to realising Swift's ambition to own

A handsome house to lodge a friend
A river at my garden's end.

7

Working in the Electricity Supply Board

We were living a very pleasant life. Being the first of my immediate circle to get married, our house was a Saturday evening rendezvous for our friends. From the very beginning of our married life, the only entertainment anyone got in our house was conversation. The intellectual diet was the latest cult book, Communism, politics at home and abroad, and the theatre. Tea, sandwiches, and a home-made cake supplied the material wants. We kept no alcohol in the house. *The Mummer's Wife* of George Moore strengthened my fear and dislike of drink. Although some of our friends had begun to sample wine as a result of visits to France, no one found it a neces-sary ingredient in an evening's domestic entertainment.

We never allowed card games in the house. I should say 'I' rather than 'we' because Mary was quite interested in Bridge, at that time known as Auction Bridge. I knew how to play Bridge but found even after a few rubbers that it became intolerably boring. Nor could I tolerate parlour games such as Charades. Regrettably neither of us were very interested in music — Mary to some extent, I not at all.

Curiously, we remained indifferent to the Censorship Act which was a talking point at this time. This was probably partly due to our lack of interest in all aspects of the Free State administration and partly because we thought, rightly as it happened, that any of the censored books which were worth reading could be obtained with-out much difficulty, though not on open sale.

Among the events which were of more than ordinary interest to Republicans around this time was the long delayed publication in 1931 of the *Irish Press*. To us who had endured the total hostility of the national press for many years it provided a welcome antidote to their political poison. Frank Gallagher, the greatest Irish journalist of his day, was its first editor and Bob Brennan, another journalist of distinction, was general manager. With contributors of the qual-ity of Seamus McManus and Aodh de Blacam (Roddy the Rover), the paper became an inspiration and powerful morale booster for the Republican cause. It played a dominant role in the success of the election campaign which was to bring Fianna Fáil to power within a year.

Having started a family, I became increasingly unhappy about my position in the Irish Tourist Assocation. From the start, my problem in the ITA had been the lack of job satisfaction; the problem of money now became important even though my salary had increased to £6 per week and I expected another substantial rise by the end of the year. At best I could look forward to a bare livelihood for myself and my family. This prospect did not in any way worry Mary. It conformed to her belief that the fewer possessions one had over and above those necessary to provide food, heat and shelter the more likely the prospect of happiness. I had a different view. I had no wish to become a collector of, say, silver, antiques or porcelain, but I would have liked to have a few functional things such as a telephone, a refrigerator or a vacuum cleaner; Mary wanted none of them. But we were very, very happy.

It has always been my misfortune to be beset by the concept of *hubris* and *nemesis,* concepts which have detracted from much of my enjoyment of life. When things are going too well, the gods strike. Life could not have been better for Mary and me when in 1930 my father died. We were expecting our first child in August and my father was delighted at the prospect. He was devoted to Mary and cycled over from Terenure to visit us a couple of times a week — much to my mother's annoyance because she thought it might be regarded as an intrusion. She had a dread of the role of interfering parents-in-law. On one of these expeditions my father got a wetting, caught a chill which turned to pneumonia and, after a short illness, he died.

When it was clear that he was seriously ill, I moved to our house in Terenure and remained until his death. My mother, though she was a woman of unusual fortitude, was desolated. It was the first time I ever saw her weeping. She had been already upset by a local priest whom she called in to administer the last rites to my father. He took her to task in quite abusive terms for not having got ready the sacramentals appropriate to the occasion. Fortunately I arrived on the scene and had no hesitation in telling the priest to leave the house at once. I telephoned the Jesuits in Gardiner Street and asked one of them to come out and attend to my father, which they did. I am always grateful to them for their charity.

I did not think I was capable of being so upset by anything as I was by the loss of my father. He was only fifty-nine years of age and I assumed he would live forever! My whole world seemed to dissolve and for the first time I realised how much I had been dependent on my parents for my emotional and material support. To add to the family upset, my grandmother, an old lady of eighty-six, to whom my father (her son-in-law) was more than a son, died from shock on hearing of his death, so that we had two funerals in one week. Fortunately, I had Mary to fall back on for the consolation so badly needed and the arrival of our first child, a son, in August did much to divert my mind from the loss of my father.

My mother was distraught. Her first concern was to have a headstone erected to my father's memory in Glasnevin. Knowing my father's detestation of headstones, which he regarded as a peculiarly repulsive manifestation of vanity (a view which I shared), I dissuaded her from erecting anything more grandiose than a simple cross. I argued that my father would regard himself as much better remembered if she bought a fur coat, a ponyskin, which she always wished for. This she did.

At our Saturday evening gatherings one of the talking points was the Shannon Scheme, the centrepiece of the Electricity Supply Board's operations. We depended domestically on oil lamps for light. We would not use gas, partly because it was made from English coal, partly because I thought it unsafe. Even at that time, we used turf for heating and Kilkenny anthracite for cooking. The ESB was spreading its supply network all over the country. We were hoping rather than expecting it would reach us soon. By this time even the most intransigent Republican accepted the ESB achievement for what it was — a boost for national morale. Dr Thomas McLaughlin, who had conceived the scheme, was quite rightly a national hero. I had never had any sympathy with the opponents of the Shannon Scheme when it was originally suggested. I thought it was the sort of undertaking that followers of Sinn Féin should welcome.

The Republican opposition to the scheme was merely verbal, based on nothing more solid than the belief that the Free State government had neither the will nor the capacity to contribute anything to the economic good of the country. This misguided verbiage did produce one of those politically adhesive phrases which never becomes unstuck. Seán MacEntee TD, one of the best known Republicans, described the project as 'a white elephant'. It was a particularly unfortunate comment coming from a man who had the benefit of an engineering training. Politicians should approach phrase-making with caution; what may seem clever to their friends may not seem so clever to their constituents or to the public.

Apart from Republican opposition to the development of the Shannon, there was also antagonism from vested interests. Local electricity undertakings were being acquired and closed down as the ESB network expanded. The monetary compensation which the owners of these undertakings received did not make up for the loss of social prestige which they had hitherto commanded locally.

I knew Dr T. A. McLaughlin. He was a few years older than I and had been a pupil of Synge Street CBS. One of his brothers had been in my class there. I met him a few times in UCD when he and Arthur Cox were trying to form a National University Graduates' Association. It was a non-political organisation and it had a useful secondary effect of at least permitting polite conversation between Republicans and Free Staters. From time to time McLaughlin and I exchanged amiable nothings, usually about my friend, John Dowling to whom as an undergraduate, McLaughlin had been very much attached. He always referred to John with condescending affection as 'poor John'. In fact there was nothing 'poor' about John Dowling. He had already established himself in an extensive dental practice. McLaughlin himself was by this time the best known man in the country, outperforming most politicians in the matter of personal publicity.

While I was interested in the general progress of the ESB and particularly in getting a connection to my home, I was ignorant about its internal workings and although I knew from my UCD contacts many of its senior staff, it never occurred to me as a possible alternative to the ITA as a source of employment.

One afternoon in the autumn of 1930, I got a call from McLaughlin's secretary asking if I would come to see 'the Doctor', as he was always referred to with affection and awe by his staff. I agreed to do so thinking that he wanted to see me in connection with the Graduates' Association. To my surprise and gratification, he told me that, as the board was having difficulties with its accounts, he was trying to strengthen the staff of the accounts department and enquired if I would be interested in joining the organisation. The prospect of quitting the ITA, an organisation I despised, to join one so nationally important as the ESB, sounded like manna from heaven, more especially since the proposed salary was to be £500 a year. There was one hurdle still to be got over; I would have to pass the scrutiny of the newly-appointed chairman, a former tax inspector named Browne. An interview with Browne was duly arranged and my appointment was confirmed but at £450 per annum. Browne, being trained as a civil servant, thought it his duty to pay everyone, except himself, as little as possible. I would gladly have accepted the job even if it paid nothing more than my current salary in the ITA.

Browne, no more than McLaughlin, gave me little information as to the nature of my appointment and when I did report for duty it was to the secretary, Patrick Dempsey. Dempsey, who was always described as 'an awfully nice fellow', was also quite vague as to my duties. On again consulting McLaughlin I was informed that each department of the Board's operations was under the control of a senior engineer and the intention was to appoint an accountant (a *Kaufman* I think was the term used) to work in tandem with each department engineer, after the German method of organisation. The role of the accountant would be to scrutinise and keep track of the engineer's expenditure.

I was not long in the Board before I realised that there was something badly amiss. I was assigned to the head of the installation department, Nicholas Matthews (universally known as 'Buckser'). Matthews was a small, fat, red-headed man of my own age. He came straight from college to take charge of the department responsible for wiring the premises of new ESB customers. He also had what amounted to a blank cheque to purchase materials for the job. Matthews was as innocent as he was upright and hard-working. The accomplished salesmen of the big electrical companies had little trouble in unloading their wares on him. Such was the system of stores accounts that much of the material which had been paid for and delivered was never used nor ever properly recorded in the books. Matthews had another difficulty. He was being pressed beyond reason by McLaughlin to have the installation programme speeded up at all costs as increased revenue was badly required by the Board. Matthews had the task of organising a body of properly qualified electricians — an impossible one for the simple reason that there were very few in the country — so that any man who was handy with a pliers and a screwdriver was employed. The results were sometimes comical. Lighting points were fixed to beds and other movable pieces of furniture. Job cards arrived from electricians showing 'Labour £500, Materials 6d', or vice versa. But McLaughlin's policy was in principle the correct one. Outlets had to be found for the electricity even at the cost of some risks.

Briefly, the accounts system in the installations department had broken down and a similar breakdown had occurred all over the organisation. Large losses would appear here and there because a transformer, or some such equipment, had legitimately been taken from stores without the transaction being put through the books. From the very beginning this lack of accounts control was impairing what was in all other respects a successful organisation.

McLaughlin had an obsession about the capability of engineers whom he regarded as the salt of the earth. As far as their technical competence went, he was not far wrong. The university engineering faculties turned out very highly trained men who were quite capable of running power stations and building the national grid.

But McLaughlin made the mistake of thinking that, without any special training, they could also serve as managers, accountants and salesmen. The ESB had a chief accountant and a deputy chief accountant who had no experience whatever of the type of accounting system necessary to control a large commercial undertaking. I soon realised that I had nothing to contribute to the fundamental problem, having as little experience of industrial accounts as the rest. But I did restrain 'Buckser' from using his open cheque book too freely. Even if his accounts staff had had the necessary management experience, McLaughlin would have paid no attention to their advice. He regarded accounts and accountants as inconvenient irrelevancies to the work of producing and distributing electricity; they were an exercise in window dressing. This proved to be a costly misjudgement on his part. *Hubris* followed by *nemesis* overtook him.

The folk memory of McLaughlin amongst Synge Street boys was of being indifferent to any of the usual schoolboy interest in games. He concentrated on his lessons with great success. Any exhibitions, scholarships or prizes that were available he won. Before my time few boys from the Christian Brothers School at Synge Street went to the university. He was one of them. The only others I knew of were Dr T. Nolan, the State Chemist, and Professor Michael Hayes, the speaker of the Dáil, and Jack McHenry, the physicist, afterwards President of UCC.

At college McLaughlin maintained his studious habits, taking little interest in either the sports clubs or the students' societies. Nor did he take any active part in the politics of the time. He was in sympathy with Sinn Féin in a detached way. His university career was no less brilliant than his achievements at school. When he had taken his Ph.D. in physics he had no difficulty in getting a post as lecturer in physics in University College, Galway. There he met the professor of civil engineering, Professor Rishworth, from whom he derived the idea of harnessing the Shannon to produce enough electricity to supply the nation's needs. The idea fascinated him. He took a degree in engineering and, being a man of action as well as imagination, he went to Germany where he succeeded in interesting the great firm of Siemens Schuckert in the project.

With the support of Siemens he successfully persuaded not only his friend McGilligan, who was Minister for Industry and Commerce, of the feasibility of the scheme, but also Gordon Campbell, who was secretary of the department and who had been trained as an engineer. The name of Gordon Campbell, afterwards Lord Glenavy, is never mentioned in connection with the Shannon Scheme but in drafting the legislation his engineering expertise must have been a considerable help to McGilligan who as a lawyer and a politician had no technical background. But it was McGilligan who had to bear the brunt of the savage and mostly ill-informed criticism to which the project was subjected and who saw it through to the conclusion.

In appearance McLaughlin was not attractive. He was rather low-sized and heavily built. He was of a shape which could never look well-dressed, however expensive his clothes. He spoke as if his tongue was too big for his mouth. He had a detached manner which varied from the charming to the downright rude depending on his estimate of the person to whom he was talking. In 1927 he became managing director of the Electricity Supply Board. He was the first Irish product of Burnham's 'Managerial Revolution' and he was the first man of no property to control millions of the nation's money. He was the best known, most admired and most publicised man in the country. He had a talent for publicity and for the cult of the personality. He wallowed in the adulation that surrounded him. He was much sought after by hostesses including the wives of the Merrion and Fitzwilliam Square doctors and of the diplomatic corps who with government ministers formed the core of Dublin 'society'.

The rising middle class Dublin society was thoroughly provincial in its standards and style of living. Its parties and weddings were ostentatious. The cocktail party was introduced and the cocktail circuit cultivated. Smoked salmon appeared on the dinner tables; indeed smoked salmon became the symbol of the risen people. To know the vintage of wines became a social accomplishment. The circles that McLaughlin frequented were the inheritors of the Republican revolution, such as it was.

But neither smoked salmon nor exquisite wines could produce accounts. The government required proper accounting from the ESB and were insisting on getting it. Official dissatisfaction resulted in the removal of the chairman, who had been city treasurer of Dublin and an intimate friend of W. T. Cosgrave, the head of the government. They substituted Richard Browne, an income tax inspector who was a golfing companion of John Costello, then attorney-general and, twenty years later, Taoiseach. McLaughlin did not heed the obvious warning indicated by this change. Despite his very high intelligence he had fallen victim of his own propaganda. He had come to believe he was indispensable. He also made the mistake of challenging on statutory grounds the authority of the government to interfere in the affairs of the ESB. He found out that any official or organisation which embarks on confrontation with a government is, by the nature of the case, bound to lose! Only a deluded man could imagine otherwise. A creature cannot be greater than its creator.

Two new members were appointed to the Board, Laurence Kettle and William Fay. Kettle had bitterly opposed the Shannon Scheme from the start. McLaughlin responded by insulting and humiliating him. Fay was a nonentity despised by Kettle and disliked by McLaughlin. McLaughlin resented the new chairman Browne, who was a man of a calibre different from his predecessor. McLaughlin drew around him a clique of adorants motivated primarily by loyalty to 'the Doctor' but his rudeness also antagonised many of the senior engineering staff who were not prepared to back him unquestioningly. In the end he found himself supported only by the sycophants. Yes-men are the blight of anyone who attains power. Briefly, the Board was in a mess.

McLaughlin, like everyone else, had the defects of his qualities. One of his qualities was his complete lack of 'side'. He was a Christian Brothers' boy, most of whom, I think, are egalitarian in that they accept the proposition that all men are created equal. This means that Jack is as good as his master but it also means that his master is as good as Jack. In the nature of things there are rich and powerful men who by any standards are good men; there is no merit in poverty. It may have been this egalitarian quality that prompted McLaughlin when we met from time to time (sometimes he sought me out) to speak very frankly about his troubles with the government and with the Board. My sympathies were with McLaughlin mainly because of my antipathy to the government and the service rather than because I thought his attitude was right.

According to McLaughlin the civil service was the main cause of his problems. Gordon Campbell having retired, he had to deal with what he regarded as cold and envious fish. I had no solution to offer for the overall accounts problem but I did point out to him that it was impossible to manage so widespread an organisation as the ESB without a large measure of decentralised control. That lesson I had derived from my past IRA experience. He was not impressed. He was the ESB. He had intended to approach Siemens for help in improving the accounts system before Browne's appointment but the Board stymied the move. When Browne joined the Board, McLaughlin raised the matter again. Browne seized on the idea, hot-footed it to Siemens in Berlin and returned with an accountant named Frederick Weckler in tow. But events had gone too far to save McLaughlin. He was forced to resign.

A great wail of sympathy swept through the ESB at McLaughlin's departure. He was presented by the staff with a magnificent model in silver of the Shannon Power Station at Ardnacrusha. The staff prepared to shuffle their allegiance but now there was only one significant allegiance — to Browne and Weckler. The remaining members of the Board ceased to have any significance or influence on either policy or administration. Technical policy and its execution were dealt with by Browne in consultation with the principal electrical engineer, P. G. Murphy, while Weckler took complete command of organisational matters.

Browne was the most distinguished looking man I ever met. Six feet tall, beautifully proportioned, he had regular, ruddy features and a magnificent head of thick white hair, perfectly styled in the fashion of the time. He dressed with extreme care and had his suits made in London by a Bond Street tailor. It used to be said with some malice or envy that he had a suit for every day of the year. Certainly he rarely wore the same suit on consecutive days. His hobbies were ballroom dancing (he took lessons in London when he went to have his suits fitted), golf, Bridge, and gastronomy. He was president of the Dublin Food and Wine Society. He was interested in antique furniture, classical music and interior decoration. He subscribed to the theory that some colours were restful and others disturbing. Blue was his favourite colour; red he disliked. He took an interest in the general appearance of the Board's offices and installations; hence the power stations are so beautifully landscaped. He spoke quietly and courteously. He made himself available to the humblest of the staff and dealt very fairly with anyone who had a grievance.

I saw much of Browne in later years when I was managing director of Bord na Móna. At that stage I discovered that he was not open to conviction on anything which ran counter to his preconceived ideas on the use of turf by the ESB, which all, it seemed to me, derived from his engineering advisers. In discussions he gave the impression that he was talking to a mirror image of himself — wondering how he looked. He was inclined to divert from the subject in hand to tell of some gastronomic adventure he had had in Jammets restaurant, or elsewhere. He was without a sense of humour; I doubt if he ever heard of the word irony. But I liked him well. A visit to him, notwithstanding our disagreements, was always an occasion of amusement to me.

Weckler was in his early forties. He was a bachelor from Stuttgart, tall, brown-haired and handsome. His working life had been spent in Siemens. Today he would be described as a workaholic. He had been in Ireland for two brief visits in connection with the Siemens contract for the Shannon Scheme. He had met McLaughlin and Arthur Cox, the Board's legal adviser, but remembered no one else. His English was minimal. To help him in this respect the assistant secretary of the Board, John Donovan, was seconded as his aide.

While Donovan was nominally assistant secretary, he was not engaged in secretarial work. Donovan was a small, frail man who had been badly wounded as an officer in the British army at Passchendaele and was kept alive by will-power, courage and an odd and cynical sense of humour. He had a spider-like facility for intrigue, and spent much of his time collecting ESB gossip particularly on the subject of the personal relations of the members of the Board each of whom confided in him. He amused everyone, was liked by everyone, but no one trusted him — a fact of which he was so well aware that he was never tempted to be malicious though indeed malice was not in his nature. Weckler's inadequate English put organisational gossip outside his reach. By the time he had learned English adequately, he was beyond being interested in any of the directors except Browne, the chairman, with whom he formed a very effective team. He was careful never to encroach on the territory proper to the technical staff without their concurrence.

Weckler set about overhauling the organisational structure of the ESB, beginning with the financial and cost account system. He treated the existing accounts staff with consideration for their feelings and understanding of their difficulties. He set up store control procedures which ensured that whatever went in or out was accurately recorded. He devised a system of billing electricity sales which eliminated disputes with customers about what they owed and made it possible to collect accounts in the last resort by means of a pliers. He decentralised the administration by establishing district offices throughout the country. He devolved a large measure of authority to the district accountants and provided a correct delineation of function between them and the district engineers. Donovan's contribution to the re-organisation was to suggest suitable candidates to man the district offices. Donovan knew most of the staff in the Board so that it was natural that those he knew best were appointed to the district accountant posts and those he knew best had been members of the British or Free State armies.

Weckler, in carrying out this massive overhaul, gathered around him a small informal staff. Of this staff the king pin was a man named John White, an old IRA man. White was an accountant who had been acquired along with the Dublin city electricity undertaking. For that reason alone he was discarded by McLaughlin so that for years his extraordinary talents went unutilised. Weckler recognised them quickly. White took charge of the development of the billing system, installed a Hollerith accounting machine, the performance of which he improved so much that it became a showpiece for the manufacturers who brought prospective customers to see it. Like Weckler, White was a workaholic. He was one of the ablest men I ever met, but had a curious defect — he suffered from pathological shyness.

While all this was going on it was my good luck to have attracted Weckler's attention and I was finally assigned to oversee the district offices assisted by a small staff of inspectors. At this point in my life I was given my first motor-car. To own a car seems to be the ambition of most young men. It wasn't mine. I loathed everything about the car; even filling it with petrol was to me a tiresome imposition. However I had to have one since my duties required me to circulate continuously between the district offices of Athlone, Galway, Sligo, Limerick, Waterford, Portlaoise and Tralee.

I had and have some psychological block about motor-cars. I am never confident that they will start. Once on the road I travel in constant terror of punctures and of the hateful task of replacing the wheel with another which I suspect is also bound to be flat. To ensure its road-worthiness requires frequent visits to a garage which I always look on as an equally repugnant chore. I suppose I was as much interested in personal prestige as most of my contemporaries but I never believed that symbols of any kind enhanced one's status and of all so-called status symbols that which I despised most was the motor-car. Old age has not changed my disenchantment with motor-cars nor indeed my indifference to status symbols of any kind which can be purchased for money.

I have views on the subject of motor-cars generally which have nothing to do with my personal fixations; I think that the smallest car on the market, provided it has reasonable storage space, is perfectly adequate for Irish family use or even for business purposes. There are no long distances in Ireland. The whole island is only 32,000 square miles in area. To reach, for example, the places furthest from Dublin involves for the motorist a journey of about 250 miles at most. An eight or nine horse-power car with a hatchback, a wide range of which are available, should be quite adequate to provide for the average family's transport requirements. With a car full of children the wear and tear on the parents' nerves in a journey of 200 miles is much the same whatever the size of the car. Small cars are quite properly taxed at a very low rate; I would like to see large cars being taxed at a rate which would make ostentation the most expensive commodity in Ireland.

This is a digression from my career in the ESB. As part of the Weckler staff re-organisation I was appointed to the post of chief accounts inspector and controller of stores. My engineering counterpart was one Paddy Flanagan who, in addition to helping to maintain a liaison with the engineering staff, advised me on the technical aspects of the stores materials — I scarcely knew what an insulator was or did. Paddy often accompanied me on my visits to the district offices. His presence made these trips all the more pleasant because he knew the country and the ways of the countryside well.

In its early days the ESB had the advantage of a staff almost messianic in its enthusiasm which was derived originally from McLaughlin's inspiration. Weckler revived and canalised this, often undisciplined, fervour into orderly procedures sustained by hard work. There were no labour problems. Hours worked counted for nothing with the technical or administrative staff and when emergencies occurred, such as a breakdown in any part of the system, total co-operation at all levels was assured. Even some members of the Board chipped in. During a blizzard in the thirties I remember seeing Fay, dressed like a skier, helping to restore the high voltage lines in Kildare. It was an edifying sight.

By the time I left the ESB in 1933 Weckler with the full support of Browne, the chairman, had laid the organisational foundation of the Board as it is today; in my opinion it is the finest industrial organisation in the country; initially its defects lay in a disunited Board membership; today its internal difficulties derive primarily from a multiplicity of trade unions. Its technical competence and record of achievement are beyond question. Only a first-class organisation, for example, could have overcome the problems of bringing electricity to rural Ireland with such notable speed and economy though admittedly the rural electrification scheme was undertaken by the ESB under duress as a result of pressure exerted by Seán Lemass.

It is sad to think that circumstances deprived this country of McLaughlin's great talent at a time when it might still have been put to good account. It is even sadder to think that the wish of every Irishman for *bás in Éirinn* was denied him. He died and was buried in Spain.

I enjoyed and benefited from my period of employment in the ESB and left it with regret. I continued to have good social relations with Weckler, White and other members of his staff as well as some of the engineers with whom I had been on friendly terms. Professionally Weckler was my first and most influential mentor; I learned from him the principles of good management, among them that no business can survive in the absence of a proper accounts system.

8

Gaeltacht Holidays

A major feature of the early years of our family life was our annual summer migration to Carraroe. I was never much interested in taking annual holidays but Mary thought differently and she also decided that she would begin as she intended to continue by spending them in the Gaeltacht. I, of course, agreed and to my great disappointment was unable to rent a house in Ring, of which I had many happy memories from my student days. What Irish I knew was Deise Irish and while 'on the run' there during the Civil War I developed a great affection for the people of the Deise. Friends of ours, Seán Beaumont, a lecturer in Irish in Trinity College, and his wife Maureen suggested that we might go to Carraroe in Connemara. They explained that they were virtually the only summer visitors to the district except for a few anglers. Neither Mary nor I had ever heard of Carraroe and when we found it on the map it looked very remote indeed, situated on a peninsula bounded by Cashla Bay and Greatman's Bay in the far west of south Connemara. The prospect looked daunting but Mary's brother, Donny, who was living in Galway, had a motor-car. We ascertained that there was a post office and a telephone in the village so that medical help would always be within reach if wanted for our child. The Beaumonts got us a house to rent but warned us that living conditions would be primitive as there was much poverty in the neighbourhood. To add to our problems, when holiday time came round I found it difficult to get away from the turmoil in the ESB. I wanted Mary to abandon the expedition but she insisted on going ahead by herself accompanied by a maid who had been hired to help with our infant son — we all had maids in those days. She arranged with her brother to meet the train at Galway and drive her, maid and infant to Carraroe.

The accommodation, or lack of it, so horrified Donny that he wanted to take Mary back to Galway there and then. But Mary wouldn't leave and even though he came back the following day, sure that her overnight experience would discourage her, she decided to stay for the rest of the month for which the house had been rented. That was in 1931 and from then until 1949, except for one year when she was having her fourth child, she came back to

Carraroe for the family holidays every year spending never less than two months, usually three months and on two occasions as much as four months there.

What shocked her brother was the meagreness of the furniture, the open fireplace, the bare condition of bedrooms and beds, the absence of cooking appliances, of drinking water nearby and of washing and toilet facilities. Water for all domestic purposes had to be drawn in buckets from a well 300 yards away and there was a dry lavatory known as the *teachín* fifty yards from the house. When I finally got down there towards the end of the month, Donny drove me out from Galway recounting en route the hazards of Mary's predicament, but on arriving we found a different picture.

Mary was delighted with herself and so, for different reasons, was the maid. The weather had been very fine and they had spent every day on the famous coral strand bathing and picnicking. Mary had got to know the neighbours and had established herself in the two village shops, John Keane's which was also the local pub and the O'Donnell's which was also the local post office. The maid had formed a romantic attachment with one of the local lads. She was as happy with the place as was Mary. She stayed with us for a number of years, always living in anticipation of the annual holiday in Carraroe. She eventually did marry her man and settled in Galway.

The outstanding feature of the house was the landlord himself. At this time a man in his middle sixties he was known to everyone as 'The Bird', a nickname derived from his earlier days when poteen got the better of him and he convinced himself that he could fly. The Carraroe poteen of his day was reputed to have had special psychedelic effects. He had a wizened, nut brown face and the merriest of eyes. He was always in good humour. His normal language, as with everyone in Carraroe in those days, was Irish but he knew some English and between that and Mary's inadequate Irish she learned his story.

He was a widower with one married daughter, Biddy, and later on, an orphaned grandchild, Julia, living with him. They lived, while we were in occupation, in an outhouse. He was the local currach builder and had also a few acres of land. He fished for pollock and mackerel and lobster. At one time he worked for the Irish Lights Commission. On one occasion while engaged in checking buoys and having had too much to drink, he was unable to get back into his currach and was clinging to a rock in Cashla Bay for nearly two days almost dead from exposure before being rescued.

'The Bird' could turn his hand to anything and when the Free State government announced that a grant of £80 would be available to help to build new houses in the Gaeltacht, he decided to build a house. He not merely built the house with his own hands but he made all the furniture including the beds. The house was two-storeyed with three bedrooms on the top floor and a large kitchen with a small room called a 'parlús' off it. The beds were made of deal frames, slotted and grooved, and flock mattresses were supported on the frames by boards — there were no springs. There were heavy home-made quilts which, with the two pillows, were something of an anacronism. They were filled with soft feathers and were the most comfortable things in the house. The place was noteworthy for its cleanliness and the absence of vermin.

Each bedroom had a wash stand — made by 'The Bird' — and a jug and wash basin. There was a bench and three upright chairs in the kitchen as well as two large chairs fitted with arm rests although they could hardly be described as armchairs. Everything, except the crockery, the mattresses and the pillows, were made by 'The Bird'. The house had been slated and the concrete mixed by him. Out of his £80 grant he had a few pounds left over.

It would be difficult to find a more good humoured man or a kinder or more generous one. I think it was his personality which so strongly predisposed Mary to Carraroe. She had no difficulty in learning to cook on the open fire and to use the pot oven. Thanks to 'The Bird' she had an abundance of turf, potatoes and eggs. She baked her own bread and got what meat she wanted in the shops. By the time we were ready to go home she had pre-empted the house for June and July of the following year.

The one aspect of Carraroe which was distressing to Mary was the poverty of the people and bad housing conditions in which they had to live. These were the days before Fianna Fáil and the introduction of the so-called dole. Little and all as it was, the Unemployment Assistance Act gave great relief to hunger and the grimmer manifestations of poverty in the rural west. Only a very low form of begrudger would have objected to the dole and other remedial measures introduced by Fianna Fáil to help the people of that time. One family near us had no less than nine children living in a two-roomed *bothán* with a few acres of land. Mary was very friendly with them and when she came back to Dublin she raised amongst her friends the price of a cow for them which came to £8. On her return to Carraroe each summer a score of eggs and two live chickens were left on the doorstep in acknowledgement of the gift.

For the first few years that we holidayed there we were almost the only *strainséirí* who frequented Carraroe. As our children arrived and reached school age each in their turn attended the local National School. Over the years they became indistinguishable from the children of the district and the older ones were, in effect, native speakers. They spent their time among the fishermen in the currachs, the hookers and glautogs at the harbour at Caladh Thadgh. The eldest ones often brought home lobsters — which could be bought for as little as sixpence each — so that at times the kitchen floor was literally crawling with the creatures. When the mackerel were running, we had as many as we could eat.

For a Dubliner Carraroe was like a new world. The people dressed differently, the men in trousers made of a cloth called *Ceanneasna,* usually with a woollen sweater and a tweed cloth cap. The women wore long red skirts, a light red if they were unmarried and a darker red if they were married. Widows wore black skirts. They wore Paisley shawls over blouses and usually went bareheaded. On Sundays the groups of people spread out along the roads on the way to and from Mass made a colourful sight. The little girls were dressed in long frocks which reached to their ankles; the male children wore skirts until they were pot trained and when they grew up a bit were promoted to short trousers. All children went barefoot in summer.

Their food consisted basically of potatoes, salt, eggs and home-made bread cooked in the pot oven. Milk was scarce and what was to be had was used for tea which was drunk in large quantities. As we got to know the neighbours and were welcomed into the houses, tea and home-made bread were invariably put on the table. Butter was a rarity and was bought rather than home-made. But the scarcest thing in Carraroe in the thirties was money. What money there was usually came from the earnings of children who had emigrated to the USA or to England. Many of the people of Carraroe had closer personal links with Boston than with Dublin. The farm holdings were so small and barren that even supplemented by fishing they could provide a living only for one son so that the rest of the family were forced to emigrate. Even those who went only as far as England rarely came back to settle down or even holiday with their families although some of those who went to Boston returned to retire and spend their declining days in Carraroe. When Fianna Fáil came to power in 1932 there was an upsurge of interest in the revival of the language and other families like ours came to Carraroe to brush up their Irish. Local residents improved their housekeeping and set about providing accommodation for these visitors who brought some badly needed cash into the community.

The feature which distinguished Carraroe as a seaside resort was its famous coral beach. There were a few other such beaches along the coast but that near Carraroe was the best known. The beach was composed of coral shaped particles, not the product of live coral but derived from calcified seaweed formed out in the Atlantic and washed ashore in millions of tons in the area of Greatman's Bay.

The beach was known locally by several names, *'Dóilín'*, *'Trá na Mná'*, *'Trá na páistí'*. It formed a magnificent bathing site, clean, safe and with transparently clear water. Even in our time there it had become a popular bathing place for Galway people and on weekends there were many visitors to be found on the strand. It was at *Dóilín* that I first saw a bikini. My eldest son, when he was about seven, discovered that it was possible to thread the coral into necklets and bracelets. He hawked them among the visitors at six-pence and threepence each and did a thriving business. In a shirt, trousers and bare feet he had all the appearance of being in genuine need of a few pence and often got them in addition to the price charged for his coral ornaments.

Mary's Irish improved and we spoke as much Irish as English while in Carraroe but, on returning home at the end of the summer and despite the fact that the children attended Irish-speaking schools in Dublin, English became the family language again. We made innumerable efforts to get the family conversing on at least a bilingual basis but never had any permanent success. The truth was that Mary and I knew more English than we could ever know Irish and to express ourselves in English was much less of an effort. Further, there was a certain artificiality in trying to sustain what would now be described as a 'meaningful' conversation in Irish for any length of time.

Over the years during which we spent the long summers in Carraroe, Mary got to know all the neighbours very well but, despite this intimacy, there were private lives and family relationships which no stranger could hope to penetrate. Glimpses of this private world would emerge accidentally from time to time. Our children, who were virtually adopted by the neighbours, would come home with innocent remarks indicative of strained family relations or some domestic secret that they had overheard.

Mary and the children would happily spend every day on the beach running in and out of the sea. In our first years there I also did a lot of swimming. Later on I fished a great deal with Charles Lamb in the local lake, Loch a' Mhuilinn, for brown trout but sometimes for sea trout on more distant lakes with Mr Scott, the father of Michael Scott, the well-known architect. He was an old man then — in his late seventies — but that did not prevent him cycling as much as fourteen miles to and from Muckanagh Lake where the fishing was very good. These cycling trips were a greater physical strain for me than for Mr Scott but his company was worth the effort. Bad weather did not bother him and we often came back from these excursions with large bags of trout but thoroughly saturated.

Returning one evening wet and cold from such an expedition we stopped at a pub for a hot whiskey but instead were offered hot rum, held to be a more reliable drink since it had been retrieved from the flotsam of a ship torpedoed on the way from Jamaica. It was powerful stuff and when we started on our seven mile journey home we had difficulty in mounting our bikes and several falls occurred in great good humour. Finally, with the help of a couple of locals, we got under way giggling like schoolboys. When we arrived at Mr Scott's lodging he fell off his bike into a ditch. I was afraid to go to his assistance owing to the difficulty of getting mounted again and the last I saw of my companion was of his waving me goodbye from the ditch and shouting that he would call for me tomorrow at ten for another day's fishing at Mackanagh. And sure enough, there he was the next morning ringing his bicycle bell at the appointed time but I did not feel game to repeat the dose. We settled for brown trout in Loch a' Mhuilinn instead. Mr Scott was a man of iron. In his youth he had been a nationally-known athlete and was the 440 yards champion of Ireland.

Carraroe had three citizens who stood out from the rest of the community. Bartley Lydon, who had a small shop and a relatively large farm, was the first in the parish to adapt his house to take summer visitors. He gave his summer guests generous help in learning Irish. He was a philosopher. He sat on a chair outside the house dispensing wisdom, in Irish, to anyone who cared to listen. He was the only local I knew to bathe in the sea but only did so in September. According to him it was only then that sea bathing did any good because at that time it was full of iodine.

John Keane was the publican and hardware store owner but he also sold food stuffs. It was a wonderful sight to see the ceiling of his shop festooned with buckets, flitches of bacon and a variety of tools. John had an ironic, not to say cynical, sense of humour and he had what were almost certainly slanderous, if amusing, observations to make about all his customers. He was a decent man. An ex-IRA man, he was the leading Fianna Fáil supporter in the district and eventually became a TD.

The O'Donnell brothers ran the post office and what would nowadays be called a supermarket. In those days they were known as *gombeen* men, a word which in Irish nationalist circles was particularly offensive. The truth was that people like the O'Donnells, far from being bloodsuckers, which the term denotes, performed an essential service for the locality. Without that service many of the people would have had to endure hunger, go barefooted and be deprived of the minimum household necessities. Furthermore, the

O'Donnells were very well liked locally and worked hard for a living. Seeing them in action made me careful of using the word 'gombeenism' in a pejorative sense.

The most unlikely person to be found in Carraroe was Charles Lamb, the painter. When he set out on his professional career the Civil War was at its height. Charles was probably unaware that the country was up in arms when he started westward from Galway on an exploratory visit to Cois Fharraige. He travelled on an outside car and only when he found every bridge and culvert between Galway and Carraroe blown up did he realise that something was amiss. He was entranced by the stark scenery and particularly by the ever-changing light, a Connemara phenomenon which has attracted so many painters. He decided that Carraroe was where he wanted to live and follow his profession as an artist. He went back to Dublin, collected his wife and returned in a genuine horse drawn caravan to Carraroe where he lived for the remainder of a long life and raised his family. At first his home was the caravan but, as his family grew, he acquired a nearby cottage. After some years he became the beneficiary of a sizeable inheritance and very wisely decided to invest it in a more substantial residence. With the aid of a well-known northern architect he designed and built a magnificent cut-stone house and studio.

Charles came from a very well-off family of house decorators in Portadown. They were a highly cultivated family whose main interest was music but they fully approved of Charles' ambition to make his career in art. He had their moral support in what would have appeared to most people an eccentric decision to settle and raise a family in remote Carraroe where at that time Irish, rather than English, was the common language and where to even English speakers Charles' Portadown accent must have seemed strange. Charles was a Catholic as was his English wife, Katherine, the daughter of Ford Madox Ford, the English novelist. Ford Madox Ford had only two children, both of them daughters. Katherine's sister had become a nun, a member of the snob English order of the Society of the Holy Child of Jesus, which had been founded by the famous Cornelia Connolly. Katherine had qualified as a vetinerary surgeon in Dublin where she and Charles met.

To find a family like the Lambs in a place like Carraroe looked improbable but they were an improbable couple. Charles was totally and solely interested in his painting. He never spoke a word of Irish in my hearing although he could not have helped knowing it. Nor was he interested in the people of the locality from whom he held aloof. Katherine on the other hand, who had abandoned her veterinary career when she married, loved the people and, until it became an intolerable imposition, she gave her services freely to those with sick animals. She learned and spoke Irish and her children were also native speakers.

Charles, like so many artists, was indifferent to wealth. At that time it was not easy to sell pictures but Charles had the advantage of being an all-round craftsman. He could make his own frames, repair damaged furniture and do any bits of plumbing or masonry needed around the house. He architected a beautiful summer house for Arnold Ussher, the philosopher, who had decided to pass the war years in the peace of Connemara.

Charles had many visitors. One of them was Francis MacNamara, Dylan Thomas' father-in-law, so well described in *Two Flamboyant Fathers*, and another was O'Flaherty-Johnson, the squireen of Kilmurvey in Aran. Curiously Charles did not appear to welcome other painters and in his home no paintings were displayed except his own. He refused rather ostentatiously to show any interest in Maurice McGonigal, for example, when he came to visit me in Carraroe. Indeed, I don't think he had many close friends except Padraic Ó Conaire. From time to time Charles went into Galway on some errand, met Ó Conaire by accident and went on the shaughran with him. After a couple of weeks' adventures of the kind to be found in *Gil Blas*, he would show up in Carraroe unabashed. Katherine looked with amusement on these digressions and realising how hard he worked she felt that he was entitled to some relaxation. I often went out with him on the turf boats to Aran but was careful to stipulate that no alcohol should be drunk on these occasions; otherwise it would be a week before he could be persuaded to leave the island and his friend, O'Flaherty-Johnson.

Many of our friends and relations came to stay with Mary in Carraroe and they were welcome so long as they realised that they were not coming to a hotel. Mary's sister, Rosemary, a girl of exceptionally striking looks who was a student at the School of Art and UCD, enlivened the household and the neighbourhood. She never went down to the shops without coming back with a tale of some comical adventure. The children loved her. Bridie Clyne, a close friend of ours was another regular visitor. She had been Frank Aiken's secretary and Man (or Woman) Friday during the Civil War and fulfilled the same role to Frank Gallagher when he became editor of the *Irish Press*. She was a raconteur of a rare order and as she was au fait with the goings-on in Dublin political circles, Mary was never short of entertainment. I was usually too busy to spend a week, or even a long weekend there, and in the early years I never really settled into it. But in the summer of 1943 due to extremely hard work, over-long hours and missing meals, I got run down and developed a carbuncle. I had always thought of a carbuncle as one of those supposedly comical complaints, like gout, that people developed on their behinds preventing them from sitting down. My carbuncle was on my neck. I became very ill and Mary had to be summoned to take over the nursing. As soon as I was on the road to recovery she returned to Carraroe to rejoin the children who had been left behind in the care of the maid and Katherine Lamb.

Private motoring had been suspended during the war and I was still physically too weak to travel by train or bus. However, Ted Courtney who was one of my colleagues on the Turf Executive and his assistant, Dan Herlihy, kindly arranged their programme of bog inspections to include Carraroe and delivered me there in comfort. It took two full months of convalescence in Carraroe to complete my recovery but by the end of that time I had learned to appreciate and enjoy the place as much as Mary and the family.

When I remarked, as I often did, on the disadvantages of holidaying in Carraroe — the absence of running water, telephone, flush lavatories, electricity or reasonable cooking facilities — Mary had a strong defence. She pointed out that even at home I was often absent for days at a time and the family saw as much of me in Carraroe as they did in Dublin. It was not until I joined the Turf Board that we had a telephone installed at home and she regarded it as a nuisance. She found it hard to make a case against running water and flush lavatories but she didn't think their absence made life intolerable. Cooking on the open fire with the pot oven was, she protested, rather a pleasure to her and the evenings were so short that oil lamps and candles supplied quite adequate lighting.

Her laundry routine was a source of great amusement to me. She brought her pot oven to a nearby pond, lit a fire under it and boiled the clothes before rubbing them out on a washboard. I suggested to Charles Lamb that the scene would make a good subject for a picture but I could never persuade him to paint it.

But what appealed to Mary most about life in Carraroe was the absence of social obligations or the routine of regular meals. She had a very leisurely breakfast in bed and that was her main meal of the day. For the rest, she ate when she was hungry and drank when she was dry. Her visits to the beach and the length of her stay there depended on the weather; she interpreted 'fine weather' liberally. She was never tied down by appointments and luxuriated in an atmosphere of complete relaxation. She did not regard her way of life as austere or even frugal nor, allowing for the fact that normal living was suspended in holiday time, did she find the lack of amenities in 'the Bird's' house in any way objectionable. How much more uncomfortable, she asserted, would be a camping holiday.

She also held very strongly that, apart from learning to speak Irish, our children should also learn through their experience of Carraroe that there was an Ireland of rural as well as suburban values and that the children they met and played with were none the worse off for being deprived of the 'good things' of life. It was a lesson that she would never allow them to forget.

Even after we ceased to holiday regularly in Carraroe we never severed our connectons with Cois Fharraige. I have frequently revisited the area, mainly for fishing, which has always been one of my favourite pursuits. My preference was for brown trout which made up in quantity what they lacked in quality as game fish. In one day my brother-in-law, Donny Coyle and I, caught a hundred brown trout averaging half a pound in the lake at Ballynahown, a few miles from Carraroe. For this reason, as well as for many other reasons, Cois Fharraige holds a warm place in my memory.

9

The Bogs — A Crusade

The Beginning

I was at a stage of my life when I was more content than ever before. I was happily married and rearing a family. My job in the ESB was interesting and varied and the organisation was expanding. My salary was reasonable. I was given a very free hand in carrying out my work and had plenty of responsibility. I liked my colleagues and my chief, Fred Weckler, was considerate and very able. From him I was rapidly learning the techniques of business organisation, management and accounting that, until his arrival, were very new to Ireland. As well as being happy in my home and my work I had a wide circle of friends from my IRA and political associations, from my school and university days. I was enjoying a full life through reading, the theatre, politics, swimming and watching football. I was also enjoying the triumphalism which so characterised us who were followers of de Valera and which was balm to the bitter scars of the Civil War. Our fears of the Free Staters were removed even though our hatred of them was not. We were determined to show them that the Civil War was not in vain. A great burst of energy was released both in the political and the economic field. It was our version of the 'great leap forward' of Mao Tse Tung.

On the political side the oath of allegiance (one of the main causes of the Civil War) was abolished. The land annuities were withheld, the right of appeal to the Privy Council was revoked, the Irish courts were made the final arbiters of Irish law, the governor-general was ignored preparatory to the office itself being abolished. We felt we had taken our place amongst the nations of the earth when in 1932 de Valera became President of the Council of the League of Nations. Special emergency schemes for the relief of un-employment were pushed through and, most important, the Un-employment Assistance Act was introduced. This was a costly measure but it relieved the poverty, sometimes amounting to destitution, which was widespread in rural areas and particularly along the western seaboard. These were merely a prelude to a long series of social reforms carried out by Fianna Fáil to ameliorate the conditions of the poor. Under the direction of Seán Lemass new industries began to spring up all over the country in contrast to the many factory closures (over a hundred since they came into power) which had occurred under the more than liberal — the *laissez-faire* — policies of the Free Staters. Clearance of the Dublin slums began and home building was being encouraged all over the country.

Despite the difficulties created by the so-called economic war (fought with economic weapons, it was a sample of British political bullying) agriculture was also developed. A great wheat-growing campaign was started and a large scale expansion of the beet sugar industry undertaken. We felt the nation at last was on the march and that the sacrifices of the Rebellion, the Black and Tan War and the Civil War were bearing fruit. It was in the middle of all this exciting national advance that Seán Lemass asked me to take charge of the scheme which the government had in mind for the development of the bogs.

My earliest association with turf was during a visit to my Longford relatives in 1916 and it consisted merely of the smell of a turf fire. Later I stayed with Paddy Smith, then a very young IRA officer and later Minister for Agriculture, on the Cavan-Fermanagh border and he took me to a bog to see turf being cut and saved. What I did know was that the word 'bog' or any phrase containing it, had become the symbol of poverty and backwardness. The 'bog-trotter' was the Irish archetype of ignorance and illiteracy. The bog-men were the descendants of the Fir Bolgs, the bog itself in the Irish mind was a symbol of aridity and barrenness. A large area of the Irish 'race unconscious' was overlaid by bog. But there was another view of the significance of the bogs in the economic geography of Ireland. Scientists and others had looked on the great waste areas of our bogs as a valuable source of wealth if they could be properly utilised. It is not easy to accept that undrained bog consists of up to 95% water and that, as the late Professor Hugh Ryan was fond of pointing out, a glass of milk contains more dry matter than the same volume of undrained bog. It is a major problem to reduce the moisture content of a bog to 89% or 90% and that is the best result which can be achieved by ordinary drainage. Thus in the past many efforts to exploit bogs commercially foundered because they were not adequately drained or because even in the relatively small areas where it was fully effective the percentage of solid matter resulting from drainage was too small to be of economic value.

Even a bog drained to 89% moisture content is uneconomic for agricultural use because the top layers must be removed to create a satisfactory growing medium. This is a costly process unless the material so removed is used either as fuel or for soil-conditioning purposes. This is the approach to bog development which was adopted successfully in Holland and Germany but it was carried out over a very long period of time. At first sight it would seem that the obvious way to de-water turf for use as a fuel or as an industrial raw material would be to extract it by pressure but the water is held in colloidal rather than mechanical combination; it has been found experimentally that almost every known pressing process would consume more energy than can be got out of the finished product. The manufacture of turf briquettes by the Peco process is an exception to this rule in so far as it successfully combines natural and artificial drying systems. This is the principle on which our own briquette factories is based.

From time to time, endless techniques and devices — wet presses, dry presses, electro-osmosis, ball peat drums, horse driven machines, sieves, wet carbonisers — had been applied to the economic production of turf, but without success. Dozens of patents exist for the utilisation of turf for specialised purposes such as carbonising, gasification, and the extraction of high grade products such as paper, artificial wood, ammonia, alcohol, animal feeding stuffs, cosmetics, medical dressings and medicaments. In the matter of medicaments it is said, but I have never seen it recorded, that bog water is a potent aphrodisiac. If that is found to be true our Irish balance of payments could cease to be a problem and we could make a substantial contribution to the conservation of the rhinoceros as a species. It is a tribute to the good sense of Bord na Móna that their efforts to produce cheap turf were never diverted into these sterile channels despite the pressure of the innumerable cranks for whom the bogs hold a peculiar fascination. Bord na Móna stuck to Swift's advice to produce turf to burn. Dean Swift made the famous remark which has been so great an inspiration to workers in peat: 'I heard the late Archbishop of Tuam mention a pleasant observation of somebody's, "that Ireland will never be happy till laws were made for burning everything that comes from England except their people and their coals".'

From time immemorial the production of turf by hand for use as a domestic fuel has been traditional in rural Ireland. Since the beginning of the nineteenth century interest grew in the possibility of developing the bogs on a more organised commercial basis and many attempts to do so were made by private entrepreneurs and landowners. Government commissions were also set up to enquire how best the bogs might be exploited. Most of these early efforts were aimed at the reclamation and improvement of the bogs for agricultural use but gradually the interest shifted in the direction of fuel production. Unfortunately, neither the efforts of private enterprise nor the reports of the government commissions bore fruit. The former failed through lack of capital and technical expertise, the latter through official opposition or inertia.

Two communications on the subject of peat submitted to the Royal Dublin Society in 1907/8 by Professor Hugh Ryan throw light on the state of the turf industry at the beginning of this century. Professor Ryan's paper is a masterly review and ranges from an examination of the origin of peat through the history of previous efforts made to win peat in Ireland to an examination of the various methods hitherto employed here and on the Continent and concluded with a systematic bibliography of peat. Reading Professor Ryan's paper, anyone who is associated with peat will realise at once that here was a remarkable man. He was one of the members of a committee set up by the British government in 1917 under the Department of Scientific and Industrial Research with Sir John Purser Griffith as chairman and Pierce Purcell as secretary. The committee's terms of reference were:

> to enquire into and consider the experience already gained in Ireland in respect of the winning, preparation and use of peat for fuel, and for other purposes, and to suggest what means shall be taken to ascertain the conditions under which, in the most favourably situated localities it can be profitably won, prepared, and used, having regard to the economic conditions of Ireland; and to report to the Fuel Research Board.

The committee's report is remarkable for its thoroughness and, in the light of subsequent events, for the sagacity of its conclusions. It recommended the purchase of a bog capable of producing 100,000 tons of air-dried peat per annum and advocated the installation of the different types of electrically driven peat-winning machines and the various mechanical devices at that time available for transport and for collection of peat. It advocated the establishment of an electric power station using peat-fired gas producers and of a chemical industry to be associated with the power station. It also recommended the erection of villages for workers in the vicinity of the bogs. It envisaged the utilisation, for agricultural purposes, of portions of the bogs not immediately required for fuel winning and the cultivation of the cutaway bog.

The fate of the committee's recommendations is an interesting example of the native hue of resolution being sicklied over by the pale cast of thought. The prospect of the State financing a power station seemed to horrify the Fuel Research Board and the committee was persuaded to modify its recommendations fundamentally. The generating plant was reduced in size to a fraction of what was originally envisaged and the electricity produced was to be used only to power the bog machinery.

They were even more unfortunate in the reception of their

recommendations with regard to the setting up of workers' houses and the cultivation of the cutaway bog. The agricultural side of their scheme was to be under the control and management of the Department of Agriculture whose opposition was clear from the start and who succeeded in killing it on what proved to be completely specious grounds.

The net result of the committee's work, as far as the government was concerned, was to authorise Professor Purcell and his assistant, Edward Duffy, to carry out experiments into the properties of machine-formed peat which might have a bearing on its economic winning and utilisation. It was also agreed to appoint Professor Purcell as peat investigation officer to the Fuel Research Department and to allow him to make a study of peat in Canada. Professor Purcell's lecture on 'The Peat Resources of Ireland' which was communicated to the Royal Dublin Society in March, 1918, and printed by the Fuel Research Department, gives a comprehensive account of the whole problem.

In 1920, a commission to enquire into the resources and industries of Ireland was set up by Dáil Éireann and Professor Hugh Ryan was appointed chairman of the committee dealing with the peat resources. The committee produced a very detailed report much on the lines of the Purser Griffith report but their recommendation went further. The experienced hand of Hugh Ryan is clearly to be seen, especially in the withering criticism of the Department of Agriculture's attitude to the Griffith Committee's proposals. The report of the 1920 Commission advocated turbo-alternators rather than gas producers for electricity production on a large scale. It also advocated experiments in the use of pulverised fuel for rotary kilns and locomotives and it put considerable emphasis on the desirability of producing nitrogeneous fertilisers and explosives.

In 1922 Professor Hugh Ryan published his translation from the German of Hausding's *Handbook on the Winning and Utilisation of Peat*. This is a complete compendium of turf knowledge as it existed in Germany in 1918; it contains a record of every patent taken out on turf in Germany. This is an indispensable part of the equipment of every turf organisation and particularly of those engaged in experimentation and research. It has saved Bord na Móna very considerable sums of money by preventing incursions into the already traversed jungle paths of turf exploitation. Incidentally, it is commonly said by turf people in Germany that Hausding himself never saw a bog. He was employed in the German Patent Office.

Sir John Purser Griffith had himself gone into the turf business and having experimented with some semi-automatic machines at a bog which he acquired at Turraun, County Offaly, he purchased in 1924 fully automatic machines, built a turf-fired generating plant and produced machine turf of first-class quality which secured a considerable market even at that time. His idea was to extend the power house to supply electricity to the neighbouring towns of Tullamore, Athlone and Birr. He believed in his own slogan: 'Burn the bog where it is born'.

Perhaps it was as well that I was too commercially inexperienced to know that the first thing I should have done on accepting my new assignment was read the literature. Even had I done so I would not have been in the least put off by the long history of previous failures. At that time nothing affecting the good of the nation seemed impossible to us. Nor was my anxiety to participate in building up a new Ireland diminished when I paid my first official visit to Seán Lemass to hear what my duties were to be. I found that he had no real interest in turf. He knew even less about it than I did; I had at least seen a bog. It began to dawn on me that why he had asked me to take on the development of the bogs was in order to get Frank Aiken, the Minister for Defence, off his back. It transpired that Aiken had been persuaded by Tom Harris, the TD for Kildare, to have turf used for heating the Curragh Military Encampment. It provided a ready and profitable market for the local producers who used to take their small loads of turf each week to Dublin to sell at the market at Smithfield. As often as not they stopped off at the Dead Man Murray's public house at Palmerstown and fell asleep in their carts leaving it to the horses to steer their way home. Aiken became fascinated by the possibilities of using the bogs as a national source of fuel. He was an idealist in every sense of the word and a convinced Sinn Féiner in the Arthur Griffith tradition. He developed a scheme for the expansion of turf production on lines which had no appeal for Lemass.

Under the persuasion of Gordon Campbell, formerly secretary to the Department of Industry and Commerce, and Professor Purcell, Lemass had already agreed to support financially the estab-lishment of a peat briquette factory at Lullymore in County Kildare. He regarded that as sufficient fulfilment of Fianna Fáil's election promise to develop the bogs. The briquette factory was technically a highly sophisticated undertaking based on what was known as the Peco process; its advanced technology removed the enterprise from the category of bog-trotters and gave it some sort of industrial cachet. The enterprise might have been successful if the promoters had practical knowledge of bog drainage or the varying characteristics of turf deposits even in the same bog. Further, despite the fact that Sir John Purser Griffth had made the bog at

Lullymore, which he happened to own, available to the new Company, his warning based on his experience at Turraun of the difficulties likely to be experienced in draining the bog went unheeded.

When Seán Lemass first asked me to take charge of the development of the bogs he told me that it would be necessary for me to enter the civil service and and that I would have to leave the Fianna Fáil organisation and take no further part in politics. This did not worry me because I felt I would still be involved in carrying out Fianna Fáil policy and anyway party politics, as they were developing, were of no interest to me. Lemass also told me that if I ran into any difficulty in dealing with the civil service I should bring the problem directly to him. I interpreted this to mean that I would be responsible to him personally. This I am sure was the original intention of the government. I had had sight of a copy of the government minute of my appointment which said so.

Unfortunately the civil service had not been consulted about the terms of my appointment or my precise status. It was said that the legislation under which the civil service was set up did not admit of such an arrangement. I knew nothing of these legal complexities and even if I had, I would not have been deterred from taking on the job. We in Fianna Fáil regarded all senior civil servants as 'a crowd of Free State bastards'; mere tools of the Cosgrave government. I did not consider them as a factor in my calculations as prospective head of the turf scheme. It took some time and involved me in much unpleasantness before I realised how I had misapprehended the situation.

The Irish civil service had been set up by a group of Irish and a few English officials who held fairly senior posts in the British civil service prior to the Treaty. They modelled the new bureaucracy exactly on the British administrative structure with the additon of a simulacrum of a foreign office which they called the Department of External Affairs. The organisation they created was of a form well suited to administering an empire on which the sun never sets or a nation with an advanced industrial economy but was totally out of place in the Irish political context and for ten years had existed as an unlanced blister on the Irish economy. Fianna Fáil intended to burst that blister and I was more than eager to take part in any surgery which proved necessary.

The creators of the civil service—Brennan, Gregg, MacElligott, Dagg, Codling, Almond, Boland, Glenavy, Leydon — were in economic terms liberals (in the Dangerfield sense) and disciples of Adam Smith. It was said of Adam Smith that his ideas had 'persuaded his own generaton and governed the next'. His philosophy was still governing the thinking of Ireland's new officialdom. They took the view that the function of the government was to maintain law and order, collect the revenues and prevent money being disbursed from the exchequer for any avoidable reason. Obviously they could not avoid paying the police and the army, but even this seemed to go against the grain. They felt no obligation to improve living standards and the limitations of their social conscience are reflected in a statement which McGilligan made in the Dáil when he was Minister for Industry and Commerce. 'There are certain limited funds at our disposal. People may have to die in this country and may have to die of starvation.' This exhibited a frame of mind not much different from the leading English economist, Nassau Senior, who, according to Cecil Woodham Smith, 'feared that the famine of 1848 in Ireland would not kill more than a million people and that would scarcely be enough to do much good.' But if the founders of the civil service contributed nothing else to the national economic aggrandisement they will, or should be, remembered with gratitude for having inflicted (and I use the word advisedly) from the outset the standards of probity and good conduct on the public service without which we might have degenerated into a banana republic or worse.

But it took us some time to discover that truth. Before Dev came to power we regarded the higher civil servants as mere minions of the Free State government and, *par consequence,* anti-national. In fact, they were a capable group of administrators within the limits of their experience in Britain. Their mistake was to think that what was administratively good for the imperial goose was good for the pastoral Irish gander. Individually, they were highly intelligent and highly cultivated men — far too intelligent and experienced for the ministers whom they served and on whom it was easy for them to inflict their social and economic ideas. Nor according to their lights were they less concerned for the welfare of the nation than were we Republicans. In the atmosphere of the time it would have been impossible for us to recognise that fact.

The secretary of the Department of Industry and Commerce in 1933 was John Leydon. He had been appointed as successor to Gordon Campbell, Lord Glenavy, by the Free Staters during the election which brought Fianna Fáil to power in 1932. Characteristically, he refused to take up the post until the new government had taken over and confirmed his appointment. The appointment elicited the jibe at the next Fianna Fáil Árd Fheis from Dr Con Murphy — who, with his family, had suffered savagely under the Free State regime — that it was the policy of Mr de Valera 'to forgive his enemies and forget his friends.'

Seán Lemass introduced me to Leydon, who brought me to his office. Without preliminaries and quite impersonally Leydon told me with cold directness that he saw no reason why I should be admitted to the civil service. He said there were plenty of established officials capable of looking after turf development. In this, of course, he was right. What he did not understand was that, however able the selected man might be, the system under which he would have to work would have made failure inevitable. Any enterprise that involves the displacement of matter is unsuitable for civil service management. It is not the civil servants who are responsible for the inadequacy of our telephone service or for the relative backwardness of our afforestation or for the slow progress of our arterial drainage; it is the system which the civil servants have to work. There was an abundance of bureaucrats and administrators. What we in Fianna Fáil wanted was action.

Leydon made it clear that he thought a political job was being made for me. He also made it clear that ranking as an assistant principal officer I would not be reporting to the minister, nor even to himself as secretary to the department. Leydon was a stocky man below average height. He spoke with a very low voice and stared at me through rimless spectacles. He looked as if he never smiled. His reception confirmed me in our view of the civil service as 'a crowd of Free State bastards'. In time I discovered that, apart from the fact that they were not bastards, they were not even Free Staters. The senior civil servants were mainly apolitical. During the ten years of the Free State regime little effort was made apart from the Shannon Scheme and the sugar beet factories to encourage industrial development. They believed that the efficient pastoralisation of the country would be enough to produce national prosperity. Leydon in the beginning of his career had, I suspect, little enthusiasm for much of Lemass' protectionist policy. He had no hesitation in putting his view to Lemass but nevertheless saw to it that the minister's directives were carried out rigidly.

I left Leydon to make contact with the next official in the department hierarchy regarding him as a large part of the blister to be lanced. It was impossible for me to foresee that in the years ahead I would come to regard Leydon as by far the greatest public servant of our time and as an outstanding Irish man of his generation. He always discounted his achievements, loyally attributing them exclusively to Lemass. This was not so. He was the crutch on which Lemass leaned, and in the absence of Leydon some of the decisions made towards the end of his political life were lacking in judgment.

Leydon passed me along to the Establishment Officer, one Tremayne Price. He had never encountered an IRA man before and was quite intrigued to meet me. There was nothing apolitical about Price. He had served in the British army and was an out-an-out Britisher in attitude and sympathies. He was anxious to leave me under no misapprehension as to his standpoint in this respect. He was a very direct and talkative man and quite unlike the run of civil servants in openly expressing his opinions. He took a note of my particulars, my date and place of birth, my educational background and marital status. He was not unfriendly but seemed to regard the turf development scheme with mild amusement. His directness surprised me pleasantly and I felt we would get on well, as indeed we did. His office was in a grubby little room over a shop in Dame Street.

Price introduced me to the Trades Section of the department which was housed in a concrete, barrack-like office in nearby Lord Edward Street. The building was filthy. There I met William Maguire who was to be my immediate boss. He contrasted with his surroundings by being extremely well dressed. To my surprise his reception was most friendly. He actually welcomed me to the department. I was probably the first IRA man he too had ever met, and, like Price, this aroused his curiosity. He went to some trouble to explain that he was entirely neutral politically. He sympathised with me for having undertaken so impossible a task as the development of the bogs about which, he said, he knew nothing. He promised me any help possible and said he had arranged an office for me in La Touche buildings in nearby Castle Street. As far as his promise of help was concerned he reminded me of the Dublin man who was 'a decent fellow when he had it, but like that again he never had it.'

La Touche building had been owned by the well-known and powerful eighteenth century family of Huguenot bankers but was then part of Dublin Castle and was in an advanced state of decay. There were no other occupants in the building and I was installed in an enormous uncarpeted room with creaky floor boards on the ground floor. The furniture consisted of a large table on which was the telephone. After a week the Board of Works provided me with a chair and so began the most important phase of my career in the public service.

These initial meetings with Leydon, Price and Maguire were sufficient to convince me that if the government wanted the bogs developed the civil service was not the organisation to use for the purpose; I made up my mind to buck the system. A bundle of about twenty files headed 'Peat' or 'Turf' arrived on my table. Each file consisted of two sheets of paper. One was a letter to the minister or the president (as the Taoiseach was then called) from people in different parts of the country urging on them the case for turf development; or some specific proposal connected with it; the other was a copy of a formal acknowledgement of receipt of the letter. The letters covered a space of ten years — a tribute to the filing system of the department. It was also a fair reflection of the interest in the turf industry displayed by the previous government and its servants.

While I was waiting for my chair from the Board of Works I worked from Aiken's office. It was from his office and under his general direction that the scheme got under way. The basis of the scheme, as it was conceived initially by him, rested on the traditional methods of winning turf by hand. Production was to be left in the hands of private enterprise and the role of the state was merely that of creating conditions calculated to stimulate maximum turf production. In an effort to make turf acceptable as a commercial fuel, particularly to the urban user, quality standards (viz. a minimum density 0·9 and a maximum moisture content 30%) were laid down and a standard bogside price was fixed for turf supplied to this specification. A multitude of local bog improvement schemes to provide better facebank drainage and road access were undertaken. Finally, in order to obtain countrywide distribution at a reasonable cost, a very attractive flat rate for the conveyance of turf by rail was introduced. It was my first contact with railway administration and even to me, who was inexperienced in dealing with people at general and traffic manager level, it was evident that they were men without hope and willing to do anything to please the government in the expectation of being bailed out of their financial difficulties.

Frank Aiken came from a south Armagh farming family in easy circumstances. He went from school into the IRA and had never the experience of earning a living. In 1923 he was a man of twenty-five, tall, heavily-built, dark and balding even then. He had most peculiar social standards. Having no money worries himself, he could not understand that people had problems in rearing and educating families. He could not distinguish between poverty and frugal comfort and thought that anyone who was not actually on the breadline was well enough off. Society owed its members no more than that.

He was a brave soldier and a competent one. No man had felt so deeply about the 'split' on the Treaty and no man tried harder to prevent the Civil War. He had unlimited patience and unusual capacity for detail. He was indifferent to the opinions of either his political friends or opponents or indeed of anyone except de Valera. He could not be insulted because he was never aware of an insult being offered. He was not sensitive to the feelings of others. Nor could he be intimidated. During the war, for example, he went to America to seek arms from President Roosevelt. With great persistence, he succeeded in seeing the great man who told him how he loved Ireland and how grieved he was that we were neutral. Aiken, unimpressed and unflattered, brought the discussion back to the request for arms. Roosevelt became angry, rang for his butler to lay the lunch table for one, Aiken refused to take the hint that the interview was at an end. Roosevelt got even more angry and pulled the table cloth, cutlery and plates off the table. Aiken, still impassive, was ushered out.

It was this same incapacity to be intimidated that made him so well suited to the post of Co-ordinator of Defensive Measures during the Emergency which included responsibility for newspaper censorship. In this role, he was, in effect, the censor. He was frequently in conflict with the newspapers, particularly the *Irish Times.* But when the war ended and the censorship was lifted, he invited the editors of the major newspapers to a celebratory dinner which all of them, except one, attended. Smyllie, the editor of the *Irish Times,* was the 'clou' of the party. All the schemes devised to defeat the censorship were revealed and all the counter ploys recounted. Smyllie was hilarious and the evening was hilarious too. Frank smiled benignly on the proceedings.

Aiken was a man of ingenuity and imagination. He was the last of the Sinn Féiners. The economic aggrandisement of the Irish nation was his obsession. Within Fianna Fáil the pressure to develop the bogs came largely from him but his *modus operandi* was based on the assumption that bog people were more idealistic than they proved to be. The Gaeltacht glasshouse scheme was also his concept but he failed to create an infra-structure to support it. He was an engineer *manqué* and in another age would have been an alchemist. He spent much of his time and money trying to upset the law of thermodynamics. He was an idealist but unlike another Don Quixote, he built windmills rather than tilted at them.

He put a lot of effort into furthering the Irish language and spoke and promoted it whenever possible. He knew a lot more about financial matters than he got credit for and less than he thought he did about international affairs. As Minister for External Affairs, he ignored the advice of his civil servants except that of his diplomatic adjutants, Conor Cruise O'Brien and Fred Boland — men of very different views and temperament. They must have provided him with the problem of making a difficult political synthesis. In later years he developed messianic tendencies in international affairs particularly in connection with Tibet, Taiwan and the proliferation of the atomic bomb.

But without Aiken there would never have been a Bord na Móna.

Building an Infrastructure

I had the idea that the marketing of turf might best be dealt with through the formation of co-operative societies and I approached the Irish Agricultural Organisation Society to see how this might be organised. The IAOS was at this time moribund. The secretary was Dr Henry Kennedy whom I had known when he had been a lecturer in mathematical physics in UCD and as secretary of the White Cross in the early days of the state. He had assumed that he was going to be made head of the civil service in 1922 but a bilious temperament had made him unacceptable despite close family ties and old boy network connections with the government. He had taken the post of secretary and chief executive of the IAOS very much as a *pis aller* and there I found him a disgruntled man, sulking in his tent, waiting for someone to come in so that he could loose a tirade against two high officials in the Department of Finance named Codling and Dagg whom he always referred to as Dagling and Codd. Alternatively, he would abuse the officials of the Department of Agriculture and particularly those associated with the Dairy Disposal Board. A *Bricriú* if ever there was one. Like the civil servants, he favoured the pastoralisation of the country. One of his favourite notions was that hay-making should be prohibited and silage enforced; he felt personally insulted when this policy was not adopted by the government.

The proposal that the IAOS should organise a co-operative marketing of the turf was more than welcome to him. It meant that he would have some contact with government circles and would have something to do other than brood on his grievances in his spacious and well-equipped office which looked all the more attractive to me after the squalor of La Touche buildings.

Henry Kennedy 'knew all about turf' having been born on a bog on the Keeper Mountain in Tipperary. He made no secret of the fact that he would have preferred to have been born elsewhere and in circumstances where his natural intellectual gifts could have blossomed into the more spacious and gracious life which he so coveted and which by his talents he believed himself to be entitled.

Dr Kennedy offered most willingly the assistance of the IAOS and we set about forming co-operative turf societies in all the bog areas. The Department of Industry and Commerce provided him with funds to increase his staff for this purpose. There were some one hundred and eighty of these societies established over the next few years and, if I derived no other advantage from the exercise, I got to know the countryside and its people very well. I had got around much on foot during the Civil War and had lived off the people of the land but now I was living with them and sharing, or at least listening to, the problems of their daily lives. I got to know many out-of-the-way townlands with their beautiful names. It is one of our national losses that these names with their significant references to natural or traditional landmarks in their Irish form are so often meaningless in their English translations. Names like Gortnahoe in Tipperary, Reenagown in Kerry, Ahascragh in Galway, Glenamaddy in Roscommon, Glenswilly in Donegal, Cuilmore in County Mayo and Carriganeema in Cork are typical of what I have in mind.

Within a couple of years it became obvious that we were engaged in a project which was inherently defective. There was no possibility of getting turf of the required standard in any quantities. Bogs vary in quality too much to yield turf of uniform density — certainly when cut by hand. It was equally impossible to educate producers in the practice of selling by weight. A moisture content as low as the specified 30% is unattainable in the case of handwon turf unless in exceptionally fine seasons. Organised on a purely voluntary basis the societies themselves failed to manage and effectively control their members' operations. The price paid for turf was insufficient to attract a major response by way of increased output or acceptable standards of quality and service. Management was in the hands of secretaries whose services were largely unpaid and whose zeal and good intentions were no substitute for business experience and competence. The secretaries were almost exclusively drawn from the Fianna Fáil Cumann and were acting voluntarily as a contribution to the national effort. Indeed the Fianna Fáil organisation had adopted the turf scheme as a political duty.

The coal merchants were less than enthusiastic about the scheme. The Dublin coal merchants in particular were well known as 'shrewd businessmen', a phrase open to a variety of interpretations. Competition from turf marketed under state sponsorship was something to be resisted and they spared no effort to disparage it. So antagonistic was their attitude, which I attributed to their anti-national sentiments, that the government was persuaded to put through the Dáil an Act which would compel them to sell a proportion of turf with each sale of coal for domestic use. It was a silly idea and produced a long and turgid debate in the Dáil. In fact the compulsory sale clauses of the Act were never implemented.

There was one section of the Act which was of fundamental importance to the whole future success of the turf industry. The minister took powers to acquire compulsorily bog and other land required for the Turf Development Board's operations. Without such powers the utilisation of large and valuable bog areas could have been prevented by unreasonable opposition on the part of owners of turbary rights. The use of compulsory acquisition to overcome this problem had been strongly recommended by the 1921 commission. I succeeded in getting these powers written into the Act in the face of strong opposition from the civil service. In retrospect I regard it as my most important personal contribution to the problem of bog development.

While the turf scheme as originally conceived by Frank Aiken did not work out on a commercial level, the publicity and propaganda which accompanied it succeeded in drawing public attention to the existence of the bogs and their potential value economically. It had the further effect of giving people living along the western seaboard and the poorest areas of the midlands the feeling that the government was taking an interest in their welfare. It did much to prepare the way for public acceptance of the turf-fired power stations, briquette factories, and peat moss factories which were yet to come. Most important of all, it provided a launching pad for the spectacular turf production campaign born of the fuel emergency during the Second World War.

While all of this was going on my relations with the civil service were becoming worse. To purchase anything more elaborate than a pencil or pen for the job required innumerable sanctions and intolerable delays. But my irritation went beyond endurance when I had an expense account of £3 or £4 held up because I had not previously received sanction to travel. I dropped the claim and stood the loss of the few pounds involved but I went to see John Leydon and spoke to him in terms to which he was not accustomed from a subordinate and which he had not previously heard even in the British navy where he had served for a time. It was not for nothing that I had been reared in the Dublin of Summerhill and Terenure and had spent so much time in internment camps. I was well versed in the invective of Dublin and how to use it. It is a fair reflection of my attitude to the civil service, commonly held by the Republican rank and file in the early days of the Fianna Fáil government, that I finished the interview by telling him that it was me and the likes of me that put him and the likes of him where he was. Leydon who was much more mature than I and had, in fact, no emotional alignment with turf or politics but whose liberal principles would have opposed the notion of state involvement in the turf industry took my outburst calmly and did not refer to it again. As always on occasions like that I felt rather ashamed of my behaviour but my travelling expenses were paid in future without prior sanction.

When it became apparent that the turf scheme as originally designed was not going to succeed and that some other method must be found for exploiting the bogs the wisdom of the civil service was invoked and Aiken arranged that an inter-departmental committee should be convened to advise on the problem. So senior representatives of the Departments of Industry and Commerce, Agriculture, Local Government, Posts and Telegraphs, the Office of Public Works, the Land Commission and the Department of Defence assembled, each one accompanied by two clerks busily engaged in taking minutes. It looked a very impressive gathering if only from the ages of those present; they seemed to me to be very old and wise. I was looking for action rather than for advice and after about three hours of talk it was clear that the combined wisdom of the civil service had nothing helpful to offer. In fact they were inclined to believe that nothing could be done. As I recall it, the only common thread running through the discussion was that all those present had been born in bog areas and therefore knew all about turf as a matter of course but were totally lacking in practical proposals. This was my first experience of many departmental conferences on a multitude of subjects and not once have I heard a satisfactory conclusion come out of them. They are a form of nonsense that does not even have the value, usual to business conferences, of enabling the participants to get to know one another. They never last beyond 1 p.m., or in the evening 5 p.m., because everyone is either in a hurry to lunch or to knock off for the day.

As far as help from the civil service in solving the turf problem was concerned I had drawn a blank. The older civil servants I met had nothing but amused scepticism to offer. Whether they were born on a bog or not they evinced the feeling of nearly all educated Irish men, reflecting their race memories, that anything to do with a bog spells inertia and ignorance. The word 'bog' had become the symbol of backwardness and contempt — 'bog-trotters', 'bog-man', 'bog Latin'. It is curious that the Irish word for bog, *portach*, has no such disparaging connotations nor does the Irish word *móin* provoke the same reaction as does the word 'turf' in English. There is a very great psychological difference in nomenclature between the 'Turf Board' and 'Bord na Móna', and it is much easier for Irish people to accept the idea of a large scale industry bearing the title 'Bord na Móna' than it would be under the title 'Turf Board'. When the time came to establish a statutory company it was not by any subtle reasoning derived from Madison Avenue evaluations that 'Bord na Móna' was chosen to be its name by Frank Aiken and my-self — it sounded well.

The scepticism of the civil servants as to the possibilities of developing the bogs on a large scale was part of the bog-trotter syndrome. What I found difficult to endure was the raised eyebrow, the amused smile and snide remark which in those early days always met me when I tried to interest anyone in the subject. With my own friends the usual response was the outright scoff. Turf still rates curiously low in the public esteem. Bord na Móna is in the big league of state companies but it has never been accepted, despite its record of success as equal in prestige to, say, the ESB, CIE or Aer Lingus.

On the political level the mere fact that turf development was inaugurated by Fianna Fáil was sufficient to evoke hostility abundant and bitter from Cumann na nGaedheal. Cumann na nGaedheal deputies had in the main reached a point of respectability where even those born in bog areas would be slow to admit it but nevertheless regarded the whole effort as hopelessly impractical. Some of them boasted of their knowledge of turf from the experience of buying and selling it — which is to say that they were in the gombeen business. Some attacked the project so violently that they developed a vested interest in its failure and for no better reason than they hoped that failure would discredit the government. I was not altogether surprised at this because I had seen a similar vein of bias and derision adopted by Fianna Fáil while in opposition in relation to the Shannon Scheme. Indeed every imaginative undertaking started in Ireland has met with its share of irrational opposition. Either it couldn't be done or it had failed before or it should be done in some other way.

I reached the final stage of exasperation, frustration and rage with the civil servants when it was decided to employ six or seven engineers to help the co-operative societies in opening new bog faces, building of accommodation roads and to make a detailed survey of some of the larger bogs. Reasonably I assumed that these engineers would be under my direct control but the civil service regulations did not permit this and the engineers were required to report to a technical department which in this case was the Geological Survey. At that time the Geological Survey was housed in Hume Street in a small building more like a museum than an office. Callers had to ring the doorbell which was opened by a porter and were reverently announced to the director, a gentle old man on the point of retirement who was horrified at having his routine upset in any way. For several reasons I regarded the situation as quite impossible. In addition to its organisational absurdity, my relations with the head of the Geological Survey were quite inhibited by the fact that he was a neighbour who was well liked by my family and to whom, as a much older man, I was accustomed to defer respectfully but the idea of taking instructions from him or seeking his advice was quite unacceptable.

No such inhibitions prevented me making clear to Leydon and indeed to Seán Lemass, what I thought of the arrangement. I pointed out that the rigidity of the civil service system made it impossible to carry out the job assigned to me and insisted that unless I got authority to do what I thought necessary to carry out the government's policy I would refuse to accept the responsibility. I suggested that if the administrative regulations could not be waived the best alternative was to set up a new organisation independent of the civil service to be run on the lines of the ESB. To my surprise Leydon agreed with this proposal though he would not contemplate giving the new body the statutory form of the ESB. The autonomy I sought was secured with the establishment in 1934 of the Turf Development Board, a limited company set up under the Companies Act and financed by grant in aid from the exchequer. This produced a radical change in the situation. No longer had we to seek sanction first from Industry and Commerce and then from Finance to buy a typewriter or employ staff. We had almost complete freedom of action to tackle the development of the bogs as we thought best and this freedom was fully availed of. In setting up the new organisation we were fortunate to have at our disposal the experience of the ESB; thus we avoided their initial mistakes in such matters as the organisation of accounts systems, store control, purchases, board procedures and the role of the board members. With the agreement of Seán Lemass I asked R. C. Barton to act as chairman of the Turf Development Board. I appointed myself managing director and secretary and Dr Kennedy as the third member of the board. I was seconded from the Department of Industry and Commerce while retaining my civil service status. Barton and Kennedy were part-time board members and were unpaid. Later at my request two other part-time members, both friends of mine, Bill Quirke and Aodhagan O'Rahilly were added to the Board.

Robert Barton was a very distinguished personality and well known nationally. He was one of the Anglo-Irish landowners who came over to the Republicans' side in the War of Independence. He had been Minister of Agriculture in the First Dáil and had been a signatory of the Treaty. His prestige in official circles was very high. He saw us through many vicissitudes in the twenty-odd years during which he held the post of chairman of the Turf Development Board and afterwards of Bord na Móna. He was extraordinarily kind and tolerant to me and many times saved me from the consequences of my extremely impatient nature and truculence in the face of opposition. He supported me in all the differences we had from time to time with the politicians and civil service and through the continuous difficulties experienced in our dealings with the ESB. He and I travelled all over the country and I heard from him the inside story of the Treaty negotiations and the personal antipathies and social behaviour of some of the delegation which resulted in that disastrous agreement. During these trips I learned much about the economic problems of agriculture and of the manners and customs of the landed gentry in the last century. And much about Europe and America at the time of *La Belle Epoque*. We discussed the political personalities of the day, the latest books and paintings — he knew all the great galleries of Europe — abstract expressionism which did not appeal to him and the outstanding figures of history. He was a strong believer in the 'great man' theory; a theory which I always disbelieved. As a chairman he was most effective. He listened but rarely participated in the boardroom discussions and when he thought that they had gone far enough he announced that he was making a minute of the board's decision. Neither he nor any of the minutes he made was ever questioned. Without his prestige in government circles and in the country generally our plans for turf development would never have been brought to fruition in the face of the opposition, stemming from scepticism rather than hostility, which emanated from the Department of Finance. Not all of the first Fianna Fáil cabinet were turf enthusiasts — some of them had been 'born on a bog'.

With the formation of the Turf Development Board we acquired the authority to recruit our own staff. We took over *in globo* from the IAOS the administrative and field staff who had been organising the co-operative turf societies. From the civil service we took over the engineers engaged in bog survey work who were theoretically attached to Industry and Commerce.

We advertised for staff for head office, the most important post being that of chief accountant which I considered to be the core of any business organisation. My ESB experience had convinced me that if the accounts went wrong, nothing went right. I had invoked the help of my friend Weckler, the chief accountant of the ESB, to design a set of accounts which would be appropriate to the Turf Development Board organisation on the assumption that it would expand over the years and, as it did so, the accounts system could take up the expansion.

I was determined to get someone for the post of accountant whom I knew to be competent and reliable. Dermot Lawlor was an intimate friend of mine. I had spent a lot of my time in his company and knew his qualities. He had taken a first-class honours degree in University College, Dublin, had made a short visit to the USA to gain experience as much of foreign travel as of accountancy. At the time the Turf Development Board was set up he was undecided whether he would go into business or become a chartered accountant.

I persuaded him to apply for the accountant's post in the Turf Development Board to which he was duly appointed. At this stage, I was combining the duties of secretary with that of managing director. It soon became apparent that, at that stage of our development, Lawlor's capacities were under-utilised and he relieved me of the function of secretary. This arrangement had the additional advantage of bringing him into closer contact with the board and its decisions and with the civil service and its peculiarities.

Lawlor was in almost every respect my antithesis — physically, temperamentally and intellectually. He was slightly built, a little below average height and not very robust-looking while I was six feet three inches and vigorous in my movement and demeanour. He was by nature very gentle. I was not. I don't think he ever read Kant but he arrived by his own intuition at the categorical imperative 'that you should do unto others as you would that they do unto you'. This principle, as he often repeated, was the lodestar of his life.

He hated violence. When the atomic bomb was dropped on Hiroshima, he got physically ill. I recognised from the beginning of our friendship that he was my intellectual superior. This suited me because I had observed in the IRA, the Tourist Association, the ESB and the civil service that an important ingredient of leadership was that the leader, or aspiring leader, should surround himself with colleagues who had qualities he himself lacked.

Lawlor had other qualities which I had not. He was patient and unflappable. He did not say much but had an infinite capacity for listening and could enliven the conversation with spontaneous shafts of verbal wit of which he was a master. He acted as a damper on my almost daily explosions arising from my frustrations with the civil service and the ESB. I never wrote an official letter or memorandum which I did not submit to him for comment before it was issued. Nor did I take any important decision without first discussing it with him and seeking his advice. In short I relied on him completely. I have to say I did not always take his advice; his caution sometimes annoyed but never offended me.

During the war years when I was much involved with the work of the Turf Executive and touring the country with Hugo Flinn, and

afterwards serving as fuel director, Dermot Lawlor managed the
Turf Development Board on his own initiative. It was a great disappointment to me when he decided to apply for and secured the
very important and highly sought post of First County Manager of
Meath. At the time there were no very bright prospects in the turf
industry. The future was uncertain but when in 1946 the government decided to replace the Turf Development Board with the
statutory authority, Bord na Móna, career prospects became much
more favourable.

I found the burden of management increasingly difficult and I
persuaded the board to invite Lawlor to re-join the staff, this time
as general manager. To my great satisfaction he agreed to accept. I
had been most uncomfortable in his absence   principally because there was no one who would argue with the frankness and
indifference to my view which I was accustomed to hearing from
Lawlor. The experience he had gained in his few years as County
Manager enlarged his administrative skills.

In the process of building up Bord na Móna even more of my
personal time was spent working among the field staff and reviewing progress on the ground. It was therefore essential that I would
have someone to handle head office affairs who had the ability and
judgement of Lawlor. When I left Bord na Móna, after twenty-five
years, taking over as my successor posed no problems to him. Apart
from our official relationship he was a close friend of my family as I
was of his.

The newly-established Turf Development Board began its search
for new and more effective methods of turf production by reviewing
the literature. The literature clearly pointed to Sir John Purser
Griffith. Sir John was a Welshman in origin but a Dublin man by
adoption. He was very wealthy and had always been interested in
the development of our turf resources. The British government had
failed to act on the recommendations of the 1917 Enquiry, of which
Sir John had been chairman, and being quite sure that he had the
answer he set out in 1924 to prove his theory. He acquired a large
area of bog beside the Grand Canal at a place called Turraun in
west Offaly and installed turf winning machinery based on the
macerating process. He built a small power station, a peat moss
plant, bought a canal barge and set up at Harcourt Terrace, Dublin,
a retail and wholesale sales depot. My first meeting with him was in
a magnificent study in Rathmines Castle where he lived. He was in
fact a very old man, nearly ninety years, and he looked to me like an
Old Testament prophet. As far as turf was concerned he was a
prophet unaccepted in his own country. There was nothing old
about his mind and he had a very clear picture of the future shape of

turf development illustrating the difference between handwon turf and the macerated turf produced at Turraun by placing sods in a bucket of water which he had by the side of his desk. The macerated turf did not absorb water, while the handwon turf did so like a sponge. His message to me was simple. The future of the bogs rested in the production of macerated turf to be burned in power stations sited on the bogs.

My first visit to Turraun was a kind of epiphany to me. I saw there *in parvo* what Bord na Móna was to become in time. The works were only accessible to a car driving along the tow-path of the canal and that was a perilous journey. In the nearby village of Pullough there was evident squalor and poverty on a scale much worse than I had ever seen even in the Dublin slums of my youth. Pullough was so isolated as to be virtually an island disconnected from the outside world. It was truly the home of the 'bog-man' tradition. The developed section of Turraun bog seemed to me at the time to be vast; the net-work of overhead electric cables, the automatic cutting machines and the peat moss plant driven by electricity in-spired me with great hopes for the future. In fact Turraun was a very small installation — no more than a pilot plant — and the area of bog worked was miniscule. Nevertheless here, in principle, was the answer to the problem and in Turraun Sir John had established, as he set out to do, that it was possible to upgrade turf to the level of a commercial fuel and use it for the production of electricity. He has spent £70,000 of his own money on the Turraun installation; in the values of the 1920s this was a very large sum indeed. Sir John was a repository of virtually all the information on bog development which had been gained abroad and had personal experience of the north German bogs. He suggested that we should visit these bogs and perhaps the Russian bogs which, reports indicated, were being worked on a very large scale.

I conveyed this suggestion to Leydon who approved of it and rightly decided that such an expedition should be under govern-ment auspices. It took some time to make the arrangements at government level. In the meantime Sir John Purser Griffith asked me to come to see him and offered to hand over Turraun Works, including the peat moss factory, the site at Harcourt Terrace and the canal barge to the Turf Development Board for the estimated value of the fuel stocks which was put at £6,500. It was a princely offer and I could not get back quickly enough to tell my colleagues on the Board as well as Leydon and Lemass. All concerned were very pleased with the offer except Dr Kennedy who was totally opposed to accepting it. His opposition seemed quite irrational and when he accompanied me to a meeting with Sir John's representative in the solicitor's office to discuss the details of the transaction he acted as if he thought Sir John was trying to swindle the government out of £6,500. It was a most embarrassing interview as Lindsay, who represented Sir John, was an upright, rather innocent and decent Scotsman who would be incapable of telling a lie much less swindling anybody. I had to make it clear that the offer, whether Dr Kennedy liked it or not, was being accepted and accepted gratefully.

This episode had considerable value in as much as it taught me that the practice of allowing a part-time board member of a semi-state body to participate in any executive function was wrong in principle and in practice. It is equally disastrous to permit part-time board members to have personal unofficial dealings with the staff of the organisation. Later on I learned that it is wrong in principle for part-time members of a board of a state-sponsored body to be permitted to go on technical missions abroad. Their participation in such missions cannot be useful and is, frequently, positively harmful to the harmony of the board. But I was only at the beginning of my boardroom education.

We took over Turraun physically at the end of 1936. The bog was 1,500 acres in extent but only about 500 acres had been developed. It was very unfortunate for the country that the first serious step towards turf development on a national scale took place in Sir John's declining years. He died in 1938 at the age of ninety. His death was a great personal loss to me because of his extensive knowledge of the technology of turf and engineering in general and his willingness to pass on this information and experience. He was not Irish by birth but he was one of those people who added a blade of grass and an ear of corn to the Irish economy and anyone who succeeds in doing that is worthy of acceptance into our rather exclusive race. I was sorry to lose what would have been a great prop to us in our forthcoming ventures. His importance as a pioneer in turf development cannot be over-rated.

The acquisition of Turraun brought turf an unexpected and valuable ally. The *Irish Times* came out strongly in support of the Turf Development Board. The editor, Bertie Smyllie, was an intimate of Purser Griffith's sons from university days and was very well briefed on the problems of our bogs. In Irish public life the *Irish Times* is unique. R. M. Smyllie, a Sligo man of Scottish extraction, had become its editor in succession to a west British pedant, who for years had edited the paper and who could not accept the fact that the establishment of the Free State represented a major change in Irish relations with Britain. The *Irish Times* was, until the days of Smyllie's editorship, a stodgy and poor imitation of the London *Times* and was read, almost exclusively, by Church of Ireland clerics, Trinity dons and the remaining occupants of the 'big houses' and their minions. Under Smyllie's editorial direction its readership extended to businessmen and bank clerks, members of rugby football clubs, academics of the national university and, even more significantly, civil servants and members of the government. Smyllie accepted that he was an Irishman owing unequivocal allegiance to Ireland. In this he differed from most of the Anglo-Irish who remained in Ireland after the Treaty. He was personally a very agreeable man who looked and behaved somewhat like Dr Johnson, holding court in one or other of the pubs close to his office in Westmoreland Street. From his seat in the bar he nightly received poets, novelists, playwrights, journalists. He was very well informed about the Dublin scene and also about Irish political affairs, although one rarely saw politicians in his entourage. He obviously had a free hand from the proprietors of the paper and his influence derived from the fact that he wrote from the standpoint of a free and independent Ireland rather than that of a province, regrettably and possibly temporarily, separated from the motherland. Smyllie was a man who liked gaiety, the atmosphere of a golf club and loved good conversation. These characteristics were strongly reflected in the paper.

Smyllie had been picked up as a British citizen in Germany at the outbreak of the First World War and he spent the war years in an internment camp called Ruhleben. Like all men who are forced to live in confinement — be it in army, or navy or prison — he learned the necessity of tolerance. He brought that tolerance to the *Irish Times* and in the columns of the paper offered the only forum available at the time where free discussion of ethics and religion could take place. He recognised, unusual for a man of his background, that the Irish language had come to stay and he threw the mantle of respectability over Irish by encouraging Irish language contributions in the column of Myles na Gopaleen. Anyone with a smattering of Irish tried to read these parts of Myles' column and there was a certain 'oneupmanship' to be gained from being able to explain his Irish language jokes to one's friends. Smyllie, in fact, integrated the *Irish Times* and what it stood for with the Irish nation and he was more than welcomed by the ruling group and by the civil servants in particular. The civil servants were in origin mainly of the lower middle classes and having attained the first aim of job security they wanted social acceptance and respectability as well. The *Irish Times* was for them and, indeed, for all the rising lower middle classes the symbol of 'ould dacency' and respectability and they read it. When anyone in the civil service offices told you that he had seen such and such an item 'in the paper', you knew that he was referring to the *Irish Times*. Favourable comment from the *Irish Times* made a minister's day. Favourable comment from the other two Dublin dailies was of no importance to them. I think that the approbation of the *Irish Times* for the policy of bog development contributed to the readiness with which the proposal to send a delegation to Russia and Germany was publicly accepted. At that time there was no opposition from the zealots and bigots to contact with godless Russia; the Church had not yet quite regrouped its forces after the coming to power of Fianna Fáil.

Foreign Mission

The arrangements for the visit were very capably handled by the Department of External Affairs after the usual battle was fought with Finance for sanction. It was said that a junior administrative officer spent weeks studying Baedeker to find the cheapest way to Moscow. Leydon invited Dr Kennedy, Professor Pierce Purcell and P. G. Murphy, the chief engineer of the ESB, to join the delegation. All accepted but Professor Purcell requested a substantial fee for his participation. Leydon characteristically withdrew the invitation without discussion and substituted E. J. Duffy, the county surveyor of Meath, who had done considerable research work on turf. He accepted and we set off on what was for me a great adventure. To my surprise I was appointed leader of the expedition. This was not perhaps a good idea as I was so much junior to Kennedy that he felt that he was being slighted. Our relations were not improved by my excessive zeal for the job on hand; early to bed and early to rise was my motto. I did not regard the delegation as being on a holiday trip. Kennedy had been in Germany often; he did not speak or write the language but admired greatly the German way of life.

I had not previously met Duffy. He had been one of Professor Purcell's first pupils and a most distinguished one. He was basically a mathematician but had a high reputation as a road builder in County Meath. As a result of his research on turf under Purcell he was well informed on the difficulties encountered at Turraun and the problems likely to be met in any large scale bog development. Despite his intellectual gifts he had no interest in or knowledge of political affairs. He was essentially a gentle person. As a young engineer he had worked in England but had never travelled beyond that. Germany was as new to him as it was to me.

Murphy was a product of the Christian Brothers School in North Richmond Street and had had a distinguished university career in electrical engineering in the College of Science. He was a first-class technologist and the high technical achievement of the ESB, particularly in the early days, was due in large measure to him. He was a very nervous and rather timid person and would probably have been much happier as a backroom boy than as a front-line executive. He had worked in Germany and spoke and wrote German fluently. Like Duffy he was detached from the world of affairs.

Apart from occasional visits to London and France I had never been abroad and literally had never met a foreigner other than English or French. My information about Germany was limited to a few historical references such as the defeat of the Roman legions of Varus by Arminius in the Teutoberger Wald which was fixed in my mind by Creasy's *Decisive Battles of the World* and the Emperor's cry of 'Varus, Varus, give me back my legions'. I knew about the Thirty Years' War, fixed in my mind by the Latin expression *Odium theologicum* and the resounding names of the generals who took part — Wallenstein, Tilley and Charles XII. I knew something of Frederick the Great, mainly because of his association with Voltaire, which I had read about in Macaulay's essay. I knew about the Franco-Prussian War, the formation of the German Empire and the exploits of the German army during the Great War and had a passing knowledge of the origins of the Weimar Republic and the coming to power of Hitler a couple of years previously. I did not know a single word of German. I had read only one German novel and that in translation. I knew nothing of how the people lived or amused themselves, what food they ate, how the houses, cities and towns looked, what the topography of the country was like. I was intensely curious about all these things no less than to find out about turf exploitation and its use. I also had a vague kind of sympathy for Germany and the Germans because they had been 'our gallant allies' in 1916 and had been so badly treated at Versailles.

We had scarcely arrived in Germany when Dr Kennedy had to return home because of a great personal tragedy and I got a message from Leydon that Purcell had changed his mind and would like to join us in Berlin for the Russian stage of the mission. In fact, not merely had Purcell agreed to waive his fees but offered to pay his own expenses. Leydon, however, let him off the hook.

In Hamburg we were taken in hand by the officials of the Department of Agriculture, the government agency which concerned itself with the bogs. While the prime interest of the department was the reclamation of bogland for agricultural use, they also supervised the various fuel projects and helped in the investigation of by-products such as wax, tar, oil and charcoal. Fortunately the officials spoke English, as indeed did most of the bog managers whom we

subsequently met. The department officials could not have been
more helpful and spent hours giving us a run-down on the state of
the German turf industry and the technical problems associated
with it.

We were taken on a tour of the city of Hamburg and shown the
sights, including San Pauli which was a rather down-at-heel version
of Montmartre and the Place Pigalle in Paris. We saw the great
blocks of workers' high-rise flats which were the pride of the city
and were exhibited as an example of what social democracy could
do for the people. The socialist city council which had built them
had just been abolished by the Nazis. To me building on that scale
for the benefit of the working people seemed a wonderful achievement and I lamented the fact that we in Ireland would never have
the technical or financial resources to emulate it. Perhaps it was just
as well considering our subsequent unfortunate experience in
Ballymun. We went to see a research station at Hamburg which was
involved in bogland reclamation for agriculture. There was an
agricultural show in progress and all the peasants came into town
for the occasion with their wives and daughters dressed in various
regional costumes. That evening we saw them relaxing in a beer
garden; they ate and drank and sang and swayed in *bruderschaft*. It
was reminiscent of a scene from *The Student Prince*. In commenting
on the gaiety and warmth of the scene to one of my cicerones, I
learned my first German word *Gemütlichkeit* and for the rest of the
trip I had every reason to believe that *Gemütlichkeit* was a most
notable characteristic of the German people.

The bogs most fully exploited were situated in north west Germany near the Dutch and Danish frontiers. Oldenburg is the principal town in the area and it became the headquarters from which
we visited many of the local turf production centres. These works
were privately owned and in most cases the production of peat moss
for export to the USA was their chief activity. There were only two
plants where turf was being used for fuel in electrical power
production — that of Herr Klasmann at Meppen and at Weismoor
near a small town called Aurich.

Weismoor was the show piece of the turf industry and was a
tourist attraction for Bremen, Hamburg and Hanover. Hundreds of
people from these cities came every Sunday to see the great glass-
houses in which so many varieties of out-of-season vegetables were
grown. In principle it was no different from Sir John Purser
Griffith's works at Turraun except that the emphasis was on hor-
ticulture and it had several acres of tomato houses heated from the
surplus heat of the power station which, in addition to providing the
full electrical needs of the plant, supplied current to Aurich. The

plant was obviously very competently run and very profitable. The manager lived in a style which was evidence of prosperity. It came as a revelation to me to find that a bog manager could enjoy such a luxurious standard of living. His house had at least four reception rooms in open-plan design; it was centrally heated and had the most beautiful indoor plants growing up the walls and even across the ceiling. I had never before seen an open-plan house. Domestic central heating was to me a completely new experience and the only house plants I knew were of the variety aspidistra. Floors were of parquet covered with large deep rugs and all the rooms were furnished with an affluence which, I imagined, was only found in royal castles. The house was surrounded by a beautifully kept lawn and flowers of all kinds. It was indeed hard to believe that such spacious living could be derived from a bog. My 'race unconscious' was stirred. Turf and bogs were not words of derision here. Weismoor could easily have been reproduced in Ireland. Unfortunately it has taken an international fuel crisis to persuade the ESB to inaugurate an experimental scheme for glasshouse crop production with the waste heat available from one of their turf-fired power stations.

I had my first German domestic meal in one of these houses. The table was beautifully laid with silver and sparkling glass; there were a couple of maidservants in attendance supervised by the woman of the house who did not sit down with the guests. We were offered a great number of different dishes. There were several varieties of fish — eel, smoked salmon, herrings in cream, cod in aspic — as well as stuffed eggs, stuffed artichokes, olives, salami, sausages, cucumber, ham. I thoroughly enjoyed sampling the different platters offered me and made a very full meal but discovered to my horror that this was only the hors d'oeuvre. Next came cold soup; I never knew there was such a thing as cold soup and this one was so unpalatable to me that only an effort of will forced it down my gullet. Then came a main course consisting of half a chicken garnished with potatoes and mushrooms. All the politeness in the world could not make me touch this dish nor anything from the great cheese board which bore half a dozen different kinds of cheese and as many different kinds of bread and biscuits. The woman of the house expressed concern at my lack of appetite. For the first time in my life I had 'dined with Lucullus' and this experience had a double effect on my gastronomic habits which lasts to this day. I acquired a taste for hors d'oeuvre whether presented under the name of starters, vorspeise, smorgas, smoørebrod or zakuski. At the same time I developed a total dislike of large meals.

The most impressive turf plant we saw in Germany and the one most likely to be useful to us was at Meppen right on the Dutch frontier. It was a family-owned plant the output of which was used mainly for the production of electricity which was sold to the town of Aurich. The type and formation of the bog was rather like our own. The production process was simlar to that of Turraun but on a much larger scale and highly mechanised. The owner and director of the bog was Herr Klasmann whose grandfather had founded the business. He too lived in a style suggestive of considerable wealth. His hobby was motor-racing and he owned a number of cars. The business was run on totally paternalistic lines and Klasmann himself might well have walked out of the pages of *Buddenbrooks*. He was absorbed in his family, knew all about the workers and their problems; the workers, of course, knew their place. He was a highly cultured person, rather reserved in manner and quite uninvolved in the current political ferment in Germany of which, at this point of our visit, I was gradually becoming aware. Klasmann looked more like an academic than a businessman. Many of the bog owners around Oldenburg were at least of the second generation and some of them had been to university or to a *Technische Hochschule*. They were far from being the ignorant backward bog men of the Irish myth.

As we travelled from plant to plant over flat countryside we passed through many villages and small towns and I was greatly attracted by their tidiness and order and the atmosphere of old-time stability which prevailed everywhere. The absence of hedge-rows, the rectangular fields, the well-planted woods and the long straight by-roads which, at that time, were mainly cobbled impressed on me a sense of order and care for the environment which we so lacked at home. It was a lesson I never forgot. I had collected the first fruits of foreign travel. I made up my mind then, that if ever I had the opportunity, I would recognise as a priority the value of maintaining a decent environment for people at work.

When it came to understanding the broad social and political scene in Germany I was badly handicapped by being unable to read the newspapers or even the street signs and advertisements. My constant enquiries about the significance of the happenings around us made me feel rather a fool. What were all the people collecting money in the street for? Who were the men parading in uniform with shovels on their shoulders? Why were all the flags on display? Who were the children singing and marching in procession and what organisation did they belong to? I had heard of the great public works with which Hitler solved the unemployment problem and of the service which all young women were required to undertake as home helps. It was strange to see so many people on the move and such an air of excitement abroad.

An old gentleman named Herr Brandy got in touch with us in Oldenburg. He had been a Prussian officer and was interested in turf development. Having heard of our bogs, he had paid a visit to Ireland after the Great War in the hope of selling us some machinery but got no encouragement except from Arthur Griffith. With the Treaty and the establishment of new regime in Ireland he decided to visit the country again to renew his connections with Griffith. On arrival in Cobh he learned that Griffith had just died and he had nothing to do but go home. When we met him in Germany he took us to lunch in a restaurant in Oldenburg. The head waiter greeted us with raised hand and a *Heil Hitler* to which Brandy replied *Grüß Gott*. Angry words were exchanged and a scene developed. Brandy appeared to loathe the Nazis and, being a strong monarchist, angrily harangued the head waiter and his fellow diners who seemed rather amused at the incident. It was explained to me by an interpreter that Brandy was just a survival of a dead age and one had to be tolerant of such backwardness, especially as he seemed to have had a distinguished military career and limped from what was evidently a war wound. The implication was that if Brandy had not been old and had not had what we call a national record, the consequences of his outburst would have been very different. Brandy ultimately came to live in Ireland, trying without much success to market a turf stove which he had invented. If we had been more experienced, we might have used him to advantage in the Turf Development Board. It took us a little time to learn that bought experience is often cheaper than made experience.

Our days were filled with inspections of bog machines and discussions which often continued long into the evenings on the different aspects of turf production. When our visit to the Oldenburg region was finished we went on to Berlin and were joined by Professor Purcell. We called on the Irish legation and our representative there, a gentleman named Bewley, seemed to me to be much more interested in Germany than he was in Ireland. He offered us drinks and when somebody asked for an Irish whiskey, he said he was sorry but he could only supply Scotch. I took offence at this and said so causing some embarrassment all round. As the de luxe atmosphere of the legation and what I felt was a condescending attitude on Bewley's part to our mission and to Ireland generally was distasteful to me, I was glad of the opportunity the whiskey gave to vent my feelings. Bewley, who was a bachelor, was a very grand person and was said to know every baroness in Berlin and every countess in Rome by the diminutive forms of their Christian names.

We spent a few days with German officials discussing the

production of insulating boards from turf; we were told that a newly-built Air Ministry was insulated with this material. We discussed gasogenes, the manufacture of briquettes by different processes and we visited some turf centres near Berlin. I was fascinated by the city and the great Adlon Hotel in which we stayed. I had never stayed in a grand international hotel before — the nearest I got to such an establishment was in Arnold Bennett's novels. I was quite overwhelmed by the size of the bedrooms and by the magnificence of the plumbing in the en suite bathrooms. The hotel porters were overwhelming in their pomposity and the place was crawling with staff — waiters, chambermaids and lackeys of all descriptions. There was a great flurry of excitement one evening when Goering with his fiancée, Fraülein Sonnemann, and an entourage of uniformed men and women in evening dress arrived and disappeared into some private rooms.

. We were taken on a tour of the city and out to Potsdam and Sans Souci where we saw the famous statue of Nefertiti. We visited the *Haus Vaterland* and were rather shocked to see telephones on each of the hundreds of tables at many of which lone women were sitting waiting to be propositioned from nearby tables by men equally lonely. The stories told about the licentiousness of Berlin seemed to me to be well confirmed. It was still the Berlin of Christopher Isherwood. Everywhere we saw uniformed marching groups and could feel the sense of energy and exhilaration pervading the city.

One of the most interesting developments in peat technology being undertaken in Germany was located at Seeshaupt between Munich and Garmisch-Partenkirchen. It was known as the Madruck process designed to briquette peat by pressurisation and the Germans were very insistent that we should see it. We travelled to Munich by train and thence by road to Seeshaupt. We saw little of Munich but I discovered the great beauty of the Bavarian Alps and saw many of the villages and small towns with their fairytale castles surrounded by woods and fields which characterise this region. It did not require much imagination to people them with Hansel and Gretel, Rumpelstiltskin, King Thrushbeard and the rest of Grimm's characters which gave me such pleasure as a child. I was very glad of the experience even though the journey was unproductive. The Madruck process though technically very sophisticated was far from proven and of no immediate practical interest.

Our work in Germany was now concluded and the stage set for the second part of our itinerary. Each member of the party approached the trip to Russia in a different frame of mind but for all of us it was a major adventure. Duffy, who was a very pious man, regarded the Russians as ogres whose only concern was to suppress religion; he wondered if it was safe to bring his rosary beads. He was not in any way reassured when I pointed out that he would certainly find ikons freely available. Murphy rather expected to find evidence of violent revolution as soon as he crossed the frontier. He would not have been surprised to see Czarist officers hanging from the telegraph poles. He had heard in Berlin dreadful stories of the liquidation of the kulaks and of the tortures of the aristos in the Lubianka prison. He felt too that we would be under constant surveillance by the GPU and, in this, he was probably correct. It did not help that he had a diet problem and was not looking forward to Russian food. Purcell regarded Russian socialism as an aberration or a joke. He refused to take it seriously and believed that the Russian state could not survive without the help of foreign technicians and capitalists and by 'foreign' he meant 'British'. He was quite sure that in a few years the Russians would correct the error of their ways and with due repentance re-establish the Czars. He was very cheerful and tolerant on the subject of Communism.

I entered on the adventure feeling excited and intensely curious and ready for anything. I had read much more about Russia than about Germany and I had followed the progress of events since the revolution of 1917. *Anna Karenina* had been one of the great literary experiences of my youth and after our Civil War it became rather a fashion among my friends to advise one another 'to read the Russians'. I tried Dostoyevsky, *The Brothers Karamazov* and *Crime and Punishment,* and I read them as one might read a prescribed text on a university course getting neither pleasure nor enlightenment from the soul searching of the 'Brothers' nor from the remorse and guilt of Raskolnikov. I read a few of Gorky's short stories without much enthusiasm and of course Gogol's *Dead Souls* which certainly gives an entertaining picture of Russia in the not too remote days of the serfs when souls represented wealth. I had seen performances of *The Cherry Orchard* and *The Seagull* and had read a good deal about the Russian theatre, especially the Moscow Arts Theatre and Stanislavsky, and had about the same kind of curiosity about Nijinsky as the present generation has about a cinema or pop star. I had never seen a ballet and was looking forward to seeing one performed rather out of curiosity than any special interest in this art form. High among my aspirations was a visit to the Moscow Arts Theatre.

From my boyhood I was fascinated by the French Revolution and through biographies, histories and novels I was steeped in its lore. My hero was Robespierre and my sympathy was with the Jacobins. I readily understood the bliss and the heaven of that time. I regarded the Russian revolution as an extension of the French revolution and I was looking forward to seeing something of the scenario in which the drama of 1917 took place as well as the way of life of the new Russia. At the same time I had no starry-eyed approach to the new Jerusalem. I had no emotional involvement with the Bolsheviks, however much they had my sympathy. My father had bought me John Reed's *Ten Days that Shook the World* shortly after it was published in 1919. It described in great detail the seizure of power by the Bolsheviks but, even more interesting for the foreigner, is a very clear account which Reed gives of the events leading from the 'Political' revolution of the Mensheviks which began in March to the 'Social' revolution carried out by the Bolsheviks a few months later. The setting for Reed's book is, of course, Petrograd (now Leningrad) but although the book had no more than a passing interest for me, the place names mentioned in it were sufficiently vivid in my memory to make me look forward with excitement to the visit to Leningrad — the Neva, the Peter and Paul Fortress, Smolny Institute, the Nevsky Prospekt as well as the names of the heroes — sometime ephemerally heroes of the revolution — Trotsky, Kerensky, Lunacharsky and Kamenev.

I was quite well aware of the fundamental difference between the French and Russian revolutions in that though in both cases the object was the destruction of the feudal class the French had no calculated social or political system to put in its place whereas the aims of the Russian revolution in this respect were clearly defined by Lenin. Our own revolution in Ireland was aimed only at political separation; we had no particular desire to disturb the economic system. We were quite prepared to accept and tolerate, for example, the slum-owning aldermen and councillors of the Dublin Corporation.

We reached Moscow after a long non-stop train journey of two days and a night. We saw very little of the countryside as the railway seemed to pass through endless stretches of forest. On arriving at Moscow we were met with the strange sight of hundreds of families in little groups camped out on the station premises. We thought that some political upheaval must have taken place but it was explained to us that these people were simply waiting for trains and, as there was no accommodation for them in the city, some had been camping out at the station for weeks. As we stepped off the train we were met by five or six men who were to our eyes unusually dressed. One was in a beautifully embroidered white Russian blouse and wore high boots corresponding exactly with our idea of a Cossack. The others were dressed in normal European clothes. Some were wearing collars and ties, some were not. But all the clothes had a second-hand appearance and the trousers seemed to be made in the style of 'Oxford bags' cut too long for their wearers. None of the party spoke English, French or German but they were accompanied by a lady interpreter who spoke English, quite without accent or even voice inflection. She accompanied us on all of our trips and we got to know her quite well. She was a tall, auburn-haired girl in her late twenties, dressed neatly as a secretary would dress in Dublin and in the same fashion. Her name was Euphrosene Simonyana. She was a Jewess from Archangel and, despite her excellent English, had never been outside Russia nor apparently had she any wish to go abroad. She seemed to have no interest in the outside world. Eurphrosene was very good natured but without a spark of humour and always seemed a little distracted. She reminded me of a famous cinema actress of the cinema of the day, Zazu Pitts. The men we met, who were as much strangers to her as to us, never seemed to take her seriously and to be constantly pulling her leg. She never showed any flirtatious interest in them and once told us that she did not intend to marry. Her kindness made our visit that much more agreeable. She was the only woman we met or even spoke to during the trip.

We were installed in the Hotel National and given rooms with private bathrooms. The hotel was very comfortable, very clean and furnished much on the style of the Shelbourne in Dublin although, to tell the truth, at that time I had only hearsay knowledge of how the Shelbourne was furnished because I had never been in it. The arrangement was that we paid for our hotel bedrooms and for any meals taken in the hotel. Fortunately our only hotel meal was breakfast which consisted of coffee and rolls for which we were charged £1. Bedrooms cost another £1 and as our subsistence allowance only amounted to £2 per day we would have starved or at least gone without cigarettes except for the generous and rather elaborate hospitality we received from our hosts in the turf organisation.

The Russians had prepared an itinerary for us which included the major bogs around Moscow and in the area of Leningrad as well as some provincial bogs. To visit the provincial bogs would have involved flying but Murphy had promised his wife he would not fly so that trip was dropped. We were all relieved at this omission as flying was not as common then as it is now, and Russian planes were especially suspect as it was the accepted wisdom of the Anglo-Saxon world then that Russians were mechanically backward. We had no other source of information.

Unlike Ireland, the development of the bogs was regarded not merely as a worthy and laudable enterprise but was something of a sacred cow, thanks to Lenin's approbation. Lenin believed that the future of the Russian economic advance depended on electric power and that electricity could be best and most cheaply produced at the source of the fuel from which it was generated. As Moscow, Leningrad and many other cities had great bogs in the vicinity Lenin actively encouraged their development. He believed in the dictum of Sir John Purser Griffith: 'Burn the bog where it is born'.

The central organisation of the peat industry was known as Glav-Torf and it was a section of the commissariat of heavy industry. It controlled the manufacture of the turf machines and a number of research stations. The magnitude of the whole enterprise was quite beyond our imagination. We spent a few days on the bogs at Klasson Turf Works which produced nearly 700,000 tons of turf per annum and we spent a few days at Shatura and a day in the experimental station near Moscow. An indication of the scale of operations can be got from the fact that even in 1934 more than seventeen million tons of turf was produced of which 38% was used in electric power stations and the rest in chemical, metallurgical, textile and other industries. Turf was little used for domestic purpose as there was abundant wood available. In the three power stations we visited at Shatura, Klasson near Moscow and Kirov station near Leningrad over five million tons of turf a year was being used for the production of electricity; any one of these stations would dwarf the production at Ardnacrusha which at that time supplied nearly our full electricity needs in Ireland. The visit could not but inspire and give us confidence to harness our own bogs. It certainly had that effect on me.

We found that the Russian bogs differed considerably both in size and character from ours in Ireland or those we had seen in Germany. By our standards they were immense and many tended to be heavily penetrated with bog timber. In these cases the hydro turf system, which uses compressed water to extract the raw peat in the form of a slurry, was commonly used as an alternative to mechanical excavation. The milled peat process, by which turf is produced in powder rather than in a sod form, was also widely employed in Russia.

Shatura bog was very much a wilderness. There was some barrack-like accommodation for the workers but nowhere to put foreign visitors and so we were offered the hospitality of the rather small house of the chief engineer. I think the family was temporarily boarded out. Purcell and I shared a room and Duffy and Murphy another. We were given the usual elaborate meal which developed into an informal late night party. Murphy and Duffy declined the invitation to participate and were so ill at ease that they actually barricaded their bedroom against, I know not what, danger. The party turned out to be most entertaining. Two officers of the guard — all Russian industrial enterprises had military guards — turned up, our sponsors from Glav-Torf and several local engineers and, of course, Euphrosene Simonyana. There were endless toasts in thimblefuls of vodka. I was a non-drinker and got by on mineral water. The vodka presented no problem to Purcell. The only effect it had on him was to deepen his naturally ruddy complexion and broaden his smile. He offered toasts to each individual present, to Glav-Torf and finally made a speech proposing a toast to the Union of Soviet Socialist Republics. The speech was superb partly because he had, in any case, an accomplished delivery and a very agreeable personality and partly because the speech was basically a variation of one he had delivered dozens of times before on festive occasions involving the Golfing Union of Ireland or the successful completion of some building contract. It struck me as very funny to see the captain of Portmarnock Golf Club and a professor of UCD toasting the USSR.

We did not see as much of Moscow as we would have liked nor as much as the Russians would have wished us to see. Partly because we had not much time to spare and partly because neither Murphy nor Duffy were very happy about being in Russia at all. As well as this the Russians were supposed to be hostile and distrustful of foreigners. I think this was purely a subjective feeling though it must be remembered that at the time of our visit the liquidation of the Kulaks had just been completed and the assassination of Kirov had produced terror all over the land.

I have often heard it said that in Russia you are only shown what the authorities want you to see. This seems to me nonsense. If you do not know a single word of the language, nor even the alphabet, which might enable you to read street signs there is no choice but to rely on the natives for guidance. We had several opportunities to stroll into the streets of Moscow but we could not go out of sight of our hotel for fear of being lost and having difficulty getting back. As we drove through the city we saw all the great buildings but the Kremlin, which for foreigners is the major place of interest, was closed to visitors. The streets were crowded with pedestrians; there was very little vehicular traffic and street cars always seemed to be overcrowded. The people on the streets differed much in appearance from their counterparts in western cities. The women were either hatless with uncoifed hair or wore scarves; all were dressed in blouses and long skirts and were quite devoid of makeup. It seems to be a manifestation of the spirit of revolution that women keep themselves unadorned. Amongst the women of our own revolution the same attitude prevailed. Cumann na mBan was an organisation

that contained many very beautiful women but when they got themselves up in uniforms and went on parade they seemed formidable
and dowdy — potential mothers of the Gracchi. The Russian men
no less than the women were indifferent to their appearance. Khaki
type jackets, loose shirts or poorly fitting western style suits were
commonly in vogue with an occasional collar and tie giving variety
to the fashion scene.

We visited the Park of Culture and Rest and saw the masses at
play. They looked far from unattractive and could well have
exemplified the happy Socialist people of the propagandist. Culture
was certainly part of the amusement provided. It was rather like a
Fleadh Cheoil on a very large scale. There were many groups of folk
dancers in varied regional costumes. There were open-air concerts
and a theatrical group was giving an open-air performance of *The
Cherry Orchard* much to my delight. Of course I could not follow a
word but I knew the story line sufficiently well to appreciate what
the actors were doing. The precise status of the company was unknown to me but it struck me that the acting was better than anything I had seen in Dublin. At that time my knowledge of the
theatre was confined to Dublin — the Folies Bergères excepted.

At this point another misfortune overtook our delegation and
disrupted it. Murphy got a telegram to say that his mother had died.
He was very distressed at the news and it was obvious that he must
return to Ireland at once. It would have been unreasonable to ask
him to travel back alone and Duffy volunteered to go with him
leaving Purcell and myself to complete the mission. Fortunately
Duffy and Murphy had seen enough of the technology employed in
the Russian bogs and discussed with experts the results of the
Russian experience in sufficient depth to enable them to prepare a
really fine report on the engineering aspects of turf production and
its use in power stations. Our schedule was interrupted to some
extent by the departure of Murphy and Duffy and it left us free for a
couple of days before setting off for Leningrad.

The Russians took us on a conducted tour of Moscow but for a
visitor who is unable to see the inside of the Kremlin or Lenin's
tomb it is not a very interesting city. There was a general air of
dilapidation about the place as if it had been starved of paint for
many years, as I suppose it had. On the other hand all the public
monuments were maintained immaculately. The crowds on the
streets seemed to contain many Asiatics and we were told that there
were one million strangers in Moscow on any given day. We visited
the Tolstoy Museum, at my request, remembering how much Anna
Karenina meant to me and how often I heard of the Tolstoy legend,
but I am afraid that the heavy Victorian furniture and the general

ambience of the museum failed to produce any emotional surge in me.

We were taken to Tretyakov Picture Gallery which houses a collection of mainly nineteenth century paintings. Every picture told its story and, indeed, they were none the worse for that. There was rather too much socialist and democratic realism grouped together to satisfy my eye which had become accustomed to less representational art. It was obviously impossible even to contemplate asking to be allowed into the Kremlin because of the political purges and the general distrust of westerners at that time but we might have asked to be taken into Lenin's tomb ahead of the mile long queue. The tomb is open day and night and the queue is always there, all the year round we were told. We did not ask but after much consultation with Purcell and much giggling and banter between us I took the daring step of enquiring if there was an antireligious museum in Moscow. There was. Could we visit it? Yes, if we did not mind. So off Purcell and I went like a pair of naughty schoolboys doing some forbidden thing for a dare.

The museum was quite small, a high oblong hall about eighty feet by fifty feet. The walls were covered with charts explaining the evolution of man and in juxtaposition the claims made by the Christian Church. There were pictures of the Church treasures shown in contrast with our Lord's exhortation to poverty. German and Russian helmets were arranged side by side each with badges invoking God's aid in war. There were pictures of the Russian troops leaving for the front being blessed by the patriarch and German troops in the same situation being blessed by their bishops. The centre piece of the whole exhibition was a large case with human remains inside — half skeleton and half mummy. It was explained that they were the remains of a saint from Kiev who for centuries was venerated because the body was incorruptible. Obviously it was not. But for us the most interesting exhibit was a picture of de Valera and the Papal Legate at the Eucharistic Congress inspecting a guard of honour of soldiers with fixed bayonets. The inscription on this exhibit was some jibe at the Prince of Peace.

We left Moscow without any consciousness of the terror campaign that had been initiated after Kirov's assassination and that was a little later to culminate in the great state trials of Bukharin, Zinoviev and other old Bolsheviks and nearly the whole general staff. I think that foreigners in any country wherever such upheavals take place have nothing to fear if they do not actively interfere or take up partisan positions; this was not difficult for us knowing no Russian.

We had a pleasant surprise when we came to check out from our hotel. So generous had been the Russian hospitality that our expense allowances were almost sufficient to cover the outgoings. Russian meals were in themselves an adventure. Every day during our stay in Moscow apart from breakfast we had two large meals, one in the middle of the day and the other very late in the evening, sometimes starting as late as midnight. The meals consisted of dozens of small dishes from which a selection could be made according to taste. The general name for this kind of food was zakuski. It included salted herrings, potato salad, different fish in different sauces, pike in aspic, smoked salmon and other smoked fish, eggs, anchovies, aubergines, green peppers, smoked ham, tongue in aspic, radishes in sour cream, pâté and caviar. Whether at breakfast or the midday or evening meal caviar was served in the abundance with which we serve butter. Previous to this the only reference to caviar that I could recall was in the tag 'Caviar to the general'. On seeing it served for the first time I thought it looked quite unpalatable but believing, as I did, that in a strange country one should eat the food and drink the drink, literally and metaphorically, of its people I tried caviar and found it the most agreeable food I had ever tasted.

We realised, of course, that zakuski on this scale was not the daily diet of the Russians in 1935; there was in fact a food shortage and queues were often to be seen in Moscow. Obviously we were getting very special treatment and I am sure that the Russians who shared the hospitality enjoyed it even more than we did. I was surprised by the evident pleasure the Russians took in their food, particularly their caviar. At home we ate things like sweets or fruit for pleasure but daily food was eaten for nourishment and to sustain life. We did not linger over the taste of blackpudding or steak, or chops, or heart, or tripe, or pigs' cheek or roast beef. We might prefer one more than the other but in general we were quite unselfconscious and uneducated in food matters. Exposure to Russian foods and eating habits gave me a new insight into the art of living. Only a few times have I again eaten caviar in quantity — once at a UN reception on the roof of the Empire State Building in New York, occasionally on long distance air flights and on a later visit to Russia.

The table was always laid in the same manner. There was for each place a set of glasses — one for vodka (a thimble size glass) and separate glasses for red and white wine and mineral water. They were all filled at the beginning of the meal and immediately a sip was taken they were at once refilled by one of the many waiters in attendance. Throughout the meal toasts were drunk to Russia, to Ireland, to the Turf Development Board, to Glav-Torf, and to one another right around the table. Purcell was the only one of our party who could cope with this challenge. I did not drink vodka but the Russians did not at all mind being toasted in mineral water.

We went from Moscow to Leningrad by train. Purcell and I were each provided with a sleeping compartment most luxuriously equipped. The carriages were much more splendidly fitted out than the ordinary European wagon-lits. Brass and mahogany abounded and, of course, the carriages were more commodious because, for strategic reasons, the Russian rail gauge was wider than the European gauge. One of the Glav-Torf people together with Euphrosene, our interpreter, came with us. In Leningrad we were greeted by officials of the Leningrad Turf Industry and installed in the Astoria, a large Intourist hotel and, by my standards, luxurious.

The electrification of Leningrad, no less than that of Moscow, was dependent on two turf-fired power stations called Kraski October and Kirov. The turf was produced by the same methods employed in the Moscow bogs, namely, hydro-excavation and milling. All the officials we encountered were scientifically trained, products of technological colleges or universities. They knew their business thoroughly and gave the impression of being totally absorbed in their work. They seemed to be inspired by something above the call of duty. This is a characteristic of people connected with the turf industry which I later observed in Germany and Sweden and it was also true of many of our own staff in the Turf Development Board and their successors in Bord na Móna. For them the turf industry became a crusade and a way of life.

Leningrad had about it no flavour of Asia. It was, and still is, as it was designed to be by Peter the Great in the eighteenth century, Russia's window to the west and the people on the streets showed in their clothes much of the relics of 'ould dacency'. Our hosts in the turf industry were dressed very much as would be their counterparts in Ireland. Possibly because by this time we had become more accustomed to Russian ways, in Leningrad we felt less constrained in our relations with our hosts. In consequence we saw, apart from the turf production centres, much more of the sights than in Moscow and, of course, for the visitor there was much more to see.

The city itself did not just grow. It was laid out with great care and beautified by magnificent monuments and buildings. It is built on the loop of the Neva river and a great thoroughfare known as the Nevsky Prospekt runs right across the city from one end of the loop to the other. To our eyes, it was a down-at-heel but nevertheless a wonderful and imposing thoroughfare, rather like the hub of a European capital on a Sunday. There was scarcely any motor-car traffic, nor even bicycles, and the tramcars looked shabby and overcrowded. There were no advertisements or lighted public signs but the monuments we saw were superbly maintained as were the great basilicas.

At the end of the Nevsky Prospekt was the admiralty building whose beautiful golden spire dominated the city. All over the city were monuments to notabilities of the *ancien régime;* the two principal ones featured were Peter the Great and the Empress Catherine. Peter the Great's monument, we are told, was one of the world's outstanding equestrian statues. Mounted on a great block of granite it was indeed impressive if only because of its enormous size. Catherine's monument was also huge and reminded me of Queen Victoria's statue outside Leinster House at home except that Catherine was surrounded by life-size statues of six men each of whom, according to our informant, had been her lover. She probably had had a happier life than Queen Victoria.

It was thanks to the very strong views of Lenin on the subject that the Bolsheviks were deterred from vandalism or iconoclasm. Everything of importance was preserved with extreme care. In the museums visitors had to wear overslippers to avoid scraping the floor. We visited St Isaac's Cathedral but except for its great size it was not comparable with the Gothic Cathedrals I had seen in Paris and Chartres. Indeed I thought our own St Patrick's Cathedral superior architecturally. I suppose I was not comparing like with like.

In Leningrad a consulting engineer from Dublin named Tweedy called to see us. I had never heard of him but Purcell knew him well. It appeared that Mr Tweedy had been interested all his life in the development of the Irish bogs and furthermore that he was a Marxist. He asked if he might attach himself to our party. Being glad to see any Irishman we arranged with the Russians that he should accompany us on our tour of the bogs and sight-seeing expeditions. Tweedy was a generous-minded soul who felt deeply about the injustices of the capitalist system and he was starry-eyed about everything he saw and heard in Russia. One of our sight-seeing trips was to Tsarkoye-Selo, about thirty miles from Leningrad. This was the Versailles of the Tsars and their principal place of residence before the revolution. To us it had the appearance of a small town consisting of palaces, churches, parks and statues. We were told that as each Tsar came to the throne he built at Tsarkoye a palace for his mistress and a basilica dedicated to Our Lady. We were also told that Rasputin spent much of his time there and, although he was killed in Leningrad, he was buried in Tsarkoye-Selo. We did not ask to see his grave. The palaces were extravagantly embellished. In fact they were designed, built and decorated by Italians. One of the palaces, in particular, an enormous pile, was extravagantly decorated in Italian baroque. Tweedy looked at it pained and horror-stricken and, in the correct Marxist fashion, declared the human waste and exploitation represented by the building was justification for the revolution. Purcell, as became the flower of the Dublin bourgeoisie, felt that the building was justified by the employment it had given.

We paid two visits to the Hermitage. This building houses one of the great museums and art collections of the world and two visits of three or four hours' duration gave us only a bare notion of its contents. We saw the famous collection of Impressionist paintings which was reported to be the equal of the collection in the Jeu de Paume in Paris. However that may be, it is extraordinary that so many of the Impressionists should have found their way into Russian hands. It was suggested by a guide to whom I put the question that they were bought by rich Russian merchants who were the earliest patrons of the Impressionist school and in the course of the revolution they were confiscated for the benefit of the community. We were taken down to a basement in the Hermitage and it was explained to us that what we were about to see was not open to the general public. Sure enough the entrance was secured by two armed guards, in this case women. With great unlocking of doors we were conducted to a small room with glass cases containing the most unusual gold ornaments imaginable. The collection included rings and bracelets and toiletries of various kinds and I was astonished to see entire battle scenes engraved on the inside of finger rings. The tiny detail and beautiful engraving could only be seen adequately with the help of a magnifying glass. We were told that these were Greek ornaments from a Black Sea find. We were very flattered to have been allowed to see them.

Our final sight-seeing trip was to the Palace of Gachina. It was not a very big palace but it featured a collection of weapons ranging from flints and slings through bows and arrows, swords, knives, daggers to Thompson automatic guns. The floors of the palace were parquet made with blocks from every known wood in the world.

Before leaving Leningrad for home we were taken on a visit to the theatre to be followed by a banquet. The theatre selected by our hosts was the Marinsky (rechristened the Kirov). I had read of the theatre as the home of the Imperial Ballet and I had a conscientious newspaper reader's familiarity with the names of some of its star performers such as Diaghilev, Karsanova and Nijinsky but that was the limit of my knowledge of ballet. As it happened the show running at the time was an opera — Les Huguenots. While I had seen a few operas in Dublin and Paris I was one of, I think, a very large number of people who regard opera as an indifferent art form. I was never able to suspend disbelief at the constant discovery of long-lost daughters, cases of mistaken identity, intercepted letters and the generally farcical plots. Anyway my musical education was so poor that except for the most popular arias, such as the Toreador song from *Carmen* and the 'Chè gelida manina' from *La Bohème,* the music of opera evoked no response. I never got through an evening at the opera without falling asleep.

But this evening in the Marinsky was different and the audience no less than the performers added interest to the occasion. There was a very large orchestra dressed with an astonishing lack of uniformity. Quite a number of them, including the conductor, were in full evening dress with white tie. Others wore dinner jackets and black ties. Some wore ordinary lounge suits with collar and tie and some wore suits with neither collar nor tie. Leningrad still clung to the old theatrical tradition and probably the members of the orchestra wearing evening dress had worked in it in the days before the revolution. There was a very large *corps de ballet* and to me the performance was wonderfully exciting and spectacular. Even the Paris opera was very much inferior to it in the perfection of product-ion. The audience, nearly as mixed in its dress as the orchestra, was enthusiastic in its reception, obviously knowing its music well.

The restaurant where we had our meal afterwards was in the roof gardens of a very high building overlooking the Neva. The meal began at midnight. The night was dead calm and the air so clear that we could see all over the city. The great buildings and monuments and the river had the quality of a Canaletto painting. We were in the shadow of the admiralty spire. Below us was the Hermitage and across the river the great buildings of the academic quarter of the city — the university, the art gallery and the academy of science — while faraway across the river was the massive Peter and Paul fort-ress, the legendary prison of Russian political subversives. Plants and flowers, the soft light of the midnight sun, the utter balminess of the midnight air, the friendliness of our hosts, and the murmur of voices around us, fused to produce for me a feeling of total peace and total pleasure. It was one of those moments that one experi-ences rarely enough in one's lifetime when the spirit is at rest.

This was the end of our visit to Russia and we returned home well satisfied with the results. We had got all the information we wanted about the Russian turf industry while profiting from the occasion to see something of a totally new political and social system then very much in its infancy. It was only eighteen years since the Bolshevik revolution and very much less since the end of the Russian Civil War and the intervention of the Great Powers.

Mechanisation of the Bogs

In a personal way the visit to Germany and Russia was something of a watershed in my life. Ever since my teens I had experience of exercising some kind of authority and carrying the responsibility that authority imposes but only on a very low plane. Heading a delegation representing one's country in foreign parts brought with it a different and higher grade of authority and responsibility. Being the leader of such a delegation conferred considerable prestige on me in the community at large and added greatly to my self-confidence.

On our return we submitted a detailed report to the government on the results of our enquiries into the production and use of turf abroad. The report was compiled mainly by Murphy and Duffy and dealt with the technical aspects of the subject. It was an excellent report, as might be expected from such competent engineers. It made no recommendations as to the policy which might be adopted for the development of our bogs. This was basically a matter for decision by the Turf Development Board whose responsibility it was to recommend a course of action for the approval of the government. My mind was made up. I believed that if the Russians and Germans could make such profitable use of their bogs there was no reason why we should not be able to match their achievement. As to the *modus operandi,* I was satisfied as a result of our observations abroad that bog development in Ireland should be based on the excavation method in use at Meppen and that turf produced should be used for electricity generation in bogside power stations. My board colleague, A. O'Rahilly was, if possible, more convinced than I of our capability to do the job.

We were extraordinarily lucky to have someone of O'Rahilly's technical quality so closely associated with the Turf Development Board. By any Irish standards he was an unusual personality. A son of The O'Rahilly, the most romantic of Easter Week men — he was killed leaving the GPO — he was in theory and practice a Sinn Féiner and a Gaeilgeoir. I met him first when he was a mere boy, and a very small boy at that, serving with the Flying Column in south Wexford during the Civil War. At that time he was brash, rude to his comrades and resentful of having to endure the kind of food and slovenliness which was a condition of life in a Column. He was quite fearless and impetuous. He was known in the Column as 'Weasels'.

I lost touch with him when I left Wexford to join Liam Lynch in

1923 and did not meet him again until 1926, this time at a Republican club party in Count Plunkett's house. He had grown so much that I mistook him for his elder brother. He had escaped arrest and jail during the Civil War. His character had undergone a complete metamorphosis. Mount St Benedict, where he had been to school, was conducted on the lines of an English public school being designed to attract the sons of wealthy Irish Catholics who might otherwise have gone to Stoneyhurst, Downside, Ampleforth or Beaumont. As it was assumed that the pupils would not have problems in earning their living the teaching system aimed at character development rather than success in examinations. It also aimed at inculcating in them a sense of being Irish; in this way it acted as an antidote to the Castle Catholicism which characterised most of the children of well-off Irish families who were sent to England for their education. Father Sweetman who founded the school was himself an 'original' and dominated his charges who regarded him with a mixture of awe and affection. They left school enriched by independence of mind and self-confidence which was sometimes not soundly based and appeared to many of their contemporaries as mere arrogance. The fact that the nuts and bolts of a secondary education, such as mathematics, science and foreign languages, were given a relatively low priority left the boys at a noticeable disadvantage if afterwards they decided to take up a profession apart of course from law which at that time presented no entrance difficulties other than financial. It is also questionable whether boys whose sense of nationalism was acquired through the ethos of an English public school, playing distinctively English games and dominated by the English Benedictines' brand of Catholicism, were really well equipped to come to terms with the Ireland of their day.

It was all the more surprising to me when I found O'Rahilly had not merely overcome the difficulties of his schooling but had taken a first-class honours degree in mechanical engineering. He had steeped himself in the works of George Bernard Shaw, Swift and Marx and was the only person I had ever met who had read *Das Kapital* through. He had adopted most of Shaw's ideas. He was anti-vivisection, anti-smoking and anti-drinking. He stopped short of vegetarianism but favoured organic food and when he later acquired a garden of some acres he cultivated it by the Indore process. Like Shaw he had simple gastronomic tastes but liked the wheat for his bread to come from his own fields, eggs from his own hens, milk and cream from his own cows, honey from his own hives and fruit from his own orchard. He had an obsession about germs — never carried money in notes and did not borrow books from a library. His linen had to be laundered at home.

I saw a great deal of him after 1926 in Republican circles and at the Abbey Theatre. He had lost none of his self-confidence but all of his cantankerousness. After a few false starts as lecturer in UCD and a spell in the bacon curing business which he quit from boredom, he started a concrete roofing-tile factory in the mews of a friend's house. Soon he had built up an extensive business. When later he tried to diversify into plasterboard he was blocked by the American multi-national companies which held the world patent on plaster-making machines. He succeeded in designing and manufacturing a machine which evaded the American patent. The NUI later recognised the measure of this achievement by conferring an honorary doctorate on him. His skill in mechanical engineering was phenomenal. Each morning on waking his mind was a *tabula rasa* and all day long he poured out ideas which were discarded when he went to sleep. One idea was never discarded and that was the pursuit of success in business. Into this he put his remarkable combination of physical and mental energy and all his life he never deviated from this objective. Just as Shaw was his intellectual model his business model was Henry Ford. He was himself a natural non-conformist but those around him were expected to conform to his ethical convictions and impulsive judgments. He distinguished sharply between the ethics of business and of private life; tolerant of the ways of the world in the one he was uncompromisingly rigid in maintaining standards in the other. He assumed these to be the views of others and was not infrequently misunderstood by his associates both public and private. He cared nothing for money, having all the things money can buy but he willingly gave his time to the public service.

O'Rahilly placed all his talents and most of his scarce spare time at the disposal of the Turf Board and became in a sense its technical conscience. During the twenty-five years that I worked in the board there was rarely a week when we did not spend one or two evenings either in his house or mine discussing turf. We frequently visited the bogs together, sometimes arriving before work begain, so as to observe progress at first hand. I never made any major decision without first consulting him or with Aiken or with both together. The evenings I was not discussing turf with O'Rahilly were, as often as not, spent discussing turf with Aiken in his room at Leinster House or at our respective homes. Aiken never tired of the subject nor of thinking up new ideas for the use or production of turf. As might be expected many of his ideas were impractical but he was never lacking in enthusiastic support for our efforts. In our worst moments he encouraged us. As far as the formation of policy was concerned he contributed as much as though he was a member of our board. In effect we were in the unusual position of having a direct presence in the cabinet. This was well known in the civil service and made it easier for us to deal with bureaucratic opposition. It was also known that the Taoiseach, Eamon de Valera, was personally interested in the success of our work. This also helped in shaping civil service attitudes towards the turf scheme.

Robert Barton, our chairman, lived in Glendalough and was not so easily accessible but I usually saw him at least once a week between board meetings to report progress and discuss matters of special importance. At moments of crisis O'Rahilly and I would drive down to Glendalough to seek Barton's consolation or advice which was always readily forthcoming.

With one exception all the members of the board were fully in agreement with the proposals we put to the government for bog mechanisation on the German model. Kennedy was, in principle, against doing anything. He had a Latin tag or some gnomic utterance to suit every occasion. *Festina lente* — 'Don't rush your fences' — 'You must creep before you walk'. He thought we should do nothing until we had gained more experience, ignoring the fact that experience cannot be gained from inaction. Mathematician though he was he could not grasp the fact that a percentage of nothing is nothing.

Broadly there are two types of bog in Ireland — blanket bog and high bog. The blanket bogs are confined to the west, are relatively shallow and occur usually at high altitude. The high bog which is deeper and more variable in quality and botanical origin is to be found in the Bog of Allen and the central plain. Except in Mayo there are no large unbroken areas of blanket bog. It is unfortunate that in the extreme west, where the need for industry is greatest, the absence of large and reasonably compact areas of bog inhibits mechanical development.

With the very considerable assistence of the 1812 Commission's report on the Bogs of Ireland, we examined most of the promising bog areas. For me the selection of bogs on which to begin operations was an extremely rewarding experience. In the process I walked nearly all the major bogs from Donegal to Kerry and from Kildare to Galway. To walk an undrained high bog was an arduous physical exercise. It involved continuous jumping from tussock to tussock. A false step often landed you in water which rose to the tops of your thigh boots and you had to be pulled out of the morass. That was why these expeditions were always carried out by groups of three or four people together. Once at Shannonbridge I had the rather frightening experience of sinking above my hips into a slough. It was easy to understand why, contrary to common expect-

ations, the great midland bogs yielded so little of antiquarian or
archaeological interest. We could well have been the first human
beings to have penetrated many of them. Even snipe would have
had problems in finding a solid resting place. Out on a bog too the
rain seemed to have a particularly penetrating quality. No conventional rainwear offered protection and on wet days you invariably
left the bog soaked to the skin. Fortunately I was in the full of my
health and never suffered any ill-effects. On the other hand to find
oneself in the middle of a great expanse of bog on a fine calm summer evening is a pristine experience. The subtle smell of the mosses
and wild flowers but above all the impenetrable silence gave me, at
any rate, wonderful sensuous pleasure. My peregrinations with the
IRA had acquired for me what for a Dubliner was an unusual knowledge of rural Ireland; my intimate associations with the bogs
greatly enhanced it. My pleasure would have been greater if I had
known something of the flora of the bogs so that I could identify
plants such as myrtle, asphodel, rosemary and sundew.

We decided to recommend to the government the acquisition of
five hundred acres of blanket bog at Lyrecrumpane, near
Knocknagosel in Kerry, and the modernisation of the plant at
Turraun so that production there could continue. As our major
pioneering project we decided to acquire and develop a large area
of high bog in the midlands using as a model the production system
adopted at Klasmann's Works in Meppen. To acquire so much bogland compulsory power was needed. We were met by the civil service with the objection, *inter alia,* that compulsory powers would
require legislation. They seemed to think that this was a conclusive
reason for dropping the scheme. So often over the years did I hear
this argument and the other equally conclusive objection that
'something was administratively impracticable' advanced as a
recipe for doing nothing. Action was supposed to stop in the face of
these difficulties. My attitude was that if the government wanted
something done the Dáil was there to legislate. I also thought that
very few projects were administratively impracticable given the will
to carry them out and the money to pay for them. I learned well and
very early in my life that there were few problems that money
would not solve. In the event the necessary compulsory powers for
the acquisition of bogland and other land required for ancillary purposes were provided in the Turf Development Act of 1935. With
the aid of the compulsory powers and the marvellous skill in land
acquisition of the Land Commission staff, some of whom were
loaned to us for the purpose, we acquired four thousand acres of
bog near Portarlington in quick time at very economic prices.

We established a good administrative organisation largely on the

The author, aged seven, with his mother and brother Patrick.

Mrs Lawlor

The author's father in 1928.

The Coyle children in their native Derry: left to right: Hugh, Eithne,
Mary, Donny, Nora, Jim

University College Dublin soccer team, winners of the Collingwood Cup, 1926. Back Row: M. Finnegan, T. Creanor, F. Friel, S. Lavan, J. Geary, F. McGahon. Front Row: P. Drury Byrne, M. Peppard, Author, J. McGilligan, T. Caffrey.

Graduation Day, 1926: Author on right, with soccer team friends: Dr Patrick Drury Byrne, Dr Frank Friel, Dr Joseph McGilligan.

Mary with three of the children on the pier at Carraroe.

En route to Aran from Carraroe: left to right: the author, Mary, Fred Boland, Mary's sister, Rosemary.

Members of the Irish Peat Commission, 1917, visiting Turraun Peat Works: left to right: Prof. Hugh Ryan, George Fletcher, Prof. Sydney Young, Sir John Purser Griffith, Prof. Pierce Purcell.

The Board of Bord na Móna 1946: left to right: Author, Prof. T. Wheeler, R.C. Barton, W. Quirke, A. O'Rahilly.

Frederick Weckler, Chief
Accountant, Electricity Supply
Board

Sir Hugh Beaver, Managing
Director, Arthur Guinness Ltd.

Under the gun of the battleship
Aurora at Leningrad: left to
right: Lewis Rhatigan, Patrick
Cogan, author.

Leningrad: armoured car used
by Lenin during the early days
of the Revolution: left to right:
P. Cogan, author.

Eamon de Valera, Frank Aiken, Patrick Barry (Works Manager) and Aodhagan O'Rahilly at Lullymore Briquette Factory.

On the occasion of the author's retirement as Chairman of CIE: left to right: Author, Frank Lemass, General Manager (standing), An Taoiseach, Sean Lemass.

Between two Presidents: Author with Şean T. Ó Ceallaigh (left) and Eamon de Valera (right).

Old Friends: At the launching of author's book **Dublin Made Me** *in 1979: left to right: Mrs Sean T. Ó Ceallaigh, Peadar O'Donnell, John Dowling and Author.*

lines of that operating in the ESB. The emphasis was on decentralised control; obviously the day-to-day bog operations could not be managed from a central office in Dublin. We were particularly careful to avoid the early difficulties which beset the ESB through the deficiencies of their accounts system. With the assistance of my old chief, Weckler, we had installed a cost accounting system which produced quick and accurate information of our running expenditures and also provided a very effective control of our purchasing department, our properties and stores. We employed an accounts staff of high quality and as a matter of policy university graduates were recruited for non-technical as well as technical posts. I think we must have been the first business organisation in Ireland to provide opportunities for employment, other than the teaching profession, for graduates from the faculties of commerce and arts.

The bog which we acquired near Portarlington was called Clonsast from one of the townlands in which it was located. An important factor in the selection of Clonsast was its location relative to the River Barrow arterial drainage system. Another consideration, derived partly from local knowledge and partly from inexperience in surveying, was the belief that Clonsast bog was timber free. Later experience showed the error of this assumption. In fact one half of the bog proved to be densely timbered, the other half less so. This miscalculation cost us dearly in money and effort until techniques were evolved to cope with it. In the early summer of 1936 our planned development work began. It involved digging by hand over five hundred miles of drain, preparing sixteen miles of railbed and arranging for the erection of thirty miles of power lines on the bog surface. In addition we had to sink wells, build offices and workshops and a hostel for seasonal workers. Railway equipment, two cutting machines (known as 'baggers' from the German 'digger') and two sod collectors were ordered from Germany. Although we were not conscious of it at the time we had started an enterprise which was unique in Ireland and unusual anywhere. We had begun to lay the foundations of an industry, by Irish standards a large scale industry, in which the native environment of the workers would be not merely undisturbed but immensely improved economically.

From the beginning very large sums of money were involved. The responsibility for their effective use fell on me as it would on any chief executive. Up to this point in time I had nothing to worry about. I had hand-picked the managerial and technical staff and had total confidence in them. I did not consider that it was the function of a chief executive to have a point of view on the relative merits of different engineering equipment or on the design of workshops. I accepted the recommendation of the engineering department on such matters just as I relied on the accounts department to see that the proper procedures were used in tendering and that we got what we paid for. We had employed a German expert from the Klasmann organisation, Heinz Mecking, to advise on the lay-out of the bog. We started with full confidence on the excavation of the drainage network but from the beginning it ran into extreme and unexpected difficulties.

The German bog technology had been built on generations of tradition rather than scientific and communicable knowledge. Unfortunately our resident German adviser had not absorbed even the tradition or was unable to apply it to our Irish conditions. He was a man in his early thirties who, as we found out later, had not been a success in the family turf business in Germany. He had been exiled to Ireland much as the blacksheep of an English upper-class family would, in earlier times, have been sent to work in the colonies. He spoke no English but he and our chief engineer, Tom McMahon agreed to exchange lessons in English and German. After a while they communicated well, McMahon speaking broken English under the impression that it was German and Mecking speaking broken German under the impression that it was English. Mecking made what, in the event, was one genuinely important contribution to bog work by insisting on the introduction of piece rates. Without this system our development costs would have been impossibly expensive; even as things stood they were running far ahead of estimate. Another innovation was the introduction of metric measurements which greatly simplified payment calculations. We must have been the first industrial organisation in Ireland to use the metric system for this purpose. We got little other value from Mecking and as German triumph followed German triumph in Europe he became increasingly uninvolved in his assignment. He set himself up as a Nazi intelligence agent photographing railway stations, river bridges, sign posts and reservoirs on the lines attributed to the itinerant German bands of my childhood. This no doubt was evidence of his patriotic zeal but he could probably have got the same information by buying picture postcards. He was obsessed with the menace of Bolshevism. It formed much of his limited conversation. It was an occasion of great amusement to me to see his incredulous reaction when I broke the news to him of the *Ribbentrop/Molotov Pact*. When war broke out he had to return to Germany — with reluctance. He thought that he would be more useful to his country acting as an intelligence agent in Ireland. He died an honourable death of hunger and oedema as a prisoner of the Russians outside Vienna.

For us his advice on bog drainage was disastrous. Misapplying his

German experience he insisted that the trenches should be excavated in a single cut to a depth of six feet. The result was that after a few days under pressure from the bog water seeping through the walls the trenches invariably collapsed. Working according to this system was like trying to perform the labour of Sisyphus. Although the engineering faculties in our universities provided their students with the wide ranging courses on the conventional engineering problems they did not, unfortunately, include bog drainage with the result that our engineers had no specialised training in this subject. We lost thousands of pounds before we discovered that a bog cannot be drained in a hurry. Nor did we realise that a bog varied in its physical composition at relatively frequent intervals. This piece of ignorance cost us many more thousands. *Ciall cheannaithe* can be expensive.

To add to our difficulties the Clonsast works manager came into conflict with our German adviser, who was strongly supported by the chief engineer, on the use of the piece rate payment system. The manager appealed directly to Henry Kennedy, whose protégé he really was, and who was only too willing to espouse the manager's cause to the point where the issue was threatening to create serious internal dissention. The manager was a thoroughly decent man but in this case was out of his depth and realising this I felt that the matter could best be resolved by transferring him to another post. In the event he declined to accept this alternative and resigned. Kennedy showed no inclination to follow suit; so with the agreement of the minister, Seán Lemass, I and my colleagues on the board compelled him to choose to resign or be dismissed. The options were not wide and he left on his own initiative. From then onwards there was no recurrence of boardroom troubles or even unpleasantness in mutual relationships during the whole of my career in the Turf Development Board and its successor, Bord na Móna. Kennedy, understandably if not reasonably, developed a vested interest in the failure of the turf scheme. For the remainder of his life he spent much of his considerable spare time trying to blacken my personal character and denigrating our efforts to further the turf industry. It will, I am sure, be apparent that I bitterly resented his activities.

Dr Kennedy's withdrawal from the Board left it with a completely Fianna Fáil complexion. It was necessary that a new member be appointed who was clearly without political affiliations. With the permission of Seán Lemass, we invited Dr Wheeler, Professor of Chemistry at UCD, to become a member. He accepted the appointment.

With nearly one year's work behind us scarcely any progress had

been made in the drainage of Clonsast bog. I began to pay for the
satisfactions I had derived from authority and responsibility and
suffered from the worries and anxieties that beset a chief executive
when things go wrong. Unlike most chief executives in this situation
I did not have the problem of facing a critical or hostile board. I
made a point of keeping in close communication with my fellow
board members during this frustrating period and also I had
frequent consultations with Aiken. The weight of my problem was
well spread. When things go wrong the principal worry of the chief
executive at any time, but especially in the depressed conditions of
the 1930s, is the fear of losing his job. I was spared this ultimate
hazard since I was seconded from and, at worst, could return to the
security of the civil service. The penalty I would have had to pay for
failure was the jibes of the people who were 'born on the bog', the
triumph of political opponents, the humiliation of feeling that I had
let down the Republic — a phrase from the polemics of the Treaty
debates. We were still emotionally involved in 'the Republic'. We
also feared letting down Dev who had so publicly identified himself
with turf development; for Aiken, O'Rahilly, Barton, Quirke and
myself he personalised the Republic. For us, the development of
the bogs was a crusade rather than a commercial project.

I was in the classical anxiety situation which, by tradition, gives
executives ulcers. I was immunised against ulcers by a number of
antidotes. I could return in the evenings to a very agreeable home.
Mary, my wife, fully accepted my comings and goings. As well as
our growing family we had the common interest of politics, books,
paintings and the theatre. We always managed to see any new production at the Abbey and the Gate. I read in bed before going to
sleep and I woke at 6 o'clock and read till eight when the papers and
breakfast came. This was a habit of a lifetime so that unlike so many
public servants I did not have to wait for retirement to catch up with
my reading. I made it a rule never to bring office work home and
never to work at weekends which, in those days, meant Saturday
afternoons and Sundays. In summer when Mary and the children
were on their annual migration to Carraroe, my weekends were
usually spent playing golf. I included in my antidote against ulcers
the capacity to turn on sleep at will. I slept for half an hour after
lunch whether at home or in the office or in a car. I never drove a
car myself if I could help it but, if driving was unavoidable, I pulled
into a side road for my afternoon nap.

As it happened the solution of the drainage problem was simple
and was found near at hand. Drawing on the experience of generations of local bogmen Pat Gorman, one of the earliest of our Clonsast workers whose natural intelligence and strength of character

quickly won him promotion to the post of foreman, advocated a radically different approach. The bog, he argued, cannot be rushed. Drains must be excavated in slow stages and the walls given time to solidify. Cuts of two to three feet deep are the maximum which should be taken at one time. This change in technique gave impressively better results and progress was rapid from then onwards.

Pat Gorman was born literally on Clonsast bog and into a family of small farmers whose holding included many acres of the bog itself. He was by any standard a remarkable personality, tall, heavily-built and a well-known local footballer. He might in another age have been Myles the Slasher, or Kelly the boy from Killane. His education finished at National School level but his imagination was not limited by education. Every day he had looked over the great stretch of bog and hoped and believed that one day something would be done to use it to the profit of the locality. The coming of the Turf Development Board was for him the realisation of a dream.

I too had a private dream about the bogs. Since I was a boy playing in Shaw's wood in Terenure and in the Old Pine Forest I loved trees, woods and plantations. From the beginning of my involvement with turf I hoped that one day the bogs would be cut away and the Bog of Allen would be transferred into the Forest of Allen. Now nearly two generations after the work began the first substantial tracts of cutaway bog are available for cultivation. It may well be that the Bog of Allen will become a prairie rather than a forest. I would be well satisfied with that. It is easy to understand the great emotional satisfaction I experienced a few years ago when Pat Gorman, then assistant manager of a vastly enlarged Clonsast bog complex, showed me over hundreds of acres of lush grassland supporting herds of cattle in an area at one time as economically valueless as the Gobi desert and whose development caused so much heart-searching and controversy.

Drainage of the mountain bog at Lyrecrumpane gave rise to no serious problem. The development and equipment of the bog was completed in time to go into production in the 1938 season. Production was also continued at Turraun. The main problem encountered at this time was that of marketing the new product. Consumers were slow to appreciate the superiority of machine-won turf and among urban and industrial users there was a decided antipathy to turf in any form. The attitude of the fuel trade was also unhelpful. It was at this stage that the foundations were perforce laid of an independent distribution network which contributed so much to the successful marketing of turf products in later years.

At Turraun the sales problem was not made easier by the fact that at this time the only egress from the bog was by canal which involved multiple handling. Although we owned our own barge, delivery by canal was troublesome and uneconomic with the result that Turraun was losing money at a time when we were looking forward to its expansion. In the event this expansion was held up more by technical than by financial difficulties. To enlarge the working area we found it necessary to cut an outfall drain under the canal leading to the Brosna River which would have been a straightforward engineering operation. We applied to the canal company for permission to go ahead. This was refused unless we entered into a bond for £100,000 to indemnify them against any damage to their property. To me this seemed mere obstruction by a gang of anti-national reactionary west Britons, which I believed the directors of the Grand Canal Company to be, although I had never met them. I discussed with our chief engineer, Tom McMahon, the possibility of solving the problem by blowing a hole in the embankment at a point miles away from Turraun and thus emptying the canal. While repairs were being effected we could construct our outfall drain without giving any indemnity. McMahon, who was a conservative-minded man, was shocked at my lawlessness so we had to await better times before proceeding with the expansion of Turraun.

By the spring of 1938 the first of the two automatic cutting machines which had been ordered for Clonsast were delivered from Germany but could not be put to work as the electricity network was not completed. This delay had its compensations, however, because it gave us a further year's grace to get the bog into workable condition. The works manager at that time was Alban O'Kelly, one of the board's earliest employees. Thanks to his inspiration and the efforts of an engineer named Finnegan and an accountant named Sheahan, who between them combined extraordinary organisational ability with extreme hard work and unlimited enthusiasm, the preparatory work was sufficiently advanced to enable the production to start early in 1939.

Finnegan was a young engineer whom, although he was much my junior, I knew from my soccer-playing days in the university. Shortly after my appointment as 'Turf Chief' as the newspaper headlines described it, I met Finnegan accidentally in the street. He congratulated me on my appointment and told me that since his boyhood in Monaghan he had been fascinated by the idea of utilising the bogs. He had regarded the neglect of our turf resources as a great national failure. When a year or so later we were advertising for engineers for the handwon turf scheme I rang him to suggest that he might apply only to be told that he had already done so. Finnegan was a *duine maith* in the sense that this term was used by Arland Ussher. Puritanical and hard-working and above all a disciplinarian, he was essentially a country man who loathed city life and had a deep distrust and contempt for head office whose instructions he obeyed or ignored as he thought fit. But so remarkable was his skill as a bog manager and engineer, and so greatly did I rate his character that I handled him on the historic basis that 'if all Ireland cannot rule this man, let this man rule all Ireland'. He seemed to have a sort of mystical communion with the bog which resulted in an unusual understanding of its character and behaviour. Sheahan, too, seemed to have the same natural affinity with the bog. Turf development was a kind of religion with him though he saw it more in human than in economic terms. In other respects he was very different in character from Finnegan. He was light-hearted, extrovert and generous in his assessment of others. He loved music and was a good musician. In the most difficult days in Clonsast his nerve and his belief in our ability to bring the work to a successful conclusion never faltered. He was the rock of morale against which all pessimism broke. Both Finnegan and Sheahan were amongst the givers of life; they were grateful for the opportunity that the bog provided to exercise their talents fully. They were without personal ambition and despised what has become known as 'the good life'.

Our interests were expanded in 1939, just as Clonsast was becoming operational, by a directive from the minister that we were to take over Lullymore briquette factory which had finally run out of financial support and had closed down. The history of the factory reaches out into an area of international intrigue to which it would take an author of the calibre of E. Phillips Oppenheim to do justice. The method of manufacture was known as the Peco process (the name Peco may possibly be an acronym) and was heavily protected by patents. It grew out of an idea conceived by a group of Norwegian engineers and businessmen for developing a smokeless fuel suitable for use in the trenches during the First World War. The fuel was produced by briquetting turf on the Scottish bogs at Dumfries by a method known as wet carbonisation. The Norwegians sold the idea to the Balfour family who financed the undertaking to the tune of one million pounds which they lost. The heat content of the finished product was only equivalent to the heat value of the coal used to briquette it. The Norwegians, unlike the Balfours, were not discouraged. They continued to experiment and evolved a method of briquetting where the turf itself was used as the drying agent. They succeeded in selling the process in Denmark before

turning their attention to Ireland where the newly-elected Fianna
Fáil government was in a receptive mood for new ideas. As this one
had behind it the great prestige of Professor Purcell, a reputed
expert not merely in turf but in engineering, and also enjoyed the
support of Gordon Campbell, later Lord Glenavy, Seán Lemass
agreed to back the project providing much of the finance through
state loans. This led to the formation of the Peat Fuel Company
who built a factory at Lullymore, County Kildare, to exploit the
process.

The Department of Finance was very much opposed to the project because to them state investment in developments of this kind
was completely against the rules of safe exchequer practice. When
the company failed to live up to its projections the department did a
thorough hatchet job. The factory was closed down and handed
over to us on a care and maintenance basis. Shortly afterwards I had
a request to see the Peco representatives. I had heard stories, probably apocryphal, of legal actions about the Peco patent rights and
intrigues with the Balfours and the Danish government, not to
speak of an alleged quarrel amongst the owners of the patent where
a gun was produced and a man was shot. As I had no wish to get
involved in these machinations my immediate reaction was to
refuse, pleading pressure of other business. I declined an invitation
to dinner but finally agreed to see them in the Shelbourne Hotel
late one evening. This was my first encounter with hard-headed
professional salesmen and I found it an amusing experience. One
was a man in his sixties, rather flamboyantly dressed. He wore a
wide cravat with a diamond pin, a flowered waistcoat laced with a
heavy gold watch-chain and rings on the fingers of both hands. He
spoke very fluent English with a slightly foreign accent. His companion was an Englishman in his thirties who said little. As I arrived
they had finished their meal and were sniffing brandy in their
ballons. Cigars were produced from a beautiful Morroco leather
case. Instead of using a match the older man produced a small, but
beautifully made, spirit lamp from which he lit his cigar observing
that it was vandalism and a form of desecration to ruin a good cigar
by lighting it with matches. I was a poor guest as I didn't drink
brandy, smoke cigars or even take coffee so late in the evening. I
listened to their spiel about the wonderful success Peco had
achieved in Denmark; how the Canadians were going ahead with a
large scale project; how Dumfries was on the point of success when
the war ended; finally, what a pity it would be not to persevere with
Lullymore just when it too was at the breakthrough stage. I was not
encouraged to ask questions nor did I want to. Finally, I was invited
to visit Denmark with a promise of the freedom of Copenhagen and

access to all its multiple attractions. Understandably I resented their whole attitude. I felt, as so often I felt afterwards in similar circumstances, that I was being treated like an executive in a banana republic. There was to be something in it for me or, at least, I could be softened up by hospitality. The encounter did not endear me to the tactics of the international salesmen.

My flamboyant visitor was not far wrong when he claimed that the Lullymore company was on the point of success. They had invented a machine called a disc-ditcher which, had it been more fully developed, would have gone far to solving the problems of mechanising bog drainage. Later, perfected by our engineers, it saved Bord na Móna great sums of money and the back-breaking labour of hundreds of men. Alas, the Department of Finance was never sympathetic to crystal balls. Reflecting on this incident I could not help wondering how many projects lay in the files of the department slaughtered at birth or aborted through their preoccupation with the preservation of external assets or their adherence to narrow and primitive accounting principles.

While the lengthy proceedings involved in the transfer to us of this new acquisition were going on, war broke out in Europe. Clonsast had not as yet received its full complement of bog machinery. It was accepted ever since Munich that war was inevitable and in preparation for that contingency we had been pressing the German manufacturers to speed up deliveries. I was in Germany the month before the war urging Klasmann to supply at least one sod collector and it had been actually loaded on a ship in Hamburg when war broke out in September. We thought it might be possible to have it re-routed through Holland, during the phony war period. Having heard that Jim Stafford, a member of a well-known Wexford shipping family, was going to Holland. I arranged a meeting between him and Klasmann at Venlo on the German/Dutch frontier to see what could be done to get the cargo out. Stafford warmly agreed to undertake the mission. He succeeded in contacting Klasmann but owing to British intervention the scheme fell through. Stafford's involvement might well have cost him dearly; but for the action on the part of our government his firm would have been blacklisted by the British as a trader with the enemy. We were grateful to him for trying. I found him a refreshing man to deal with. In another age he would, I felt, have been a cheerful buccaneer.

The Fuel Emergency

In the year that followed Munich virtually no precautions were taken to provide against the scarcity of raw materials which was sure to occur in a war situation. The government, or more correctly the civil service, believed that Britain would continue to meet our needs in vital commodities. It did not take long to find out the truth of the old Irish triad: 'three things to beware of: the horns of a bull, the hoofs of a horse and the smile of an Englishman'. The truth is that our economic connections with the outside world were largely second-hand. A typical example which caused strong feelings at the time was that of tea which had always been bought through the Mincing Lane tea brokers instead of direct from the producing countries. So great was the faith of officialdom in our British commercial connections that the possibility of their failing to supply their long-standing Irish customers was never envisaged. The wartime tea shortage inflicted much hardship particularly on old people.

The higher civil servants had never mentally detached themselves from their *chers collègues* in Whitehall. I remember sitting beside a very important department head who said, with deep regret and some resentment, that if the British were still here he would have had a knighthood. I pointed out that if the British were here he would not be occupying his present position nor would he have made the acquaintance of the smoked salmon he was eating. Though their horizons had been enlarged by events such as de Valera's election to the post of President of the League of Nations, many Irish people still looked through English eyes on the outside world. They were looking through an opaque glass; they saw little and cared less about Europe or the world at large.

As usually happens in critical national situations, men arose capable of dealing with them. John Leydon, whom I suspect was disappointed more than most by the attitude of his *chers collègues* in England, was one of these men. He felt betrayed. His happy relations with his English counterpart, 'Dear Jenkins' cooled and any lingering 'liberalism' which he retained, disappeared. He became the complete Sinn Féiner and like all converts he was more than zealous in promoting his new faith.

As head of the Department of Supplies under Seán Lemass he scoured the world for the feedstuffs and fertilisers required for agriculture as well as for fuel and raw material for industry. He put together a small fleet of possibly not too seaworthy cargo ships and

tankers to ensure the importation of the minimum supplies necessary for economic survival. He organised a rationing scheme to
ensure that clothes, fuel and the more essential food products were
equitably distributed. He was an iron disciplinarian and quite ruth-
less in dealing with the numerous spivs and blackmarketeers which
a rationing system inevitably spawns. For his wartime performance
Leydon surely deserved well of his country.

Coal supplies remained normal up to the spring of 1941; in fact
some increase in imports took place due to appeals made to consumers and to the activities of Fuel Importers (Éire) Limited, an
agency appointed by the government to stockpile coal reserves.
The agency had on its board representatives of the coal trade and of
large users such as the Gas Company, the ESB and the railways. Its
chairman was the shrewdest of the coal merchants, John Reihill,
who at the time was managing director of Donnelly's, a coal importing firm owned by the Stafford family of Wexford into which Reihill
had married. Reihill's origins were obscure but his oddly clipped
accent suggested that he came from Liverpool. Generous subscriptions to the Fianna Fáil party funds had brought him to the notice of
Seán Lemass. He formed with Lemass what amounted to a symbio-
tic relationship and this relationship in due course extended surprisingly to Leydon. It would be impossible to imagine two men
more dissimilar in character and motivation. Reihill lived and died
in the faith of big business (Irish-style) leaving behind him a
thriving coal and oil empire. Coal imports fell drastically from 1941
and thereafter Fuel Importers (Éire) Limited were mainly concerned with the organisation and management of depots for the
storage of turf in Dublin and other east and south coast centres.

After Lemass and Leydon, the man who in my opinon did most
to help the nation's economic survival during the war was Hugo
Flinn TD, parliamentary secretary to the Minister for Finance.
Hugo Flinn was a Corkman who though educated in Ireland spent
much of his early life in the family fish business in England where he
also trained as an electrical engineer. On returning to Cork he
joined Fianna Fáil under the powerful political influence of Tom
Dowdall, an intimate of de Valera. He was, or at least seemed to us
old IRA men, an improbable member of the party. He differed
from the rest in his accent, his well-tailored clothes, his upper
middle-class mode of life, his independent means and above all his
total absence of shared experience which, until the intrusion of
Taca, was the great emotional bond of the party. But in the Dáil he
brought great strength to the party as a parliamentary debater. He
acquired exceptional debating skill in England as a member of the
Catenians or some such organisation which made it their business

publicly to defend the Catholic faith against the ignorant sectaries with which Liverpool abounds.

When I met him first he was a man in his fifties, white-haired, strongly built and exuding energy and truculence. He had the physical lineaments of Winston Churchill when Churchill was playing his role of John Bull. His appearance did not belie his manner or his behaviour. When he was appointed to the Office of Public Works he found that neither the chairman, Sir Philip Hanson, nor many of his colleagues nor members of the senior staff were on speaking terms. He put that situation right in an unceremonious and inurbane manner. Sir Philip left complaining that when he joined the Office of Public Works it was an organisation for gentlemen run by gentlemen, but now! Hugo Flinn was a man who was always bored with his own company; he did not seem to have any close friends either inside or outside politics. He should, by any standards, have held a ministerial post. The fact that he did not was probably because de Valera thought he would not fit into the cabinet team which he believed should consist of like-minded people. In this sense Hugo Flinn was certainly an outsider. He became something of a national figure through a campaign he conducted — mainly in the *Sunday Independent* — for the abolition of income tax. The fact that he used the *Sunday Independent* to air his political views detracted considerably from the *gravitas* which was expected of cabinet material at that time.

How Hugo Flinn came to take charge of the Emergency turf campaign was never quite clear but the choice was certainly a fortunate one. His strength lay in informality of approach and improvisation. The main elements of the campaign originated in his inventive mind and were pursued with vigour and determination. It was his idea, promoted by John Collins, one of his senior officials, that the County Council organisation with its trained administrative and engineering staff and its massive workforce, largely unemployed due to wartime shortages, should be switched over to turf production on a countrywide scale. It was his idea too that the overall responsibility for turf transport should be given to the Office of Public Works to be exercised through close liaison with the railway and canal operators and through control of the petrol supply. Also on his initiative the services of the Land Commission and of the Special Employment Schemes Office were enlisted to acquire and open up new bogs to facilitate private production. It is doubtful whether these or Hugo Flinn's other proposals were ever considered at cabinet level but he carried sufficient influence with the ministers immediately concerned to ensure that the necessary authority and funds were available to put them into practice. It is also reasonable to assume that the plan of campaign had Dev's general approval.

Hugo appointed a committee, of which he was chairman, to co-ordinate the work of the different interests involved. The committee, known as the Turf Executive, consisted of T. C. Courtney, J. P. Candy, J. C. Gamble, T. J. McLaughlin and myself. As it happened it could not have been, from the point of view of personalities, a more agreeable or more harmonious combination. Despite very different temperaments we got on exceedingly well. The executive met as often as Hugo Flinn was in Dublin, which was rare enough. Temperamentally he preferred to be where the action was. Much of his time was spent circulating through the bog areas, particularly in the west, inspecting work in progress, ironing out problems with local officials and urging them on to greater efforts. Apart from this, he really enjoyed motoring. He was an insomniac who could sleep only in a car. A Dáil question — malicious of course — produced the information that his monthly mileage was about four times as much as an average deputy.

T. J. McLaughlin acted as secretary at the Turf Executive meetings. McLaughlin, no longer a young man, had spent all his life in the civil service. Like so many of his kind he wrote civil service English of great clarity; according to Courtney the minutes were completed before the meeting ended. He had been associated with Hugo since the pre-Emergency days and was never surprised by his vagaries and brusque mannerisms which were much in evidence. Hugo had no regard for subordinates' personal dignity or feelings or for their convenience. If he wanted someone to accompany him on one of his country tours the victim's family obligations had to take second pace. My personal relations with him were reasonably good, perhaps because I was not officially under his control or perhaps, as he said, I was easy to get on with provided I got my own way. At meetings of the Turf Executive none of us had much opportunity to contribute to the deliberations. We listened to Hugo's pronouncements and instructions and watched with amusement McLaughlin's cold eye and sardonic expression as he wrote and wrote.

Courtney, who had been an officer in the Free State army, supervised the County Council turf production schemes. He was something of a hypochondriac; driving in a car with him it was possible to discuss his long intestine all the way from Donegal to Kerry. Nevertheless he was a man of considerable charm and popularity. He was esurient which did not improve his health nor add to his energy. Fortunately he had the most loyal of deputies in Dan Herlihy, the most zealous and meticulously minded public servant I ever met who never stopped working even at the weekends. I was later closely associated with Courtney and Herlihy in CIE. Under their direction, County Council turf production got off to a flying start in 1941 and was reputed to have reached one million tons in its first season though much was lost due to the misguided policy of late cutting and the inadequacies of the transport system.Thereafter geographical and transport limitations rather than productive capacity based on bog and labour supplies became the determining factor in the County Council operations. Production was organised on a more rational and selective basis with the emphasis on quality rather than volume. Nevertheless the County Council scheme made a contribution of over three million tons to the wartime fuel supply before finally winding up in 1947.

During the Emergency it became necessary to ration all forms of fuel. Turf presented a special problem because, being so widely produced and rarely sold through the regular trade channels, its distribution was not readily controllable. Without some restriction on its physical movement many Dublin people, for example, with family connections in the vicinity of the bogs would have no difficulty in getting all the turf they wanted at the expense of the common pool and there would be wholesale opportunites for evasion and blackmarketing. I proposed to the rationing authorities in the Department of Supplies that the country be divided into turf and non-turf areas. In the former, roughly corresponding to the midland and western counties which taken together were self-sufficient in turf production, turf would be sold without restriction. Rationing would apply only in the non-turf areas, consisting basically of the six eastern counties, and to make possible its enforcement the movement of turf into these areas would be allowed only under licence. The response to my proposal was completely negative. The trite old objection of administrative impracticability was trotted out and this was supposed to end the matter. For the senior official concerned administrative impracticability was more or less a disease; anything that disturbed the even tenor of his way fell into this category. He was one of those elderly boy clerks who had reached his position by a combination of 'Buggin's Turn' and total risk avoidance. He had no intention of jeopardising his career prospects at this stage by backing innovations. In his heart he believed, despite all evidence to the contrary, that our British friends would not see us pressed to extremities and any attempt to make good the fuel shortage from our own resources was so much wasted effort. Fortunately Hugo Flinn supported my view on the matter and I had no difficulty in persuading the Minister for Supplies, Seán Lemass, to issue a statutory order restricting the movement of turf on the lines indicated. In all modesty I consider this to be my most important personal contribution to the Emergency turf campaign. Not only did it provide a workable basis for rationing and price control but in many ways it became a cornerstone of our wartime fuel policy.

Because of its novelty and Hugo's close personal involvement, the County Council scheme attracted much publicity as well as some controversy. In terms of quantity, however, by far the largest contribution to the Emergency turf supply came from private enterprise. A massive drive was launched to maximise turf production under private auspices. The main effort was concentrated on the traditional turf-winning areas where there had always been a limited production for sale. To extract the full productive potential of these areas the establishment of a guaranteed market was essential and a formal undertaking to this effect was given by the government from 1942 onwards. More important than any specified guarantee was the manner in which it was implemented. Though the theoretical demand was almost limitless there was no properly developed marketing machinery and limitations of transport and cost created all sorts of blockages in distribution. To cope with this problem a special section was set up within the Turf Development Board whose function it was to provide an organised marketing system which relieved producers of surplus stocks and directed their flow along the most economic lines to the points of consumption.

To complement the efforts of the traditional turf-winning sector attempts were made to mobilise a host of new turf producers able and willing to cater independently for their own requirements. Since compulsion, on the lines of the compulsory tillage campaign or otherwise, was clearly unworkable reliance had to be placed on purely voluntary methods of appeal motivated by individual or national security. The co-operation of community councils and other local bodies was enlisted to translate this appeal into appropriate forms of activity. Responsibility for the planning and execution of this publicity drive was entrusted to the marketing section of the Turf Development Board whose local staff organised over one hundred meetings each year aimed at setting up new production units and ensuring that all available bog facilities were fully utilised. The response to this campaign can still be seen in the scarred mountain tops around Glencree and Sallygap which testify to the determination of thousands of Dubliners to achieve self-sufficiency in fuel. It is fair to say that their efforts were duplicated by urban dwellers all over the country whenever bog accommodation could be found within striking distance of their homes. By one means or another private production was increased by one million tons annually during the war years. For what was up to then a primitive and unorganised industry this was no mean achievement.

At no time did Hugo Flinn's brief include control of the Turf Development Board which continued under the jurisdiction of the Department of Industry and Commerce. As the agency officially responsible for turf development and already engaged in large-scale production, he saw the board as playing a central role in the Emergency campaign. He explained to me that what he had in mind was a crash expansion programme aimed at opening up the vast untapped areas of the Bog of Allen to produce handwon turf as a strategic source of supply for Dublin and the east coast counties.

I pointed out to him the magnitude of the problems involved; that huge tracts of bogland would have to be acquired, drained and made accessible; that since the area was thinly populated an army of workers would have to be imported, fed and housed; that a control staff of engineers and accountants would have to be built up from scratch; that very large expenditures would be involved which could not be financed from the board's own resources. I began to sound rather like some of the civil servants — the 'No' men — whom I so much despised. Hugo was quite undismayed by this litany. Brushing aside the physical and administrative difficulties, he was at least able to assure me that the necessary money would be forthcoming from the Department of Finance and on the strength of this we embarked on what became known as the 'Kildare Scheme'.

The scale of the operation and of the organisation required to manage it can be judged from the fact that it covered an area of 250 square miles lying roughly in a triangle bounded by the towns of Enfield, Edenderry and Droichead Nua. Alban O'Kelly, then our works manager at Clonsast, was appointed to take charge. He was a scion of the well-known County Galway family, the O'Kelly's of Hymany. Maria Theresa of Austria had conferred the title of Count of the Holy Roman Empire on one of his ancestors in the eighteenth century. Alban was very proud of this title though he did not make use of it publicly. He was deeply involved in genealogy, and was well versed in the history of the County Galway 'Big Houses', — the Bowes, the Lyons, the Martyns, the Blakes and many of the lesser squirearchy. To drive with him around the west of Ireland was an adventure as he recounted story after story about the exploits, many disreputable, of the great county families. He was an active member of the Knights of Malta and held high rank in that Order. I learned from him all about the Knights of Magisterial Grace and the Knights of Honour and Devotion. I listened, amused and amazed, that a man with such an acute sense of humour could take seriously what to me was nothing more than humbug and fancy dress. These minor eccentricities did not take from O'Kelly's qualities as a natural leader of men with an easy and pleasant disposition and a remarkable talent for management. His achievements in the Kildare Scheme and in many other demanding posts deserve more than a passing tribute. His energy, knowledge of rural Ireland, of bogs and bog technology but above all his ready acceptance of responsibility and dedication to the job marked him out as one of the finest of the fine men produced by Bord na Móna.

By the autumn of 1941 a comprehensive survey of the Kildare bogs had been carried out and a development plan drawn up. Completion of this preparatory work which involved the acquisition and drainage of 24,000 acres of bogland and the construction of an elaborate road network was compressed into eighteen months. Much of the credit for this and for the efficient management of the scheme must go to Michael Maguire, our chief engineer, and to the team of young engineers whom he recruited mostly fresh from college, whose inexperience was outweighed by their enthusiasm and self-confidence. To many of them this exercise marked the beginning of successful management careers in Bord na Móna.

The scheme was based on the use of imported labour and pro vision had to be made for its accommodation. Fourteen residential camps, each with a capacity for up to 500 workers, were erected by the Office of Public Works and equipped with catering, sanitary and recreational facilities. The Office of Public Works, released for once from the trammels of bureaucracy, showed their true competence and though hampered by the shortage of building materials the work was finished in record time. It was a great feat of sustained effort and improvisation which demonstrated, in reverse, the truth of my belief that no government body concerned with the displacement of matter can be fully effective while working within civil service rules.

Intensive recruitment was undertaken especially in the western counties with a view to building up a labour force of 4,000 men. Much difficulty was experienced initially in getting the workers to settle down to camp life and the problem was compounded by our own ignorance and inexperience. The firm of caterers who had been hired to handle the commissariat proved hopelessly inadequate and we were forced to take on the job of producing 12,000 meals daily without any knowledge of what this involved. We looked to the army for guidance but their advice was unhelpful. The daily rations of a soldier were no more than 'a daisy in a bull's mouth' to men doing eight hours a day of heavy bog work.

The camp buildings themselves were soon reduced to conditions more typical of refugee camps. As I well knew from my experience of internment health, comfort and hygiene can only be achieved by strict self-discipline. In army camps cleanliness and order are imposed by virtue of military regulations. No such internal discipline prevailed in the turf camps with the result that after a few months of occupation there was a serious fall-off in standards. Father Wheelwright, de Valera's half-brother from New York, paid us a visit at that time and to my great embarrassment insisted on going through one of the camps at Timahoe. What he saw would have provided a field day for a visiting journalist seeking material for an article on the 'Dirty Irish' though, in fact, the situation had no connection whatever with our native living habits. The results would have been identical even if Dutchmen or Swedes, with their high housekeeping standards, were living in the same environment.

We were fortunate at this stage in recruiting a man with experience of this type of industrial colonisation. Bill Stapleton had been a member of Michael Collins' inner circle during the War of Independence, had served as a colonel in the Free State army and subsequently managed the camp site on the Shannon Scheme. He quickly took stock of the situation and set about re-organising the camp regime on more socially acceptable lines. Rations were virtually doubled, trained cooks and kitchen staff hired and orderlies appointed to serve meals, make beds and clean up generally. A proper medical service was provided, organised and run by Dr Thomas Murphy, then a young doctor and now president of University College, Dublin. We were lucky to have found a man of Tom Murphy's quality as medical officer. His humour and compassion and disregard for bureaucratic rules helped greatly to maintain morale in the camps. Stapleton himself spent day and night circulating among the camps, tasting food, inspecting latrines, organising concerts, theatre and football competitions. It would have been sensible to employ female help for such tasks as cleaning, bedmaking and serving at table, but two years elapsed before our fear of ecclesiastical disapproval was overcome sufficiently to do so. We did not realise how greatly the good spirits of men in the mass is dependent on the society of women.

Even with improved camp conditions there was still an atmosphere of industrial unrest and labour wastage remained high. In the hope of creating a more stable labour force we suggested to the trade unions that an effort should be made to have the workers organised but their reaction was completely negative on the grounds that rural labour was incapable of being unionised. A man named Seán Dunne had other ideas; he saw an opportunity to establish himself in the role of a militant labour leader. Dunne's name first appeared in the newspapers in connection with the theft of lead from the roof of the house allegedly to use to cast lead shot for the IRA. He was a man of energy and intelligence with no fixed principles but with undisguised ambition for public recognition. He organised demonstrations and hunger marches on behalf of the turf workers, himself always in the lead but never available to discuss alleged grievances with the management. His activities in Kildare, which consisted of stirring up as much trouble as possible before disappearing from the scene, laid the foundation for his future career in agitation. He founded the Federation of Rural Workers but left it under a cloud. The Dublin unemployed became the next focus for his attention; with their support he entered politics and was elected to the Dáil. He found in that assembly all the advantages of the right of sanctuary provided by the Church in medieval times. A wealthy marriage brought him immediate respectability and a Mercedes car. He became a journalist and a lover of journalists who represented his death as a national tragedy. Of such stuff are heroes sometimes made. His was a saga from lead to riches.

The Kildare Scheme went into full production in 1943 and yielded almost 600,000 tons in the period to its closedown in 1947. Most of this turf was sold in Dublin where, presumably because it was produced and harvested under better than average conditions, it gained a high reputation for quality. Mechanised production was also maintained throughout the war at the board's permanent works at Clonsast, Turraun and Lyrecrumpane and though output was limited important operational experience was gained as well as confidence in the mechanised process. This high grade machine turf served a particularly valuable social purpose in that it was allocated entirely to the cheap fuel schemes organised by various municipal authorities for the benefit of the urban poor.

Lullymore briquette factory, which we had taken over in 1940 on a care and maintenance basis, also began to twitch into life under the management of P. J. Cogan who had previously worked in one of the alcohol factories which had been forced out of production during the war. Cogan was not only a man of great technical skill but also had qualities of patience, determination and judgment unusual in a relatively young engineer. Thanks largely to his ingenuity the factory was gradually brought back into production and had reached its full capacity by 1945. In our wartime fuel economy Lullymore briquettes had an importance out of all proportion to the quantity produced, being supplied only to industries of the highest priority and even helping to maintain the railway services at a time when they were threatened with total collapse.

It must be admitted that the turf supplied to the non-turf areas during the war years came in for a lot of justified adverse criticism. Turf mass-produced in what were often completely virgin bogs is bound to contain some substandard material. Likewise handwon turf, even when properly harvested, reabsorbs moisture when exposed to the elements and inevitably deteriorates in quality while in transit to the consumer. Understandably many people, wrestling with the problem of home heating, could not tolerate or excuse these shortcomings. Being so publicly associated with turf, it was only natural that I became the target for these complaints which pursued me even into private life. I shared the experience common to doctors, particularly psychiatrists, who are forced to listen on purely social occasions to tiresome accounts of the backaches and nightmares endured by their fellow guests. The nadir of my guilt was reached when I was presented with a soaking sod of turf by Mary, my wife, with the invitation to 'look at this'. What the public failed to recognise was that they were living in a siege economy. People could not accept that they were at worst being inconvenienced. Sometimes there was real hardship but at the end of the day it could truthfully be said that no one died of cold during the Emergency or had to eat uncooked food. This is a big boast and, in my view, it is one which could not be sustained were it not for the energy, drive and total disregard for red tape which characterised Hugo Flinn. With all his irascibility, rudeness and indifference to the feelings of his subordinates he was truly the man in the gap. The nation's debt to him has been little acknowledged. When he died in 1943 I was appointed Fuel Controller. This was not really a replacement; in truth he had no successor. The Emergency turf campaign in which he was so deeply involved in the closing years of his life was by then fully established and carried on under its own momentum.

Post-war Developments

Had it not been for the Emergency the Turf Development Board might well have met the same fate at the hands of the Department of Finance as the Peat Fuel Company of Lullymore. All our original projections had gone awry although by 1943 we were beginning to produce substantial quantities of machine turf and our performance was improving despite the lack of machinery resulting from the war. Nevertheless when we received a departmental circular requesting us to submit plans for the future development of the turf industry after the end of the war I did not take the matter too seriously. I had a feeling that the circular had originated in the mind of one of the bright young junior administrative officers in the department who were then referred to as 'flyers' and would probably now be known as upwardly mobile executives. I was surprised to be summoned soon afterwards by Leydon who wanted to know when he might expect to see our plans for post-war turf development. I had to confess that I had not given the matter much consideration. He was insistent that the plan should be prepared and submitted without further delay and also expressed the hope that whatever proposals were put forward would be comprehensive. At this point I reminded Leydon that the question of using turf for power generation had been approved by the government before the war. I was rather surprised at the warmth with which he received the idea. Indeed it was a matter for some surprise that Leydon should be taking so much interest in bog development although our personal relationship had changed radically since those earlier confrontations. My view of civil service officials, though not of the system, had changed. I realised that the intellectual level of civil servants generally was much above the common average. Apart from the Church and the professions there was in those days no other outlet for bright boys unless they had a family business to fall back on. But even among civil servants Leydon, because of his clarity of mind, disinterestedness and impersonality in his dealings with people, appeared to me different from the rest of officialdom. Without his encouragement I do not think that I would have had the temerity to put forward a post-war plan on the scale eventually formulated. I reflected that if Dr McLaughlin could succeed in creating an enterprise of the magnitude of the Shannon Scheme (in the context of his time and place it was an enormous achievement) we in the Turf Development Board should not be deterred from embarking on an undertaking of similar dimensions in relation to the bogs. Besides the temper of the times was favourable. The Department of Finance was in no position to oppose any worthwhile attempt to utilise the national resources. The weakness of their economic judgment was exposed by their mismanagement of the external assets as the following quotation from *Ireland in the War Years and After*, edited by Kevin B. Nowlan and T. Desmond Williams, shows:

> Now the really interesting thing is that in 1939 — when the world was clearly sliding towards war after the German annexation of Czechoslovakia in March — the Currency Commission held on to its sterling and bought no more gold. To an outsider it does look as if a gentleman's agreement had been reached on the basis that if Ireland continued to hold sterling the British government would do its best to assure some level of supplies.

Since my first association with turf I regarded the very existence of the waste boglands as an affront to our national pride. It was as if one was living in a well-kept house surrounded by a neglected garden overgrown with grass and weeds. A country whose bogs support only grouse and snipe was to me a backward country. I was also obsessed by the idea that our lack of industrial progress was due to having never outgrown our reliance on British technology. If the Russians and Germans could master the problems of large scale bog operation I believed that it should also be within the capacity of Irishmen. With the assistance of a particularly bright young engineer named Claude Warner a graduate from University College, Galway, who dealt with the engineering calculations and financial costings, we drew up for consideration by the board a set of proposals which provided for the production of one million tons of machine turf in twenty-four selected bogs, modernisation of the briquette factory at Lullymore, erection of a peat moss factory at Kilberry, establishment of an experimental station to promote research and development of turf production and utilisation. Warner, as well as having unusual technical and mathematical skill, was something of an 'original'. His taste in dress which ran to green trousers, yellow pullovers and linen jackets foreshadowed in the forties the product of Carnaby Street in the sixties. He also had a refreshingly independent mind which accepted none of the national *idées reçues* without question.

Even my own board colleagues were rather sceptical of our ability to achieve the planned annual production of one million tons of machine turf considering the current output level was less than 100,000 tons. For myself, I had no doubts on the matter. Without even having heard of Pascal and the heart having reasons that reason does not know, I had never regarded reason as an infallible guide to action. It was intuition rather than rationalisation which prompted my decisions and judgments. It was my good fortune that Bord na Móna was conceived before the days of the computer. One of my colleagues undertook on behalf of the board that on the day when the target figure of one million tons was reached they would present me with a gold watch. I am glad to record that this promise was duly honoured and within the time limit originally envisaged.

Our post-war plan, which later became known as the First Development Programme, was submitted to the government in December 1944, approved in principle and published a year later in the form of a White Paper. Among other things the White Paper provided for the erection of two generating stations designed to absorb the output of the two largest midland bog groups and it stipulated that except where justified on exceptional technical grounds all future electricity production projects should be based on the use of turf. The entire programme received formal legislative sanction in the Turf Development Act 1946 which established Bord na Móna as an autonomous statutory corporation and defined its mandate. The efforts of eleven years to create a framework in which the turf industry could be properly developed had at last been crowned with success.

In the aftermath of the war in Europe our most pressing concern was to complete the mechanisation of Clonsast bog so that it could be brought into full production in time to meet our commitment to the ESB. We were also conscious that a large range of specialised machinery would be needed over the following few years to equip the twenty-four new bogs then under development. Understandably, our thoughts turned initially to our German associates — the Klasmann organisation at Meppen — on whose methods our programme of bog mechanisation had been modelled and who had supplied most of our pre-war requirements. Meppen was situated in the British zone of occupation and we applied through the Department of External Affairs for permission to visit it. The British were quite willing to facilitate us but they insisted, even though Ireland had been neutral during the war, that the proposed delegation should be dressed in British civilian uniforms. I made it clear to Dev, who was Minister for External Affairs at the time, that I was not prepared to wear any sort of British uniform nor would I authorise any of the board's staff to do so. Dev made a not-too-strenuous effort to overcome my objections but it was evident that he sympathised with my point of view. So the idea was dropped for the time being.

As extensive use had been made of the Swedish bogs during the war it was suggested that the help of Swedish manufacturers might be enlisted in our search for bog machinery. In the summer of 1945 the wartime restrictions on travel were still in force and application had to be made to the British Foreign Office for the necessary travel facilities. The British were quite accommodating even to the extent of offering to provide air transport. Aodhagan O'Rahilly who, because of his family connections in Sweden, was in a position to be particularly helpful, agreed to accompany me and we flew out from London in a converted British bomber.

It was my first experience of flying unlike O'Rahilly who was a veteran air traveller. Our plane bore little resemblance to the commodious passenger aircraft of later days. The seats were hard, the floors uncovered, no stewards were in attendance and neither food nor drink was available though at one stage the crew kindly shared their tea and sandwiches with us. Despite the ascetic conditions both Aodhagan and I were good subjects for flying and certainly in no way nervous. We had complete reliance in the capabilities of the crew knowing that they would probably be the first victims of any carelessness or incompetence. Possessing the happy knack of dozing off at will and in almost any circumstances (especially at conferences where the proceedings became intolerably boring) I was able to sleep through most of the eight hour journey.

Arrangements for our visit had been made in advance with the Swedish authorities and we were rather taken aback to find no one to meet us on arrival at Gothenburg and, even more surprisingly, no one could who speak English. We were deluged with official forms, completely unintelligible to us, most of which later turned out to be ration cards and as almost everything was rationed in Sweden they were a most valuable commodity. We finally reached Stockholm and were taken in hand by officials of the Ministry of Fuel who made us welcome as the Swedes do so well. During the war Sweden had been isolated from the outside world in much the same way as Ireland. We were, in fact, the first civilian visitors they had met and we were treated like men from another planet. So far as turf was concerned their main interest seemed to be in the manufacture of 'turf-coal' for use in gas works. An engineer named Pilo, who was in charge of Stockholm Gas Works, was the originator of the idea and was promoting it enthusiastically. O'Rahilly, having examined the process in depth, came to the conclusion that it stood no chance of success.

This was my first visit to Stockholm. I was fascinated by its order and cleanliness, its stately buildings, its tree-lined thoroughfares and its beautiful situation on an island-studded sea. Pilo went to great pains to exhibit the city and we sailed in his yacht around the archipelago. We were lavishly entertained and for the first time in my life eating became a really pleasurable experience. Having sampled many national cuisines my vote to this day would be in favour of Swedish Smorgas — open sandwiches of unimaginable variety with as many as one hundred different kinds featured in the more elaborate menus.

Most of the Swedish bogs are in the southern part of the country around Malmo. Most notable was the briquette factory at Sosdala which operated on the same principle as ours at Lullymore but up to that time more successfully because of the superior quality of the turf available. The turf production centres in this area were technically rather less advanced than those we saw in pre-war Germany. The main emphasis was on peat moss production, turf fuel being a secondary consideration.

We were in the office of one of these peat moss factories when the discussion was interrupted by the arrival of a heavily built, middle-aged man who addressed us in a loud, cheerful voice speaking thickly accented English: 'Are you boys from Dublin? Do you know Daddy Orr and the College of Science?' We were astonished at this apparition. Daddy Orr was a legendary and eccentric Professor of Mathematics in the College of Science who was alleged to have believed himself to be the square root of minus one. It was surprising, to say the least, that his fame has spread to an obscure peat moss factory in a remote corner of Sweden. Our cheerful visitor was Konrad Petersen, a nephew of the Petersen of Kapp and Petersen, the famous pipe manufacturers of Dublin. Konrad was a Latvian from Riga; as a young man had taken part in the revolution of 1905 when Latvia was a province of Imperial Russia. When the revolt failed he took refuge with his uncle in Dublin where he remained until the establishment of Latvia as an independent state after the First World War.

Konrad took a degree in engineering at the College of Science and worked on a number of engineering projects including a survey, carried out by a group of private entrepreneurs before the First World War, into the possibility of harnessing the Shannon for electricity production. This project came to nothing and the idea remained dormant until revived by Dr T. A. McLaughlin in 1924. During his long stay in Ireland Konrad became culturally an Irishman. He was closely associated with the trade union movement, was involved in the 1913 strikes and was on personal terms with Connolly, Larkin and Countess Markievicz. He also formed close links with many of the literary and theatrical figures of Dublin at that time including, in particular, the famous Daisy Bannard and the man whom she afterwards married, the Republican journalist Fred Cogley.

Back in Riga with his Irish wife, a Miss Yeates from Clonliffe Road, Konrad found employment in the peat moss industry which ranks as one of major importance and operates extensively in all the countries bordering the Baltic. At the outbreak of the 1939 war he was in charge of the government department dealing with bog development. Like all Balts of the succession states, he welcomed the Russian withdrawal under pressure from the German army in its drive towards Leningrad but they soon discovered that there was little to choose between the occupation forces of the two nationalities. For the Jewish population the German occupation spelt total disaster. Petersen gave us a most horrifying account of an incident which he had witnessed. Several hundred Jews — men, women and children — were herded into a huge pit which they themselves had been compelled to dig in the fields outside Riga. They were then machine-gunned by German SS men and the soil from the pit was bulldozed over their corpses. We found it difficult to credit the reality of such barbarities. We had heard of Buchenwald but not of the gas chambers nor of the hundreds of similar outrages aimed at the extermination of the Jews all over Europe. We tended to be suspicious of atrocity stories believing that they contained a large element of propaganda and it was a long time before the truth of the Jewish holocaust came to be accepted by uninvolved people such as ourselves. Even now it is difficult to understand how a highly cultured and civilised nation, which the Germans undoubtedly are, could have connived at the genocide of the Jews. I saw a lot of Germans and of Germany in the years after the war. I have never met a German who in the depths of his or her heart repented of their monstrous treatment of the Jews.

Much as he disliked the German occupation the prospect of renewed Russian domination of his country was even more abhorrent to Petersen. When the Germans were forced to evacuate Latvia in the face of the Russian counter-attack he decided, like thousands of others from the Baltic States, to seek refuge in Sweden with his wife and child. With the help of two friends the hazardous journey across the Baltic in an open boat was safely accomplished. With his wealth of experience he had no difficulty in getting employment in the peat moss industry. We took him and his wife to dinner in Malmo and to say that his life story kept us entranced until the small hours would be an understatement. Despite all its vicissitudes he had enjoyed life to the full. In the course of his business career he had travelled all over Europe and America on an official passport. In reference to some of his nightlife adventures I enquired whether his activities were not inhibited by the possession of an official passport. Petersen's reply was very much in character; far from acting as a constraint it had provided him with opportunities to spread his wings in safety. This was a way of thinking completely alien to ours; not indeed that either Aodhagan or I were anxious to spread our wings in pursuit of the fleshpots. Compared with Petersen, a full-blooded European *bon vivant,* we were a pair of Irish prigs abroad.

Our bog at Kilberry, near Athy, was being developed at that time for peat moss production. As this was a specialised process in which we were inexperienced we asked Petersen if he would be willing to come to Ireland to take charge of the project. The offer was readily accepted and in due course he was installed as manager of Kilberry factory where he spent the rest of his working life. He could never reconcile himself to the different standards of remuneration which applied to bog managers here and on the continent nor could he easily adjust to the rigidity of the board's disciplines. But he laid the foundations of what was one of Bord na Móna's most successful operations and became a highly respected local personality.

Apart from acquiring a works manager, we succeeded during the Swedish visit in contacting sources from which the factory equipment required for Kilberry could be procured. But on the broader question of machinery for our turf fuel bogs the search for potential manufacturers was completely negative. Our attention then turned to Northern Ireland. Some years before the First World War Hamilton Robb, the Portadown linen manufacturers, had decided to run their factory on power from turf-fired gas producers. The process was technically successful but after the war when abundant and cheap coal became available the use of turf was discontinued. In the early days of the Turf Development Board we had been in touch with Hamilton Robb about their experience in using turf for motive power. The owner, William Mullen, replied with a very warm invitation to us to visit Portadown. He had been thinking of recommissioning the gas producer plant and suggested that we might like to inspect what remained of it.

Our party consisted of Aodhagan O'Rahilly, Bill Quirke and myself. At that time the board had not made the rule which deterred the members from exercising what are normally executive functions. In making the trip our main interest was new methods of turf utilisation but we were also conscious of a wish to maintain contact with the Six Counties for national reasons. It so happened that our visit coincided with the date of Hamilton Robb's annual staff party and we were invited to attend. Each worker on entering the factory was presented with a miniature Union Jack partly as a souvenir of the occasion and partly to be waved at appropriate moments during the after-supper speeches. Poor Mullen was overcome with embarrassment on realising that we could not refuse to accept the Union Jacks offered to us without grave discourtesy to all concerned. We quickly reassured him that neither this nor the politically tendentious speeches which followed caused us any offence. However, we could not help being tickled by the absurdity of the whole situation as we speculated on the snide comments of the opposition parties in the Dáil if it became known that three well-known Fianna Fáil supporters were seen flaunting Union Jacks in Portadown.

Nothing much came of this visit apart from the start of a warm personal relationship between Mullen and myself. Through him I got introductions to a number of Belfast engineering firms including Harland and Wolff. None of them could be persuaded to take any interest in supplying our machinery requirements. To them the whole idea of bog development was a matter for derision worthy only of a backward and economically impoverished country such as they held the 'Free State' to be. Most of the engineering firms I visited seemed to be managed by men who had come up from the shop floor. They wore hard hats and carried two foot rules and a battery of pens stuck out from their breast pockets. Unimaginative and set in their ways, anything which did not conform to their normal *modus operandi* was rejected out of hand. I could not help recalling Joseph Campbells's poem *The Orangeman:*

> A gingerfaced man
> With a walrus moustache
> His eyes, like his soul
> Of the colour of ash.

By this time the British engineering industry was beginning to disengage from its wartime commitments and return to commercial production. Our first breakthrough came when, thanks to J. W. Dulanty, the Irish High Commissioner in London, we succeeded in interesting a small Aberdeen firm in the manufacture of our more pressing requirements. This led to arrangements with other British manufacturers for the production of bog machinery from blueprints prepared by our own engineers. These designs were based on the German prototypes but many improvements dictated by Irish bog conditions were incorporated. The number and variety of the units required and doubt about the prospect of a continuous, long term market presented problems from the point of view of the manufacturer. At home an important advance was made when a young engineer named Peter Thomas took over the management of the engineering firm of Thompsons of Carlow and, recognising the potential value of the turf development programme, he expanded the capacity of the works to cater for a large part of Bord na Móna's machine requirements. In the years that followed the policy of utilising native manufacturing facilities was sustained and expanded till the point was reached where almost all new equipment was built by Irish firms or in the board's own workshops.

In 1947 we were informed that the rule requiring the use of uniforms by civilian visitors to the British zone in Germany had been relaxed so that we were free to visit Meppen. Lucas Collins, our chief mechanical engineer, and I travelled out via London and Ostend. The officials of the Foreign Office who briefed us in London were extremely helpful. All visitors were required to hold a nominal military rank and we were designated Lieutenant Colonels for the occasion. We were each given £50 in occupation marks and arrangements were made with the British army headquarters in Minden to supply us with a chauffeur-driven car. We would be allowed to travel freely and accommodation would be provided for us in the officers' messes attached to the army posts throughout the occupation zone. Each of us was allowed to bring 3,000 cigarettes together with three pounds of tea, coffee and cocoa all of which were worth their weight in gold. Cigarettes at that time had become a medium of exchange in Germany and we were told that 3,000 would buy a Volkswagen car.

Our friends in Meppen had not suffered unduly from the war. Living in the country the food supply was adequate and their involvement in fuel and power production had kept them afloat financially. But our cigarettes and other gifts were like manna from heaven; they had not had access to real coffee, for example, since well before the war. The local town of Oldenburg had been comparatively little damaged. We were fed and housed there in the Grand Ducal Palace which had been converted into a mess and club for the benefit of the 'Officers and Gentlemen' of the British army some of whom betrayed their poor social origins by being abominably rude to the Germans. The services of no less than two string orchestras had been provided for their delectation.

The devastated cities of Hamburg, Bremen and Hanover presented us with a relatively different picture from the undamaged town of Oldenburg. As we drove through mile after mile of total destruction the problem of clearing the sites, not to mind rebuilding the cities, strained imagination. Our visit was suddenly cut short when I fell sick with a high temperature. The only medical attention available was at the British military hospital in Oldenburg and the doctor there insisted on detaining me for treatment. By this time the fever was running so high that I was almost in a semi-conscious condition suffering from delusions of being abducted to Russia and never seeing my wife and family again. Under the care of a Scots nurse — a big, kind, matronly woman — I recovered quickly and after four or five days was fit to leave hospital. In retrospect I believe my illness was of psychosomatic origin produced by the dreadful sight of a nation in ruins, its towns and cities destroyed, its population hungry and ill-clad and the air of misery which prevailed everywhere.

We made a further visit to Germany the following year to inspect some new turf projects originated during the war. The main items of interest were drainage machines of new design and a peat wax extraction plant at Hanover. We were also taken to see a plant for the production of synthetic petrol from brown coal near Brunswick. At the time of our visit it was closed down awaiting dismantlement and removal in accordance with the policy of the occupation authorities. Despite the affinity of turf to brown coal there was no evidence that the process could be adapted for turf and in any case its operation would have been beyond our technical resources. By this time the rubble of the shattered cities had been largely cleared away. International aid programmes had improved the lot of the German population; there was less evidence of poverty and malnutrition. The non-fraternisation regulations had been considerably relaxed. But the general industrial collapse and the restrictions imposed by the occupying powers ruled out any prospect of obtaining machinery from this source. Indeed several years elapsed before the pre-war links with our associates in the German turf industry were effectively restored.

With the end of the war in Europe it was generally expected that coal would again become freely available. In fact, coal imports continued to be scarce and unpredictable and it was several years before supplies were back to normal. During this period the importance of continuing the Emergency turf campaign as a security measure should have been evident but, against this, there was mounting pressure on the part of the county councils, whose work programmes had been disrupted by the war, to disengage from the turf business and resume their normal activities. This line of action was firmly backed by the Department of Local Government whose minister, Seán MacEntee, was vehemently opposed to any further involvement of his department in turf production. Unfortunately Hugo Flinn was dead and there seems to have been little interest in the social and economic consequences of an abrupt termination of the scheme. However, the issue was apparently causing serious disagreement at government level and the upshot was that early in 1947 I was asked by the Taoiseach, Eamon de Valera, to arrange to have the functions of the county councils in regard to turf production taken over by Bord na Móna. I pointed out to him the objections to this proposal. The county councils had at their disposal a countrywide organisation with an experienced workforce and a fully-equipped staff. Bord na Móna would be unable to put an equivalent organisation in the field — certainly not overnight — and the possibility of a smooth operational takeover was at best very questionable. Moreover the board was fully occupied in getting its own post-war development programme under way and its progress could be seriously held back by too thin a spread of resources.

Dev was not a man to be put off by objections of this kind once he had decided on a course of action. He knew only too well that, like so many others, my devotion to him was such that I would go to any lengths to carry out his wishes. He went so far as to hint at the possibility of a cabinet crisis if the matter was not satisfactorily resolved. Feeling as I did, there was no choice but to accept the inevitable.

It was agreed that the transfer of the county council bogs would take effect from January 1948. The task of shouldering the preparatory work and of subsequently managing what was referred to as the County Production Scheme devolved on Alban O'Kelly who demonstrated once again his extraordinary powers of organisation. In a matter of months district offices were opened up to cover the main turf production centres. These offices were fully manned with control staff at all levels and arrangements were made for the recruitment and disposition of bog labour. To improve the quality of the turf and cut down on hand labour several of the bogs were equipped with semi-automatic cutting machines which had been widely used in Germany and Scandinavia. However, the scope and character of the scheme suffered a radical change, even before it got off the ground, with the establishment of the coalition government early in 1948.

The first coalition government might seem at first sight to have been a political aberration on the part of the electorate until it is realised that the electorate had no anticipation of the consequences of their voting until faced with the actual results. Then, to everyone's astonishment, and to the horror of the Republicans, it was found that the disappointed leader of Clann na Poblachta, Seán Mac-Bride, ex chief-of-staff of the IRA, was about to bring to power a moribund Fine Gael party under a Fine Gael Taoiseach, named John A. Costello, a lawyer of no political distinction. Costello was a survivor from the Irish Parliamentary Party. He was regarded by Clann na Poblachta as innocuous and malleable. In fact, in government he did not know whether he was coming or going. On a visit to Canada he impulsively announced his intention to declare an Irish Republic. It was commonly believed that he misread a script presented to him by one of his advisers on the occasion. The idea of John A. Costello — a Fine Gael Taoiseach — declaring Ireland a republic, raised three shouts of derision amongst us Republicans. MacBride's party was composed largely of Fianna Fáil supporters who were (in my opinion rightly) convinced that the party was becoming atrophied and arrogant as a result of prolonged tenure of office. With his illimitable self-confidence, MacBride had put forward ninety candidates for election but only got ten seats. With the aid of those members of the Labour Party who could not otherwise hope for the spoils of office and a group of rural politicians calling themselves Clann na Talmhain, who might have figured in an Abbey farce, they formed the worst government the country has seen to date or is likely to see again.

Seán MacBride was born in France in 1904. French was his mother tongue. He came to Ireland with his mother in 1917. He was brought up in situations where he met only the important people in the Independence movement. He behaved from boyhood as if he was one of them. He was accepted as such by everyone he met. A tall man, with thin non-descript hair, his features were finely wrought but his hollow cheeks and deep-set haunted eyes gave him something of the appearance of a character in a gothic novel. He spoke to his equals *de haut en bas* and to his superiors with polite deference but whether to his equals or superiors he spoke in a peculiarly soothing manner. He was extremely brave and had an aristocratic indifference to money. On the question of Separation, MacBride never lost the Fenian faith. He loathed the British but his sympathy with Gaelic Ireland was minimal. He was industrious in whatever interested him but sustained effort did not appear to be one of his characteristics.

A strong interest in his life seemed to be the pursuit of power. He worked best in an organisation when he was the leader. His knowledge of history seemed to have been acquired by verbal tradition. His political judgment was often poor. It reached the abyss when he helped bring Fine Gael back to government buildings — a great disservice to the nation. He became in later life a political traveller on the international scene and seemed to like meeting everyone of importance in the world political arena. He knew everyone of consequence and journeyed almost everywhere.

He became well known internationally mainly for his work on Amnesty International. He was awarded a Nobel Prize and, by the Russians, a Lenin Prize. Whatever one may think of MacBride's role in Irish politics, Nobel and Lenin Prizes are not conferred on people of no merit. Any Irishman to whom they are given reflects credit on the nation. I think the government and the National University have been remiss in not acknowledging Seán MacBride's international distinction. The University of Dublin (Trinity College) did make amends, to some extent, by conferring an Honorary Degree on him.

The campaign which preceded the 1948 election was the dirtiest in recent memory. Clann na Poblachta, which really dictated the campaigning, relied on the simple slogan 'Put Them Out'. Clann na Poblachta's attack was directed not merely at the personal qualities of government ministers but at their wives. Major economic projects which had been introduced or supported by Fianna Fáil were denounced as a national extravagance inspired by the vanity of the ministers or, in some cases, by their officials. The turf development programme did not come under attack presumably because many of the opposition deputies represented constituencies, especially in the midlands, which stood to benefit from our work.

One of the results of the coalition government was to edge Jim

Larkin junior out of politics. He retired to the relative seclusion of union activies — a field much too narrow for his intelligence, realism and integrity. He was a loss not merely to the Labour party but to the nation.

The coalition came in with hatred in their hearts of all things associated with Fianna Fáil. They fulfilled their election promises to the hilt. They dropped the transatlantic airline project without even examining its merits. They sold off the Tourist Board's hotels for next to nothing. They took Bus Áras away from CIE, preventing the company from saving £250,000 per annum which would have resulted from the concentration of all its Dublin city operations under one roof. They abandoned the plan to reconstruct Dublin Castle, thereby losing many thousands of pounds by failing to provide adequate accommodation for the civil service.

Leydon, who had been associated with the airlines, offered his resignation. He was persuaded to stay on in an advisory capacity but his services in this role went unused. Reynolds, the chairman of CIE, was pushed out but he had made sure of compensaton for loss of office. It was made clear to O'Brien of the Tourist Board that when his warrant of appointment expired in a year's time he would not be re-appointed. He had no private means nor any entitlement to compensation or to a pension in spite of a life devoted to the development of tourism. It is fair to say that Dan Morrissey, the Minister for Industry and Commerce, a decent and compassionate man, exerted himself on O'Brien's behalf but O'Brien had too many personal and political enemies determined to bring about his downfall.

In the light of these developments I was naturally concerned about my own fate. Like O'Brien, I had no entitlement for loss of office nor any pension rights, since I had resigned from the civil service, but my warrant of appointment had still three years to run. While I was quite properly identified with Fianna Fáil — I had few friends outside the party or amongst Republicans of differing hues — I was not a member of the party and it was well known both inside and outside Bord na Móna that I was strongly opposed to staff appointments being influenced by political affiliations. Besides, Bord na Móna had taken such deep roots in the rural economy that it would have been politically inexpedient to liquidate it merely because I was so emotionally involved in Fianna Fáil. In fact,the only curtailment in our operations was a drastic overnight cutback in the County Production Scheme in what amounted to a complete closedown of the handwon production programme. Faced with a directive to virtually dismantle the machinery so skilfully built up by Alban O'Kelly to replace the county council organisation I asked to see the minister, intending to point out to him the consequences in terms of unemployment of the government's action, but he refused to meet me. Leydon had ceased to be an effective force in the administration and his successors were of that variety of civil servant who are only concerned with keeping right with the minister. But the minister saw me quickly enough when the *Irish Press* of 9 March 1948 came out with a banner headline —

HANDWON TURF SCHEME TO GO.
EMPLOYMENT CLOSED TO 15,000 WORKERS

Our chairman, Bob Barton, and myself were called to the minister's office. The acting secretary of the department, Shanagher, was present to take notes. Morrissey launched a violent attack on me, accusing me of having leaked the information to the press in order to embarrass the government. It apparently required the newspaper headline to bring home to the minister and his colleagues the serious effects of the closedown. Even though the bogs where semi-automatic machines had been installed were to continue in production, disemployment of thousands of workers would nevertheless be involved.

Morrissey was so offensive that my first inclination was to resign on the spot and walk out. But Bob took control of the conference and in a quiet but very superior manner reduced Morrissey to civility. I think Morrissey rather regretted his bad-tempered performance for thereafter he consulted me frequently; indeed we ultimately became good friends and he became one of Bord na Móna's most enthusiastic supporters. On one occasion he even arranged for me to attend a cabinet meeting so as to present my own case for an increased capital investment necessitated by the second development programme which was duly approved. Unfortunately the decision to reduce the scope of the County Production Scheme proved irreversible. Among the turf workers in the west of Ireland it resulted in a spate of emigration to England.

Fianna Fáil returned to power in 1951. In an effort to restore the wartime prosperity of the western seaboard, based on the turf production for a guaranteed market, we proposed the establishment of a number of small turf-fired power stations to serve the main turf centres. After a careful survey of the potential turf supply four locations were selected — Cahirciveen, Milltown-Malbay, Screebe and Gweedore — each with a capacity of 30,000 tons a year. The project was approved in principle by Seán Lemass, who was then Minister for Industry and Commerce, but it got held up by a prolonged argument between the ESB and the department. Eventually it was decided that the ESB should be financially responsible for the erection and operation of the power stations. In fact it had never been intended by us that the financial cost of the project should devolve on the ESB — its value was seen in social rather than in commercial terms. Further years elapsed before the stations were ready for commissioning. Inevitably the delay resulted in a loss of local interest and support for the project and since the stations could not be economically operated the ESB did little to encourage turf production. Nevertheless twenty-five years after the event they are still working.

The County Production Scheme bogs equipped with semi-automatic machines continued to produce about 100,000 tons a year up to 1953 by which time the fuel situation was back to normal. The scheme, even in its attenuated form, was an interesting experiment. It was the first attempt in Ireland to mechanise the small privately owned bogs. Maceration, which is the key feature of the mechanised process, improved the quality of the turf and made it more readily saleable. On the other hand only a very litte degree of mechanisation could be achieved with semi-automatic cutting machines and it did little to reduce the labour and cost of turf harvesting. In more recent times a somewhat similar scheme promoted by Comhlucht Siúcre Éireann using more advanced machines and producing turf for home use rather than for sale has met with greater success.

The Turf Industry Comes of Age

One of the most important features of Bord na Móna's post-war development programme was the establishment of an Experimental Station. Indeed the board's success in implementing this programme owes much to the existence of research and development facilities which could be brought to bear on the specific problems of the Irish turf industry. By locating it in Droichead Nua, County Kildare, we ensured that the Experimental Station had easy access to the major midland bog areas. At that time Droichead Nua was a dull country town with anything but an attractive appearance. The main street was bounded on one side by a high, blank, dirty wall which had once enclosed the largest British cavalry barracks in Ireland. It had served as an internment camp during and after the Civil War. I had been a prisoner there for nine not too uncomfortable months in 1923. The board took over part of this property and by the end of 1946 structural alterations and staff recruitment had advanced sufficiently to enable the work of the station to get under way under the direction of H. M. S. Miller, a young English mechanical engineer just out of the British army, whose Irish wife was anxious to rear their family in Ireland. Workshops, laboratories and a design centre were added as the project took shape.

From the start the priorities of the Experimental Station were clearly defined and concentrated on practical results rather than pure research. They included, in particular, the mechanisation of drainage and harvesting operations still largely done by hand labour; the improvement of existing machine designs to give better yields and productivity; the study and testing of new natural and artificial drying methods. As a starting point for these investigations a comprehensive study was made of world literature on current turf production and utilisation techniques and the latest advances in machine design. Much of this desk research was the work of John Hennig, a German who left Germany because of the Nazi regime. With his remarkable grasp of foreign languages, he built up a comprehensive library and information service, establishing connections with practitioners in bog work in many countries.

As time went on research emphasis shifted towards the problems of turf utilisation, the combustion characteristics of turf and the development of turf burning apparatus. Manufacturers were encouraged to produce specially designed turf-fired appliances both for domestic and industrial use and many such units were placed on the market. A fuel advisory service which was widely availed of was established as a back-up for the board's sales promotion efforts. Experimental work in bog reclamation and afforestation was put in hand.

In a wider context the Experimental Station provided us with a clearing house for new ideas, inventions and innovations and the opportunity to test them without interference in day-to-day operations. In Ireland there have always been people who believed that they were the possessors of a philospher's stone capable of transforming the bogs into 'brown gold'. We had self-made experts nurturing private theories about how the bogs should be developed as well as enthusiasts in quarternary research who thought they should not be developed at all. This was a view shared by sportsmen who did not want the grouse disturbed and by environmentalists who opposed any interference with nature as God made it. There were people who were convinced that turf could be dried artificially by the use of pressure systems, that it could be used for the production of town gas and chemical fertilisers, that it could be converted into charcoal, wallboard and insulating materials, that it would yield industrial waxes and a wide range of medicinal products, that mixed with coal dust it represented the last word in domestic fuel. The ingenuity of the amateur turf technologists was endless. And by and large they were right. These methods could be used and these products made, but not economically. We were under constant pressure to pursue one or other of these fruitless byways. With our own research unit it was possible to challenge the practicality of these ideas or to show that they had already been tried out somewhere else in the world. While conscious of the need to keep informed about activities taking place on the fringe of the turf industry we refused to be diverted from our basic objective epitomised in the words of the chairman, Bob Barton: 'To produce the largest possible amount of turf of the highest possible quality at the lowest possible price.'

A notable achievement of Miller and his colleagues in the experimental Station was the organisation of the first International Peat Symposium which was held in Dublin in July 1954 and was attended by two hundred delegates from fifteen countries. It covered every feature of the turf industry ranging from bog classification and survey to reclamation and by-products. It could be said that the proceedings of the Symposium raised turf, for the first time, to a level of serious scientific interest. It also acknowledged the major and unique contribution which Bord na Móna had made to this branch of international knowledge. Public opinion at home became conscious, with some sense of pride, of our role as one of the world's leaders in this field. I was gratified at the close of the Symposium to receive from the heads of the national delegations a presentation in the form of a silver tray inscribed in these rather extravagant, honorific terms: 'To C. S. Andrews Esq. in acknowledgement of his service to mankind throughout the world by his contribution to the development of peat as a source of energy'.

Apart from the personal satisfaction I derived from the success of the Symposium and the prestige it conferred on Bord na Móna, I felt that it had also contributed something towards expanding our national horizons. Since my schooldays I had a deep emotional conviction that the only way by which Ireland could survive as an entity distinct from the Anglo-Saxon world which surrounded it was by identifying itself with the continent of Europe culturally, and if possible, commercially. I did not then foresee the establishment of the European Economic Community but I felt very strongly that unless we absorbed something of the traditions and manners of Europe and acquainted ourselves with its art, architecture and literature we would inevitably degenerate to the level of a province of Britain, second-rate suppliants for small privileges. This, as I see it, is the situation which now obtains in our **Six** Counties which has become a community of run-down industries shaped in its attitudes and aspirations by fundamentalist clerics. By sponsoring this conference of scientists and technologists I believed that the nation was doing honour to itself as well as broadening its field of vision. Exchanges of this kind were particularly valuable in the 1950s when oppressive censorship and the activities of extremist Catholic groups were sapping the national morale.

It is not so long since almost our sole links with the outside world were in missionary work. Today it is a cause of unending satisfaction to me to see our politicians and civil servants of a younger generation playing an important role in EEC affairs; our engineers helping in the development of Third World countries; our doctors and nurses establishing hospitals and clinics in Africa and the Middle East; our businessmen competing successfully in world markets. And unlike our missionaries who were more or less permanent exiles, they work from a base at home. My peregrinations in Europe have helped to rid me of at least one misconception about my fellow countrymen. We have so often been labelled a lazy, feckless, if lovable people, that we have ourselves come to accept this designation. Because Bord na Móna used the same machines and the same methods of measuring output as our opposite numbers in Germany it was possible to make an exact comparison of standards of performance. It must come as a surprise to those who believe in our traditional image that the productivity of the Irish worker was much higher. Furthermore our bog management staffs worked longer hours for lower rewards than their counterparts in Germany. Indeed they displayed a pride in and a commitment towards their work such as I have never observed elsewhere with the possible exception of Russia.

As early as 1948 it had become apparent that Bord na Móna's post-war development programme would be completed well within the time limits originally set. Progressive survey work also showed that this initial programme fell far short of exploiting all of the economically usable bogland. In the light of these surveys we were able to draw up proposals for the development of several additional bog areas in the midlands and west which would bring our original planned capacity up to two million tons of turf annually. These proposals were duly approved by the government and the necessary development capital was provided by the Turf Development Act 1950.

This Act was also important because it authorised the board to provide housing for its workers. In these relatively early days the high seasonal element in turf production presented considerable problems. Very large numbers of temporary workers had to be recruited each year for harvesting work and since this labour was imported, in most cases from remote sources, it had to be housed in hostels. Under these conditions it was impossible to create a settled workforce. Progress in mechanisation of harvesting operations gradually reduced the need for heavy seasonal recruitment and in time the hostels were phased out.

There remained, however, the need to establish a hard-core labour pool of sufficient size to maintain the key bog services and the solution was found in the provision of houses for workers willing to make a living in the turf industry. Over the next few years nearly six hundred of these houses were built in groups varying from eight to one hundred and fifty depending on local needs. In most cases they amounted to sizeable village settlements.

We were determined from the start that the houses would be models for rural living. The house plans and the layout of the sites were designed jointly by our own building engineers and our consultant architect, Frank Gibney, and the whole project was under the general supervision of Dermot Lawlor, the general manager. Their combined efforts resulted in the creation of villages of a quality far surpassing anything of the kind previously built in Ireland. They did not, however, materialise without a hitch.

The minister responsible for steering the 1950 Act through the Oireachtas was Dan Morrissey, a man of considerable ability and intelligence who had risen from the position of a council roadworker to his present eminence. He had been converted from one of his early political beliefs, shared also by some of his government colleagues, that Bord na Móna was founded by Fianna Fáil to provide jobs for its supporters. Like all converts he had become an enthusiast for his new faith. On being notified that we were about to get the housing project under way he summoned me to the department for a discussion on the matter. He was accompanied by Shanagher, the Department Secretary who, apart from an elaborate display of note-taking at which he was adept, having spent all his life recording other men's ideas, contributed nothing to the occasion. It transpired that Morrissey was strongly opposed to the idea of grouping the houses in the form of village settlements; he insisted that they should be built as individual units scattered around the periphery of the bogs. It took an hour of argument to convince him that if this policy were adopted the provision of services such as sewerage, running water and electricity would be uneconomic and that there would be no possibility of developing a proper community life. Finally a compromise was reached. We would be free to build the houses in groups as originally intended but baths, which the Minister regarded as an unnecessary luxury for turf workers, should be omitted from the house plans. The minister's instructions in this respect were carried out to the letter but not in the spirit. The houses we built were equipped with bathrooms which contained no baths; when in due course a change of government took place we felt free to make good this deficiency. This incident made me realise that in Ireland, or at least certain parts of it, there was still resistance to being dragged into the twentieth century even by such decent and well-intentioned men as Morrissey.

Another idea which it was felt might add to the internal attractiveness of the houses regrettably came to nothing. When the first village was completed I approached the Irish Countrywomen's Association with an offer to place one of the house at their disposal to be furnished, at our expense, in whatever manner they considered most appropriate for a rural household. No limitations were placed on their selection except that the items should be as far as possible hand-crafted and in all cases be of Irish manufacture. The association expressed enthusiastic support for the idea and delegated one of their members, who was a professional architect, to organise the details, but unfortunately nothing ever materialised. I felt resentful at the time about the association's failure to make good its promise. An exceptional opportunity had been lost to raise the standard of home furnishing not only in the Bord na Móna houses but possibly throughout rural Ireland.

Despite all this, the village schemes won universal approbation as one of Bord na Móna's best social achievements. They have stood the test of time and served their purpose well. They represent the fulfilment of a process aimed at industrialising a rural population while at the same time improving rather than disrupting its environment.

Back in 1936 when Government approval was received by the Turf Development Board for the establishment of a turf-fired generating station my immediate reaction was to bring the good news personally to Dr McLaughlin of the Electricity Supply Board. As founder of the Shannon Scheme he had been the first Irish product of the Burnhamite managerial revolution and I hoped to emulate his achievement in the field of turf development. By this time his star had faded somewhat and my visit found him in a state of slightly diminished glory. I was naturally quite excited by the new project and having given him an outline of what was involved I waited in anticipation of his good wishes and encouragement. But instead of an expression of goodwill I was told, not very politely, that the idea of producing electricity from turf was nonsense and that we would get no co-operation from him. There was no reason apparent to me at the time why McLaughlin should adopt this attitude. He had always been friendly to me. Besides, he was under a considerable obligation to me since Phyllis Ryan (afterwards Mrs Seán T. Ó Ceallaigh, wife of the President of Ireland) and I had persuaded Seán Lemass to re-appoint him to the board of the ESB from which he had been forced to resign by the Cumann na nGaedheal government, most of whose members were his personal friends and which he had strongly and publicly supported. In his heyday McLaughlin had organised what amounted to a branch of the Cumann na nGaedheal organisation among his senior staff to support McGilligan in the Dáil election of 1927.

It was characteristic of the man to bite the hand that fed him and, although I was unaware of it at the time, he had conceived a hatred of Seán Lemass to whom he always referred as 'the hatter of Capel Street'. McLaughlin's cold reception was so unexpected and so disconcerting that I almost lost my temper. I confined myself to saying that what I was seeking was merely his goodwill and general support and not his technical advice as I was aware that he knew as little about the use of turf for power generation as I did. Rather less, in fact, because I had seen power stations operating on turf on a relatively small scale in Germany and on a scale in Russia which we could never hope to emultate.

This information did not impress McLaughlin who regarded the Russians as barbarians. He knew as little of Russia as he did of turf. He carried his antipathy to turf to the extent of invoking a letter from the great Swedish engineer, Borquist — the ESB adviser on water power — in which Borquist expressed the view that anyone who believed that turf could profitably be used in power generation knew nothing about mathematics. McLaughlin sent a copy of the letter to a couple of his friends in the Fianna Fáil government, one of whom held the view that turf production was an occupation suitable only for small farmers, and the other who, though himself from a technical background, was overawed by the high-powered academic qualifications of the engineers in the ESB.

The senior ESB engineers were even more strongly opposed to using turf for the generation of electricity than McLaughlin but on more reasonable grounds. They argued that the relative cost of turf to coal (oil at that time was not in the picture) would make the use of turf prohibitively expensive. They feared too that under Irish weather conditions turf supplies would be unreliable. They believed that one large centralised power station located at Ringsend would have considerable cost advantages over a series of smaller stations spread around the country. In my opinion, there were factors in the ESB opposition to turf which were not technically or commercially based. Dr Henry Kennedy was a member of the ESB board. He had been rather ignominiously forced to resign from the Turf Development Board and had developed a vested interest in the failure of the turf scheme. Again, in the political climate of the time, the harnessing of the Shannon had rightly been seen as a political achievement of the Free State regime. The development of the bogs was regarded as a Republican response to this achievement and the higher echelons of the ESB were ardent Free Staters though not having contributed to the pre-Truce conflicts they described themselves as apolitical. Perhaps there is something in the training of an electrical engineer that limits his imagination and his national or social conscience, compelling him to exercise his professional skill in a vacuum. For whatever reason, from the day that I brought the good tidings to McLaughlin in 1936 until I left Bord na Móna in 1958 we experienced nothing but opposition, bitter and sometimes virulent, from the technical directorate of the ESB to the policy of using turf in the power stations.

Even when agreement appeared to have been reached in principle, resistance fastened on matters of detail. For example, it had been decided in 1936 that the first turf-fired power station should be located in the vicinity of Clonsast bog near Portarlington. Objections to this proposal were raised on the grounds that all possible sites in the area were unsuitable because of poor foundations and insufficient cooling water; that the access roads were incapable of carrying the heavy plant required; that large transmission losses would occur owing to the distance from the main load centres; that the construction cost would compare unfavourably with that of coal; that turf at an estimated cost of 10/- per ton would be marginally uncompetitive; that the time lag involved in the development of the bog and the erection of the station would be excessive.

The outbreak of war put the Portarlington project in abeyance. Even when it was revived in 1945 the original ESB objections still stood though in the new situation they had become patently unsustainable. Their opposition was eventually overcome by a directive from Seán Lemass whose wartime experience had changed his attitude from lukewarm indulgence of Aiken's whims to a firm, personal commitment to turf development.

In the years following the end of the war, Bord na Móna succeeded in making rapid progress with its planned development programme. The time scale originally foreseen for completion of the work was reduced and a big expansion of the original programme by the inclusion of new bogs was being considered. This expansion depended in part at least, on the willingness of the ESB to provide increased turf-fired generating capacity but we found it impossible to tie them down to a broad long-term commitment. We were faced with a two-pronged objection: on the one hand additional units were required urgently to meet predictions of a growing demand for electricity, and on the other no further turf-fired stations could be built pending some years of operational experience at Portarlington. By this time also oil was beginning to come into the picture and it was argued that a coal/oil station would have the advantage of greater flexibility over one based exclusively on turf. Once again the intervention of the minister, Seán Lemass, had to be invoked. Under pressure from him the ESB was forced to draw up a ten year generating programme sufficient to absorb the tonnages to be supplied by Bord na Móna.

Ten year's experience in Lullymore convinced Bord na Móna that, on the basis of their relative heat values, milled peat could be produced more cheaply than machine turf because the production process could be completely mechanised. For this reason we put it to the ESB in 1951 that it would be to our mutual advantage that milled peat should be used in any future turf-fired power stations. The proposal came up against strong technical opposition from the ESB who declared that milled peat was unburnable despite the fact that it was used on a large scale as a power station fuel, especially in Russia, and had been fully reported in the relevant technical literature. The government called in the Battelle Memorial Institute, a firm of American consultants, to advise on the matter and their report fully supported the Bord na Móna recommendation. The first of a number of milled peat power stations was commissioned at Ferbane in 1957. In point of fact they were designed and operated by the ESB without encountering any real difficulty.

Much of the conflict between the ESB and Bord na Móna could have been avoided if it had been possible to bring about a closer working relationship at technical level. We had been agitating for years for the formation of a joint technical committee but it was not until 1952 that this body, composed of senior engineers from both sides, was established under pressure from Seán Lemass. This personal contact between the engineers helped to create an atmosphere of mutual confidence and made easier the solution of day-to-day problems but it failed to eradicate the antagonism to turf of the ESB board members. In retrospect it is astonishing that the news media never became aware of the recurring feuds between the two organisations and, on the contrary, we were held up as an example of the value of co-operation between state agencies. Editorial comment to this effect raised many ironic smiles.

In 1956 I had what was to be my last major confrontation with the ESB. I was in the middle of a German bog with our German consultant, Herr Klasmann, when I was summoned to the office to take a telephone call from Dublin. The second coalition had come back into power some months earlier and by this time Bord na Móna had become something akin to the government's 'favourite son' among the semi-state bodies. This was partly due to the fact that Bill Norton, the Minister for Industry and Commerce, represented Kildare which was heavily dependent on the bogs for employment and partly to the fact that he and I had always been on friendly terms.

The telephone call was from Norton and the gist of it was that there had been a serious setback to the turf development programme which required my presence in Dublin urgently. On my return I found Norton in a state of distraction the source of which was a communication from the ESB to the effect that the levelling off in the electricity demand had created a surplus in their plant capacity and no additional power units would be required in the foreseeable future. The effect of this cutback on Bord na Móna's operations would be to reduce by 50% the planned output of two of the larger bogs then under development and to eliminate two others completely. It also put at risk the jobs of six to nine hundred workers.

One of the areas most seriously affected was a wilderness in the heart of County Mayo which we had christened *Tionnsca Abhainn Einne*. I persuaded Norton to visit the area and see for himself the implications of a large scale loss in local employment. On our return a conference between Browne, the ESB chairman, and myself was arranged by the Department of Industry and Commerce. In these recurrent crises I dealt directly with Dick Browne whose imperturbable though futile amiability so amused me that I found it impossible to get angry. With Browne I never had any unpleasantness and this personal relationship was strengthened by the fact that Weckler, the ESB chief accountant, and his close associates were helpful and sympathetic to Bord na Móna. The conference failed to persuade the ESB to alter their stance. But Norton, whose capacity for Fabianism amounted to genius, decided to ignore the implications of the ESB embargo at least for the time being and that work on the bog development programme should be allowed to go ahead unimpaired. For myself, however, I had lost all confidence in the willingness of the ESB to honour any undertaking where the use of turf was involved.

I suggested to Norton and the department that our dependence on the ESB could be reduced by switching over the product of the milled peat bogs in part to briquette production. My proposal was met by two objections; that there was no market for large scale briquette production and that the capital of £3 millions required to build two moderately sized briquette factories was not available. I got the impression that if the government could be assured about the marketing problem they could be more readily persuaded to put up the capital. Help came from a most unexpected source.

At this time the managing director of Arthur Guinness Son and Company was Sir Hugh Beaver. He was a man of many parts and diverse interests. Among other things he was chairman of the British Institute of Management and from time to time he and his management colleagues organised group visits of inspection to various industries. I met him at a seminar of the Irish Management Institute in Killarney. I had made a speech on decision-making in which I advocated the intuitive approach — the hunch — as likely to be no less effective and certainly quicker than decisions based on laborious, contrived, logical reasoning and analysis. I assumed of course that the intuitive process was based on extensive experience. What I said, or perhaps the way I said it, caught Beaver's attention and he asked me to meet him. I had no wish to meet anyone from the Guinness establishment. I looked on the firm as an alien organisation making its profits in Ireland and disposing of them in public beneficences in England, procuring titles and honours for the Guinness family. The senior management staff of Guinness was, by definition, non-Irish. Besides I had a couple of personal grievances against the firm. Mary, my wife, had worked before she married as a 'lady clerk' (the male clerks were known as 'young gentlemen') in the brewery. She had been forced to resign because of her activities in Cumann na mBan. In the early days of the Turf Development Board Frank Aiken had arranged for me to see the 'Head Engineer' of Guinness in the hope of persuading him to use handwon turf in their furnaces. I was received with amused indulgence such as might be extended in *Castle Rackrent* to a client of the big house.

Nevertheless I met Sir Hugh Beaver and almost immediately recognised him as a person quite different from my preconceived ideas of the Guinness top management. We discussed intuitive decision-making with which he had a good deal of sympathy. He knew Ireland very well; his mother was an Eyre from Eyrecourt in Galway. He had come to Guinness from outside the organisation. His firm having built the Guinness factory at Park Royal he so impressed the board that quite late in his career he was invited to join the company as chief executive.

Beaver introduced modern methods of management, decapitating the 'Head' engineer and generally letting fresh air into the organisation. He told me that he regarded the firm's attitude of aloofness from Irish affairs as deplorable. He intended to change that situation and he hoped that they would be able to contribute something to the economic development of the country. He knew of our efforts to develop the turf industry and expressed a wish to take a group of his management friends on a tour of the bogs.

The visit was duly arranged. Sir Hugh and his party were taken on a tour of the Kildare bogs including Lullymore factory where extensive renovations were in progress aimed at increasing production to 50,000 tons. Beaver was impressed by the cleanness and compactness of the briquettes and thought them an admirable fuel. He told me that if we ever encountered a sales problem we could count on his co-operation.

When the question of building additional briquette factories arose and the absence or otherwise of an assured market became a major issue I remembered Beaver's promise of assistance and telephoned him in London to ask for an appointment. He had intended to come to Dublin the following day but as he would be staying for one day only and had a very full schedule he invited me to meet him for breakfast at the Guinness guest house in James's Street. Having heard my problem he repeated his assurance of help in disposing of any surplus briquettes. In connection with the shortage of capital, which I had only mentioned *en passant,* he inquired whether a loan of half a million pounds would be of any assistance. His offer was so generous and unexpected that I was momentarily nonplussed. I thanked him profusely but pointed out that government permission would have to be obtained to accept the offer. I could hardly get out of James' Street quickly enough to bring the news to Norton in his office in Leinster House. Norton was equally surprised and gratified at the result of my approach to Beaver. He had no doubt that the Guinness offer should be accepted but suggested that I should clear it with Gerard Sweetman, the Minister for Finance. 'You mean *you* will have to clear it with Sweetman,' I replied.

There was good reason for my reluctance to have any avoidable dealings with Sweetman who was about the most objectionable politician I had ever encountered. Years earlier, as a young senator, he had reported me to the Committee of Procedure and Privileges for having stared him down to his great embarrassment, when making a speech in the house. We never spoke again. He reminded me of Flashman of *Tom Brown's Schooldays* — arrogant and a bully. I also believed that despite his family name, he was a west Briton in his sympathies. Norton who shared my opinion of Sweetman — they were political rivals in the Kildare constituency — suggested that I should discuss the matter with T. K. Whitaker who had just become secretary of the Department of Finance. Whitaker readily approved of the Guinness investment and suggested that I should inquire about the possibility of getting the loan increased to one million pounds. This I did. Beaver undertook to put the new figure to his directors and within days he telephoned me to signify their agreement. The Guinness initiative and their interest in Bord na Móna's operations left the government with little alternative but to sanction the briquette factory project and provide the additional money for its capitalisation. Before I left Bord na Móna two years later the construction of the new factories at Derrinlough and Croghan was well under way. We were no longer wholly dependent on the vagaries of the ESB.

Sir Hugh Beaver was anxious that co-operation between Guinness and Bord na Móna should be further developed. We discussed at length where in the scientific field our interests might coincide. I happened to mention a problem we experienced arising from the spontaneous combustion of milled peat stockpiles due to anaerobic reaction. Sir Hugh pointed out that the basis of brewing could be said to be anaerobic reaction and suggested that this could usefully form the subject of a joint research project. Arising out of this discussion it was agreed that we should jointly sponsor the foundation of a Chair of Industrial Microbiology in University College, Dublin, which would give special attention to the problems and possibilities of peat. Sir Hugh's interests were not confined to the commercial world. He was also a patron of the arts and several young Irish painters benefitted from his support. Unfortunately for Ireland he died too soon.

In Russia Again

When we were leaving Russia in 1935 it had been agreed with our Glav-Torf hosts that the link between the two turf organisations should be maintained. In the years that followed, both before and after the war, we made several efforts to re-establish contact with the Russians but there was no response to any of these initiatives. We were therefore pleasantly surprised when in 1956 word came through from our ambassador in London, Fred Boland, that the question of an exchange of visits between representatives of the turf industries of both countries had been raised with him by the Russian ambassador, Maisky. At home the coalition government was in power and Bill Norton was Minister for Industry and Commerce. The invitation to exchange visits with the Russians put the government in something of a predicament as it was a time when the Catholic sectaries were at their enthusiastic worst. These militant organisations had whipped up a noisy frenzy about atheistic Communism and the Church of Silence and the fact that our constitution did not recognise the Holy Roman Catholic and Apostolic Church as the one true Church. Russia was their hate figure so that anything which might foster relations with Russia was likely to provoke noisy opposition. When a Russian delegation paid us a return visit the following year the *Maria Duce* people mounted a protest demonstration outside the Bord na Móna offices in Pembroke Street, and to avoid giving offence to the Russians we had to pretend that it was a welcoming party.

Norton was the leader of the Labour party and nominally a socialist though, in fact, he had no interest whatever in socialism. He was a good humoured and good hearted cynic. He would have enjoyed being a minister very much except that from time to time he was expected to make decisions. Usually he avoided making them by setting up a commission or a committee to examine any problem that was too embarrassing to be ignored. He had just as low an opinion of the religious sectaries as I had but, such was the temper of the times and so low was the public morale, that even a tiny but very noisy minority of true believers could embarrass the government. Supported by the knowledge that the opposition would raise no objection — with his approval I got an undertaking to this effect from Seán Lemass — Norton finally gave his consent so that exactly twenty-one years after our first visit a delegation from the Irish turf industry again set foot in Russia.

This time the delegation went with a very substantial sense of achievement. Bord na Móna, the organisation responsible for the development of the turf industry, had been given the status of a statutory authority. Already it was producing machine turf at the rate of one million tons a year. It had one briquette factory in full production and there were two more on the drawing board. Four turf-fired power stations had been established, a peat moss factory was producing for export and considerable progress was being made in the automation of bog operations. Above all the board had learned thoroughly the extremely difficult technology of bog drainage and it had found, at some expense, that without perfect drainage cheap turf cannot be produced in quantity.

The 1956 delegation consisted of myself, Patrick Cogan and Lewis Rhatigan. Cogan, in his middle forties was deputy chief engineer of the board and Rhatigan, in his middle thirties, was manager of one of the largest bog groups. I was in my middle fifties, about the same age as Professor Purcell at the time of our 1935 visit. With twenty-one years experience in the turf business behind us we had something of value to offer the Russians particularly in the field of milled peat production where we had acquired considerable expertise. The Russians had become aware of our achievements from the proceedings of the 1954 International Peat Symposium in Dublin. The Swedes had taken a very active part in this Symposium and it was through them that the Russian curiosity about our operations was aroused. The Russians had not been invited to the Symposium because having failed to reply to our previous communications it was assumed that they would be uninterested. If the truth was known we were probably glad to shelter behind this pretext not being anxious to bring down on our heads the abuse of the Catholic fanatics. We were, I am afraid, less courageous than Bill Norton. During our visit the Russians frequently reminded us of our remissness.

Cogan and Rhatigan were engineers of very different backgrounds, Cogan's fundamental training was as a mechanical fitter. He had no formal engineering qualifications but he had broadened his experience by working on the Drumm Battery project and later in the Irish Alcohol Company where he had reached managerial level. While on a training course abroad he had got a thorough knowledge of German. He was a man of unusual intelligence with a rare capacity for penetrating humbug and a disbelief in human perfectibility. He read little but appeared to have antennae which drew information from the air around him. He would talk the language of the logical positivists without having ever heard of A. J. Ayer or indeed of logical positivism. Cogan understood human motivation better than anyone I ever knew. No human frailty surprised him and he had an extraordinary capacity to distinguish between what people said and what they really meant. He believed that in everyone there was a large measure of self-deception or theatricality. A strong sense of the absurd provided him with an inimitable store of anecdotes which, told in a dead-pan manner, made him the most entertaining of companions. Wherever he was outbursts of laughter were sure to be heard. He belonged to that unusual type of Irishman who preferred female to male society and he had the capacity to evoke the confidence of women. They were always anxious to tell him their personal problems and to seek his advice.

Cogan was not distinguished for his punctuality or speed of decision and he had a tenacity amounting to obstinacy in sticking to his viewpoint which often tried the patience of his colleagues sorely. As impatience was totally alien to him this did not in any way disconcert him; he had almost endless self-control and stamina. This was a quality which was of very great value in his frequent dealings with trade unions. It is part of the stock in trade of every union official that nothing, however sensible, proposed by management can be agreed to until it is subject to prolonged discussion amounting in practice to assertions and counter-assertions endlessly repeated. Only in this way can the trade union representative show that he has the interest of his members at heart; without this touch of exhibitionism his job would be at risk.

Cogan did not smoke, took very little alcohol and then only for politeness, but had a peculiar addiction to tea. He was not interested in sport, the theatre or the cinema but was a dedicated radio fan. He was a do-it-yourself hobbyist and enjoyed doing handyman work around his home. Close family ties were of great importance to him though I was never able to understand how he found any time for either family or hobbies because he worked all seven days and many evenings of the week for Bord na Móna and never, so long as I knew him, took a holiday. He seemed to have illimitable energy. His influence on the development of Bord na Móna was decisive in many ways. It was he who was largely responsible for the design of the briquette factories and for introducing the milled peat production system. Despite his achievements he did not look for rewards either in money or status. If only for that reason Cogan was a man not usually found in Ireland or indeed anywhere else.

Rhatigan came from a background of comfortable farmers and school teachers. He took a degree in engineering in UCD and, according to his own account, had been a very rackety student. In his case the rackety life scarcely went beyond drinking a few bottles of stout on Saturday nights or some gaudy occasion. He joined Bord na Móna on leaving college — at that time jobs were scarce and he wanted to get married — and was posted to Coolnagun bog in a remote part of Westmeath. In the course of time he became manager of our works at Boora and it was there that he came to my attention. Apart from his strength in management and engineering he was distinguished from his peers on the staff of Bord na Móna by an orderliness, equal to the highest Swedish standards, which characterised both his office surroundings and his work. He had an admirable concern for the working environment and was noted for good housekeeping — planting trees and shrubs and laying down lawns and, even more important, maintaining them. He had a perfectionism which was quite un-Irish and refused to accept the belief so commonly held that 'it will do bloody well'. From whence his quite extraordinary sense of order derived I do not know. He had never been outside Ireland so that the Russian visit was an adventure which held out great expectations for him. His expectations were more than fulfilled and the trip proved to be a high point in his life.

In contrast to the rather deferential attitude we displayed during the 1935 visit we had gained extensive experience in the intervening years in dealing with foreigners. We had wide ranging contacts with all the countries concerned with the utilisation of bogland and had numerous visits from technologists from Britain, Sweden, Denmark, Canada, Holland and Germany. We had, at the request of the Stormont government, given advice on the development of the Northern Ireland bogs and were on close terms with the Highlands and Islands Development Board in Scotland. Bord na Móna staff had travelled frequently on technical missions to Sweden, Denmark and France and we had especially close business relations with the Germans from whom much of our knowledge of bog mechanisation had been originally derived and who were later involved in the manufacture of plant for our briquette factories. In short when we returned to Russia in 1956 we felt none of the diffidence with which we approached them in 1935. This time I had also taken the precaution of learning the Cyrillic alphabet and a dozen or so Russian phrases.

The difference in our approach to the visit resulting from increased maturity and self-confidence was exceeded, if anything, by the difference which had taken place in Russia itself since 1935. The change that was to affect us most agreeably was the evolution of 'Communism with a human face' which followed Kruschev's speech denouncing Stalin and the errors of his regime. We arrived shortly after this denunciation and I noticed from the moment of our arrival and first meetings with our Russian hosts a marked difference even in the manner of greeting from the constrained, though courteous, way we were treated in 1935. This, of course, may well have been merely a subjective feeling.

We arrived late at night at the magnificently planned and brilliantly lighted Moscow airport where a delegation of senior members of the Ministry of Power Stations, accompanied by our interpreter, met us on the tarmac, took us through customs with the minimum of formality and conveyed us to the Savoy Hotel. Conspicuous at the airport was a mammoth gilded statue of Stalin; they had not yet got around to deculting him. The drive through the city was in itself an experience. There was very little traffic nor even many pedestrians on the streets which were laid out like boulevards lined with fully grown trees. On all sides we could see blocks of high-rise apartments, many still under construction. Moscow University which was flood-lit stood out as one of the show places of the city which promised to be exciting to explore.

Immediately on arrival at the Savoy Hotel we were informed by our hosts that for our sojourn in Russia we were to be their guests and that they would be responsible for all our hotel, travel and entertainment expenses. It took days to persuade them to let us cash travellers's cheques so that we could buy small personal items such as stamps and postcards. If we wanted to smoke, cigarettes were handed to us by the packet. It was after midnight when we were installed in the hotel and then we sat down to supper. I was re-introduced to caviar and after twenty-one years of abstinence I found it as agreeable as ever. During supper we were presented with an itinerary which had been prepared for our visit with the suggestion that we might consider it overnight and that it could be altered or extended in any way to meet our wishes. I was delighted to see that the programme included a visit to Sverdlovsk, once known as Ekaterinburg, which was familiar to me as the town where bands of exiles *en route* to Siberia were assembled, and also where the Russian imperial family was liquidated in June 1918. Later it was developed as an industrial complex which contributed a large part to the Russian war effort.

The Savoy Hotel where we stayed while in Moscow might well have served as the location for Visconti's movie version of *Death in Venice*. I noticed when discussing my 1935 experiences in Russia that it was the trivia of the visit that mainly interested people and I was frequently asked, for example, whether there were plugs in the wash-basins or if it was true that the Russians did not use toilet paper. I can say beyond doubt that all the wash basins we encountered were fitted with plugs and that the toilet paper conformed to the claims of the American manufacturers' advertisements — it was strong, soft and soluble.

We were taken after breakfast to the office of the Ministry of Power Stations where we were received by Mr Jermakov, the deputy minister, and by Mr Bausin, the vice-minister for turf. We were to get to know Mr Bausin very well during the visit and later in Ireland. To our great surprise we learned that arrangements had been made for us to meet the minister, Mr Malenkov. I recalled that Malenkov had been a member of Stalin's entourage and inner cabinet. He had taken part in the liquidation of the Kulaks and the great state trials that resulted in the elimination of the old Bolsheviks who, with Lenin, had founded the Soviet state. With Stalin, Molotov, Beria and Voroshilov he had been a member of the five-man state defence committee ultimately responsible for the conduct of the war and was Stalin's personal representative directing the Battle of Stalingrad. After Stalin's death he played a major part in the liquidation of Beria. He succeeded Stalin as party secretary and prime minster but, after a year, resigned the position at his own request, according to the official report.

This was to be my first encounter with a great international figure who had been one of the most powerful men on the world stage. Naturally my reaction was one of great curiosity — it was almost as if I had been invited to meet Robespierre or Fouché. Malenkov turned out to be a man small in stature and rotund. He reminded me at once of Bill Norton and had the same pleasant humorous manner. Due possibly to this similarity I felt very much at ease with him and was in no way overwhelmed by what was to me an important occasion. The meeting lasted for rather less than an hour; much of the conversation, apart from dealing with the general problems of turf production in Ireland and in Russia, was good humoured *blague*. As we spoke, I began to wonder what were the qualities that had made him a leading figure in world politics. I had devised criteria for my private evaluation of important people whom I met for the first time. Supposing, I asked myself, that they were applicants for a job in Bord na Móna, would I employ them and, if so, in what capacity? My second test question was equally simple-minded. Assuming the opportunity arose, would I like to entertain them in my home for an evening? Malenkov, shorn of the trappings of office, I would have rated as suitable for employment as manager of a peat moss factory. On the second score I decided that to spend an evening at home with Malenkov was not my idea of stimulating company as he was unlikely to have enough to say to hold my interest. The truth is that I have never subscribed to the concept of the superman. Further, wherever I went, whoever I met, I asked myself as Shylock asked about Jews — 'Hath not a Jew eyes? Hath not a Jew hands, organs, dimensions, senses, affections, passions?' I have always believed that all individuals are, as human beings, equally important. My approach to them has been the same, high or low. Two only, among all the people I met, did I put in a class apart: they were Peadar Clancy and Gunnar Myrdal. Clancy, whom I met only once, was leader of a hunger strike in Mountjoy in 1920. Myrdal was the famous Swedish scholar, politician, journalist and international statesman.

Following the meeting with Malenkov we went on to discuss our proposed itinerary with vice-minister Bausin. He again emphasised that the programme which they had drawn up was flexible and could be adjusted in any way we wished. On the 1935 visit to Russia it would not have occurred to us to suggest any variation in the specially prepared itinerary. We had accepted the generally held belief that the Russians only showed what they, the Russians, wished their visitors to see. This time we had the temerity to enquire why the thermal mechanical dewatering plant which they had developed and was a process of special interest had not been included in the programme. They explained that it was located at a rather inaccessible place called Borgsitogorsk, north-east of Leningrad, but if we were prepared to extend our visit to Russia by a few days a visit could be arranged. We were prepared. Our first working session consisted of a documentary film and talk on the Russian turf industry and we then visited a vast agricultural exhibition which included an impressive display of turf machinery. In the evening — the Bolshoi being closed for renovation — we were taken to see a musical comedy called *The Countess Maritza*. To me it was no more or less boring than any other musical comedy. The enthusiasm with which the performance was received was surprising. When the curtain came down on the final act many of the audience advanced down the central aisle to the stage clapping and shaking hands with the cast, more particularly with the beautiful and obviously very popular leading lady.

After the theatre we were taken to a restaurant for a typically long drawn out Russian dinner. Our fellow diners were the ordinary people one met on the streets — a young mechanic, a clerk taking his girl out for the evening, a few obviously married couples and many Chinese. At that time there was a large Chinese population in Moscow composed mainly of students. So much did they seem part of the city, and so well accepted were they as honoured guests, that the break between Russia and China, when it came, was as much of a surprise to me as the Molotov/Ribbentrop pact had been.

We were due to set out for Sverdlovsk on the first of our bog visits in the late afternoon of the following day so that we were able to spend the morning sight-seeing. The Russians are very proud of the Moscow underground rail system. Work on its construction had just began when I was there in 1935. It was now one of the show pieces of Russia. As an underground railway it is markedly different from the dirty, smelly subway systems we know of in London, Paris and New York. The stations look like great airy palaces studded with ornamental columns and decorated with mosaics, sculptures and paintings. Each station represents a different aspect of Soviet life and achievement. Marble from various parts of Russia are used throughout. One station is dedicated to Soviet recreation, another to Soviet military victories, another to the different peoples making up the Soviet Union, another to Soviet agriculture and so on. The underground carries millions of people daily; yet not a scrap of paper nor a dropped cigarette butt nor a muddy foot mark was to be seen. Only a team of workers in continuous circulation could have managed to keep the platforms so spotlessly clean. Most western architects would probably look with distaste on the rather old fashioned architectural style of these buildings nor would the pictures and sculptures displayed there have much artistic appeal to viewers not dedicated to Soviet realism. Throughout the ages the human spirit has expressed itself in great buildings — the Pyramids of Cheops, Knossos, the Parthenon, Chartres Cathedral and St Peter's in Rome. I think that the Moscow underground, if only for the imagination and effort used to produce it, could be placed in that category of human achievement.

Accompanied by our interpreter and a representative of the ministry we were put on a regular scheduled flight to Sverdlovsk. We flew very low and hence it was a bumpy journey. We touched down at Kagan on the Volga, the capital of the Tartar Republic. Like all Soviet domestic airports it consisted of a massive heap of concrete; the conventional statute of Stalin had not yet been removed. Indeed his portrait still hung in all the state offices we visited. After a few days it became irritating to have to look at this benign omnipresent father figure, knowing the villainy of which he had been guilty. That is a contemporary judgement; history will, I think, judge him differently. He left, if not to his own generation, certainly to later generations of Russians, opportunities to attain a much more fulfilling way of life than was possible before he came to power. For those who remember the fate of Bela Kun and the Hungarian revolutionaries after the First World War and more recently of Allende in Chile it is hardly surprising that Stalin made sure that there were no Thermidorians.

At Sverdlovsk we were greeted on the tarmac with a great show of friendliness by officials of the Sverdlovsk Peat Trust and taken to our hotel in the older part of the city. When I got to my room I found I had been provided with a full suite including a study, sitting-room and bathroom. The hotel had remained unchanged in its furnishings since the First World War. There were plush curtains, an enormous Victorian sideboard, heavily made chairs upholstered in tapestry, a grand-father clock and a very old upright piano. Several sentimental paintings of rural life hung on the walls as well as a profusion of gilded mirrors everywhere. The plumbing and the electrical fittings had been modernised and there was central heating, a shower in the bathroom, electric points and a radio. I had a great double bed with a high canopy but the mattress unfortunately was antiquated — it was hard and lumpy. At the bedside there was a statuette of the Venus de Milo, intended, I am sure, to produce beautiful bedtime thoughts.

We were up early next morning. Our hosts suggested that we might like to see the industrial area of the city. Knowing from experience that, unless one has some direct interest in the proceedings, factory visits are usually tiring and boring I declined the offer.

The invitation was however significant of the change which had taken place in the official attitude to foreigners. In Stalin's day any foreigner found in the vicinity of a factory was likely to be arrested. So, early in the morning we found ourselves following the footsteps of the Czarist political prisoners who were assembled at Sverdlovsk before being distributed to their places of exile in Siberia. We entered Siberia on the railcar of a bog railway. The landscape on all sides consisted of enormous tracts of bogland broken here and there by forests of pine-trees. Along the railway new workers' villages were under construction. We stopped to look at one of them where work was well advanced.

The scene was evocative of an American frontier settlement as shown in the movies. The difference was that modern technology was expediting the building process. The dwelling houses were log cabins, many already occupied, but the most prominent feature was a large concrete building which served as a community centre. We were told that the provision of these community centres was the priority in the creation of a new village. It seemed to be symptomatic of the emphasis the Russians place on the education of the masses. The centre comprised a large assembly hall which was also used as a cinema and theatre. There was a conference room and for so small a place an astonishingly large library. Looking through the shelves and being able to spell out the authors' names I discovered a representative collection of English classics in Russian translation — among them Shakespeare, Swift, Smollett, Defoe, Fielding, Dickens, Thackeray. I noticed a copy of Fielding's *Joseph Andrews* and when I told the librarian, a woman, that Andrews was my name she insisted on making me a present of the book. Having travelled about twenty miles on the bog railway we reached a large, well settled village called Losinoye which was one of the local headquarters of the Sverdlovsk Peat Trust. On the way we saw a remarkable tree-felling operation at a point when a forest was being cleared for bog development. The trees were being felled mechanically not singly but in swathes like we cut wheat. The trees in question were not saplings; one which we measured had been forty-three feet high and twenty-six inches in diameter.

Since we had arrived in Russia the sense of 'humanity on the march' had taken possession of Rhatigan who was fascinated by the great new buildings of Moscow and by the underground railway. He listened with awe to the accounts given to us of the extent and operational variety of the Russian turf industry. The vast plains of Tartary covered with thousands of acres of wheat over which we flew was a phenomenon completely new in his experience. But above all he was deeply impressed by the sense of purpose of the people we met. His considerable imagination was stimulated and a suppressed idealism, which until then he was unaware of, was released. The climax came when we got off the railcar at Losinoye to walk to the village institute, as the community centre was called, for lunch. A few people from the vicinity began to gather around and follow us along the roadway. One old peasant woman who had been collecting wild flowers came over to Rhatigan, who was obviously the youngest of us, stopped and addressed him in what was clearly a speech of welcome and with a graceful bow presented him with her bunch of flowers. It was a highly emotional gesture. Rhatigan was overwhelmed. His conversion to the Russian way of life was complete. His whole perspective of life had changed utterly. I too felt very touched by the incident but Cogan, in his usual down-to-earth fashion, thought that the peasant woman could have used the flowers to better advantage to decorate her home as no doubt she had originally intended. By the time we reached the institute all the inhabitants of Losinoye — men, women and children — had assembled to escort us to the entrance clapping us as we went. There was no mistaking their spontaneity and friendliness — partly, of course, arising from curiosity. The scene, as I observed it from the building, was most colourful with the women in their multi-coloured headscarves and blouses, the men heterogeneously dressed but mainly in shirt sleeves, the children with bits of ribbon in their hair, or holding bunches of wild flowers like children in a Confirmation procession at home. The meal was as sumptuous as all these meals were. For the locals they were a form of expense account entertaining.

Losinoye was one of the three major turf centres visited during our stay in the Sverdlovsk region. The production methods employed were fairly conventional although the bogs were heavily timbered and climatic conditions were greatly different from ours. The bogs are frost-bound for much of the year; even at the time of our visit in July the excavating machine brought up occasional chunks of frozen peat. What was most impressive was the immensity of the whole undertaking. The working area operated by the Sverdlovsk Peat Trust covered 25,000 acres with an annual output of three million tons a year and there was much more bog under development. The turf was used to fuel a group of local power stations and in a gasification plant in Sverdlovsk.

The local plant officials received us everywhere with great personal openness and hospitality. We stayed overnight at the house of the manager at Losinoye sleeping three in a room. The house though small was furnished and equipped in modern style with central heating, aluminium framed beds and spring mattresses. The following day we visited Monetroye Works and were invited to lunch at his home by the manager. The lunch table was a spectacular sight prepared by the woman of the house assisted, no doubt, by the neighbours. The centrepiece was a sucking pig surrounded by red caviar. There were at least a dozen plates of hors d'oeuvres, the Russian zakuski, containing salted herring with mustard sauce, potato salad, pike in aspic, egg mayonnaise, stuffed tomatoes, ham, radishes, liver paste, chicken livers, beetroot and lettuce. Remembering my unfortunate experience in Germany many years previously I ate sparingly of the zakuski since I would certainly be expected to get through a generous helping of sucking pig. To drink we were served with vodka, wine and mineral water. For dessert we had an apple tart followed by Russian tea with lemon but no milk. It was a most generous display of hospitality far beyond the call of duty. I think I am unlikely to see again a meal so beautifully presented.

We had an unexpected experience on the way back to Sverdlovsk having completed our tour of the bogs. We had been discussing Stalin and the part he had played in the Second World War. The official from the Peat Trust who accompanied us talked very freely and we discussed the attitude prevalent in Russia since Kruschev's historic denunciation of Stalin. With some diffidence I mentioned the association of Sverdlovsk with the liquidation of the Czar and the imperial family. Our host was quite frank and dispassionate on the subject, pointing out that the killings were necessary to prevent the royal family falling into the hands of the Czech Whites who were advancing on the city. He mentioned casually that on the way back to Sverdlovsk we would pass the house where the shooting had taken place and agreed quite readily to my request that we should stop and see it. It was a very large and massively-built, two-storied house just off the public road which had formerly belonged to a merchant of the city. Some families occupied the upper floors of the house but the basement was sealed off and made inaccessible to visitors. The Czar, his wife, their son and four daughters and their attendants, a doctor, a cook, a waiter and a maid had been shot before each other's eyes by eleven executioners using pistols, in the cellar of the house on the night of 16 June 1918. The head of the execution squad was a local commissar named Urovsky and we were told that he died peacefully — a highly respected citizen — in Sverdlovsk only a couple of months before our visit. This was the bloodiest regicide in modern times and we stood looking at the house overcome by a feeling compounded of morbidity and awe at the enormous importance of the political drama which had been played out there. Our feelings were certainly justified on both accounts. By any standards the liquidation had been carried out with frightening callousness and brutality. The executions had been ordered by Lenin to deprive the counter-revolutionaries of a living rallying point. The bodies of the imperial family and their relatives were cremated in a near-by forest. Their ashes and what remained of their few personal possessions were thrown into a mine where they were discovered when the Whites captured Sverdlovsk shortly afterwards.

Our final visit before leaving Sverdlovsk was to the Malmask gasification plant where 300,000 tons of turf a year was used to produce gas for industrial purposes. The process was a highly sophisticated one and we had the impression that despite the big scale of operation it contained a large element of experimentation. It seemed to be a hang-over from the war when economic considerations did not count and there was no profit and loss account. The return flight to Moscow, though smoother than the outward journey, was long and tiring and it was midnight before we reached the Savoy Hotel. At that time conditions on Russian domestic flights were below the standard provided by western airlines; there were no seat-belts, no drinks, no food, no smoking. Fortunately the next day being Sunday we were able to take some time off. Remembering from our catechism that 'like good soldiers of Christ we should never deny our religion on any occasion and be faithful unto death', we announced to the interpreter, Alexandrov, that being Catholics we would like to go to Mass on the morrow. Alexandrov assured us that there would be no difficulty about this as religious services were available in many places in Moscow. It took some little time to explain that we were Roman, not Greek Catholics. Not until I used the term 'Latin' Catholics did he fully grasp the distinction and realised that not all religious services were equal in our estimation. Had we appreciated the complexities of the problem presented to Alexandrov we would cheerfully have modified our religious principles. It took him nearly an hour on the phone to locate a Catholic church and enquire about Mass times. Eventually it was arranged that he would pick us up at the hotel at eight o'clock the following morning but it was then discovered that the church was only a hundred yards away and Mass was not due to commence till nine. To fill in the time we made a short motor tour around the city.

The trip took us along the Moskova river. Even at that early hour we saw *bâteaux mouches* with their decks crowded with trippers out for the day. Some of the new monuments were striking even though built in the style of socialist realism; one in particular, a group sculpture of male and female workers holding high the hammer and sickle, symbolising the future advance of collectivisation. Even at that hour too a long queue had formed to pay their respects at the Lenin/Stalin mausoleum. We had an opportunity to view the great Red Square at a time when it was empty of traffic and to appreciate the massive dimensions of the Kremlin.

On our return to the church our Russian friends asked, with marked diffidence, if it was in order for them to accompany us to the ceremonies or would it be preferable to wait outside. We assured them that their presence would be quite welcome. The church was small but beautifully decorated with flowers. The congregation was small, perhaps two hundred people in all. One third were obviously foreigners, presumably from the diplomatic corps. The others were mainly poorly dressed elderly women. I noticed that the prayer books they held were old and tattered. The state publishing house obviously did not encourage the propagation of 'superstition'. All through Mass there was organ music and the choir sang magnificently. There was no sermon. We were embarrassed when the collection plate came around since we still had not cashed our travellers' cheques and had no Russian money. Our hosts, appreciating the situation, very decently put several notes on the plate. On the way out I asked Alexandrov his opinion of the ceremony. He replied, 'Personally I do not believe in God but I thought the music and singing very beautiful.'

The next two days were devoted to visiting bogs in the vicinity of Moscow. Our first stop was at Orechevo Zuevo where we saw a medium-sized briquette factory which was in operation since 1937 but differed in design from the Peco system we had adopted at home. However, the Russians admitted the superiority of the Peco system since they had already built six Peco-based briquette factories in other bog areas and planned to build several more. Old as the Orechevo factory was it was noticeable that its surroundings were beautifully landscaped and maintained. We moved on that evening to the great bog complex of Shatura. I had visited Shatura in 1935 and could not help being impressed by the progress of the enterprise. The Shatura Peat Trust now controlled no less than nine separate production centres with a seasonal workforce of 10,000 people and an annual output of more than three million tons for use in local power stations. Apart from physcial expansion, the working conditions and amenities had been greatly improved. There was a finely appointed hostel and canteen including guest rooms where we stayed overnight. A whole new town had been constructed to accommodate the permanent workforce. As in the case of Orechevo, it was apparent that care was devoted to the working environment and the landscaping and general cleanliness around the plant were of a high order.

We had a particular interest in the working of hydro peat production systems designed for heavily timbered bogs, as Bord na Móna was operating one experimentally at Derrylea near Portarlington. Though this system was used extensively at Shatura and its technology had been highly developed, the Russians were not happy with the results and we saw nothing which would justify the continuation of the Derrylea experiment. As I listened to my colleagues discussing a multitude of technical problems with their fellow engineers at Shatura — and at times indeed dominating these discussions — I could not help feeling, with some pride, that we too had come a long way since 1935. The idea also struck me that where turf engineers are concerned there is very little difference between the Irish and the Russian varieties.

The Shatura visit had been extremely strenuous and we were glad of a short break in the official travel programme to recharge our batteries in Moscow. It also gave us a chance to compare notes on our experiences in the privacy and comfort of the hotel. Apart from the relative absence of tension and constraint, I had observed several other ways in which the face of Russia had changed since 1935. There was a near clinical attention to communal cleanliness and a greater emphasis on punctuality. In 1935, for example, time seemed to have no relevance in the making of business appointments whereas now such arrangements were adhered to punctiliously. In 1935 much heavy manual work was done by women and while this was still the case we noticed in the course of our factory visits that women held a sizeable proportion of the technical and professional jobs. On the occasion of my first visit there was still in Moscow a large element of the Asian city, but this had all disappeared. Single storey shops and offices were replaced by multi-floor blocks. Streets had been widened to open up new vistas of public buildings and monuments. Moscow now presented in some ways the appearance and atmosphere of an American city.

Alexandrov was finally persuaded to introduce us to a bank where travellers's cheques could be cashed. The rate of exchange was miserable and we got very poor value for sterling. The bank teller did his calculations on a abacus, which we would have associated with children's toys but was still in universal use in Russia at this time. As we wanted to do some shopping Alexandrov suggested a visit to GUM, the great departmental store of Moscow. It was a vast domed building surrounded on the inside by balconies built well above ground level. The balconies contained rows of shops each dealing in one type of merchandise such as furniture, clothing, footwear, radios, electrical appliances and so on. The quality of the goods on display was not impressive. They may well have been technically up to the standard of similar products elsewhere but were lacking in design and finish. Prices were completely beyond the reach of our currency resources so that our shopping was meagre. I settled for in alabaster ash tray. GUM may lack the elegance and presentation of the great western cosmopolitan stores such as Harrods, Printemps or Saks Fifth Avenue, but the Russian man in the street who is pragmatic in these matters might well say that an inelegant refrigerator is better than none at all.

The only other visits we found possible to fit into our official timetable in Moscow were to the Kremlin and the university. I was particularly anxious to see the Lenin/Stalin mausoleum provided some way could be found to avoid queuing for admission. Our hosts were only too glad to comply. Alexandrov explained that it had been originally intended to include the mausoleum in our itinerary but they felt that it might perhaps be inappropriate. This diffidence seemed to reflect the Russian feeling that all foreigners are so hostile to the regime that a visit to the Soviet Holy of Holies would cause them embarrassment.

The Kremlin was originally a fortress. In the course of time it was transformed into a city but one of palaces, cathedrals and museums. The cathedrals — one the Assumption, the other the Annunciation — are the most striking buildings. In the time at our disposal there was no possibility of exploring the Kremlin, even cursorily, in its entirety. We confined ourselves to inspecting the treasures which were housed in the armoury. Every conceivable form of jewellery and every imaginable precious stone and metal which had been used for the adornment of the aristocracy was on display. The famous Fabergé Easter eggs with their delicate workmanship in gold and diamonds, emeralds and pearls which the courtiers gave to one another and to their mistresses as Easter presents could be counted in hundreds. The robes and dresses encrusted with jewels and trimmed and lined with furs represented for me the ultimate manifestation of luxury and vanity. It seemed to me that human beings could never be morally or intellectually large enough to fit these magnificent garments nor indeed to justify the palaces in which their owners lived. As for the cathedrals, their excessive ornamentation and over-elaborate liturgy and ceremonial must surely have inhibited rather than fostered the worship of God. The wearers of the robes and ornaments and the denizens of these palaces and cathedrals must have lived their lives as characters in an opera. The only propensity to self-adornment shown by their successors in the Soviet regime is an over-ready indulgence in medals and military uniforms. Still it is impossible to imagine that some future Krupskaya or Svetlana will one day appear in an ermine robe surmounted by a diamond tiara.

The visit to the mausoleum was clearly a matter of special interest and excitement even for Alexandrov. To him it was a pilgrimage to be undertaken as reverently as Irish people would treat a pilgrimage to Knock or to Lourdes. Moreover the objects of his veneration were visible. We went to the head of the queue, presented our credentials to the guards and were admitted at once. Cogan, who on our visit to the armoury had been more interested in the craftsmanship of the Fabergé eggs than on philosophical reflections about aristocratic extravagance, regarded the preservation of what he called the stuffed effigies of Lenin and Stalin as an absurdity. I warned him of the dire consequences that would follow any show of irreverence though in a sense I shared his attitude having myself no belief in relics. To keep relics in the form of whole corpses seemed very much a waste of effort as well as a strain on credulity. Rhatigan still in his Russophile euphoria was as excited as Alexandrov. Stationed at the entrance to the hall were guards with reversed rifles through whom we and the hushed queue were directed to the staircase leading down to the chamber. As we descended the black marble staircase of twenty-two steps the silence became almost tangible. We entered the inner chamber where some trick of lighting appeared to suffuse every particle in the atmosphere in a soft red glow. Before us the mortal remains of Lenin and Stalin lay clothed in brown habits, the backs of their heads covered by a cowl. Lenin's arms were stretched by his side. Stalin's left forearm was resting on his chest. It would be impossible, unless for one of Cogan's temperament, not to be impressed by the solemnity of the scene and the sense of reverence that emanated from the pilgrims. There was very real emotion. I avoided Cogan's eye until we were safely outside the building where his irreverence got the better of him. He had followed, he told us, many a red light in Amsterdam and Hamburg but none of them led to dead bodies; only living bodies were of interest to him at the end of a red light trail.

The university which artistically is one of the showpieces of Moscow would have merited a longer visit than we were able to afford. Apart from the vast dimensions of the assembly hall and the library and the multitudinous lecture halls, the feature that I found most interesting was the students' living quarters. The rooms were tiny but were masterpieces in the efficient use of space. Bed, table, bookshelves, clothes press, lavatory and a cooking stove were fitted into the the living area. Each was connected with the library by a chute so that the students could get what books they wanted without leaving their rooms. Indeed, apart from attending lecturers and procuring eatables, it was never necessary to leave their rooms and that, we were told, was exactly the practice of the Chinese students who believed in unremitting study. The student accommodation which we saw seemed to have a predominance of Chinese residents. In the allocation of rooms there was no segregation between men and women and both sexes lived side by side. If sleep-walking was prevalent nobody noticed or cared. Even as late as 1956 we found it difficult to react to this situation without raised eyebrows. The size of the university, its lavish equipment and its seemingly superb organisation emphasised the importance placed by the Russians on education. Education was completely free; given natural ability there was no financial nor other barrier to prevent a child from a village school in a tiny Siberian settlement, such as Losinoye, from enjoying the facilites of this great university. Assuming that any of their pre-revolutionary landlords still survive, as some few must, it would be interesting to hear their comments on the living conditions and opportunities of the Russian peasantry today.

We left Moscow on an overnight train journey to Leningrad. The Moscow-Leningrad express is one of the luxury trains of Europe. It has not changed much in its appointment since the days when it was used by Anna Karenina and Count Vronsky. We each had a separate compartment and the sleeping berths were superb. On arrival we were met by the director and some of the staff of the Scientific Research Institute of the Peat Industry which is headquartered in Leningrad and was our main focus of interest there. We were put up at the Astoria Hotel which was also a survival of the old regime. Though to a large extent modernised, much of the old furniture and fittings was still intact. In the dining hall there was an enormous chandelier and damask curtains. Each of the upstairs corridors had a sort of cubby hole occupied by an ancient lady who performed no discernible function. It was suggested to me that she was there to ensure that ladies and gentlemen didn't mistake their bedrooms.

The function of the Scientific Research Institute, which is under the control of Glav-Torf, is to improve existing turf winning systems and to develop new ones. It is affiliated to the University of Moscow and among other things produces each year three hundred specialist engineers for work in the turf industry. The range and sophistication of the Institute's testing equipment and laboratory facilities were very impressive. Weather conditions in any combination of wind, rain, sun and humidity could be simulated. Bog of any moisture content with adjustable water tables could be reproduced on a laboratory scale. A special group of technicians was working on the problem of spontaneous combustion in peat. Rather to our surprise the fundamental research programme did not include any work on peat colloids as it was considered to have no practical value. The Institute also operated 3,500 acres of bog at Tos, near Kalinen, which was used as a testing ground for new bog machinery and equipment. This field station had its own workshops for building prototype machines and even a small cast iron foundry. We spent several days with the Institute personnel both in Leningrad and Tos discussing problems of common interest and examining various research projects. Much of the work was related to the specifically Russian conditions but we came away with some useful ideas. Our most memorable impression was the imagination and inventiveness which characterised the activities of the entire establishment. The resources in money and manpower which were committed to turf science was a clear indication of the high standing of turf in the Russian industrial economy.

Our itinerary had allowed us a fair amount of time for sightseeing. On our first evening we ventured out briefly without benefit of guide or interpreter keeping the hotel well within our compass. One of the things that surprised us was a women's hairdressing establishment operating in a basement. The women we had seen in Russia generally did not bother about hair-do's. Along the Neva river fishermen lined the banks exactly as one saw *les pecheurs de la Seine* in Paris. They seemed to be having as little success as their French counterparts. We were struck by the great numbers of Chinese on the streets as well as groups dressed in regional costumes. In the days that followed we got to know the city better. Leningrad, like Moscow, had changed greatly since my visit in 1935. Vast areas had been destroyed during the siege of the city by the Germans but the Russians with inspired pride had rebuilt the historic buildings exactly as before. They profited by the destruction to remodel the city by elminating large numbers of decrepit houses and streets creating wide boulevards and vistas where the historic buildings could be seen to the best advantage.

We spent a morning driving around the city merely admiring the great edifices and monuments, their beauty enhanced by the River Neva and innumerable canals. Leningrad has been called the Venice of the North. Like Venice it is not flattered by comparison with any other city. It is certainly the most beautiful I have ever seen, excelling even Washington, Paris or Venice itself in its planning and in the diversity and splendour of its public buildings. For my part I was very conscious that, in our own time, this city was the scene of a historic drama which had brought about a fundamental change in relationships to most of the world's population. I became even more conscious of the greatness of Lenin. A man with so high an intelligence and such an iron will to action rarely appears in history. When a leader of equal stature does emerge, as in the person of Alexander the Great, Caesar or Napoleon, personal glory and aggrandisement has been his motivation. Lenin was moved by loathing of the exploitation of the many by the few. For himself he sought neither glory nor riches. He certainly would never have tolerated the absurd cult of personalities which developed under Stalin's regime nor, could he have prevented it, the worship of his own mortal remains now lying in the Moscow mausoleum. He hated war. He was prepared to make peace at almost any price as he demonstrated at the Treaty of Brest-Litvosk. But to sacrifice the fruits of the revolution was a price he was not prepared to pay. When war was forced on him by the intervention of the Great Powers and by Czarist reactionaries — Wrangel, Denekin, Kolchak — he lead the revolution to success undaunted by the appalling difficulties of what appeared to be a desperate situation.

I felt that I should, while in Leningrad, make a private pilgrimage in his honour. I asked Alexandrov if he could arrange such an excursion. He was delighted that foreigners could take so much interest in one who was, so to speak, the founder of his religion although Lenin would surely have regarded this as a low form of superstition. In the course of the tour we saw the armoured car from which Lenin spoke at the height of the Bolshevik take-over. We stopped outside the Smolny Institute where he had his headquarters. We visited the square which saw the start of the fighting and the attack on the Winter Palace, the last citadel of the Kerensky provisional government. With its fall Lenin became the head of the Russian state. The signal to begin the attack was given by a blank shot fired from the cruiser *Aurora,* which had been ordered into Leningrad (or, as it was then called, Petrograd) to support the Bolshevik forces. The *Aurora,* now a museum piece, was still preserved though not open to the public. Alexandrov, by bluff and cajolery, got us permission to board the ship and we had our photographs taken standing under its famous gun. That picture together with the photographs taken of our party beside the armoured car, in the square of the Winter Palace and at the Smolny Institute are the only mementos of my foreign travels which I would feel justified in offering to visitors to my house for their delectation. In the ordinary way I regard it as a social crime to inflict pictures of one's travels on one's friends.

Unfortunately we failed to get to the Finland Station where the train in which Lenin arrived from Germany to take command of the revolution could still be seen. Through some mixup in the instructions we were taken instead to see the giant sports stadium which has a crowd capacity for 110,000 people. The stadium, even empty of specators, was an impressive structure made more so by the sight of a small group of men on the pitch, training horses in the *haute école* exercises. It seemed to me an improbable form of sport to see in Russia.*Haute école* equestrianism is so much the preserve of aristocrats.

We were taken on an extended and rather tiring tour of the great Hermitage museum. Left to myself I would have gladly opted out of the visit although I would have enjoyed an hour looking over the French Impressionist collection in which I had a particular interest. It is very doubtful if much benefit can be derived from this kind of cursory inspection of a museum or art gallery of the magnitude of the Hermitage. Rushing through a collection of items illustrating the heroic military history of the Russian people or an equally massive array of silverware including scoops, goblets, drinking vessels, jugs, bowls, salt cellars, dishes and the like is to me artistically indigestible and therefore counter-productive. However we decided to go, if for no other reason than that our hosts would have been otherwise disappointed but made sure to get to the picture gallery as quickly as courtesy allowed. It had an extraordinary effect on Rhatigan, still bewitched by the new socialist world he had discovered. Until then he had no interest in and no knowledge of art and had never even visited a gallery in Dublin. He was moved to fascination by the splendor of the Titians, Rembrandts, Renoirs, Sisleys and the rest. He felt he had missed a dimension of living. On his return home he set about remedying this omission. He immersed himself in art appreciation and began what in time became a substantial private art collection.

For me a more interesting experience was our visit to the Peterhof Palace, now called Petrovorets, on the Gulf of Finland about twenty miles from Leningrad. On the way we passed several large country residences similar to the big houses once owned by the landed gentry in Ireland. These houses belonged to the trade unions and were used as holiday homes for their members. Russian trade unions are always represented to the western world as something of a joke, mere window dressing to conceal the oppression of the workers by a brutal, power drunk bureaucracy. The Russians have a different view of the role of their trade unions. They exercise many of the welfare functions undertaken by the state in western countries. They have no real bargaining powers in the western sense nor do they have the right to strike. The Russians maintain that, since the workers own the enterprises which employ them, to engage in what we euphemistically call industrial action is unnecessary and illogical; merely militating against themselves and against the state of which they form part. It is perhaps well to remember that a denial of the right to strike is not entirely unknown in Ireland; in fact it applies to much of the public service. Driving along the coast we saw crowds of holiday-makers bathing or sailing in dinghies, rowing in fours and eights or just lolling around for pleasure. It occurred to me that our trade unions in Ireland might well interest themselves more in providing leisure facilities for their members and, in particular, get more fully involved in catering for the needs of those who are retired or infirm. It is arguable that their substantial funds might be better employed in these ways than in erecting palatial offices such as Liberty hall.

Petrovorets was built by Peter the Great and is his version of Versailles. During the war the Germans had burned the Grand Palace and had systematically destroyed the hundreds of fountains and all the statues in the surrounding parks. It must have been an appreciable diversion of the German war effort to have engaged in systematic barbarism on such a scale. At the time of our visit the façade of the Palace had been reconstructed and every single statue, whether in bronze or marble, was back in exactly its original positon. All the fountains too were restored and were in full working order. They were a remarkable sight and were being thoroughly enjoyed by the great assembly of holiday-makers.

The highlight of our tour of the Leningrad area was a visit to the Kirov Power Station, a short distance outside the city. This huge enterprise was one of the more spectacular focal points of the Russian turf industry. It was originally built in 1932 and even in the pre-war years had a capacity equivalent to Ireland's total electricity consumption. It was rebuilt in the early fifties on a much larger scale. At the time of our visit the station used a combination of sod peat and milled peat and the annual consumption was close on four million tons. Supplies of peat were drawn from bogs up to 150 miles distant, not surprising considering that the station's annual intake would have absorbed the entire present day output of Bord na Móna. The design and layout of the plant was mostly conventional and had long since been proved technically. For anyone doubtful of the policy of using turf for generating electricity a visit to Kirov could hardly fail to carry conviction.

The final item on our schedule was a visit to the Thermal Mechanical Dewatering Plant at Boksitogorsk. Glav-Torf had not included this in our original itinerary and the reason soon became apparent. Boksitogorsk was a new town built in a heavily forested area about 150 miles from Leningrad and not easily reached by road. We travelled by train to the nearest railway station and were driven a further twenty miles to the town. The rail journey was in stark contrast to the de-luxe conditions of the Moscow-Leningrad express. The carriages and locomotives were clearly relics from the last century. The carriage seats were little more than benches and wooden bunks were fitted for overnight travel. The train was crowded with shabbily dressed peasants — evidence presumably of the difference between rural and urban living standards. The final stage of the journey by car from the railway station was along a dirt road running through a forest which gave an eerie feeling of primitive wilderness. Wolves howling behind us or a bear crossing the track would not have been out of place in this environment.

As it turned out, little practical benefit was gained from the visit. The plant produced compressed turf by a combination of thermal drying and mechanical pressure and some chemical by-products were also extracted in the process. Though established for several years it was still treated as experimental. We came to the conclusion that it offered nothing which could not better be achieved by the Peco system. One interesting feature of the plant was that it was operated almost wholly by women, although in fact all the works we visited employed a high proportion of female labour. The people we met moving around the town seemed unusually lethargic and for the first time I saw drunks in Russia. On the other hand the officials connected with the plant were exceptionally friendly. We were lodged in a modern hotel and entertained to a lavish meal with an elaborate array of zakuski dishes followed by a main course of baked pike. Apparently the nearby river was famous for pike and the most popular local sport was fishing for pike with rod and line. One man gave me a long and vivid account of how he had landed a twenty-pound pike. As one angler to another I did not have the heart to tell him that I had heard it all before.

Our fifteen day stay in Russia had now come to an end. We returned to Moscow for a final exchange of views with Mr Bausin and his colleagues in the Ministry of Power Stations and were presented with a film of the Russian turf industry as a memento of the occasion.The following summer Mr Bausin led a delegation from Glav-Torf on a return visit to Ireland. Happily the bridges built in 1956 between Russian and Irish turf industries have survived to this day to their mutual advantage.

When I returned from Russia I went to see Dev to report on the trip. I think my version of Russia was something of a surprise to him.

10

Eamon de Valera —
A Personal View

In whatever task I was engaged while working in the public service I was inspired by Dev. I did not think him infallible nor incapable of error but for me he represented the kind of Irishman I should aspire to emulate in his patriotism and integrity in public life.

In 1927 I was co-opted to the national executive of Fianna Fáil and served on it for several years. Dev presided at the meetings of the executive; indeed for all practical purposes Dev was the executive because his rulings were never questioned. In any case the members were so much of one mind that there was little room for controversy. From time to time, prompted by my socialist beliefs, I put forward proposals for setting up nationalised clothing and shoe industries but in the political circumstances of the time these ideas must have seemed naïve and unrealistic. One equally unrealistic proposal which I advocated was that of shutting down the bar in Leinster House; excessive drinking during Dáil sessions had led to the downfall of one prominent Fianna Fáil senator. Another issue on which I had strong views was the importation of petrol and its distribution at the pumps. When Fianna Fáil finally attained power, Seán Lemass made a determined effort to get control over our oil supplies but was out-manoeuvred by the oil companies.

It was about this time that I got to know Dev. He looked on me as something of an *enfant terrible* to be treated with indulgence. In his mind I was always associated with Liam Lynch, the late chief-of-staff of the IRA, whose adjutant I was when he was killed in the closing days of the Civil War. He always had a friendly word for me and over the years until his death I had ready access to him. Having the equivalent of a fool's licence, I could say almost anything I liked to him. He, on the other hand, seemed to enjoy my forthright opinions, sometimes expressed in uninhibited terms. In this respect he used to say that I came up to the standard of Seán Moylan, who held ministerial posts in various Fianna Fáil cabinets and had a reputation for using strong language.

When I was invited by Lemass to take charge of the turf development scheme Dev was at pains to impress on me the importance which he personally attached to the project. The big County Clare boglands around Shragh and Doonbeg were one of his electoral strongholds and he regarded the people of these localities as personal friends; they were known to him individually by name. He also assured me that he would always be available to help with any special problems I encountered. This show of interest and goodwill was important to me.

Almost everything has been written about the public life of Eamon de Valera that can be written. In my opinion he was the greatest political figure in our history. Even applying Taine's formula for appraising historical personalities — 'the race, the milieu and the moment' — and beginning with the father of separatism, Wolfe Tone, he outshone Emmet, O'Connell, Fintan Lawlor, Davis, Mitchell, Smith O'Brien, Stephens, Parnell, Pearse, Arthur Griffith and Michael Collins. While he had fewer flaws than most of them he had as much compassion for human frailties as any of them.

As a political thinker he was the superior of Davis or Pearse. As a popular leader he was comparable to Parnell. He was as close to the common man as O'Connell or Collins. He had a quality necessary in any Irish leader when dealing with the British, and one which unfortunately not all of our leaders possessed; he was immune to flattery. In his dealings with the British he was very wary of this hazard. He did not disagree with me when I once suggested that much of the apparent weakness of the Treaty delegates might have been the result of the flattery and hospitality of London society. The historians might well apply their minds to this feature of the Treaty negotiations.

Holding that opinion of him, it is with diffidence that I say that over the years I got to know him well and in all humility I would like to claim that he regarded me as a friend. When I knew him first I called him 'Sir' but later I always addressed him as 'Chief'. His impression of me as an *enfant terrible* persisted even when our acquaintance ripened into old age. Even in my late fifties he sometimes teasingly addressed me as 'Child'.

I got the impression that Dev suffered from a sense of guilt because he felt that he had neglected his family in dedicating his life to his country. Several times he told me, and no doubt others as well, that when joining the Volunteers in 1913 he had put it to his wife (he always referred to her as 'Sinéad' and she to him, in conversation with me anyway, as 'Dev') that she would have to take complete responsibility for rearing their children, and a wonderful job she made of it.

His life was lived in accordance with the doctrine of frugal comfort which he preached. The fact is that until he became President of the Executive Council in 1932 and proclaimed that no man was worth more than £1000 a year he probably had no option to frugal comfort. His material resources until then must have been very meagre and his family must have been brought up in austerity but there was never a suggestion of complaint. Occasionally on our way back from a trip to the bogs he did me the honour of inviting me to his home in Blackrock for a meal. The meal consisted of rashers and eggs, bread, butter and jam and was no different from what Mary or my mother would have cooked for me at home. In later years when I was invited to tea in his private quarters in Áras an Uachtaráin, the same simple food was presented. Mrs de Valera supervised the services of the meal with the warmth and charm which so captivated President Kennedy.

Dev seemed to me to be a man extraordinarily free from intolerance or rancour. He was hated by a substantial number of people but when they met him personally, even those who hated him intensely inevitably fell for his charm; his charm lay in his ability to make people feel that they were of some importance. It always puzzled him why W. T. Cosgrave would never offer as much as a nod of recognition when they met in public. I pointed out that in a letter to Joe McGarrity he had referred to Cosgrave as a 'ninny' and in his deep heart's core Cosgrave knew that the description was appropriate but could not forgive the perception which prompted it; it was like catching a man with his trousers down.

When opening a conversation with me Dev always used Irish but, because I usually had more to say than I could readily express in Irish, we soon reverted to English. During his years in Áras an Uachtaráin he occasionally rang me at home for a chat (I suspect out of boredom) and on these occasions we always spoke Irish. I asked him why he did not wear a gold *Fáinne*. He explained that on one occasion he had commissioned Seán a' Chota, a well-known Gaeilgeoir and flamboyant character from Kerry, to compile a list of unusual words and phrases in use in the Dingle Gaeltacht. In order to avoid any ambiguity about the financial terms and, lacking confidence in his own ability to do so in Irish, Dev had used English in negotiating the deal and felt that his lapse from grace had disqualified him from wearing a gold *Fáinne*. As a substitute, Kathleen O'Connell, his secretary, was persuaded to sew a ring of coloured thread as a permanent fixture on his lapel. Kathleen was a better secretary than seamstress but a daughter-in-law of Dev's solved the problem by dipping a fountain pen cap in face powder and using this to form a perfect circle on the lapel which would be easily stitched around. Cardinal Conway brought him some authentic cardinal red thread from Rome to enhance the job. The emphasis of this story, as Dev told it, was on the cleverness of his daughter-in-law rather than on his own extreme conscientiousness in fulfilling an obligation. It was the only reference I ever heard him make to his family. His children were unusually gifted but unlike most parents with distinguished children he never mentioned their achievements.

Dev was very proud of the constitution. I heard him say that it was entirely the work of John Hearn, the legal adviser of the Department of External Affairs, and that his own contribution amounted only to dotting the 'i's' and crossing the 't's'. When framing the terms of the constitution he spent hours in consultation with Dr McQuaid who was a close friend and adviser on theological matters. McQuaid pressed him hard to insert a clause proclaiming the Roman Catholic Church to be the one true church. Though he fully realised the political hazards of such a sectarian assertion Dev was equally troubled in conscience about its omission. He consulted the Papal Nuncio who, in turn, discussed the matter with Dr Byrne, at that time Archbishop of Dublin. Dr Byrne advised him to act in accordance with his own judgment and the clause was dropped.

Dr McQuaid succeeded Dr Byrne as Archbishop of Dublin and it was generally believed that Dev was responsible for the appointment. It appears that their close friendship was disrupted by disagreement over Dr Noel Browne's 'Mother and Child' scheme. Dev had read the White Paper setting out the terms of the scheme and reacted to it favourably. Dr McQuaid, on the other hand, was adamant in his opposition to the scheme and believed that it was calculated to bring about the destruction of family life. Dev considered this to be a far-fetched conclusion and felt obliged to say so whereupon Dr McQuaid got very angry and left the room. The incident left Dev sorry and upset; intimacy between the two men was never so close again. 'A broken friendship can be soldered but will never be sound.'

Dev had his roots deep in rural Ireland and was always eager to recall memories of his childhood in Bruree. One incident from his early days in politics was recounted with relish. Addressing a meeting somewhere on his home ground and boasting of his agricultural prowess — milking cows, making hay, digging potatoes, snagging turnips and so on — his speech was interrupted by a relative's voice shouting from the background 'and a damn bad warrant you were at farm work'. The colloquialism fascinated and amused him. It has often been said that Dev had no sense of humour. A sense of humour is a gem of many facets. Certainly if the joke involved a pun or some play on words it would have to be explained to him whereupon he would always laugh heartily as much at his own obtuseness as at the point of the joke.

Dev was deeply interested in the progress of bog development and took pains to make his support known in public. Year after year from the beginning of the scheme he honoured us with a visit to the bogs every Good Friday. In the early days, before members of the Oireachtas were debarred from the boards of semi-state bodies, the party usually consisted of Frank Aiken, Senator Bill Quirke, Aodhagan O'Rahilly and myself. Quirke had a repertoire of picaresque stories, mainly about his adventures with Dan Breen, which Dev found highly amusing. There was a picnic lunch on these occasions and we tried hard to persuade Dev to drink a bottle of beer as proof of his assertion that he was not a teetotaller. His beer drinking exploits produced a lot of badinage. In Rockwell, he told us, he used to slip out to a local public house for a bottle of stout though he maintained that the stout was only an excuse to meet the barmaid on whom he had his eye.

On these visits to the bogs Dev made a point of greeting the staff at all levels with interest and friendliness and without the slightest hint of condescension. He had a wonderful and most natural simplicity of manner. Needless to say he never discussed his major problems with me but equally he showed no resentment at my occasionally injudicious comments on some of his decisions. I ventured to suggest that the constitution was less suited to our needs than an American style constitution would have been. Considering the study and research which he and his collaborators had devoted to the examination of the constitutional systems of the world my opinion did not deserve to be taken seriously but Dev did not appear to take exception to my assertatively expressed views. I remember, on another occasion, telling him that I thought that the biggest mistake of his political career was the establishment of the Banking Commission. The remark was intended as a joke though I genuinely believed it to be true. Dev's reply, also delivered as banter was that my biggest mistake was the closedown of the Harcourt Street line 'with its lovely little stations'. I assured him that had we realised that he felt so strongly on the matter we would have preserved at least one of the stations in his honour, before they were all vandalised.

During the war Dev toured the bog areas of the west in support of the Emergency turf campaign and I usually accompanied him on these occasions. During one such trip to Kerry in 1944 he invited William Warnock, our ambassador in Germany, who was at home on leave, to meet him in Killarney for a report on his mission. I was

present when Warnock recounted the horrifying story of the bombing of Berlin. His description of the casualties and destruction
caused by the bombing raids was truly shocking. It struck me how
fortunate we were, thanks to Dev's determination, to have escaped
involvement in the war and how courageous Warnock was to have
remained at his post in the midst of the Berlin holocaust.

During these tours it was usual for the local notables to assemble
at the various stopping points to greet the Taoiseach and offer him
hospitality. This always consisted of a simple meal in deference to
Dev's well-known tastes. Invariably several bottles of whiskey were
placed at convenient intervals along the table but, again in deference to Dev's taste, there was always a long delay before anyone
had the courage to open them. In fact, Dev never showed disapproval of other people's indulgence in drink. He was very tolerant of the 'habit as he was of all other manifestations of the human
condition although he once acquiesced in the expulsion from the
Fianna Fáil party of a TD who was guilty of a sexual pecadillo. As it
so happened, the expulsion was short-lived. At the next election
the culprit stood as an Independent, headed the poll and was re-
admitted to the party.

When Dev made his famous speech about 'frugal comfort' and
'comely maidens' it was met with either indulgent smiles or sophisticated derision. Nevertheless of all his public pronouncements, it is
the one least forgotten. In fact it encapsulated the ideal way of life
derived from the ethos of the Republican movement which
developed in the years following 1916. 'Frugal comfort' did not
equate, in Dev's mind, with the concept of a family sitting on *sugán*
chairs, around a turf fire, under a thatched roof, listening to a *sean-
achaí,* preparatory to saying the family Rosary. Nor were the 'comely maidens' of his imagination dressed in Macroom cloaks and red
petticoats reaching to their ankles. His vision of Irish life was much
less romantic. He looked forward to a country where every family
would be comfortably housed, warmly clothed, properly fed and
well educated but a country where conspicuous waste was not
indulged in and, if practised, was not admired.

The dilution of this ideal had already set in when Dev's speech
was delivered in 1943. The decline started when some of his ministers could no longer afford to live on their incomes. Some of them
met and associated with a class of people for whom frugality had no
attraction. What Dev did not foresee, and would never have
approved of, was the growth of a political generation whose
rewards are fur coats, big cars, indoor swimming pools, vintage
wines and any other form of ostentation which fashion demands.

Dev was a deeply religious man but not evidently pious. He did not evangelise anyone. He presented me with a little prayer book inscribed *Do'n Dr Tod MacAindriú ó Eamon De Valera, le n'a chur ar bhealach a leasa, 1959* — (to put him on the right road). This is the only time he showed interest in my immortal soul.

He bore the personal hostility of the bishops, thinly disguised at the time of the Eucharistic Congress, with a patient shrug. He knew that some of his colleagues had not forgiven the hierarchy as easily as he had and could readily understand their attitude, even that of one close associate who became a follower of Madame Blavatsky. But he did not encourage anyone to speak critically of the Church. Once he showed open annoyance with me at a meeting in Kerry when I joined a group of TD's who were discussing with him some row over school management involving the local parish priest. I interrupted the discussion with some off-the-cuff remark like, 'You will have no peace until you get rid of the clerical managers and give the national teachers full responsibility to run their own schools.' Dev made no comment but he froze me with a look. Whereupon I subsided.

The difficulties arising from the economic war created a serious employment problem, particularly among school leavers. In most countries the vacuum would have been filled through military conscription but this solution was unavailable to us owing to possible repercussions in Northern Ireland. I suggested to Dev that a Labour Corps should be formed to provide employment for young people leaving school on public works and amenity projects. This idea was adopted and took shape in the form of the Construction Corps organised and administered by the army. I was invited by Dev to take charge of the running of the Construction Corps with the rank of army colonel. I found it difficult to take this proposal seriously as there could hardly be anyone less attuned to army life than I was. The Construction Corps was officered by old IRA officers who had no regular military training and its personnel consisted mainly of young people recruited from the inner city areas who were physically unsuitable for heavy manual work and did not take kindly to camp life remote from their normal environment.

In one respect Dev failed me. It is true that the bulk of the money subscribed to the foundation of the *Irish Press* was raised by Dev himself in the USA, but at home in Ireland thousands of members of the party put in much effort to collect a substantial part of the capital in small subscriptions. Dev never personally took one brass farthing from the *Irish Press,* but I was surprised and dismayed that he handed over control of the paper to his son, Vivion, rather than to the Fianna Fáil party. I never had the nerve to ask him why he did it. He may have feared that the party would in future depart from the ideals which the paper was founded to propagate.

Except for mathematics, Dev had no hobbies. Sometimes he took long walks and at least once went on a pony-trekking expedition with Frank Aiken but this interest did not last. He often regretted that he had little opportunity for reading, particularly history. His opponents accused him of having made a study of Machiavelli, as if that in itself was a crime. I asked him about his interest in Machiavelli but found that he had only a vague knowledge of his writing — not more than the average literate person — and in particular no familiarity with *The Prince*. I am certain that in the pre-Treaty discussions with Lloyd George he never consulted, as he might profitably have done, the chapter from *The Prince* entitled 'Of those who have attained the position of Prince by villainy'. Equally, he might usefully have provided the members of the delegation who negotiated the Treaty with a copy of the chapter that deals with 'How flatterers must be shunned'.

To my knowledge, Dev never took a holiday, with or without his family. His round-the-world-tour with Frank Aiken was a burden rather than a vacation which only men of their physique and dedication could have sustained. Until he moved to Áras an Uachtaráin he never had any leisure and little occasion for relaxation. He kept to the letter of the resolution he made when joining the Volunteers — to devote his whole being to Ireland. We never saw his like before and are unlikely to see it for a long time again.

11

The Nation's Transport

Reform of Córas Iompair Éireann

With the power station programme at an advanced stage of completion and with the erection of the new briquette factories in train —
one at Derrinlough near Ferbane, and another at Croghan near
Daingean in County Offaly — my contribution to Bord na Móna
effectively came to an end. The organisation was soundly based and
working smoothly apart from the day-to-day problems which beset
all such enterprises. Further expansion could only follow a pattern
of development which was by now well defined. My function as
chief executive was reduced to keeping up the momentum though
much of my attention was also devoted to the promotion of good
public relations. Such an administrative role did not suit my temperament so that during my last few years in Bord na Móna I was not
by any means fully stretched. Probably all concerned would have
benefitted had I been taken out of the organisation and given some
other task while I had some more years of active working life left.
But I was identified so publicly with Bord na Móna and it was
reflecting such credit on the government that their reluctance to
sever my connection with the board was understandable.

After our return from Russia in 1956 I made this point to Seán
Lemass in the course of a casual conversation at a government
reception in Iveagh House. I didn't think again about the matter if
for no other reason than there was no post of any interest to me on
the horizon. But Lemass did not forget the conversation and he sent
for me one day in the summer of 1958 and, to my great surprise,
asked whether I would be interested in taking on the chairmanship
of CIE. The 1958 Transport Act had just been passed and the new
chairman would have to give effect to its provisions. His only mis-
giving in making the suggestion was the difficulty that would arise in
replacing me in Bord na Móna. I never believed that I was immortal
or otherwise indispensable and I was always conscious of the
obligation of every chief executive to provide for his successor. I
was able to assure Lemass that there was at least one man whose
experience, temperament and intelligence made him much better
equipped to manage Bord na Móna as a well established going

concern than I could ever do.

I was on the point of telling Lemass that I would be delighted to accept the offer when he mentioned that he proposed to appoint two other whole-time directors to the CIE board. I paused at this stage and asked if I might have a day or two to think it over. I decided, to start with, to get my wife Mary's reactions on the matter. She said that I must do as I thought fit but warned me that the chairmanship of CIE was a very exposed job and she hoped that I would not get too upset at the public criticism it would surely entail. She also was uneasy at the possibility of having to participate in formal entertaining or public functions both of which had been conspicuously part of the activities of CIE in the time of my predecessors. The substantial increase in remuneration which I anticipated did not impress her as she believed, almost as an article of faith, that one can pay too high a price for money.

Bob Barton was absent in America at the time so I sought advice from Aodhagan O'Rahilly. He agreed that Dermot Lawlor, who had served for many years as general manager, would be quite capable of replacing me in Bord na Móna and that his management style would probably suit the organisation in its present state better than mine. I told him about the proposal to appoint two whole-time directors in CIE and that my reservations, based on my experience of a similar situation in the ESB, were so great that I would not accept the chairmanship if the idea was persisted in. He, knowing me well, thought that this was the correct approach.

I went back to Lemass and assured him I would gladly undertake the post but not if two other whole-time directors were appointed. I felt I could not do justice to the job unless I was the complete boss subject, of course, to the broad overall control of the board of CIE. I also asked him if I might assume that I would be employed on terms no less favourable than the incumbent chairman, both in respect of remuneration, pension rights and the considerable fringe benefits attached to the post. I was not sure what these amounted to but I knew that they were very much better than I enjoyed as managing director of Bord na Móna. I did not trust the civil servants not to avail themselves of the chance to worsen the terms of the appointment; they were notoriously jealous of the higher salaries and perquisites of the heads of the semi-state companies as compared with their own. Lemass accepted both stipulations and within a week I got my letter of appointment.

Since the occupation of the Four Courts by the Republicans in 1922, I was associated with Seán Lemass in the IRA, in Sinn Féin, in the starting of Fianna Fáil, in the civil service and the public corporations. In 1922 he was the Four Courts' garrison adjutant and had a great reputation from the Tan times as a very active street fighter. At that time there was in the IRA a hierarchy of status based on 'records' achieved during the Black and Tan War. It was imprescriptible but nevertheless acknowledged. Using an analogy from the soccer world, the likes of Tom Barry, Ernie O'Malley, Frank Aiken and Michael Kilroy were at the top of the League of Ireland while the likes of Seán Lemass, Moss Twomey and Paddy Rigney would be the leaders of the Leinster Senior League. I would have placed myself near the bottom of that league.

Lemass had a quality most uncharacteristic of an IRA man of his time in that he was very careful of his appearance — no dirty trench coat and cloth cap for him. He was very well groomed — highly polished boots, leggings and Sam Browne, well-cut civilian suit and neatly tied tie and a hat. In the jails and camps, I believe, he paid the same attention to his appearance, regarding it as a morale builder. To do that was not easy in the circumstances and in itself marked him as an exceptional personality. It was also the outward manifestation of his orderly mind.

Meeting him here and there in 'safe houses' during the Civil War, when he was Director of Communications, he always gave the impression of a critical taciturnity; until he became Taoiseach he rather cultivated that taciturnity. As a minister he developed the technique of listening and saying nothing except 'quite' at intervals. This was disconcerting and could be very disheartening to enthusiasts with an idea or to suppliants looking for a tariff or grant. He rather enjoyed their discomfiture but quickly understood what they were about — he was unusually quick on the uptake — and even quicker at giving a decision. The ability to make a quick decision was his most valuable asset. He used to say he was a slapdash decision maker and probably he was. He had an amused contempt for colleagues or subordinates who were affected by *aboulia* — a word which always amused him. But his decisions, slapdash or not, produced Aer Lingus, Irish Shipping, the briquette factories, the power stations and the villages on the bogs, rural electrification and the whole fabric of modern Irish industry. Before him there was only the ESB and a vestigial beet sugar industry. In the government he was the defender and supporter of these enterprises and, if he was less of a socialist at the end of his career than he was at the beginning, he always regretted the failure of his efforts to bring the national oil supply under public control.

He gave the appearance of being almost totally without emotion, but his involvement in the problems of the old IRA and of the Dublin working people — from which the Dublin IRA was mainly drawn — belied that. He was certainly deeply committed emotionally to labour legislation. The Conditions of Employment Act, which he virtually wrote himself, will surely be part of his epitaph. He was deeply sympathetic to the trade unions and did everything to heal the split between the Congress of Irish Unions and the Irish Congress of Trade Unions. He always hoped that the chaotic conditions of the Irish unions would be reduced to order from within, and he would not contemplate any legislation which would reform them from without. In his dealings with the unions there seemed to be a lacuna in his mind; he displayed a sentimentality and naïveté that seemed to deny reason and ignore the public good. This was surprising because on other issues he never appeared either sentimental or naïve.

To his subordinates he was always civil, loyal and aloof; he did not believe in being too close to his staff. In matters of discipline involving human frailty he was understanding and uncensorious. He expected his staff to know that he appreciated their efforts, and indeed he did, but he had that inability to say thanks so common to Irish people. Hence he often appeared ungracious.

He rarely expressed resentments and kept clear of the Civil War recriminations which followed Fianna Fáil's entry into the Dáil. It was well known that the liquidation of the transatlantic airline and the tourist hotels by the first coalition bitterly disappointed him. At one point in his career he was the victim of a slander campaign which, through lack of truth and common decency, hurt him deeply. Like so many IRA men he despised intellectuals and academicians — and not without cause, considering how little they contributed to the setting up of the Republic and how much they contributed to its undoing.

He read widely in history and economics and was very well informed about the European and American political scene; he felt that we never got as much help as we deserved from the Irish in America and had not a high opinion of the utility of their political intervention in the homeland. He professed no real feeling for literature, art, music or the theatre and he often said that he would have liked the life of a research biologist. He had a total inability to suffer fools and hence he had the reputation amongst many people of being unapproachable. There was an exception to his reputation for unapproachability; all the members of his old pre-Truce Second Battalion and of the Four Courts' garrison were welcome to see him at any time and he was always ready to help them.

Punctuality was an obsession with him. So was thoroughness. He never accepted the proposition, so common among us 'Ah, sure it will do well enough'. The only prototype of Seán Lemass to be found in the history of Ireland is Wentworth.

His attitude to the Irish language has been called into question, and it is true that he did little about it, '*ach ní fhéadann an gobadán freastal ar an dá thrá*' and anyone who worked so hard at building the economic life of the country just had not the time to interest himself in the language. In fact, his heart was with Irish but he was not the man to carry the torch. The argufying, dissensions and cast of mind of the Gaeilgeoirí of the time would have been antipathetic to him.

His attitude to women in public life was not liberal — an attitude possibly derived from his experience with Cumann na mBan when Fianna Fáil was being formed. Cumann na mBan was extremely hostile to the New Departure and its advocacy of the policy of entering the Dáil. What was worse, from his point of view, its attitude appeared irrational and emotional. On the other hand, he appointed the first (and only) woman head of a government department.

He had little real rapport with rural Ireland and, considering the amount of travelling he did when building up the Fianna Fáil organisation, he had surprisingly little intimate knowledge of the countryside and its people. He was essentially the Dublin Jackeen with the ready wit and derisive humour so common in the city. In his later years he became an enthusiastic angler. He also became much more genial and approachable but I do not think he had any intimate friends. I had the impression that the only person outside his family to whom he was really close was Hugh Early, his driver during most of his official career.

To return to CIE: its origins go back to 1924 when twenty-six separate railway concerns were, by Act of the Oireachtas, amalgamated with the Great Southern Railway. The object of the amalgamation was to secure economies in operation and more cohesive management. It was hoped to arrest the progressive deterioration both in the finances and the services provided by the railways due to the competition of motor transport on the roads. Additional legislation was passed between 1924 and 1958 aimed at helping the railways to survive but despite the fact that private enterprise, at its freest, had control of the system until CIE was established with the merger of the Great Southern Railways and the Dublin United Tramway Company in 1944, the railways continued to decline.

Their failure to prevent the rot did not proportionately diminish the very high esteem the railway managers had of their own importance; they were the *crème de la crème* of the Irish business community. When Fianna Fáil came to power in 1932 the GSR directors asked Seán Lemass to meet them. Having agreed to accept the invitation he was informed that they had arranged to receive him in the board room at Kingsbridge at a given date and time. They had to be reminded that arrangements of this kind were not theirs but the minister's prerogative. They lived in a dead age.

The first chairman of Córas Iompair Éireann, Percy Reynolds, was so savaged by the political opponents of the government that he got no chance to make the necessary changes in the organisational structure. His successor, T. C. Courtney, with whom I had been closely associated on Hugo Flinn's turf executive, was not helped by the lack of firm direction from the government who were awaiting the report of the Beddy Commission. Nor was he helped by the hostility of the trade unions, his less-than-friendly relations with the civil servants and his inheritance from the war years of run-down equipment.

When I took over in 1958, the CIE board consisted of two retired trade union officials, the owner of a moderately-sized textile firm, a successful cattle dealer, a highly qualified engineer who described himself as a professional director and my predecessor as chairman who had retained his membership of the board.

I had only had a slight acquaintance with the board of the Tourist Association, the members of which received no remuneration for their services but enjoyed what little prestige was attached to their appointment; they took no part in the day-to-day running of the association. The board of the ESB, when I was employed there, consisted of a chairman who was full-time, three whole-time members and two part-time members. The whole-time members disliked one another with varying degrees of intensity. One of the part-time members despised all his colleagues equally and the other was indifferent to them. Bord na Móna presented still another variation on the theme in that it had a part-time chairman, a number of part-time members, and a full-time managing director. At one time I thought this to be the best possible combination but in fact it owed its success to the intimate relations and unity of purpose which characterised the members of the board. Bord na Móna was *sui generis*.

The part-time members of the boards of the semi-state companies are a variable commodity and are given their appointments for a variety of reasons. The commonest of these is that they have participated in or supported the activities of the political party in power, but frequently because they have subscribed heavily to political funds. Some are appointed because they are friends of particular ministers or TDs. A trade unionist is usually appointed for cosmetic reasons. From time to time an academic is appointed to provide an intellectual cachet or to reflect some cultural interest on the part of the minister concerned. Sometimes the statutes require that the government makes the appointment, sometimes a particular minister. It is not important. No appointment is ever made without the agreement of the Taoiseach and the government whatever the statutes say.

A practice had become common before I retired of appointing to semi-state boards retired civil servants who, when in office, dealt with the affairs of these same bodies. I think this is an objectionable practice. There is no reason why a retired civil servant from the Department of the Environment should not be appointed to CIE or Bord na Móna but it seems to me that there are evident reasons why a retired civil servant from the Department of Energy should not be appointed to the board of, say, the ESB. I think such appointments indicate a depreciation of the currency of public life. Equally, I regard it as bad in principle that the secretary of the Department of Finance should automatically become chairman or a member of the board of the Central Bank on his retirement.

Membership of a semi-state board confers distinction and status. That reward should be enough. I do not think that part-time board members should be paid. To many, if not to most of those appointed to these positions, the remuneration is of no significance in their total income. For others it is merely an agreeable supplement which they could well do without; no hardship would be caused to their families nor would it adversely affect their way of life. For the first years of its existence, the members of the Turf Development Board worked without payment and did so with enthusiasm and success. Even without remuneration it is certain that there would be no lack of suitable candidates for membership of semi-state boards — indeed it might lead to an improvement in present standards. Working on official commissions is a much more arduous task than working on these boards and there is never any difficulty in obtaining suitable honorary members.

The basic function of the board of a state-sponsored company is to ensure that the chief executive is carrying out the policy of the government as laid down in the statutes. It could not be repeated too often that in no sense are members of the boards of semi-state companies 'directors'; they 'direct' nothing. There are predictable outbursts of indignation from deputies (when they are in opposition) that the Oireachtas has no control over the semi-state companies. But the function of the boards of these companies is precisely this — to control them on behalf of the government and make them instruments of express government policy.

Experience soon confirmed my belief that the re-organisation of CIE was a crash operation which could not be successfully carried out unless, as was the position in my case, the chairman was chief executive; an operation of this kind required the virtually complete authority of one man. The board was, of course, entitled to be kept informed on what the chairman was doing; he could not take major decisions or spend large sums of money without reference to the board but the board was not in a strong position to oppose whatever line of action he adopted. In the event of serious fundamental disagreement between the board and the chief executive, I suppose either they or he would have to resign. In my term in CIE there were no such disagreements.

Seán Lemass's brother, Frank, was the general manager of CIE when I was appointed. He was a chartered accountant by profession and had been with CIE since its formation, having come in with the Dublin United Tramway Company in the 1944 amalgamation. He was a man of very high intelligence but had limited administrative experience. The many vicissitudes which confronted CIE had not afforded him a chance to give fully of the great talents which he had to offer. The ethos of the place did not encourage initiative. Fortunately for both of us, Frank Lemass and I established a close rapport from the beginning. He was much more knowledgeable than ever I could be about the detailed working of CIE and about transport in general. I never took an important decision without consulting him beforehand. Indeed I never took any such decision without discussing it in advance with the senior staff on whose area of responsibility it might impinge. But when a decision was taken I expected it to be accepted by everyone without further argument.

I approached the task of managing CIE with great confidence, and with a lot of goodwill from the public, the civil servants and the trade unions. The Irish Transport and General Workers' Union wrote to welcome me and wish me well. Jim Larkin junior, of the Workers' Union of Ireland, whom I knew slightly, called on me. He was far and away the most competent, best trained and most intelligent of the trade union leaders with whom I came in contact. He was a very tough negotiator but deals made with him stuck. Unfortunately his union had very few members in CIE.

There were 20,000 employees in CIE. The company's operations extended into the remote reaches of the country. Every skill and trade was represented in its work force. My first act was to visit all the major railway and road transport centres and as many of the smaller installations as time permitted. I saw and spoke to as many of the staff as possible. I made a particular point of visiting the bus depots in Dublin. Being reared largely in Terenure amongst employees of the Dublin United Tramway Company, I regarded the busmen as my own people.

I returned from my tour with two impressions. The first

concerned the physical condition of the plant. The exterior of the buildings bore evidence of decay, office equipment was mostly obsolete and in some cases the premises appeared not to have been cleaned for years. In an office attached to one of the larger stations there was a wall full of cubby holes stuffed with delivery dockets dating from before the First World War. At every station there were masses of valuable scrap material including in some cases obsolete steam engines of which the copper alone would fetch a high price. At Inchicore we had the largest engineering workshop in Ireland. It was just a like a scrap yard. Even the latrines were open-ended which meant that the backsides of the men at stool were visible to everyone. The stores had stocks of materials which had not moved for generations. They included hot water bottles which had been used to heat the feet of first-class passengers before the introduction of central heating.

It was clear to me that, as a priority, the appearance of the company premises required improvement if for no other reason than to indicate to the public and to the staff, whose morale was not of the highest, that a change was on the way. We had the buildings painted outside and inside. Station masters were encouraged to cultivate their gardens and good housekeeping was insisted on. It took a long time to get rid of the obsolete engines, miscellaneous scrap, useless stores and accumulated apparatus. The task was finally accomplished by detaching an engineer and giving him carte blanche to dispose of the junk in any way he judged fit and at any price he could get. Much of it was a hangover from the major railway companies amalgamation of 1924 and the change-over from steam to diesel locomotion.

The second fact that I observed in the course of my initial tour was that there was in CIE a reservoir of unused talent with no outlet. There was no shortage of ideas and honest effort but it lacked direction and co-ordination. In management terms it did not make sense that the four main branches of the organisation — the rail and road passenger and freight services — should be working in the same territory but without any real local liaison. In addition there was virtually no devolved responsibility; if a clerk was wanted at an office in Tralee or Galway, permission for the appointment had to be obtained from headquarters in Dublin. I also noticed that for an organisation involving so much engineering work few professional engineers were employed.

Clearly a fundamental re-organisation of the management system was called for. So the country was divided into five areas each of which would be controlled by an area manager with complete personal responsibility for the activities of the company within his jurisdiction. The areas were in turn broken down into a number of sub-areas to be run by district managers who were also given a large degree of local autonomy. Of the original area managers appointed, three were mechanical engineers by profession and one a chartered accountant; all of these were recruited outside the organisation. The fifth was a member of the existing staff who had exceptional qualifications in the theory and practice of transport.

Before being assigned to their posts they worked together for six months on a specially designed training course during which they visited all the major installations of CIE, spent some time in the different head office departments and completed their training by spending a month each with the Netherlands and Swiss railways. They were an enthusiastic group and succeeded in making their enthusiasm felt throughout the organisation. We employed a firm of industrial consultants to set up the local office administration and to produce the necessary documentation including management accounting and budgetary control systems.

At headquarters two deputy general managers were appointed, one to co-ordinate the work of the areas and another to deal with the central services — accounts, personnel and commercial departments. The public relations department was strengthened and its functions expanded. The CIE hotels were extended and modernised. A central planning office was established to control the integration of rail and road services and a research and development unit to investigate the introduction of more efficient handling and transport technology. A training centre was set up in Dublin which provided courses in marketing, hotel management, public relations, work study and languages. All middle management staff were required to attend these courses. The training centre encouraged the use of Irish throughout the organisation and used only Irish in its internal day-to-day work. That I regarded as a considerable advance on our efforts to promote the use of Irish in Bord na Móna. The internal training system was a little publicised feature of CIE but it was operated by the director, Micheál Ó Cíosóig, with enthusiasm and proficiency and contributed greatly to building up a highly competent staff at all levels. The skills so acquired were disseminated through the national economy when outside firms began to draw on the wealth of managerial talent which could be tapped from CIE. As time went on some of the most important management positions in the private and public sectors were filled by CIE personnel.

It was a radical re-organisation in that it introduced for the first time into the national transport service a system of decentralised and devolved management. Not the least of its effects was the great boost it gave to staff morale. Hitherto the promotion process in CIE was slow and limited. Now staff, whose highest ambition might have been to become chief station master at Kingsbridge, found themselves men of authority in the local administration of the company and men of consequence in their communities.

The 1958 Transport Act had incorporated the principal recommendations of the Beddy Commission in regard to the future operations of CIE. The act, among other things, abolished the 'common carrier' obligations which meant in practical terms that the company was able to trade freely and compete for business by the introduction of a flexible rating system. CIE was also empowered to close down sections of the line which were unlikely ever to prove economic. To meet the cost of the re-organisation particularly in the matter of redundancies CIE was to receive an annual subvention of £1.75 millions for a period of five years after which it was expected to be in a position to pay its way.

Side by side with the establishment of the new management structure we launched an intensive sales campaign in search of new traffic. Important new freight contracts were secured with the help of package deals, passenger traffic was stimulated by the development of special fares and charters and the opportunities created by CIE's new commercial freedom were fully exploited. The dieselisation of the locomotive system was completed and the pruning of unprofitable operations made it possible to effect many economies in manpower. The workforce was reduced by over two thousand men with the benefit of what were, for the time, exceptionally high redundancy payments. Business took up, the standing of the company was greatly enhanced as the fruits of the re-organisation became apparent to the public in the form of new and more efficient transport services. By 1961 we were within a quarter of a million pounds of breaking even financially.

We received a good press. The newspapers gave full recognition for the success of our efforts. When we boasted that we got the trains to run on time they refrained from exclaiming Mussolini! The approbation of the newspapers added greatly to the internal morale and self-confidence of the staff; they felt that they formed part of an organisation which was publicly respected. We never, to the extent I could prevent it, used the word 'image' in CIE. In my opinion the creation of 'images' in business and in public life is too often what the dictionary defines it — an artifical representation of the object. There is a suggestion of fraudulence about the process. Politicians are successful or otherwise depending on how they deport themselves on TV; acting ability becomes a necessary qualification. Beer advertisements on TV create the fantasy of the primrose path of dalliance with the promise of a woman at the end of it. The performer has become a cult figure irrespective of his real merits.

Under earlier legislation the two canal systems had been acquired by the state and their ownership vested in CIE. By this time all commercial traffic on the canals had ceased and it was clear that as a means of transport of commodities they were obsolete. Their enforced acquisition was nothing but an economic burden which should never had been inflicted on CIE. By 1961 the financial position of CIE had improved to the extent that we felt some money could be devoted to the development of the canals for amenity purposes at least in Dublin. I saw the city manager and proposed that CIE would landscape the canal banks from Ringsend to Inchicore if the corporation would agree to maintain them. We would also undertake to keep the canal channel clean. My proposal, which I recall was made over lunch in the old Red Bank restaurant, was drowned in a deluge of official verbosity. Any further interest I had in the matter was directed to getting responsibility for maintaining the canals transferred to the Office of Public Works. I did not succeed.

Seán Lemass became Taoiseach in 1959. His first cabinet differed very little either in personnel or ethos from those appointed by Dev but it only lasted a couple of years. Jack Lynch, as Minister for Industry and Commerce, was responsible for CIE during my first two years in office. When, after the election of 1961, Seán Lemass became his own man a difference in the *modus operandi* of government was noticeable. The setting up of the Ministry of Transport and Power and the appointment of Erskine Childers as minister and Dr Thekla Beere as secretary was not unwelcome to me. I knew both of them very well. Erskine did not enjoy the same measure of esteem among his colleagues in government or the officials in the various government departments as he did among the public. He was inclined to write long letters of advice or comment to his colleagues on matters affecting their departments which aroused amusement rather than annoyance. He felt, because of his Cambridge accent and general sophistication, that he was regarded as a political outsider in which feeling I think he was right. Erskine loved public speaking and spoke beautifully. In the beginning he was inclined to interfere personally in the management of the state-sponsored bodies and once was humourless enough to declare that he would like to act as chief executive to all of them simultaneously. A ministerial role of that kind was neither practical nor legal. Whatever his shortcomings he was very loyal to and strongly supported all the companies that came within the jurisdiction of the Department of Transport and Power.

Thekla Beere who became secretary of the new department was a rare woman. The daughter of a clergyman she had put herself through Trinity College by scholarships. She was a Protestant who had integrated with not merely the Irish state but the Irish nation. Amongst her other distinctions she was a founder of *An Óige*. She was a hard worker and liked by her colleagues. Her promotion to the post of departmental secretary aroused no criticism or jealousy. Everyone was pleased at the appointment because she was a woman and a Protestant. If she had been passed over everyone would have said it was either because she was a woman or a Protestant or both. She was a friend of mine and while theoretically the executive of CIE need have little contact with the civil servants it would be the unwise chairman who stood on his rights and ignored them.

Apart from the effect of the new Department of Transport and Power, a change in the style of government was noticeable. I was acquainted in a personal way with all the members of the early Fianna Fáil cabinets and some of them were my very close friends. Over the years I never heard one of them make an adverse comment on their colleagues although I knew, as did many others in the public service, that all was not sweetness and light among them. They didn't all love one another as brothers but they acted, as far as outsiders were concerned, as if they did. They were tied by a powerful bond of loyalty, shared experience and personal affection for Dev. No such considerations pervaded the successive cabinets of Seán Lemass. Snide remarks about one another were common enough. Accounts of cabinet proceedings were leaked and often discussed with outsiders. In Dev's time it would be impossible to imagine cabals in either the cabinet or the party but they were certainly organised during Seán Lemass's time. These cabals were not organised against Lemass himself. His prestige was too great and he was not likely to be diverted from his purpose by threats of resignation. Patrick Smith, the Minister for Agriculture, had his resignation accepted and his place filled with a promptitude typical of Lemass. But there was always personal tension in his cabinet which finally crystallised in the contest for the succession.

In my opinion Seán Lemass came too late to power. He was a tired man. Furthermore he had not behind him the sort of disinterested advice which the leader of any large scale organisation requires and which he had enjoyed through all his ministerial life in the person of John Leydon. Collective responsibility was not one of the principles of government to which Seán Lemass subscribed. He came to office a poor man and was a poor man when he left it but in his later years he accepted the ability to make money as a criterion of success in others. It is a standard which enables successful businessmen and speculators to buy their way into politics. I do not think that any politician of any party ever received a personal bribe but I do believe that heavy subscriptions to party funds have redounded to the benefit of the subscribers.

The 1957 report of the Beddy Commission evisaged a substantial reduction in railway mileage the closure of uneconomic sections of the line. For years Frank Lemass had been pointing to the need for this reduction but the complex procedures involved and the likelihood of strong local opposition prevented CIE from taking action. The 1958 Act gave CIE a free hand to close down lines and stations for which it saw no prospect of economic operation, provided satisfactory alternative road transport services were made available.

An investigation of uneconomic routes and services was begun in 1959. The investigation followed a set procedure. Before any proposal to close down a line or station was submitted to the board a study in depth was made of its current performance together with an appraisal of its future prospects in traffic and financial terms. Enquiries were addressed to government departments and local bodies seeking information about any future developments which might affect its potential. CIE had to give an assurance that there would be sufficient road transport facilities to ensure a satisfactory substitute service.

Following these criteria a list was prepared of the lines most likely to prove irremediable. At the head of this list was the Harcourt/Shankill branch which was closed down early in 1959. Not surprisingly, since the service was used to a negligible extent, its closure evoked virtually no comment or criticism except from the *Irish Press* which seemed to have developed a sentimental interest in the line. Over the following two years about half a dozen additional branch lines were abandoned. Here again the decision gave rise to nothing in the form of public protest or resistance. There seemed to be general acceptance that the lines in question had outlived their usefulness and could no longer be justified.

When, however, the proposed closedown of the West Cork, West Clare and Waterford/Tramore lines was announced early in 1961 loud agitation broke out. In the case of West Clare the campaign was relatively light-hearted. It amounted to an appeal that the line be retained as a memorial to Percy French who had immortalised it in a ballad with the famous refrain, 'Are you right there, Michael, are you right?' In Waterford the agitation, though noisy, was not taken up seriously by the general public who were well aware that the line no longer served any valid purpose.

In West Cork the resistance was of a different kind. Local politicians, traders and professional people launched an organised attack on the competence and motivation of CIE. The campaign had the blessing of the Church. Protest meetings were held and CIE was bombarded with demands for a stay of execution. Political pressure was brought to bear on members of the government to support the retention of the line. My telephone brought endless calls from interested parties to receive deputations. One TD was particularly offensive. I heard him out politely until I thought he had outstepped the bounds of toleration at which point I replied in kind. I made an exact note of the dialogue including my own scatological advice to the man concerned and sent it to our minister, Erskine Childers, with a protest that I was not paid to take abuse from Dáil deputies.

Our refusal to receive deputations from members of the Oireachtas and local councils was represented as 'an attack on the democratic process'. That phrase was to me a very weary cliché in the vocabulary of agitation. Two other popular clichés of abuse 'dictator' and 'fascist' were freely used. At this stage the campaign changed its character and became something of a contest of wills. Some people seemed more concerned with overcoming the refusal of CIE to receive deputations than with the actual preservation of the line. I was well aware that a number of ministers and their official advisers considered our attitude to be unduly stiff necked. One of the top civil servants went out of his way to remind me of the appropriateness of the Latin proverb *Suaviter in modo, fortiter in re.*

Fortunately our stand in this matter was fully supported by Erskine Childers and the Department of Transport and Power. The 1958 Transport Act had been passed almost unanimously by the Oireachtas and CIE had been given the task of carrying out its provisions including the closure of manifestly uneconomic services. Having reached a decision on the objective merits of the case to abandon a particular line it was the duty of CIE to give effect to this decision without deferring to local pressure groups in the interests of political codology. We felt it to be intolerable that deputies, who by definition are assumed to be persons of responsibility, should take part in local agitations aimed at frustrating policies laid down by the legislature. Some must have known full well that the West Cork line had seen its day but were not above scoring political points and winning some local popularity at the expense of CIE. I was transmuted by them from a 'fascist' to a 'communist', but remained a dictator.

How often during my lifetime have I seen misguided efforts of this kind played out to a fruitless conclusion. I think it is the duty of public representatives to tell people the truth rather than encourage them to develop grievances based on incorrect information or misdirected emotion. Their attitude in this case could not be excused by lack of information because whenever services were discontinued CIE took steps, by pamphlet and newspaper advertisement, to make the public fully aware of the grounds for the decision. Usually these agitations were initiated by a small number of people.

Continuing studies disclosed several additional sections of the railway network where the revenue earned fell short of even their direct operating costs and during the next two years a dozen branch lines were abandoned and others had their services curtailed. In general these closures provoked no significant protest. Even those people immediately affected were disposed to accept that decisions of this importance were not taken by CIE capriciously and simply for the sake of change. Furthermore it had to be conceded, on the basis of any fair assessment, that the substitute road services were adequate and efficient, that the travelling public suffered no real inconvenience and that no local development was adversely affected. To quote from an *Irish Times* leader writer:

> The fact must be faced that small lines carrying little traffic are uneconomic and that their work can be done more efficiently as well as more cheaply by buses and lorries. These small lines, if allowed to remain, constitute a drag on the national transport at large; the great excess of them in Ireland thirty or forty years ago contributed greatly to the financial ruin of the Great Southern Railway. It is easy to plead, but far from easy to prove, that they possess an 'invisible value' in that they act as feeders to the main lines. Even in that capacity they are far more expensive than road services which, in nine cases out of ten, can do the same work more satisfactorily. Compared with a bus journey these little local services are often picturesque, free and easy and lovable but that is all that can be said of them.

Disappointment

When I took over CIE as chairman, I was aware that the relations between the company and the trade unions were not good; it was a fact which had received much newspaper publicity. I was warned by the civil servants who were closely associated with the affairs of CIE of the advisability, as a first step in my regime, of changing the CIE personnel dealing with labour relations. In Bord na Móna the unionisation process had developed slowly due to the widely scattered nature of the bogs, the seasonality of the work and the fact that most of the workers had a rural background. This did not, of course, mean freedom from labour difficulties. For example, there was much resistance initially to the application of piece rates to bog work and later on the agitation led by the demagogue, Seán Dunne, caused serious disruption among the Kildare hostel workers. But with the help of a well-organised conciliation procedure, most of the disputes which arose were settled locally and head-on confrontations with the unions, who were eventually persuaded to organise the workers, were normally avoided. In the first twenty years of Bord na Móna's existence there was never an official strike.

I went into CIE with a determination that, whatever else worked, good labour relations practice would prevail. I knew the unions were satisfied with my appointment as chairman. But I had the naïve belief that the unions' attitude towards the great semi-state bodies like the ESB, Bord na Móna, Aer Lingus and CIE corresponded with my own. To me these were nationally owned and community based enterprises. I thought that the unions accepted these organisations as being in a different category from private businesses or public companies. It was not until the finances of CIE and its standing with the public showed a radical improvement in 1961 that I realised how wrong I was.

There were early signs of trouble ahead. I had barely arrived at Kingsbridge when the Irish Transport and General Workers Union demanded additional money because the capacity of the Dublin buses had been increased from 78 to 84 seats. It did not seem to me a good reason for increasing wages. It was my first lesson in the principle of labour management which says that no change, however trivial, can be made in working arrangements without a demand for increased pay. I had taken the civil service advice and brought in different CIE personnel to handle the negotiations. It seemed to have been a successful move because a satisfactory arrangement was reached amid mutual congratulations between the new regime and the ITGWU.

Unfortunately the union came back a week later to tell us that the men would not accept the settlement. I could not understand this change of front. I thought that once agreement had been reached with their representatives the deal was final. It was explained to me that the negotiators were not the union; the last word lay with the union membership and the settlement terms had been rejected after a ballot of the men concerned. It followed that the negotiations did not resume at the point in the wage structure from which they originally started but rather from the point where they left off.

With that sort of negotiation CIE had no chance. The management were on a hiding to nothing. The amount involved in this instance was relatively trivial and was not worthwhile bringing to an issue. The effect the incident had on me was to diminish my trust and sympathy with the unions or rather with the ITGWU.

But, by and large, with interest focused on the internal re-organisation, the opportunities for promotion and the growth in the staff morale and in public esteem, we had a quiet time on the labour front until early in 1961. Some months earlier the unions had presented us on behalf of the bus crews with a claim for increased pay for weekend working which we considered unjustified and rejected. The unions brought the matter to the Labour Court for investigation. A state organisation like CIE is bound morally, if not legally, to accept the findings of the Labour Court — largely in our favour as it happened — and this we did. The unions rejected the Labour Court award and made it clear that if their demands were not fully met future weekend services would cease. The Minister for Industry and Commerce, Jack Lynch, summoned the union and ourselves to a conference aimed at averting the strike. (Strikes are never stopped, they are only averted.) The intervention of a minister in a strike involving a semi-state body, after the Labour Court has adjudicated on the matter, could only have the effect of diminishing the authority of the court and of encouraging the unions to hold out for better terms. Ministers I found from experience to be primarily concerned to get strikes — particularly those in public utilities — off their backs allowing them to revert to more agreeable political activities. In this case the minister's intervention dissipated any hope of having the Labour Court award accepted. Ministers' interventions in strikes can never be anything but disastrous.

The conference went on for hours with constant repetition less of arguments than of *ex parte* assertions. By the time 1 a.m. was reached I felt too exhausted to continue but in reply to my plea for an adjournment, John Conroy, the president of the Transport Union, retorted, 'Let's work on through the night. It is too important a public issue for officials to spare themselves.' As I well knew, the senior staff of CIE had for months on end been working a twelve hour day, many of them a seven day week, so this unctuous display of public spiritedness left me unimpressed. It took me some years to learn, vicariously I may say, that this tactic of 'working through the night' is a common and not ineffective form of union pressure on parties involved in industrial disputes.

In an effort to reach a settlement we offered a further increase on the terms recommended by the Labour Court but the unions would accept nothing short of their original demand. The issue involved was not so much a wage claim as such but how far the bus crews were entitled to be compensated for working 'unsocial hours'. The unions laid much emphasis on the inconvenience to the men's families caused by weekend working and as one of them said to me as an afterthought 'and then of course there is the religious dimension', a remark which forced me to laugh in his face. He had the grace to laugh too. In fact, far from having conscientious objections, the men prized weekend working greatly.

We could not accept that it was reasonable for the employees of an essential public service to choose when they would or would not work. I warned the unions that if the men refused to undertake weekend duty they would be locked out and this was what happened. The minister made a last minute bid to break the deadlock with a proposal to refer the case to an independent arbitrator whose verdict would be binding on both sides but this was also rejected by the unions.

The unions had good reason to think that we would not enforce the threatened lock-out. 'Lock-out' was a dirty word in Dublin since the days of William Martin Murphy before the First World War and not merely in the ranks of the trade unionists but among the public at large. For someone like me whose normal sympathies would be with the bus workers — many of whom I had grown up with in Terenure, many of whom were with me in the IRA — to take such a decision produced a severe cauterising of conscience. The fact is that we in CIE thought the union leaders did not seriously believe in the merits of their case and were giving no guidance to their members. We believed too that the proposed weekend strike was an easy way for the union to have its meat and its manners. It could stage a cheap strike, showing militant leadership, without dipping into its very substantial fund for strike pay.

The lock-out started and gave the political opposition and all the loud-mouths in the country an opportunity to invoke the names of Big Jim Larkin and William Martin Murphy and draw analogies between 1913 and 1961, between the Dublin United Tramway Company of that day and the new CIE. This analogy was particuarly distressing for me. I was by conviction a Jeffersonian democrat. I believed that 'all men are created equal'. I believed too that we had in Ireland a classless society except for the remnants of the Anglo-Irish gentry, and their imitators. After the Treaty many of these left; those who remained, with some notable exceptions, accepted the state but rejected the nation. The Free State regime warmly adopted this alien element, gave them seats in the Senate and proceeded to re-build a native ascendancy around them. The election of a Fianna Fáil government in 1932 put a stop to this process. This restoration of the classless society is one of its rarely recognised contributions to the national well-being. What class consciousness exists in Irish society is merely tuppence halfpenny looking down on tuppence.

As well as being a Jeffersonian democrat, I was a socialist and regarded the semi-state industries as socialism in its practical form. For me the public service was the most honourable form of employment and I looked on CIE as the property of the whole nation. I felt that the trade unions should recognise that the board and management of CIE and the other semi-state companies were of the same social origin as themselves and had nothing to gain by treating their employees unfairly. That was not the view of the president of the ITGWU, John Conroy. He once told me that if CIE treated its workers like human beings all would be well.

The bus stoppage went on for a month with the political pressure on the government mounting all the time until finally the Taoiseach, Seán Lemass, decided that the lock-out should be lifted and the bus services restored. Jack Lynch phoned me to say that 'the Boss' (i.e. Lemass) wanted me to take the men back. I told him I would refuse to do so unless I got a directive either from the Taoiseach or from himself as Minister for Industry and Commerce to end the lock-out and that the terms of the directive be published. At Lynch's suggestion I decided to discuss the position personally with the Taoiseach and reiterated my demand for a formal public directive. I said to Lemass that in every man's life there comes a time when he must make a stand. There would be no compromise on the question of the lock-out unless it was made clear that the decision had been taken out of the hands of CIE.

I was playing from strength. For the first time in my life I did not have to take my livelihood into account in arriving at decisions; I was entitled to a pension. Besides, the bonds of mutual respect which had long existed between us would have made Lemass reluctant to force the issue to the point of refusal. Moreover the acknowledged revivification of CIE from its moribund condition made him even more hesitant to bring about the chairman's dismissal. With typical decision, without discussion, he said, 'All right. I'll tell the minister to issue the directive.' When I got back to my office there was a message from Jack Lynch asking me to come to see him. We agreed on the form of the directive and he promised to send it to the press. Later he phoned to say that he had read over the directive to 'the Boss' who agreed with the wording but did not think it was necessary to publish it. I replied that unless it was published the lock-out would not be lifted by me. He phoned me back again in due course to say that publication had been arranged.

With the creation of the new Department of Transport and Power in 1961 responsibility for CIE passed to Erskine Childers. I welcomed this arrangement because it seemed to me that Jack Lynch was not particularly interested in the affairs of CIE, finding it a political burden. I got the impression that he found me also something of a burden; my abrasive manner was offensive to his nice, gentle personality.

Work was resumed but a legacy of bad feeling persisted between CIE and the union leadership, particularly with John Conroy. Conroy was quite untypical of the great union traditions established by Big Jim Larkin, O'Brien, Foran, Tom Kennedy and the other founders of the trade union movement in Dublin. He had become a Buggin's turn president of the ITGWU, moving up the ranks. He was a man of narrow integrity. He would not accept a lift from any member of the CIE management for fear of being compromised in the eyes of his colleagues although they had no such scruples. Conroy's predecessor as president of the ITGWU, William McMullan, was a member of the board of CIE at this time. Conroy conceded nothing to the idea that companies owned by the state were different from private business. He could not accept that the board, management and staff who were running CIE were his own people writ slightly larger. Conroy's frame of mind exasperated me. In his eyes all employers were enemies. His idea of trade unionism, it seemed to me, had not developed from the nineteenth century.

In the years that followed conflict recurred between CIE and the bus workers. After three years of discussion with the unions we decided in 1962 to introduce one-man bus operation starting with private hire and day-tour coaches where the use of conductors or couriers was clearly superfluous. Generous terms had been offered including a guarantee of no redundancy or loss of earnings, increased pay for the drivers and a clear limitation on the type of service to which the new crewing arrangement would apply. The result was a lightning and unofficial strike which halted bus services totally in Dublin and partially in the provinces in a week. The unions having first refused to countenance the strike eventually decided to make it official and it was on this basis and a promise of Labour Court intervention that a return to work was achieved.

In the Labour Court hearings that followed the unions not only accepted the principle of one-man bus operation but also the terms under which it would be applied. When, however, a year later the next stage of the new manning arrangement, extending it to a number of scheduled provincial routes, was reached the union refused to honour the agreement unless it was guaranteed substantial improvements in fringe benefits for all bus workers. CIE refused to give way to this quite arbitrary demand whereupon the unions withdrew their labour leaving the country without bus services for nearly six weeks. The strike ended with the establishment of a joint commission to investigate the claim for improved fringe benefits. In effect it took four years of continuous effort including every known form of negotiation, conciliation and Labour Court mediation, as well as two strikes, before CIE succeeded in implementing the one-man bus programme on a limited scale. The blame for this debacle must lie squarely with the unions which failed to carry out their agreement and gave no real leadership to the men.

The Worker's Union of Ireland headed by James Larkin junior had relatively few members in CIE but enough to provide a base for expansion and there was something of a groundswell among the bus workers in favour of transferring to Larkin's union. I myself suggested that he should make a bid to absorb the entire bus crew membership but he felt that this would place too great a strain on the resources of his small union. Eventually there was so much dissatisfaction with the ITGWU that a section broke away to form the National Busmen's Union.

I remember once suggesting in the course of a talk with Larkin that there was no labour relations problem that could not be solved if all concerned acted on the basis of reason. He replied sardonically that if reason prevailed in Ireland we would become a country with a very prosperous population of a million people living off the cattle trade. On this or some other occasion I expressed regret at his decision to leave politics. He told me that the choice was not his; he had been forced out of politics by the right wing of the Labour party and specifically by those who were associated with the first coalition government.

I believe that any successful organisation must be pyramidal in form. At its apex must be one man or woman whose decision is final. Two American presidents expressed this principle in different ways: Truman when he said, 'The buck stops here'; and Lincoln who, when some proposal had been discussed by his cabinet and unanimously rejected in a vote around the table, announced, 'The ayes have it' — the 'ayes' being himself. This, in my belief, is the basic principle of management and it is something which the Irish trade union bosses lacked with the exception of James Larkin junior.

The ITGWU was the biggest union and the biggest single organisation in Ireland. There was no one in it who could say 'yea' or 'nay'. The union officials were not sufficiently trained in the management skills which a large organisation requires. Union staff as a whole held their posts or chances of promotion tenuously, walking on eggs in an effort to placate their members and divested of all real authority. It was difficult for the executives of semi-state companies to deal with trade unions of this provenance without often feeling a sense of despair or, to use that favourite trade union word, frustration. It seems to me that if the unions — and in this the ITGWU by reason of its size and resources should set a headline — spent money on the education and development of their future leaders rather than on financially rewarding projects such as the new Liberty Hall they would be better equipped to deal with labour problems and to obtain for their members a larger share of the national cake.

The establishment of the National Busmen's Union gave a new twist to the already complex labour relations situation in CIE. The busmen were now represented by no less than four separate bodies intensifying inter-union rivalry and making a unified approach to labour management almost impossible. It was further complicated by the fact that the NBU was not recognised by the CIE group of unions or by congress and even the Labour Court hesitated to deal with it officially. In 1965 the NBU started a series of one-day strikes in support of a claim for increased pay and a five-day week. We held this demand to be in breach of the national wage agreement and rather than allow these sporadic stoppages to continue it was decided to lock out the strikers. The other CIE unions, although not directly participating in the strike, refused to pass the NBU pickets causing a near total disruption of all public transport services for a period of three weeks. A settlement was reached, after Labour Court intervention, at some financial cost to CIE but nothing comparable to the extent of the original claim.

It inevitably had a carry-over effect. Within a year the Dublin city bus services were again grounded for two weeks by a strike of garage maintenance workers, initiated by the Worker's Union of Ireland and tacitly supported by their colleagues in the other three unions, in support of a claim for equivalent treatment to the bus men. Eventually a formula was worked out which provided for limited pay increases to the garage staff thinly disguised in the form of so-called performance allowances.

The immediate financial loss to CIE arising from these recurring stoppages was serious but more important was the lowering of morale within the organisation and of its standing in the public mind. Confidence in the reliability and efficiency of CIE services which had produced progressive growth in traffic in the preceding years was badly shaken. Our efforts to sell the concept of public transport as an acceptable alternative for road users and carriers no longer sounded credible.

Apart from the bus men, relations with other sections of the workforce were on the whole satisfactory. There were no less than thirty-two unions operating in CIE and it is a tribute to the labour liaison officers, who were appointed as part of the management re-organisation, that disputes other than those affecting the bus services were kept to a minimum. Their purpose was to keep the employees at all levels informed of the progress and future plans of the company and to invoke ideas for improvement of local work practices. There were in all thirty-seven joint consultative councils made up of employee and management representatives as well as a top consultative committee consisting of senior trade union and company executives with the general manager of CIE acting as chairman. Joint consultative councils were not an original conception of CIE; they derived from a movement started in England after the First World War. But whether because of the scale on which they were established or the vigour and effort with which they operated I know of no organisation which used them more advantageously than did CIE.

There is much discussion nowadays about worker representation on the boards of semi-state bodies. I would question whether such representation can be more effective in creating a sense of participation in the affairs of a company than a well-run joint consultative scheme. In any case I think it wrong in principle that shop-floor workers, or any other class of employees, should be treated as a special interest group entitled to separate board representation. There are no *prima facie* grounds for thinking that the mere fact of coming from the shop floor, or any other staff level, qualifies an employee to contribute a special wisdom to board deliberations. Part of an employee's obligation is to devote whatever talents he has to the betterment of the job. If he has anything of special merit to contribute the joint consultative council system will ensure that it is brought to light and used to the best advantage of all.

It is worth noting that the CIE board at this time included two men who had spent their lives in the trade union movement. J. T. O'Farrell had been executive secretary of the Transport Salaried Staffs' Association and William McMullan was a former president of the ITGWU. Neither of them saw himself as representing any special interest even though their natural sympathy would have been with the workers. No member of the board of a semi-state body is entitled to represent anything but himself nor should he have any role, outside the boardroom, in the running of the organisation unless such a role is required by statute.

O'Farrell and McMullan were the only two members with whom I had any close association outside the boardroom. Because of our joint involvement we travelled together to meetings of the Clearing House and the County Donegal Railways. They were to me the most entertaining companions. O'Farrell, by reason of his office, had formed close links with the trade union movement and the Labour party in England no less than in Ireland. He had been one of a trade union delegation which was brought as a propaganda exercise on a visit to the western front during the First World War. He had known J. H. Thomas, the Labour minister, who had inflicted the economic war on us in the thirties and had formed a very low opinion of him, correctly as it so happened, because Thomas was eventually forced out of public life for revealing cabinet secrets.

In 1920 O'Farrell had been connected with the organisation of the general strike which forced the British to release the hunger-strikers (of whom I was one) from Mountjoy Jail. I doubt whether he had supported it with much enthusiasm. He expressed the opinion that had the stoppage gone beyond the two days it actually lasted it could well have collapsed. I would hope that the diaries which he claimed to have kept dating back to the outbreak of the First World War have survived his death and find their way into the national archives because O'Farrell was a highly observant and reflective man. As a member of the first Free State Senate he was immensely proud to have been on terms of familiarity with the remnants of the Anglo-Irish gentry and even more pleased and flattered to have made the acquaintance of 'intellectuals' such as Yeats and Gogarty. He shared their personal loathing of Dev and regarded all Republicans, as they did, as little better than thugs. I was probably the first ex-IRA man ('Irregular' to him) with whom he had spoken since the Civil War. When I knew him first I think he half expected to find me fidgetting with my gun over coffee. But as time went on we became very friendly.

William McMullan, on our visits to his native Belfast, kept me regaled with tales about James Connolly, the 1916 leader who was executed after the Rising. As a young man he had met and worked with Connolly in Belfast trying, sometimes with success, to get Protestant and Catholic workers to make common cause against the bosses. As a Protestant, he had access to much inside information from loyalist sources about their pograms but despite his personal antagonism to these activities he had to be very careful in the face of the Orange gunmen and their paymasters.

McMullan's reminiscences, if ever they are published, should be revealing. If he is as frank on paper as he was in our conversations much light will be thrown on the operating methods of trade unions. He was particularly well informed about the split between

William O'Brien and Jim Larkin. Larkin was his great *bête noire;* he could discourse at great length on the subject of Larkin's iniquities and repeat himself at the least opportunity. Such opportunities arose at the monthly lunches which followed our board meetings. These functions followed a custom carried over from the days of the Great Southern Railway Company and were supposed to assuage any ill-feeling which might have arisen at the meeting. In my time as chairman I saw no ill-feeling so that in this sense at least our lunches served no particularly useful purpose.

Our failure to bring the bus workers along with us in the really massive effort to revive CIE was the biggest disappointment of my public service career. I found my inability to cope with them distressing especially since I believed them to be sound and enlightened nationally. Much of their waywardness — it could not be called militancy — was due to ineptitude and lack of union discipline but the attitude of the rank and file was sometimes so irrational that it suggested the possibility of contributory factors not easily discernible. I suggested to Fintan Kennedy, by this time president of the ITGWU and James Larkin junior of the WUI that CIE and the two unions should jointly commission the Tavistock Institute of Human Relations to make a study of the underlying causes of the poor morale of the busmen. The Irish National Productivity Council agreed to participate in the project. Dr Hans Van Beinum of the Dutch Board of the Tavistock Institute came to direct the investigation.

Dr Van Beinum's report did not throw much new light on the problem. Wages, as we suspected, were not the dominant issue; busmen's earnings were not bad by the public service standards of the time. The major sources of discontent seemed to derive from the stresses peculiar to the job itself and the demanding conditions under which the men worked, as well as lack of opportunities for advancement and promotion. Busmen do not appear to differ much from the rest of humanity in their motivation.

Working experience and personal observation over many years have convinced me that the trade union movement badly needs reorganisation if it is to be effective in serving its members and contributing to the national prosperity. As at present constituted, with as many as one hundred and twenty unions catering for a total membership of 300,000, it can do neither. Many trades are represented by two or more unions and the same applies to unskilled workers. This overlap of interests undermines both unity of purpose and of tactics. Switching of membership is a source of constant union friction and in the long run must make for weak leadership. The ideal of 'one big union', once so strongly advocated in trade union circles, seems to have been completely discarded. Nor can it be in the interest of either labour or the country that many of our unions are still foreign based. I consider this to be particularly unfortunate in the case of the National Union of Journalists whose members play a dominant role in forming public opinion in Ireland.

Another glaring weakness in trade union management is the failure to control picketing procedures or even more militant demonstrations such as 'sit-ins'. There can be no objection to respecting a picket placed in pursuance of an official strike. But unless the unions insist on their members ignoring and indeed condemning unofficial picketing there can be little hope of orderly development of labour relations. The unofficial strike supported, as it so often is, by a near mystical respect of the picket line is an evil in the body politic and should be treated as such. It is capable of doing great harm to workers not involved in the dispute, to the public at large and to respect for union authority. All this is, no doubt, widely recognised within the trade union movement but it lacks the strength to apply the necessary constraints internally. For that reason I believe that the community has a right to demand that unofficial strikes should be banned legally. Clearly this could not be done without trade union agreement and support but it is a development which would probably be welcomed by many trade unionists as it certainly would be approved by the general public.

These weaknesses in trade union management and organisation were at the root of the labour problems which beset CIE in my time. They were certainly not due to the 'reds under the bed' or Communist influence, such as the unions' spiritual advisers in Merchant's Quay were prone to suggest. Nor do I think they were caused by any failure on the part of CIE management which since the company's inception had always followed enlightened labour policies.

*   *   *   *   *

From the Great Southern Railways CIE inherited hotels in Galway, Killarney, Kenmare, Parknasilla, Mulrany and Sligo. From the Great Northern Railway it inherited a hotel in Bundoran. As in the case of the canals CIE should never had been burdened with these subsidiary enterprises although, unlike the canals, the hotels made a profit. The functional relationship between the Railway companies and the hotels ceased once the bus and the motor car took over the type of tourist who at one time travelled by rail and for whose use the hotels were designed. However, they were still valuable assets and as part of the re-organisation programme which followed the 1958 Transport Act we decided to enlarge and modernise them in order to cater for the increased traffic which the tourist industry was endeavouring to develop. For decoration purposes we were able to avail ourselves of the Arts Council scheme under which modern Irish paintings were supplied at high price for display in public buildings. The scheme gave a considerable boost to Irish artists and we were proud to be associated on a large scale with it. It was decided to hive off the hotels to a specially-formed subsidiary company called Óstlanna Iompair Éireann.

The Ulster Transport Authority had inherited four hotels from the Great Northern Railway but had done nothing to modernise them. I had established close personal links with Sir Arthur Algeo, the chairman of the UTA, and we often discussed areas of mutual co-operation which might be of advantage to our two companies. It occurred to me that one obvious method was to amalgamate the two hotel groups.

I raised the matter with the Taoiseach, Seán Lemass, and with our minister, Erskine Childers, and both felt that the project was worth pursuing. I was authorised to approach the UTA with two options; we would buy their hotels for £1 million (a figure rather above their market value) or we would set up a joint company with equal shares to operate the hotels, north and south, as an integrated group. Algeo strongly supported the idea of amalgamation and he personally favoured the second of the two proposals but the deal was, of course, subject to the agreement of his political superiors. The minister responsible for UTA affairs in the Six Country government was William Craig who indicated privately to Algeo that he would not be wholly opposed to the idea of the joint venture.

As a next step Mary and I were invited, not for the first time, to spend a fishing weekend at Algeo's home in Ballymoney and it was arranged that Craig and his wife would meet us for Sunday lunch. In the course of the afternoon drive around the countryside the minister, Algeo and myself had a further discussion on the hotel project.

Craig's view was that this was the kind of co-operation between north and south which should be encouraged. He did not think there was any political principle involved and undertook to put the proposal before his government colleagues at Stormont. Unfortunately they were not equally open-minded. Approval could not be obtained for either of our proposals and the idea was summarily dropped. The UTA hotels were subsequently sold to an English hotel group for £600,000.

I had excellent relations with Sir Arthur Algeo's other UTA colleagues. They were always co-operative and friendly. They showed an interest in happenings in Dublin and often visited the city not only for events such as the Horse Show, the Spring Show, the big race meetings and rugby internationals, but also for occasional theatre outings and art exhibitions. I had the impression that in many ways they were envious of life in Dublin and, dyed-in-the-wool Unionists though they were, regarded Dublin rather than London as their capital city. Orangemen or not, they never appeared to me to be hyphenated Scots-Irish; even less did they appear to me to be Englishmen. Indeed I often detected evidence of resentment against the English officials who virtually controlled their public service. I certainly never felt alien to them. I recall being entertained at his house in Derry by a leading member of the Orange Order and was amused rather than repelled by his innocent pride in his collection of Orange regalia.

When Queen's University conferred an honorary Doctorate of Economic Science on me the Stormont government gave an official dinner to the honorary graduands on that occasion at which the prime minister, then plain Terence O'Neill, presided and Mary, my wife, was his dinner partner. A fellow graduand was Yehudi Menuhin whom we met again at a reception and lunch given by the university. Menuhin and his wife were charming and unassuming people. In an after-dinner speech Menuhin demonstrated that he was not only a great musician but also a philosopher who exuded love of humanity and a desire to improve the human condition. At the official dinner which was attended by most of the Stormont cabinet Mary and I were treated with friendliness and courtesy by our hosts. The one exception was Brian Faulkner who later succeeded Terence O'Neill as prime minister and met his own political downfall in the aftermath of the Sunningdale Agreement. Our introduction to him was less than agreeable; on learning that we were from Dublin he barely acknowledged our existence and curtly turned away.

The people I met and knew in Belfast while chairman of CIE were members of the northern establishment. But at another level in CIE close connections developed between Belfast and Dublin. Since the 1960s the CIE and UTA busmen have together organised weekend social outings rotating the venue annually between the two cities. These visits include a soccer competition played for the 'Inter-City Transport Trophy' followed by a dinner and cabaret. Customarily many of the visitors are accommodated in the homes of their colleagues over the weekend. Some of the Dublin bus depots such as Ringsend and Conyngham Road have established special links with their opposite numbers at Ardoyne and Smithfield in Belfast. Despite the political upheaval in 1968 this camaraderie between the bus workers continued. It would surely be helpful if people in other walks of life followed the example of the CIE busmen in making similar reciprocal arrangements. I am sure the Belfast and Dublin busmen suffer no loss of cultural identify as a result of their cross-border excursions.

The conclusion, it seems to me, to be drawn from my contacts with the northern establishment and business dealings with my UTA colleagues is that as Irishmen we got on perfectly well together. Our common nationality forges a powerful bond of mutual understanding and appreciation. England continues over the centuries to be the source of our political ills. Given a British withdrawal with benevolent goodwill, I believe an accommodation could be reached with our northern fellow countrymen. The political divisions between us may be rooted longer in history but in other respects the situation is not much different from that which De Gaulle found, and for which he provided a solution, in Algeria. At least in Ireland there is no colour bar to national unity.

But I doubt whether we who look forward to that unity have given sufficient thought to the price which may have to be paid for it. I believe that our constitution, particularly as it has been interpreted by the Supreme Court over the years, has served its purpose well. But some of its provisions would be unacceptable to the Protestant community of Northern Ireland as indeed they are objectionable to the Protestant minority here. To alter these articles in the hope of softening unionists' attitudes in advance of a British withdrawal, or at least of a clear declaration of intent, would to my mind be quite ineffective. But granted British co-operation and a genuine desire on their part to facilitate change, I am convinced that the terms of an All-Ireland constitution acceptable to all parties could be negotiated.

* * * * *

CIE did not succeed in maintaining the position of near solvency it reached in 1961. Operating costs continued to grow under pressure from inflation and expensive wage settlements but were not matched, as in the early years, either by the increased productivity or the increased traffic revenue necessary to finance them. Most sections of the company's operations were profitable, though on a declining scale, but these profits were more than cancelled out by losses incurred in the railway system.

We carried out a comprehensive cost/benefit study, code-named 'Pacemaker', of alternative plans on which public transport policy might be based. It was shown that so long as the railway network was retained even in an attenuated form there was no possibility of breaking even. It was also shown that in financial terms the most economic way of providing a public transport service was exclusively by road. But governments cannot reach decisions merely on financial considerations. The ultimate form of the public transport system must be a political decision resting with the government of the day.

I retired from CIE on my sixty-fifth birthday. I had no reason to regret my association with the national transport service and I felt every reason to be pleased with the re-structuring of the company which provided many of its staff with the opportunity to realise their full capabilities. I also felt grateful to the Minister of Transport and Power and my colleagues on the board for giving me a very free hand in managing the company and supporting my decisions unreservedly.

12

Among the Broadcasters

In May 1966 I was in Orly Airport, Paris awaiting the arrival of a Dublin plane for a return flight home. The plane brought copies of the Dublin evening papers, one of which carried a headline saying that I had been appointed chairman of RTE to succeed my namesake Eamonn Andrews. He had resigned because he disagreed with the authority on the prominence given to the Irish language in television programmes and because there was opposition in the authority to the employment of non-nationals in posts of responsibility. It was assumed that 'the employment of foreigners' referred to a Swede — Gunnar Rugheimer — who was the controller of programmes at that time.

I was due to retire from the post of executive chairman of CIE in October but I had no notion that the government were going to offer me the part-time chairmanship of RTE. Although the Irish Televison Service had been operating for the previous five years I had no particular interest in television in the sense of speculating on what influence it might have on the Irish character and culture. Radio broadcasting had not had much effect beyond the rapid diffusion of news; people did not seem to be any better or worse in their manners and morals and the long and profound arguments about the medium being the message or the massage passed me by.

I was reared at a time when neither telephones, motor-cars nor electricity were in common domestic use. I have experienced or seen all the scientific achievements which have altered for better or worse the human condition since my youth. I am no longer amazed at moon landings, computers and even nuclear energy. But I am still astonished at being able to see a military parade in Moscow, a student demonstration in Tokyo or a World Cup Final in Mexico when these events are actually happening.

I was interested generally in all the semi-state companies and had watched the creation of RTE with more than casual attention. No semi-state company got off the ground more quickly and with so few teething troubles thanks largely to the skill of the Post Office engineers and the employment of some expert assistance from abroad. The opposition to the use of foreign experts, which partly provoked Eamonn Andrews' resignation seemed to me to be ill-advised. There can be no objection to seeking foreign advice when it is needed and can be used to advantage but I do not think that foreigners should be permanently employed in posts of responsibility other than in very exceptional circumstances.

On the other hand I had no sympathy with his complaint about the excessive use of Irish. Looking at RTE I thought it could possibly have done even more than it was doing to promote the use of Irish for everyday communication. Whatever my views on these matters, I did not want to appear to be rushing into Eamonn's post. He had been part-time chairman of the authority since its beginning. He was respected and liked by the public. He had been a spectacular success on British television. He had become a national figure in England and his deportment, way of life and evident Irishness in that role reflected credit on his native country.

When the Taoiseach, Seán Lemass, spoke to me about taking the post he told me he was sorry that Andrews was leaving but assured me that his resignation was not due to any conflict with the government. He did say that there had been some difficulty between the controller and auditor general and the authority about the mode of vouching staff expenses but he thought that this difficulty had been overcome and anyway it had never become a government issue. Incidentally when I looked at the problem later I concluded that the controller and auditor general had been in error in principle.

Seán Lemass expressed very little interest in RTE except to say that some of the staff seemed to be 'losing the run of themselves' in thinking that the government had no function in relation to the National Broadcasting Authority, a point of view that no government could accept. His attitude in this respect was one with which I was fully in agreement. The government was the ultimate authority and in formulating these policies the government had before it all the facts, just as it bore all the responsibility for the consequences of the decisions made. Facts on which major issues are resolved often present to those on whom the burden of responsibility lies an aspect different from that seen by the leader writers of newspapers or by 'the man in the street'.

The Taoiseach had said that RTE

> was set up by legislation as an instrument of public policy and as such was responsible to the government. The government had overall responsibility for its conduct and especially the obligation to ensure that its programmes do not offend against the public interest, or conflict with national policy as defined in legislation. To this extent the government rejected the view that RTE should be, either generally or in regard to its current affairs' programmes and news' programmes, completely independent of government supervision.

This point of view was even more strongly held by me because I had had very definite and sometimes sorry experiences of the consequences of resistance to government policies by some of the semi-state bodies and even by civil servants.

The director-general of RTE at the time of my appointment was Kevin McCourt. I already knew him and knew him to be a man of integrity and decency. By hard work and laudable ambition he had ascended the commercial ladder, equipped himself with a qualification in accountancy and had become one of Ireland's most successful salesmen on an international scale. He had succeeded in putting Carrolls' tobacco products on the world market. Finding his scope for advancement limited in Carrolls he had accepted a post with a Canadian multinational aluminium company as their European representative based in Holland.

But he wanted to get back to contribute to the new Ireland which was emerging at that time. At great monetary sacrifice he had accepted the post of director-general of RTE. Coming from the world of business to that of the public service he had some difficulty in adapting himself to dealing with officialdom. He found it particularly difficult to accept the situation common in the public service that, no matter how hard you worked or how much positive and evident success you had, there was no commensurate monetary reward nor even expressed appreciation, apart from the possibility of promotion if and when the opportunity occured. For the director-general of RTE there was obviously no further room for promotion in that organisation.

He also found it difficult to put up with the constant gripes which he had to endure, often from individual ministers including, regularly, his own. He was very upset by the resignation of Eamonn Andrews who had also come from the world outside the public service and who had little use for or sympathy with the restraints and practices of officialdom. I liked and respected Kevin McCourt (as we say, he hadn't a bad turn in him) but unlike him my roots were deeply in the public service. I was probably more critical of some of its procedures than most but I had long since accepted the proposition that there were no rewards to be expected from hard work or success even if there was no punishment for those who failed to make the grade. The one exception to the latter half of this rule was in the very highest echelons of the semi-state bodies. The top posts in these bodies were filled or sanctioned by government authority and only for a fixed term, usually five years. At the end of this term the people concerned were at the mercy or prejudices of the government of the day.

The RTE authority at the time of my appointment numbered

eight, only one of whom I knew very well: Mrs Seán T. Ó Ceallaigh, widow of the late president, was an old friend of mine. There were two provincial journalists, a Dublin businessman, a university professor of history, the usual trade union representation common to all state companies, and the head of Gael Linn, Donal Ó Móráin. I was particularly glad to see Ó Móráin on the authority since I felt that he and his organisation had accomplished more for the Irish language than any other body since the Gaelic League in its heyday. None of the board members had any special knowledge of either television or radio work.

The first television programme was broadcast on 31 December 1961. When I joined RTE in June 1966 it was still a very young organisation and in a state of flux. When I arrived to take up my duties at Montrose — a very beautiful function-built building — I found that I had been provided with an office, a secretary and a chauffeur-driven car. These did not seem to me appurtenances necessary to a part-time chairman. I had no intention of performing any duties except to preside at meetings of the authority, undertake any representational functions which were required of me and be available for consultation with the director-general as he felt necessary. My proposed plan of action did not work out quite that way.

I made some changes in the procedure of the authority, reducing the number of meetings from two to one per month. This allowed the agenda to be circulated well in advance and it gave time for the items on the agenda to be fully documented so that, in the main, the authority had merely to say 'yes' or 'no' to the proposals being put to them by the director-general. They usually said 'yes', partly because the supporting documentation was detailed and clear-cut leaving little grounds for argument and partly because some of the members never went to the trouble to read the written submissions and discreetly remained silent. These procedures also reduced the time necessary to reach essential decisions leaving much more time available to the members to discuss and criticise the programmes which they had seen or heard about in previous weeks. At this point of the meeting everyone came into their own, even those who had contributed nothing to the formal agenda nor read the supporting documents. Programmes, once they had been broadcast, were something on which everyone could pass judgment. Whatever was said had to be said before lunch; it was made a rule that the meeting should conclude by lunch time and not be allowed to run on into the afternoon. Post-prandial meetings have many evident demerits.

The members of the authority were pleasant people to be associated with and lunch was a most agreeable function. It provided us with an opportunity to meet the heads of the departments, though the affairs of RTE were rarely mentioned on these occasions. Indeed at no time was there any official communication between the staff and members of the authority. This I considered to be a *sine qua non* of good management. I did not regard it as a function of the part-time members of a semi-state organisation to appoint or appraise the staff or get involved in its day-to-day operations. These, broadly speaking, were the functions of the director-general and with him also rested the responsibility for implementing the policy laid down by the authority. It was, moreover, his duty to take the initiative in formulating this policy as clearly it was not within the competence of a disparate group of individuals such as constituted the authority (or any other similar board for that matter) to produce a serviceable broadcasting policy though they were never short of suggestions for this or that programme or of criticism of programmes already made. They did have an opportunity for a broader and more critical appraisal of the work of the organisation when the director-general submitted the autumn and summer schedules for approval but in practice his proposals were usually accepted.

When I came to RTE, Rugheimer, the foreigner to whom so much exception had been taken, was on his way out. I regretted this as he seemed from what I saw or heard of him, to be a man whom I would certainly like to have working in a dominant role in RTE if only temporarily. His departure required the appointment of a successor as controller of programmes. The director-general consulted me about several potential candidates but while I knew one of the people involved I could not pronounce on his relative merits nor indeed had I any precise knowledge of the job specification. I was no help to him beyond suggesting that the post should be advertised publicly which was done without success. It was then suggested that the appointment be given to Michael Garvey, a member of the existing staff. I looked at Garvey's curriculum vitae and I raised no objection to the director-general's choice. I was then consulted about the vacant position of head of news for which James McGuinness had been nominated. I knew him well and was very friendly with him and his family — he was something of a protegé of mine. He was a very proficient journalist having been editor of the *Irish Press* and also had experience of working on American newspapers. If he was appointed it was bound to be attributed to influence on my part. On the other hand, it was not reasonable that he should be at a disadvantage merely because he was a friend of mine. I had seen that trend being followed all too often in Fianna Fáil, particularly in its early days, so that ministers might have the self-satisfaction of feeling incorrupt, or more likely, out of fear of being accused of patronage. Great injustices have been done to many men because scruples of this type prevailed in Fianna Fáil. The government, and those close to them, felt particularly susceptible to this sort of criticism especially from the Fine Gael opposition who, for the first ten years of the existence of the State, had filled every appointment of importance and many of no importance with their supporters. There was a large measure of truth in the jibe directed at de Valera by a leading Republican, Dr Con Murphy, at a Fianna Fáil Árd Fheis when he said, 'The policy of Mr de Valera is to forgive your enemies and forget your friends.' I think that Dev worked on two assumptions. He believed that any totally committed Republican should not expect political preferment; it was not the aim of Fianna Fáil to provide jobs for its members. On the other hand, he seemed to suffer from an obsessional fear of being unjust to his political opponents.

I made only two other interventions in staff matters. I thought the authority required the services of a highly qualified secretary and, rather to the annoyance of the director-general, I thought it proper that the authority itself should make this appointment. The post was advertised and I was delegated to carry out the interviews *solus*. I selected Oliver Maloney, who in the course of time and long after I had left the organisation, became director-general. I also urged on Kevin McCourt the need to appoint a deputy to himself. Fortunately for the organisation he selected John Irvine who, because of his long-standing association with the service, had become a repository of broadcasting experience. As a civil servant he had had considerable influence in drafting the Act setting up RTE. The appointment was a popular one as John Irvine was probably the best liked man in Montrose. If he had a fault it was that he was without ambition.

In 1966, RTE though only a few years in existence and despite its limited resources of money and manpower had already achieved high standards of performance and was held in esteem nationally. The organisation had done a marvellous job in recording the visit of President Kennedy. It had covered the general election of 1965 in detail to everyone's satisfaction. Its home-produced programmes, such as *The Riordans,* were both interesting and instructive while *The Late Late Show* was certainly entertaining and at the same time, timidly perhaps at first, began an area of open discussion not usually available to the public at that time. The technical staff were highly competent people who were at pains to keep up-to-date with all the latest advances in telecommunications. A well-organised sales and accounting staff to handle the commercial end of the service had also been established.

The TV production staff had to be recruited from musicians, actors, teachers, journalists, writers and graphic artists who, except for those who had worked in the radio division, had no previous broadcasting experience. There was usually a trendy priest in the background. A few whole-time academics — to the extent to which such people exist — were recruited in a part-time capacity to add prestige to the discussion programmes. Generically, the production staff were known as the 'creative people'. Some of them were creative people in the sense of having written and published books or plays or having composed or performed music but in general the word 'creative' applied to them was perhaps a misleading classification.

But they had a characteristic in common; like the civil servants they were almost all above the average in education and intelligence. Unlike the civil servants, they were almost all endowed or inflicted, depending on one's point of view, with temperament and, unlike the civil servants, many of them claimed to be 'concerned' which was the vogue word of the time. They were a difficult group for a director-general to cope with — to use the word 'control' in this context would probably be considered dictatorial. 'Concerned' citizens seemed to me to be divided into different categories. Some were idealists prepared to go to the scaffold to eliminate the injustices of society. Some were dissatisfied because their jobs did not give them the power and influence they felt capable of exercising on contemporary events. Some were parlour pinks enjoying the social cachet attached to radical chic in pubs and suburban drawing rooms. Many of them were convinced that they were living and working in a society which was rotten to the core; they believed that they had a mission to change it through the use of television. They felt as medieval knights must have felt when they rode forth on crusading expeditions. It was difficult to see how they expected so rotten a society to provide them with the expensive and complicated facilities of a television network and pay them while they rushed into the fray to establish the new Jerusalem.

One curious example of the power of television is the creation of what is known as a 'television personality'. The personality in his private existence may well be an established historian, medical doctor, learned theologian or leading politician but, if he appears often enough and performs well enough on television, any eminence achieved in his ordinary working life becomes of secondary importance to his new role of 'television personality'. In fact he becomes an actor and is judged as such, achieving a status in the community which bears no relation to his professional competence. Sometimes he makes the mistake of believing in the importance he acquires as a TV personality and persuades himself that the star rating he enjoys qualifies him to act as a leader or formulator of public opinion. It doesn't often work out in that way.

One such manifestation of image-making is the status often attained by newscasters. I do not think many people would hold that the ability to read a news bulletin requires a hard period of apprenticeship or a particularly high IQ or even anything more than a slight acquaintance with the subjects treated. Yet newscasters' faces grace the cover of the *RTE Guide* and they are in demand, much as ministers are, to open supermarkets and do similar public chores not because of any private intrinsic merit, which many of them undoubtedly have, but merely because they read the news and in the process have become household names. Acceptance of that criterion as a standard of value in the community is, I think, deplorable. As for the non-professional practitioners who take part in TV programmes, they do so for one of three reasons. Either they have a point of view to evangelise, want to earn money or appear for reasons of vanity and self-indulgence. Only they themselves know which is the true motivation.

Kevin McCourt was a man of tolerance and kindness. He liked to manage by persuasion. He had come to the conclusion that, among other things, changes were necessary in the running of the station orchestra. The authority agreed with him. The conductor of the orchestra, a Hungarian named Tibor Von Paul, objected strongly. All McCourt's persuasive efforts were unable to induce Von Paul to come to a reasonable accommodation. While this situation was coming to a head I became chairman and found myself under extreme political and personal pressure to reverse the decision of the authority and the director-general which had not yet been implemented. I was unwilling to intervene and indeed, having heard the circumstances of the case, I formed the opinion that Kevin McCourt had been quite right in relieving Von Paul of his post. Failure to block the decision involved me in the break of a life-long personal and political friendship. It was a high price to pay for the chairmanship of RTE and one which I would not have paid had I been in a position to anticipate the problem. I had never met Von Paul and knew nothing of the workings of the station orchestra nor any member of it.

I liked power and the exercise of power. I was well aware that the roles of part-time chairman and that of chief executive which I had held for many years in Bord na Móna and CIE were quite different in this respect; nevertheless I found it difficult to accept cheerfully the position of merely suggesting courses of action rather than saying '*Fiat!*' I disliked the restriction of RTE foreign news coverage almost exclusively to British and American sources. When some members of the authority complained that our news coverage of the war in Vietnam was imbalanced I had sympathy with this view. This was followed by a suggestion that RTE should send a team to Hanoi to report on events at first hand which was agreed without objection and indeed rather cursorily. There was no discussion of the expense involved or on its desirability in the context of the international situation.

It was unfortunate that my very close and intimate relations with the Minister for Foreign Affairs, Frank Aiken, had been fractured by the Tibor Von Paul affair; otherwise I would have discussed the matter with him and avoided any clash. But as soon as our intention to send a news team to North Vietnam became known, rather excessively strenuous objections to the project were conveyed from Foreign Affairs to RTE through Erskine Childers, our minister. I had not very much confidence in the reservations expressed by Foreign Affairs because I knew Frank Aiken's mind was concentrated solely on the issue of Nuclear Disarmament and anything that might divert his efforts or conceivably detract from them, such as a visit by RTE to Hanoi, would be unacceptable. On the other hand, I realised that the responsibility for conducting our foreign policy rested with him. I began to have misgivings about embarrassing the government in its foreign relations.

I believed strongly that it was the duty of the television authority to support official policy but I also felt obliged to ensure that the objection to the North Vietnam project was based on a government decision and not the personal view of an individual minister — particularly one whose judgment on such matters I regarded as being far from infallible. The proper course to follow would have been to insist that if the government wanted the project abandoned they should exercise their statutory powers by issuing a formal instruction to this effect. I decided against this partly because of my own misgivings and partly because I knew from my experience in CIE how difficult it was to extract a written instruction of this kind from the government. In the end I compromised, but this turned out to be an error of judgment. I spoke on the telephone to the Taoiseach, Jack Lynch, and asked if it was in fact the decision of the government that RTE should not send a team to Hanoi. He confirmed that this was so. I told him that in that case we felt obliged to issue a public statement to that effect. He agreed that we could issue the following:

> The Radio Telefís Éireann Authority wishes it to be known that the Taoiseach informed the chairman of the authority that, in the opinion of the government, the best interests of the nation would not be

served by sending a news team to Vietnam and that it would be an embarrassment to the government in relation to its foreign policy.

The newspapers had a field day as always happens when RTE appears to be at odds with the government. I think this is as it should be. But in other respects, especially in regard to its internal staff difficulties, the treatment that RTE gets from the newspapers seems more often open to question. The newspaper commentators seem to be obsessed by the internal affairs of RTE which are of no more general interest than the staff upheavals that occur from time to time in the newspapers themselves. But such interest from the newspapers guaranteed that the disgruntled 'creative' people would have a platform to air their grievances.

A group of creative people were restless, possibly a manifestation of the *Zeitgeist* of the sixties. They despised the management and held the authority in contempt. One example of their determination to go their own way irrespective of the consequences was the decision to send a news team to report on the Nigerian Civil War under the auspicies of some Biafran publicity agency. They did not bother to tell the controller — their immediate boss — much less the director-general in advance. He heard of the expedition when it was already in Lisbon awaiting transit to Biafra. He told me over lunch about the situation. On my strong advice and his own judgment of the probable repercussions he decided to recall the team. Instructions to this effect had scarcely been issued when I had a call from Garret Fitzgerald who appeared to be in some way involved with the Biafran lobby here and who asked me to confirm if the visit had been cancelled. I told him to clear his mind of any idea that government pressure was being exerted on RTE. As far as I knew the government were completely unaware of the incident. The director-general's decision to recall the team had been done with my full support and I was sure he would agree on reflection that to have done otherwise would have been irresponsible considering the delicacy of the situation. In the eyes of the Nigerian government, with whom Ireland had diplomatic relations, the Biafran secession was an act of rebellion and, whatever the rights or wrongs of the case, the position of Irish missionaries in Nigeria was such as to warrant caution in circumstances where the national TV authority might be accused of hob-nobbing with rebels.

Another instance of what I thought to be injudicious, if not irresponsible, mentality of the 'creative people' was a programme dealing with the activities of the Garda Special Branch. Here again neither the controller of programmes nor the director-general were informed before the programme was made. I asked to see the film and thought it trivial and lightweight in content and unsuitable for transmission. To reinforce my judgment I arranged to have it viewed by the members of the authority who came to the same conclusion and decided that the programme should be cancelled. The director-general, tolerant though he was and anxious for harmony in his staff, thought it necessary in view of these incidents to transfer the responsibility for the *Seven Days* programme from the controller of programmes to the head of news. The move brought immediate uproar. The *Seven Days* team (who were probably the most intelligent and sophisticated of the 'creative' people) refused to accept the new arrangement and were suspended. Strike notice was served on the authority. A lampoon was posted in the canteen which reflects the attitude of some of the staff to the management and the authority:

To all, Whether it concerns them or not:
The director-general wants to inform the staff that following controversial statements by Daithi Lacha, in the current series of programmes, he has decided to transfer responsibility for the series to Mr Michael O'Hehir, head of sport. The reason for this change is a logical one in that the animals concerned have been known to run on occasions and would, therefore, fit more easily in the sports department. There was no question of interference with the head of children's programmes, who would still have full freedom to play the National Anthem at 5.30 p.m. every day.

In regard to *Quicksilver,* it is confirmed that this programme will now be under the direct control of the Archbishop of Dublin, following the unfortunate slip of a competitor in using the word 'feck' on the programme. The director-general wishes to deny that this change-over from money prizes to indulgences is an unwarranted intrusion in the affairs of the producer.

The fact that the *Late Late Show* is now being transmitted without sound is one more example of the technical daring which makes Montrose the courageous leader of the Irish people. Fury without sound is a far more civilised form of entertainment. Should panelists continue to use untoward facial expressions, it is eventually intended to dispense with vision also. . .

All those who still have opinions are advised to cash them in at the chairman's office before 28 June when a referendum will be held.

My withers were unwrung by this piece of juvenalia. The absence of radio and television from the air was unlikely to create any social unrest and even less political commotion. There was little enthusiasm for a strike amongst the RTE staff. Mortgages and school fees had to be paid, salary levels were reasonable and working conditions good. The unions probably realised all this. Quite properly they invoked the conciliation procedures set up by the authority and trade unions to deal with such disputes. The conciliation committee recommended that the suspensions should be lifted and the

Seven Days programme should be transferred to the news room.
The evolution of RTE had moved on a little.

Shortly after this incident Kevin McCourt resigned to return to
the world of business where his great skills received due recognition
and reward. In appointing a successor the authority took considerable trouble to ensure that whatever choice was made would be
seen to be uninfluenced by extraneous considerations. That is to
say that candidates whose political, social and religious views were
well known were not precluded from competing for the post.
Neither I nor the other members of the authority had any intention
of appointing anyone but the best candidate available.

We set up a selection Board consisting of myself as chairman,
three other members of the authority — Professor Moody of
Trinity College, Fintan Kennedy, president of ITGWU, Donal Ó
Móráin, managing director of Gael Linn, two outsiders, Maurice
Gorham, a former director of Radio Éireann, and John Garvin,
former secretary of the Department of Local Government (and a
leading authority on James Joyce). At the very outset a problem
arose. As is common in such cases it was stated in the advertisement
inviting applications that the names of the candidates would be
treated in confidence. Our minister, Erskine Childers, asked to be
shown the names of the applicants but I pointed out that they were
confidential. The minister was obviously under some pressure from
his government colleagues because after successive cabinet meetings the request was renewed. He was clearly very upset at not
being able to provide the desired information and finally told me
that he had received a specific instruction from the Taoiseach on
the matter. I told him to tell the Taoiseach, or if he wished I was
prepared to do so, that the promise of confidentiality could not be
breached in any circumstances. The reasons for the government's
interest in the identity of the candidates was all the less understandable because this information, even if disclosed, could not affect the
appointment. I was at a loss to understand why such a fuss was
being created and could only conclude that what began as reasonable curiosity became a contest of will, as so often happens in that
type of situation.

We did all the things proper to selection boards and finally
appointed Thomas Hardiman as director-general. Hardiman was
the almost perfect end-product of a Christian Brothers' education
through Irish at Coláiste Mhuire. He took an engineering degree in
University College, Dublin and went directly into the telecommunications section of the Department of Posts and Telegraphs.
He was closely involved in the establishment of the technical foundations of the television service. At the time of his application for the

post of director-general, he was director of engineering in RTE. Whoever got the post would have been the target for critical comment. The chief criticism of Hardiman was that he was not a 'communicator'; his training and background had been scientific. It had been my experience that the best university discipline on which to build management or administrative skills was engineering or science and it was clear from our interview that Hardiman was quite familiar with C. P. Snow's other culture. Furthermore he knew everyone of consequence on the staff of RTE, their ambitions, capabilities and peculiarities.

Hardiman knew his Irish history well and spoke Irish fluently. He had read widely and was something of a philosopher and a Latinist. He had a more than ordinary interest in music. He knew the importance of the media in promoting the distinctive character of Irish nationality and culture and was determined that RTE would be used to that purpose. He absorbed himself in his job. In manner he was polite and unassuming. He neither smoked nor drank alcohol. He was a devoted family man. He had all the qualities of a prefect prig. But he was far from being a prig. His sense of humour and evident success in retaining the respect and goodwill of his colleagues deny any such characterisation. He was fearless in the expression of his opinions and quite immune to outside pressures either from the politicians, the special interest lobbies which abounded or from the many cenacles within the organisation.

Hardiman had a characteristic which sometimes amused and sometimes irritated me. He was garrulous to a point which often led to over-stating his case and at authority meetings he frequently failed to let well enough alone. He would have preferred to manage by consensus but soon ran into a situation where some of the 'creative' people objected to the organisational framework in which they were required to work. They generated a ferment in which meetings of small groups took place all day long, the 'philosophy' of televison was discussed in memoranda, teach-ins and seminars. What the controller of programmes did or did not say became a major issue.

Hardiman dealt with the situation firmly. He kept me informed about the 'goings-on' though this was not necessary because I could read about them in the newspapers. The journalists were, as usual, well informed and, as usual, obsessively interested in the internal workings of RTE. Hardiman told me that there were threats of resignation. My advice to him was that, if any such threat materialised, he should present the party concerned with a paper and pen, invite the recipient to put the resignation in writing and accept it there and then. Any manager altering his decision under

the threat of staff resignation is inviting trouble for himself and his
organisation. In any case I do not believe in the doctrine of indis-
pensability.

That hardline approach would be contrary to Hardiman's nature
but in the end he received and accepted with a great deal of reluctance the resignations of some members of the staff. One man did
not bother to resign; he just walked out. Sad to say those who left
the service were highly intelligent people, well informed and
animated by the best of sociological and national convictions. But
they were not prepared to bear the yoke of discipline that membership of any organisation demands. They suffered considerable
financial loss and preferred to immolate their careers in pursuit of
principle. I had seen an identical situation arise, *mutatis mutandis,*
in Bord na Móna many years previously.

Hardiman soon stamped his authority on the organisation.
Equally he acquired the respect of the RTE authority and among
his international colleagues in the world of broadcasting he became
a figure of importance. His interest in things Irish and fluency in the
language enabled him to deal effectively with the turbulent Irish
language lobby; I think he even satisfied them that Irish was getting
its proper place in the programmes.

Hardiman became director-general of RTE in the spring of 1968
and by the autumn of 1969 he had the organisation working
smoothly. Standards were improving all the time as the production
staff gained experience and creative talent both inside and outside
the organisation was employed to better effect. The public affairs
coverage in particular achieved a wider scope and a better balance.
More discrimination was exercised in the selection of the 'bought-
in' material and the Irish language programmes became more
sophisticated and informative. The general election of 1969 was
covered by the external broadcast unit. It was a major feat of staff
organisation, involving the co-operation of the technical staff with
producers, directors, designers and journalists. The effort though
expensive was brilliantly successful.

RTE, because it shares to some extent a common audience with
British televison, is exposed to comparison with the BBC and ITV
services and the comparison is usually to its disadvantage. What the
critics ignore, however, is that RTE is not in the same league financially as its British counterparts nor can it draw on anything like the
same pool of talent. Before my appointment to the RTE authority I
had some experience of television in the USA and in Japan (in
colour, for the first time) and later during visits abroad for conferences of the European Broadcasting Union I had the opportunity of
seeing it in several continental countries. In my judgment the

performance of RTE was well on a par with the standards prevailing elsewhere. I felt that Irish radio and television audiences were getting good value for money, much more indeed than they paid for. I thought it deplorable that our national broadcasting service should depend on advertising for so much of its revenue. Raising the licence fees to a realistic level, more in keeping with the value derived from it, would go far towards making RTE financially independent.

Whatever the case may be for or against commercial broadcasting I was strongly opposed to the use of the medium for advertising cigarettes and drink. Before I left RTE a decision had been made to phase out cigarette advertising and in due course it went. Hard drinks advertising had also been banned but beer advertising was still allowed to continue on a large scale, cleverly presented. Considering our history of alcoholism and the contemporary problem of increased drinking among young people it seemed to me disgraceful that the national television service should be acting in the role of a drug pusher. I argued strongly with Hardiman in favour of a change of policy in this respect but could not persuade him to accept my point of view though he was personally a teetotaller. I raised the matter informally with the authority from time to time but getting little support from the other members I let the idea drop. My failure to make an issue out of it, even to the point of resigning if the decision went against me, has been a source of regret to me to this day.

In the autumn of 1969 a programme was sent out on television aimed at uncovering the evils of illegal money-lending in Dublin. It made first-class viewing and created something of a sensation. I happened to see the programme at home and thought it to be an excellent piece of investigative reporting. It perhaps exaggerated the extent of the money-lending racket and furthermore the propriety of using concealed cameras and tape recorders in a documentary of this kind might well be questioned. The measure of overstatement, particularly in the presenter's summing up of the situation, might also be a matter for contention. I intended to express this opinion, which I felt would be shared by the other members of the authority, to the director-general at our next meeting. It never occurred to me, however, that these or any other possible defects in the programme were incapable of being dealt with within the normal management processes of RTE. I was wrong in thinking this. I could not, nor could anyone else, foresee that the programme would be interpreted by the Department of Justice as a deliberate attack on the competence of the Gardaí although I knew that the department was paranoid on the subject of RTE.

Our minister at that time, Paddy Lalor, was a comparatively new appointment. He told me about the resentment expressed by the Department of Justice. I gave him my own views about the contents of the programme and the method of presentation and assured him that the authority would take whatever action was appropriate to rectify the matter. I also told him that one of his ministerial colleagues had gone to the trouble of ringing up to congratulate RTE on its performance. I thought that was the end of the affair.

But when subsequently the question of the prevalence of money-lending was raised in the Dáil the Minister for Justice attacked, at what seemed to me unnecessary length and vehemence, the authenticity of the programme and indeed the good faith of those responsible for making it. The opposition revelled in the confrontation between the department and RTE and when the authority issued a statement expressing confidence in the competence and good faith of the staff they demanded a public enquiry to determine where exactly the rights and wrongs of the matter lay.

On hearing the word 'enquiry' mooted I went to see the minister and pointed to the unfortunate experience which had attended public enquiries held in somewhat similar circumstances in the past. I recalled, in particular, the scandalous waste of public money on the quite sterile enquiry into the Locke Distillery affair, where the sale of the distillery had, for merely political purposes, been blown up to appear like a major financial scandal. I knew, because he had told me so on different occasions, that Seán Lemass had determined never again to agree to a public enquiry where the matter at issue stemmed merely from party politics. Such enquiries can contribute nothing to the public weal.

I urged the minister in no circumstances to agree to an enquiry, emphasising once again that if there was anything objectionable in the programme, it was the function of the authority to have it dealt with by the established internal processes of appraisal. But when the Taoiseach, Jack Lynch, intervened in the debate to say that all would have been well if RTE had only made it clear that the programme was fictitious, I desisted from offering any further advice. The opposition got their enquiry which lasted fifty-one days and cost the taxpayer £250,000. It proved nothing and changed nothing. In my opinion, the opposition in asking for an enquiry and the government in granting it were guilty of an act of political irresponsibility. A public sworn enquiry was disproportionate to the needs of the occasion. Its only effect was to create much personal anxiety to individual members of the RTE staff and to disrupt the organisation for months.

There are many misconceptions amongst the public as to the role of the RTE authority. The idea that the members of the authority

are only 'a shower' of party hacks is often expressed, and sometimes believed, even by people who are far removed from the sub-
culture of the public house where so many habitués proclaim what
they would do if they were Taoiseach, President of the United
States or in control of the Kremlin.

The authority consists of a part-time chairman and eight other
members all of whom are appointed by the government. In my day
it happened that Fianna Fáil was in power. I had been a well-known
supporter of Fianna Fáil since its foundation and had been
emotionally involved in the fortunes of the party, though not an
actual member since entering the civil service in 1933. With some
members of the government I had close personal friendships; they
were in the main veterans of the Legion of the Rearguard. (I
suggest, in passing, that the rather splendid rhetoric of the phrase
had been devalued when it was set to music with a lyric composed, I
think, by a journalist named Jack Sheehan. The song provided too
much opportunity for ridicule and the phrase 'Soldiers of the
Legion of the Rearguard' dropped out of the Republican vocabulary.) With the departure of Dev in 1959, to be followed by Seán
Lemass's regime, my attachment to the party had begun to weaken.
Finally, Taca and its implications diminished still further any
emotional interest I had and by the time Seán Lemass resigned in
1966 this vestigial interest had vanished. I continued to vote for
Fianna Fáil because I could not bring myself to do otherwise and
anyway I thought no administration could be worse than the coalition governments which had twice cast a blight on the nation.

As to the other members of the authority, some were openly
supporters of Fianna Fáil but others were not and one in fact was an
ex-Fine Gael TD. The assumption voiced so often in public that the
authority enjoyed no real autonomy and merely reflected partisan
interests was also nonsense. During my term of office I can only
recall three occasions when government pressure was brought to
bear on RTE. In two of these cases the pressure was successfully
resisted; in the third the government's representations were
accepted and acted upon not at its behest but because they were
considered to be well founded. In fairness it should be said that in
none of these cases did the issues involved impinge on political
party interests.

That is not to say there were no efforts by individual ministers to
interfere in RTE affairs. These intrusions were not aimed positively
at persuading RTE to express a particular viewpoint or advocate a
particular course of action. It usually took the form of individual
ministers ringing up to record a complaint about programmes that
they found in some way objectionable. These complaints were

frequent and extremely irritating. But Kevin McCourt dealt with them by using the soft answer which turneth away wrath while Tom Hardiman did so by overwhelming the complaintants with words. He enjoyed arguing and was never willing to let his bone go with the dog.

In my own case the ministerial grouses surfaced every Thursday and Friday, the days on which the cabinet met, relayed to me by Erskine Childers, the minister responsible for RTE during most of my term of office. It appeared to me that the complaints showered on Erskine by his fellow ministers were so many and trivial that they were, for the most part, pulling his leg. Erskine, who had not much sense of humour or sense of proportion, approached me after cabinet meetings in great distress. I could not persuade him that it was not part of my duties to monitor broadcasts nor as part-time chairman did I have the functional responsibility for managing the affairs of RTE. I advised him to tell his more persistently critical colleagues to go to hell and if this did not put a stop to their silly complaints I proposed that he and I should see the Taoiseach and ask him to exercise a restraining influence. Unfortunately Erskine was not willing to act on my suggestion and during the remainder of our joint association with RTE these unending complaints continued to be a source of extreme annoyance. Intervention on my part would have been out of place as well as ineffective. If there was any substance in the complaints the director-general would have dealt with them. He would certainly have heard about them because it seemed to me that no programme ever sent out on television failed to provoke adverse comment from some quarter irrespective of its merits.

Erskine was constantly being warned by the Department of Justice about the prevalence of left-wing influence in RTE. When Hardiman became director-general, I invited Erskine to dinner to meet him. In the course of the meal Erskine handed me a rough sheet of paper containing about a dozen names all of whom were recognisable either as employees of RTE or as participants in occasional programmes. According to Erskine, the people on the list were known to be 'lefties', if not card-carrying Communists and should be treated as suspect subversives. I could not help laughing as I read through the list. Some of those named were contemporaries of my own whom I knew to be respectable socialists. Most of the others were known to Hardiman as people who had socialist sympathies and might possibly be classified as Maoist, popularly regarded as a pejorative description at the time.

Erskine refused to disclose the source of the document but I had no hesitation in asserting that it had been compiled by the Special

Branch under the inspiration of the paranoid Department of Justice. I assured Erskine that no attention would be paid to the allegations nor would I give the list to Hardiman for the record. As a young man I and many of my associates suffered from harassment by the Special Branch. Some of my friends had to emigrate as a result of this treatment. I was quite determined that, to the extent I could prevent it, no one would ever suffer economically or otherwise for their political opinions. The Special Branch maintained a presence in the RTE offices at Montrose but their job was to ensure the security of the building and not to institute a system of thought control or act as purveyors of political gossip. I sent a rather violent letter of protest to Erskine with a request that it be shown to the Taoiseach. He did not do so but at least secret lists were never mentioned to me again.

Part of the duties of the chairman (even a part-time chairman) was to represent RTE at various functions at home and, if desirable, abroad. As a new boy I was expected to introduce myself to the broadcasting scene and indeed I wanted to see something of the personalities of the European Broadcasting systems. I visited a number of these organisations with McCourt and Hardiman but as I grew older travelling became a chore. At home television parties or conferences and the milieu they created were of no interest to me. The idea of spending hours upon hours at the Cork Film Festival or at the Jacobs' Annual Awards dinner wearied me. I had another point of view about the Jacobs' function. I did not think it any part of a public servant's task to promote the sale of biscuits or any other commodity and for that reason I disapproved of RTE's participation in the award scheme.

I did not serve out my full term as chairman of RTE. In 1970 my son, David, was appointed chief whip of the Fianna Fáil parliamentary party and, rather than risk a situation which might give rise to a conflict of interest, I decided to submit my resignation to the Taoiseach without much regret. I had the feeling that it was accepted with even less. Effectively my resignation from RTE marked my final break with the public service and the end of my official career.

13

In the Establishment

After the war when Bord na Móna, now a statutory body, became a recognised success, my prestige and status in the community increased greatly and it was with something of a pleasurable shock that I realised the truth of what my friend, Joe Griffith, said to me: 'Do you realise you're a national figure?' One consequence of being a national figure was that it opened for me new areas of experience. Hitherto any leisure I had was spent among my family and my friends. Now I began to receive invitations to government receptions, to dinners in Iveagh House and Áras an Uachtaráin. Áras was not new to me; since Seán T. Ó Ceallaigh became President I had often enjoyed his hospitality but that was on a personal basis because I was an old friend of himself and his wife, Phyllis. These new invitations were of a different kind and doubtless derived from the fact that my name had been put on some list compiled in the protocol section of the Department of External Affairs. In the beginning I was flattered to receive invitations even to functions attended by several hundred guests but Mary refused to come along to any of them; social gatherings *en masse* were distasteful to her and she was not prepared to go to the trouble of dressing up for the occasion. However, they served the useful purpose of putting me on personal terms with the secretaries of the government departments and the heads of the state-sponsored bodies.

After a while these functions bored me and I made a point of declining invitations unless they had some positive connection with the affairs of Bord na Móna or CIE. External Affairs must have passed on the invitation list to the embassies because while I was in Bord na Móna, and even more frequently when I was in CIE, we were invited to embassy dinners. Mary, with reluctance and as a matter of duty, came to the dinners which were in fact often enjoyable affairs. The ambassadors were sometimes career diplomats and sometimes political appointments. We generally found that the career people were far more interesting. I had the impression that the career diplomats when posted to Ireland were either on their way up or on their way out but they were always well travelled and some of them were very scholarly men. They were all most agreeable and friendly but I was quite well aware that I was their guest because my name was on the official invitation list and not because they liked the colour of my eyes. I rarely established personal relations with any of them and I rightly surmised that when they left Ireland I would not hear from them again. The one exception was John and Mary Moore but we had been friends of theirs before they came to the American embassy.

Some of the political appointees were very wealthy men and had elected to come here for the horses in which they were more interested than the people. One in particular, whom I met a few times, might well have been high amongst the Houyhnhnms. To communicate with him satisfactorily one felt it was necessary either to whinny or to neigh. For his part he regarded the Irish as yahoos. One advantage of attending these official dinners was that you weren't left to wonder what went on at them and, better still, you didn't have to wonder why you weren't invited.

During the war Mary and I were frequently invited to all sorts of functions at the German embassy and we always made a point of attending. At this time many of the regular embassy set had dropped the Germans from the visiting lists so that the ambassador, Dr Hempel, was glad to fall back on people like us who were genuinely neutral in our attitude towards the war. Dr Hempel and his wife belonged to the old school of diplomats, in manner very polite, correct and imperturbable. When the German armies overran France and were dominating almost all of Europe they never, by as much as a flick of an eyebrow, displayed emotion. This was strongly in contrast with the behaviour of some of their staff who exuded triumphalism which we found thoroughly unpleasant.

It is curious that, except for Madame de Laubespin, the wife of the Belgian ambassador, I don't recall meeting one interesting woman amongst the diplomatic corps. That was probably due to lack of interest on their part rather than mine. I remember Madame de Laubespin because, apart from great charm, she was deeply interested in the works of Teilhard de Chardin which for a long time fascinated Mary and myself until I read a devastating commentary on his philosophy by the Nobel prize-winner, P. B. Medawar, when my interest diminished but not Mary's. De Chardin reinforced her already strongly held religious beliefs.

One function which we attended gave me special pleasure. I had no expectation whatever of being invited to the state banquet given in Iveagh House by Seán Lemass in honour of President Kennedy. It was to be followed by a reception to which we might reasonably have been asked and to which Mary certainly would not have gone. It was quite a distinction to have been a guest at the banquet because very few public servants were included and I knew that all the socialites in Dublin were canvassing for invitations even to the reception. As we came out from dinner — which was a prolonged affair — I recognised among the milling mob waiting for the reception to begin a great many people who regarded me, and the old IRA to which I belonged, as little better than murderers. I was maliciously amused. Such are the petty and very unworthy satisfactions of life.

I was invited to a dinner by Bishop Conway (not then Cardinal) to meet Bishop Wright of Boston (not then Cardinal either). Bishop Conway's other guests were Dr Hillery, then Minister for Education, now President of Ireland, Ken Whitaker and one other whom I cannot remember. Dr Wright was part of the Kennedy family entourage. He had very little regard for Jack Kennedy because of his penchant for women but he thought Bobby Kennedy was intellectually and morally much superior to his elder brother. He talked most interestingly about the family but it was not what he said so much as the way in which he said it that made the evening memorable for me. Dr Wright spoke in an accent similar to that of Monsignor Fulton Sheen, whom I had heard on the radio or television. But his command of the English language was such as I never heard before and am unlikely ever to encounter again. He never appeared to search for the right word and as he spoke you could nearly hear the full stops, the colons, the semi-colons, the hyphens and the inverted commas being inserted in their appropriate places. As balanced sentence followed antithetical sentence and metaphor followed simile, it sounded as though he was reading from a chapter of Gibbon or an essay by Macaulay. I am sure that when Dr Wright was preaching in Boston nobody missed Mass.

One result of attending all these functions in Áras an Uachtaráin and elsewhere was that I was in a position to indulge in name dropping on a grand scale. I could truthfully say I met President Kennedy, General de Gaulle, U Thant, Radhakrishnan (President of India), Cardinal Agaganian, the Papal Legate to the Patrician Congress, Senator Edward Kennedy, Senator Everett Dirksen the Majority leader in the American Senate, Gunnar Myrdal the Swedish statesman and writer, and Pedro Arrupe the head of the Jesuit Order. Equally it is certain that no one of them would ever remember having met me nor, even if I exchanged more than a handshake or a few words with them, would they have brought away with them any memorable thoughts or sayings which might be credited to me.

I shook President Kennedy's hand and said, 'You do us great honour by your visit, sir.' To which he replied, 'Thank you,

Doctor,' having got my name from the usher who announced the names of the dinner guests. Dev paid me the compliment of inviting me to a lunch at Áras an Uachtaráin in honour of General de Gaulle. I had about twenty minutes conversation with de Gaulle with whom I was assigned to take after-lunch coffee. I asked him how he enjoyed his visit. He made a few complimentary remarks. I mentioned that I had been in Paris when he came to power and could recall the universal excitement in the streets with the cars honking 'Algerie Française', at which he smiled. After a few more banalities from me, I was moved on to make way for someone else. I had met de Gaulle.

Frank Aiken asked me to engage U Thant after a dinner in Iveagh House. I spent at least an hour in comversation with him, asking questions about the work of the United Nations. I would like to have learned from U Thant something of Lee Kuan Yew of Singapore whom I thought to be an outstanding statesman of our time but I drew a blank. In fact the whole conversation was a blank. U Thant must have been 'engaged' in this fashion almost every night of his life. His eyes were glazed with boredom and so would mine have been except that I never suffered from glazed eyes; I am always too aware of the other person's.

Cardinal Agaganian I met several times but never got beyond the point of kissing his ring. His visit produced a regular outbreak of ring kissing due to the concentration of the higher clergy for the occasion. A colleague of mine got so conditioned that when Dev appeared amongst the ecclesiastics and held out his hand to be shaken my friend dropped to his knees and kissed Dev's hand, not noticing that he wore no ring. Unfortunately a press photographer spotted and recorded the absurd incident. He sent a copy of the photograph to my colleague but very decently refrained from publishing it.

Radhakrishnan, the President of India, and his staff were consigned to my care on a visit to Killarney. We travelled by the state railway carriage. The President ensconced himself in a corner of a compartment and didn't communicate with anyone; he remained in a state of meditation all the way to Killarney. His entourage, of whom there were about six, including two beautiful women secretaries, were as gay and light-hearted as the President was austere. They brightened the journey considerably. The tour of the lakes was miserable. It rained in the best Killarney fashion. Fortunately the president was familiar with monsoons.

It had been arranged that the Killarney Urban District Council would offer the President a reception but the plan went wrong. Either the reception committee mistimed the arrangements or the weather was too bad. When we arrived at the Town Hall it was clear that something was amiss so we drove on. Killarney did not feel any great deprivation at having failed to honour the President of India. Echoes of that other Kerry town resounded in my ears — 'Knocknagoshel, arise and claim your place amongst the nations of the earth'. Radhakrishnan was not merely the President of India, a country of five hundred million people, but also a world figure in the realm of learning as well as politics. He had been awarded innumerable international honours, among them the German *Pour le merit* and the British 'Order of Merit'. The Pope had conferred on him the highest Vatican distinction, the 'Order of the Golden Fleece'. Moscow University elected him to an honorary professorship and conferred on him an honorary Ph.D. He was an intellectual giant among men. It was not surprising that he appeared forbidding — but not to the Killarney Urban District Council.

I met Father Arrupe at a reception in the Jesuit college in Milltown and spoke to him about Japan where he had spent many years and from which I had just returned from a visit of inspection to the Japanese Railways. I had hoped to meet him in Japan but he had left before I arrived. Father Arrupe was a frail, small man who spoke quietly. It was difficult to believe that this was the famous Black Pope.

Queen's University, Belfast, is much more lavish in its honorary degree ceremonies than either Trinity or UCD, so I had several opportunities to speak to Yehudi Menuhin mainly about his reaction to the constant travelling his profession entailed. I gathered that his wife, who was an exceptionally beautiful and gracious woman and to whom he was conspicuously devoted, accompanied him on most of his journeys. As well as being a musician he was a philosopher and he made a brilliant, if rather too subtle, speech at the dinner offered to the new graduates.

The Indian concept of *darshan* whereby mere physical contact, such as hand-shaking, with the great ones confers some quality of grace never affected me. I was certainly never over-awed by them or their reputations. It was interesting to have 'met' them but that was all. However, one visitor from the international scene left a lasting impression on me. External Affairs asked me to see a Swede, whom they described as important, named Gunnar Myrdal. I had never heard of him but I never forgot him. He was an outstanding man of our time — statesman, editor, writer, economist and philosopher: At one time I was told he was a rival of his countryman, Hammersjold, for the post of director-general of the United Nations.

He came into my office accompanied by a secretary with a greeting that sounded like a bellow. He sat me down in front of him (in my office) and at the end of an hour's questioning I had told him all I knew about Ireland. He already knew a lot on the subject because he had thoroughly briefed himself. He had not been in the country long but made one comment about Dublin which illustrated his acuteness of observation. He asked me if I realised that Dublin was indistinguishable from an English city in that the names of all our main thoroughfares act as memorials to our former overlords. I could have told him that an effort to change the street names of the Grafton Street area had been made when Fianna Fáil first came to power. It failed because of the fear of offending 'business interests' which seemed to many of us at the time an example of bending backwards to placate a section of the public who wished little good to the new government. Gunnar Myrdal was the most impressive visitor from abroad I ever encountered.

It was expected of senior public servants to serve, in an honorary capacity, on different committees, commissions and councils. I always regarded it as an honour to be asked. I never refused. I was well rewarded by the acquisition of new and detailed knowledge about different aspects of the country's problems which satisfied my curiosity and by meeting new people and new minds which satisfied my gregariousness. The first commission on which I served was the Drainage Commission. It was presided over by a tough-minded solicitor, an ex-IRA man from Tralee, who had been brought to Dublin by the new Fianna Fáil government to cope with the Department of Justice where the scales had become badly maladjusted. Dan Browne was a friend of mine which made it easier for me to secure the objective uppermost in my mind — to get the River Brosna placed at the head of the list of the arterial drainage projects. Were it not for the Brosna drainage scheme, turf production on a large scale on the Bog of Allen would have been impossible.

I served for many years on the Senate of the National University. Dev was the chancellor at that time and Michael Tierney had just succeeded Arthur Conway as president of University College, Dublin. Before I became a member of the senate I had heard, and assumed to be true, allegations of nepotism and jobbery in university circles, but in all the years I served on the senate I saw no evidence of it and I never knew the senate to make a bad appointment. To the contrary, I have seen the senate reject recommendations from the governing bodies of the colleges which did not conform to the required standards. As chancellor, Dev presided over the meetings but the strongest personality in the senate was Tierney. Like so many academics, he had been a disastrous failure in politics but he was a Greek scholar of some consequence as well as an experienced educationalist and he knew the soul of Ireland better than most men. Rough mannered and irascible, he had a reputation for liberality when it came to allotting funds for scholarly projects. He was the creator of the Belfield campus which will be his memorial.

I served on the Arts Council under the chairmanship of the Jesuit art connoisseur, Father Donal O'Sullivan. His main interest, in fact his only interest, was in promoting modern painting by young Irish artists which was much to the advantage of those who fell into that category but not so good for those who favoured a more conservative style. However the reverend chairman had his way and I was glad to take what pictures he approved at half price for use in the CIE hotels. Between an excellent collection Father O'Sullivan acquired for the Council itself and the pictures acquired on behalf of the hotels, Irish painters got a great boost economically. Our erudite and energetic secretary, the novelist Mervyn Wall, looked after the interests of the amateur theatre effectively. *En passant,* I never thought Mervyn's novels got the public appreciation they deserved, particularly the Fursey books.

While chairman of CIE I had an opportunity to contribute in a small but important way to another art form. In the course of an inspection of what was left to us of Busáras after most of the premises had been taken over by a government department I was shown what seemed to be a large furniture store. In fact it was originally designed as a small cinema which Dublin corporation had refused to licence as suitable for that purpose. Dermot Kelleher, the executive who was showing me around and who was interested in show business in an amateur way, put forward the idea that while not usable as a cinema it could readily be transformed into a good 'little theatre'. As a habitué of the 'little theatre', I approved enthusiastically of Kelleher's suggestion. I thought it would be a particularly suitable venue for Sunday night poetry readings or performances on the lines of Austin Clarke's Lyric Theatre which always attracted an audience.

Kelleher and the CIE architect, Patrick O'Shea, made an excellent conversion job of the very limited space. The new theatre was named the 'Eblana'. It was opened for the Dublin Theatre Festival of 1959 with Synge's *Deirdre of the Sorrows.* Miss Phyllis Ryan took over as the theatre's artistic director and producer. Her *Gemini* productions have flourished there over the years, as have many other theatrical groups. We had several Sunday night poetry readings including a remarkable rendering of an Irish translation from Homer by Monsignor Browne, the polymath and Gaelic scholar, which was presented superbly by the Monsignor's niece, Máire Mac an tSaoí.

The most important commission I served on was that on higher education, presided over by the chief justice, Cearbhall Ó Dálaigh, afterwards President of Ireland. The purpose of the commission was to review the national system of higher education and to make proposals for its future structure. It was a wide ranging brief and the commission was numerically a large one. It consisted of people representing most major interests in the country — farming, medicine, religion, the universities and their colleges, the national and secondary teachers, the semi-state bodies and Irish language organisations. It was about as representative a body as could be got together and its members were persons of distinction and achievement in their different fields.

The commission was especially fortunate in having for its secretary Séamus Cahill, a classics graduate from University College, Cork, who was seconded from the Department of Education. Sometimes when I hear criticism of civil service indolence I remember the long hours of work and the intense and scholarly effort undertaken by Séamus Cahill in the service of the commission. His phenomenal labours received no recognition from the government. On the contrary, while the commission was drawing up its report it was subjected to a contrived and insulting attack by a junior minister on the spurious grounds of dilatoriness. In the face of a threat of mass resignation by members of the commission the Taoiseach, Jack Lynch, repudiated the junior minister but the commission was pressurised into submitting a preliminary report. Its most important recommendations were that the three constituent colleges of the NUI should be re-established as independent universities and that Trinity College, Dublin, would remain a separate institution.

Within a few weeks of receiving the preliminary report and without waiting for the full report and recommendations, Donagh O'Malley, the Minister for Education, in a well pre-publicised television broadcast announced in an atmosphere of high drama that it was the government's intention to merge Trinity College and University College, Dublin, into one establishment. Thus without giving consideration to the views of the commission, its major recommendation was rejected out of hand. All the hard and prolonged effort of so many first-class minds was largely wasted.

Cearbhall Ó Dálaigh was deeply disappointed at the casual destruction of so much of his work. It is extremely doubtful if the minister's broadcast was authorised by the government as a whole. I and a number of others of what might be regarded as the Old Guard of Fianna Fáil wondered to what level governmental behaviour had sunk when a minister could indulge in such a display of irresponsibility and survive. We also wondered why the press gave an almost hysterical welcome to what at best could only be described as O'Malley's inspiration. Whosoever inspired him was clearly ill-informed. If one thing more than another emerged from the deliberations of the commission on higher education, it was that Trinity College and University College, Dublin could not be amalgamated successfully.

Of all the men, Irish or foreign, whom I have encountered Cearbhall Ó Dálaigh was unique. His essential characteristic was that of an Irish patriot. He was a separatist. He believed that so long as the British remained in the six counties, the nation could not burgeon. That did not mean he was anti-British; he only wanted them to leave Ireland. But he wanted an Ireland where the native language and literature, music and arts would play a dominant part in the life of the nation. He was more aware than most men of *The Hidden Ireland* of Daniel Corkery. It was an Ireland in which his inner life was led. He had a scholarly knowledge of the Irish language. He spoke it with what some Gaeilgeoirí regarded as an affected accent. But what he was doing was giving every vowel and every consonant its precise value. His Irish would, I imagine, have been that spoken by educated people if the language had developed uninterruptedly over the centuries.

Cearbhall Ó Dálaigh was extremely but unaffectedly courteous. He had absorbed all the good manners of the Europeans with whom he associated. He was essentially a European and wished every Irish person to regard themselves as European as well as Irish. He spoke Italian, French and Spanish as well as a smattering of some other languages. But Italy was his second country. Its religion, its art, its customs, its food were very precious to him. He even took a glass of Italian wine at his meals, not because it was wine but because it was an Italian custom.

I do not know if he had been influenced by Castiglione's book *The Courtier*. But he acted as if he had.

> The courtier must be at home in all sports, among them running, leaping, swimming and wrestling; he must, above all things, be a good dancer and, as a matter of course, an accomplished rider. He must be a master of several languages; at all events Latin and Italian; he must be familiar with literature and have some knowledge of the fine arts. In music a certain practical skill was expected of him which he was bound, nevertheless, to keep as secret as possible. The mutual interaction of these gifts and accomplishments results in the perfect man in whom no one quality usurps the place of the rest.

He was very fond of young artists. He encouraged them in their play writing and their poetry. He bought many of their pictures. He displayed a bizarre sense of humour, one manifestation of which was his often repeated assertion that he believed the earth was flat — he was a flat-earther. His public life showed many of the characteristics of Saint Thomas More — the loyalty, the devotion to the state and the moral strength that enabled them both to sacrifice their careers on a matter of high principle. I suspected that he dreamed of a Gaelic Utopia and he certainly was possessed of the spirit of the sixteenth century humanists. Had he lived then he would have been a Renaissance man befitting the company of More and Erasmus.

I was closely associated with the Institute of Public Administration from its early days. It began in the fifties when two senior Excise officials in the Custom House, James Waldron and Pat Doolan, organised informal *conversaziones* to discuss the problems of the higher civil service and national issues generally. Simultaneously a few younger civil servants, led by Charlie Murray, Tom Barrington and Desmond Roche, started *Administration,* a journal designed 'to give civil servants an outlet to express opinions on professional matters and eventually to form an institute of public administration'. At the same time Sir Hugh Beaver, managing director of Arthur Guinness, with the support of John Leydon of the Department of Industry and Commerce was advocating the formation of an institute for the development of business management and it transpired that a group of young businessmen were engaged independently in a similar project.

Eventually these influences came together and efforts were made at co-ordination. Leydon made a strong plea for the establishment of a single organisation which would provide a forum for both business and public service interests. In the end it was decided, not without some acrimony, to set up two separate bodies — the Irish Management Institute which was oriented towards commercial management and the Institute of Public Administration which pursued broadly similar objectives in regard to the public service.

The IPA catered for members of the civil service, the semi-state bodies and the staff of the local authorities and John Leydon was elected as its first president. Thanks to the persistence and dedication of it founders the Institute flourished. Lectures and conferences were organised, training courses established. *Administration* was enlarged to become a magazine of authority and significance and a publishing house was set up to publish books of social and administrative importance. Most senior civil servants and local authority managers participated in the development of the Institute and it has since achieved a status of which the pioneers have every reason to be proud.

I gave what support I could to the evolution of the Institute particularly in the formative years. When eventually John Leydon retired from the presidency I was flattered and honoured to be invited to succeed him. One particular satisfaction I derived from this association was the opportunity of getting to know the city and county managers. I have long felt that, apart from the semi-state bodies, the local authority management system was the most successful innovation we had established in the field of public administration. It is unfortunate that no equally radical change has been made in the working of the civil service proper.

Such a change did, in fact, almost come about at the beginning of the Second World War. Impressed by the success achieved by Fred Weckler, the chief accountant, in re-organising the ESB I suggested to the government that he be entrusted with the task of reforming the civil service. I urged this course in discussions with Frank Aiken, who was then Minister for Co-ordination of Defensive Measures, and with Dev himself. It was finally decided to set up a committee with the following terms of reference (drawn up by Aiken): 'To examine and report on the organisation of and administrative methods in each department . . . and to make such recommendations in relation thereto as are considered conducive to greater efficiency and economy'. The committee was to consist of Dan Browne, a Land Commissioner, H. P. Boland a former assistant secretary of the Department of Finance, Fred Weckler and myself.

The decision to appoint this committee aroused manifold emotions in the Department of Finance — shock, horror, despair and even momentary compliance. But they soon recovered their nerve and by a masterful display of Fabian tactics delayed the establishment of the committee until they were rescued by the outbreak of the Emergency in 1940. In that situation it was felt that any attempt at civil service re-organisation would be untimely. The problem then facing us was that of national survival.

It is still my belief that the structure of the civil service as we inherited it at the time of the Treaty was fundamentally unsuited to Irish needs. In my opinion no patching of the system can improve its effectiveness; it requires to be scrapped and to be replaced by a body with a completely different orientation.

The function of the civil service is to give effect to the legislation as passed by the Oireachtas. In carrying out this function its day to day operations are subject to the Parliamentary Question — the PQ — which from the day he takes up duty until the day he retires is a *dopple-gänger* of every civil servant. In theory a minister replying to the PQ in the Dáil must have an answer which justifies the course of action which is being questioned. He must never be in the wrong or admit to having made a mistake. It is the minister, personally, who has to take public responsibility for the acts of his departmental staff. The system is geared to ensuring that the minister is not embarrassed by having to admit an error.

The net result is that, whether he is a clerical officer or the secretary of a department a large proportion of the civil servant's psychic energy is spent in avoiding the possibility of a mistake or taking a risk which could be detrimental to his career. No civil servant, not even the department head, takes the ultimate responsibility for his advice as it resolves itself in action; a civil servant never takes action, he only makes recommendations. Much of the paper work that goes into the system serves no indispensable purpose unless it is accepted that the purpose is to enable the minister to answer the PQ without embarrassment.

Civil servants are often accused of having soft jobs but in general this is not true. They work hard — the higher officials extremely hard. But it is questionable whether the bulk of the work which they do has any value other than to prop up the concept of ministerial accountability. Considering their high level of intelligence and education, civil servants are well capable of taking on much more responsibility than is now entrusted to them. I think they should have such responsibility. In a democracy, the PQ is a necessary part of the parliamentary process but it is not necessary to offer the pretence to the Dáil and to the public that the minister or his servants never make a mistake. Theoretically, resignation is the penalty for ministerial mistakes. I use 'theoretically' advisedly.

The semi-state bodies and the local authority managerial system were established to enable nationally desirable objectives to be implemented free from the constraints of civil service practice. I see no reason why government departments should not be given the same measure of responsibility as the semi-state companies with the secretaries of departments exercising the same authority as the chief executives of these organisations. There are certainly enough capable people in the public service to carry through the radical structural changes which I have in mind. A mixture of conservatism and inertia is the real obstacle to progress in this direction. What is needed is the political will to overcome them.

I was associated with five different semi-state bodies at different stages of their development. When I was in the Irish Tourist Association it could scarcely be said to have had a management structure; it had not developed to the point when it required one. When I first joined the ESB it was badly in need of a properly structured management system. Fred Weckler established one and introduced management methods based on European practice. It was my good luck to have been close to Weckler when the new regime was being established in the ESB. When the re-organisation was completed he appointed me chief accounts inspector and controller of stores. This post gave me an opportunity to learn how Wecker's management methods worked in practice.

When the Turf Development Board was founded I set out on paper, with the help of Weckler, a form of management which would provide for the normal process of expansion; new production centres as they became operational would be absorbed into the system. This worked so successfully that even during the Emergency when the situation required a massive increase in turf production at short notice the scheme was readily accommodated within the existing administrative and accounting system. In the case of the Turf Development Board we had, of course, the advantage of starting with a *tabula rasa* and of working in an expanding organisation. The fact that all managerial appointments and the senior members of their staff were known to me personally was a great help to me as chief executive in co-ordinating the work.

CIE was far from being a *tabula rasa* nor was it an expanding organisation. But the very amorphous character of the organisation, as I found it, together with the abundance of staff eager for and capable of taking responsibility made re-organisation all the easier. Furthermore redundancy terms very much in advance of their time helped in effecting staff economies. Devolution of responsibility through the establishment of local and regional administrative units, as applied in the ESB and in Bord na Móna, was the central feature in the new CIE management structure.

My association with RTE was that of part-time chairman. This post carried no managerial responsibilities apart from presiding at meetings of the RTE authority and making what contribution I could to the formulation of broadcasting policy.

It is not difficult, once its objectives have been defined, to design a management framework to fit any organisation. The real problem is how to animate it. The success achieved depends more than anything else on the personal qualities of the chief executive. Chief executives adopt different approaches to the animation process. I regard management as an art rather than a science. For the head of a semi-state body the capacity to read computer print-outs or to analyse balance sheets would be a poor substitute for a feeling for the social climate and the political constraints in which such bodies operate. Knowledge of the people with whom he is working is indispensable. Data processing systems played little part in my own decision making. I had confidence in the ability of the senior departmental managers to evaluate and find solutions for their operational problems. Acceptance or otherwise of such recommendations as came to me for decision was basically an act of informed intuition.

In decision making I believed in the truth of the old tag 'He gives twice who gives quickly'. In Bord na Móna my close personal contacts with the works managers made it possible to deal with most of their problems on the spot and even where further consultation with headquarters was required they could be sure of a quick decision. In CIE it was not physically possible to be so close to the staff on the ground. I had an standing arrangement with the general manager, Frank Lemass, to meet in my office at 10.30 each morning with a list of items requiring decision. Most of them were finalised then and there, only rarely was a matter postponed for further examination.

Organisations as wide-ranging as Bord na Móna or CIE employ people from every known trade and profession — engineers of all descriptions, chemists, architects, lawyers, accountants, sales and publicity men, fitters, electricians, carpenters and so on. I made a conscious decision never to attempt to acquire any of these skills or even pretend to any knowledge of them. The role of the chief executive is analogous to the conductor of an orchestra whose functions do not include the ability to play all or any of the orchestral instruments.

Like every chief executive I favoured certain personal methods (principles is too pretentious a word) of management. Apart from surrounding myself with abler men I believed strongly in pushing responsibility as far as possible down the line. I think that every man or woman works better if they are made to take responsibility for their actions. As a corollary, I did not question the right of a subordinate to make a genuine mistake or blame him when an effort was unsuccessful. Equally I insisted that once a decision had been arrived at by competent authority at whatever level it should be carried out unquestioningly.

At board level I never treated one member of the board differently from another and avoided lobbying. The position in Bord na Móna was unique to the extent that I had close personal relationships with some of the members so that, unavoidably, the affairs of the board were discussed outside board meetings. The procedure at these meetings was kept as informal as possible apart from ensuring that they began and ended on time. In my dealings with staff also I made a fetish of punctuality.

I was always available to my senior colleagues or indeed any member of the staff who sought an interview. I made a point of recognising merit or special effort. I discouraged the use of memoranda or written reports in favour of the telephone. I put much effort into eliminating paparasse. That was easier to do in Bord na Móna than in CIE where dedication to the printed form was a strong traditional practice. The consultants engaged on simplifying paperwork invited me to inspect a large room where all the forms then in use had been accumulated. Pasted closely side by side on all four walls they might well have set a trend for a new art form but organisationally they were a disaster.

The individual predilections of managers are bound to be reflected in the organisations they control. In Bord na Móna, for example, I made it a rule that all our works and housing schemes should be given Irish place names and that only these names should be used officially. At our Oweninny Works in Mayo, which was a Breac Gaeltacht, a determined effort was made to establish Irish as the working language. All the bog machines were marked with their Irish names and a simple phrasebook of commonplace working terms was published. We got little encouragement from the local people and, I am sorry to say, even less from our own engineers. The engineering school at UCD of which they were largely the product was not noted for an interest in the Irish languge nor indeed for any other expression of nationalism. The professor of engineering, Pierce Purcell, and his successor, Professor Hogan, never seemed to have shaken off the effects of their early working experiences in Britain.

I have always been ashamed of the street names of my native city. The great patriots except O'Connell and Parnell are commemorated, at best, in secondary streets while, as Gunnar Myrdal observed, its principal squares and thoroughfares are named after onetime British overlords — Grafton, Westmoreland, Rutland, Fitzwilliam, Mountjoy. I felt that something should be done to identify Dublin in the eyes of visitors as an Irish city. When the opportunity arose I made arrangements to have the bus destination scrolls shown in their Irish translations; there is no record of anyone having lost his way because of that. I also changed the names of the principal railway stations in Dublin and the other cities to commemorate the men of 1916 for most of whom no memorial has been erected. These relatively minor attempts to reverse the tide of anglicisation evoked much abuse at the time but I never lost any sleep over it.

14

A Valuable Perquisite

When I was in the Irish Tourist Association, Jack O'Brien devised the slogan 'See Ireland First'. It is an injunction any Irish person should heed before undertaking foreign travel. Knowing Ireland well provides a standard of comparison with the sights, the manners and customs and the political systems that are to be observed abroad. It also helps to get Ireland into perspective in relation to other countries. I had the good luck to have visited every part of Ireland before embarking on extensive foreign travel and undoubtedly this has greatly enhanced the satisfaction I derived from my experiences as a tourist abroad.

I had, when in the IRA, visited Donegal, Cavan and Monaghan and the Leinster and Munster counties, mostly on foot, which is the best way to get to know the people and the countryside. While I was in the ESB I acquired a car and in the course of my duties visited all the large and most of the small provincial centres in the country. So that even at that early stage of my life I knew Ireland very well indeed.

But the ambition of most young people is to travel abroad. In imagination Mary and I often speculated on the pleasures of visiting Rome or Venice or Athens or a dozen other places we came across in our reading. In the thirties it was impossible for us to look forward, even in the future, to going further afield than France. These were the days before package tours and student tickets. Foreign travel has until recently been one of the major prerogatives of the wealthy. It required leisure and money beyond the reach of the common man.

The mission to Germany and Russia undertaken by the turf delegation in 1935 marked a radical change in the civil service attitude towards foreign travel. Irish public officials did not go abroad except perhaps to see their *chers collègues* in London who were the repository of all official wisdom. Any travel beyond London was regarded as a holiday trip at the public expense; to say such trips were not encouraged would be an understatement. They just did not arise.

Francis Bacon wrote one of his essays on the subject of travel and what he said is as true now as it was in the seventeenth century, though his advice on what to seek in foreign travel was addressed to the aristocrats of his day for whom expense was no object:

> Travel, in the younger sort, is a part of education; in the elder, a part of experience. He that travelleth into a country before he hath some entrance into the language, goeth to school, and not to travel. That young men travel under some tutor, or grave servant, I allow well; so that he be such a one that hath the language and hath been in the country before; whereby he may be able to tell them what things are worthy to be seen in the country where they go; what acquaintances they are to seek; what exercises or discipline the place yieldeth. For else young men shall go hooded, and look abroad little. It is a strange thing that in sea-voyages, where there is nothing to be seen but sky and sea, men should make diaries, but in land-travel, wherein so much is to be observed, for the most part they omit it; as if chance were fitter to be registered than observation. Let diaries, therefore, be brought in use.

Bacon supposed that his traveller would be accompanied by a highly educated and polyglot tutor who would have boned up on the history, antiquities and customs of the country to be visited. He writes that:

> things to be seen and observed are: the courts of princes, specially when they give audience to ambassadors; the courts of justice, while they sit and hear causes, and so of consistories ecclesiastic; the churches and monasteries, with the monuments which are therein extant; the walls and fortifications of the cities and towns, and so the havens and harbours; antiquities and ruins; libraries; colleges, disputations and lectures, where any are; shipping and navies; houses and gardens of state and pleasure, near great cities; armories, arsenals; magazines; exchanges; burses; warehouses; exercises of horsemanship, fencing, training of soldiers and the like; comedies, such whereunto the better sort of persons do resort; treasuries of jewels and robes; cabinets and rarities; and, to conclude, whatsoever is memorable in the places where they go.

I could not have foreseen before that first visit to Russia and Germany that it would have been my good fortune to travel under the guidance of people who had no language problems and who knew the monuments and antiquities of their countries better than any tutor could. As the years went on and I travelled more extensively abroad I had for Cicerones on sundry occasions the representatives of government departments, national fuel organisations, national tourist boards, national railways. When I travelled on official business, whether by ship, road, rail or air it was with a degree of comfort which only a very rich man could normally have afforded.

The decision to develop the bogs on the German pattern involved me in frequent visits to Germany and apart from my business interests I managed to see much of north-east Germany and Hamburg, including its famous 'fun' district, similar to the Place Pigalle in Paris, and its infamous Reeperbahn, where the prostitutes offered themselves from the house windows; you could pick and choose. Except in Amsterdam, I have never seen this facility in any other city I visited. During these pre-war visits to Germany I was quite conscious of the rise of Hitler and was not particularly unsympathetic to the Nazis, principally because they had solved the problem of unemployment and also because the movement in its early stages introduced an element of egalitarianism which had been singularly lacking in the class-bound German social structure. I was in Germany just a month before the outbreak of war and it was evident from all the immense engineering work that was going on along the Dutch frontier that war preparations were being pushed ahead frantically. As we learned later they were constructing the Siegfried Line. But the Germans we spoke to were even then persuaded that there would be no war, that Hitler's intentions were peaceful and this at a time when everyone outside Germany rightly regarded war as inevitable. My critical comments about the persecution of the Jews to people whom I regarded as cultured and sophisticated products of German society were shrugged off with the reply that in the protection of the nation someone has to suffer.

There was no foreign travel during the war but much of my time was spent touring the bogs in an effort to stimulate Emergency turf production. Often I travelled with Hugo Flinn but more often by myself in an eight-horsepower Ford car which, despite my misgivings about all things mechanical, always started and never had a puncture! A curious illusion has been created by the motor manufacturers that the car you use is supposed to be a reflection of your personality, of your standing in the community or of your success in life. I would readily confess that it would be difficult to find anyone more greedy than I for recognition of status in the community but I find it impossible to regard the ownership of a car, or of property of any kind, as a genuine criterion of success. Even government ministers are not satisfied with the prestige justifiably associated with their position; they show off their success by appearing amongst their constituents in a large car which must not only be black but shiny as well. It argues the acceptance of low standards of values. I was expounding this view to a friend who retorted, 'Is it because thou art virtuous there shall be no more cakes and ale?' To which I replied, 'Yes! Virtue is more important than cakes and ale.' And so I think. Like most people of my day, I have succumbed to some of the lures of the consumer society but I am not happy about my weaknesses.

Mary had made friends with some Breton refugees and when, after the war, foreign travel resumed they offered to arrange holiday accommodation for her and our three youngest children in a place called Douarnanez in Brittany. She and a friend took the cheapest route to Douarnanez. After a gypsy-like trek by ship, rail and road, they arrived at their destination having been compelled to spend one night in a *maison de passe* in Rouen and another night en route sleeping five in a room. The holiday which lasted two months was a success. In the following year her Breton friends offered Mary the free loan of a house in another Brittany village, called Piriac, which she readily accepted and this time their stay extended to three months.

I was too busy to join the family in Douarnanez but I did get down several times to Piriac for a few weeks to find Mary installed as a member of the community giving voluntary classes in English in the convent school and on friendly terms with the Curé and the nuns. She met two Parisian families in Piriac with whom she formed an enduring friendship. Some years later when my daughter who was attending school in Paris became seriously ill, these French families took charge of the situation and behaved to us as an Irish neighbour would have done in a similar emergency.

While I was in Bord na Móna, I visited officially Sweden and Denmark as well as France, Austria and Germany. I made and remained very close friends with a Swedish family. They have holidayed with us in Ireland and I and my eldest son, who worked in a Stockholm Hotel, have stayed with them in Sweden. Mary, despite many invitations, never visited Sweden. Even the charm of our friends Bjorn and Irene Holmgren could not persuade her to go. Mary believed that the Reformation had been a disaster and she saw in Sweden the history of the Reformation writ large. She believed that the Swedes like the WASPS, who form America's permanent ruling class, held Catholics in contempt. I used to tease Mary on her inability to outgrow the bigotry of the Northern Catholics into which she was born. From my limited experience I formed the opinion that Sweden was the nearest humanity was likely to get to Utopia. It was governed rationally and with tolerance. It succeeded in combining egalitarianism and the monarchy — a rare exercise in political syncretism. But I would not like to live in Utopia, nor anywhere else but Dublin.

When I joined CIE in 1958, foreign travel took on a new dimension for me. On taking up office as chairman I was presented by British Railways with a gold pass which entitled me to free travel all over the British Rail system and on ships owned by British Rail for my lifetime. The same facility extended to Mary if she was travelling with me and we found that an equivalent concession applied on all European railways, and indeed on any railway in the world, by virtue of international usage. One would need to have a very large income to be able to purchase travel facilities of that order. And I availed myself of them in full.

Since our honeymoon the only holiday Mary and I had taken on our own together was in 1954 when we celebrated our twenty-fifth wedding anniversary by spending a month in Cannes. Ordinarily we could not have afforded to spend a week in Cannes but we had become friendly with a French Canon, Monsignor Héon, who arranged for us to be received into a guest house run by a branch of the Loreto Nuns where it transpired, members of the Lyons *haute bourgeoisie* were accommodated for holidays. Our fellow guests were rather elderly couples who might well have walked out of the pages of Mauriac. They were highly cultivated and interested in poetry, painting and religion. Except for the cost of the air fare, the holiday was very cheap and we repeated it several times in subsequent years. After I became chairman of CIE we were able, by courtesy of the French railways, to travel in luxury by *Train Bleu* from Paris to Cannes each with a separate wagon lit. It is a wonderful experience to wake up to the glorious early morning sky of southern France.

Thanks to the generosity of the international railway authorities, Mary and I had several successful and enjoyable holidays together in Europe. We once travelled by rail via Paris, Milan, Belgrade and Sofia to Istanbul and returned by Athens and Vienna where Mary fulfilled an ambition to see Vienna and hear an opera in the Opera House. As we could only get one ticket for the Opera I availed myself of the opportunity to visit the Vienna Woods. Knowing very little German I was forced to keep my own company and out of sheer boredom I casually entered a church where a magnificent ceremony was in progress. I could not understand what was going on but the function culminated in exposition of the Blessed Sacrament. That made me feel that I was at home among my own people, a feeling I always experienced when attending Mass in any foreign country. But that was in the days of the Latin Mass. Irrespective of my feelings about the Irish Church or the practice of going to Mass in Ireland I always went out of my way to attend Sunday Mass when abroad. If she was with me Mary, who was punctilious in regard to religious duties, would not have allowed me to forget. The only place we failed to find a Catholic church was in Istanbul.

Only twice did Mary accompany me on official as distinct from private visits: once when the Dutch railway authorities invited us to be their guests at the centenary celebrations of the Dutch railways, and again when the SNCF (French National Railways) and the French government combined to entertain us for a week in Paris on the occasion of the centenary of the *Union Internationale des Chemins de Fer*. The Dutch are marvellous hosts and we succeeded in seeing most of Holland, its historic sites and many of its customs and traditions. In Paris, on the other hand, we experienced entertainment in its most elaborate forms with the grand escalier of the Opera lined by Republican Guards in full dress uniform and a banquet in the Orangerie at Versailles where the waiters and attendants were dressed in the livery of the days of Marie Antoinette. I have to confess that I was bored by both the big occasions. To me these grandiose functions were suggestive of an operatic stage set or of the performances of the Royal Court of Lilliput and man at his most absurd.

We visited Greece and Crete twice, the Cretan visits being inspired by Mary Renault's *The King Must Die*. We visited Spain, going by train from Paris via Madrid where we stayed for a few days sightseeing including a visit to a bull fight. The spectacle was extremely colourful and the excitement intense. What I knew of bull-fighting was derived solely from Hemingway's *Death in the Afternoon,* admittedly an inadequate textbook on the finer points of the sport but I found nothing to shock or amaze me in the treatment of the bull. The manner of its death was no more cruel or inhuman than the pole-axe used in every village butcher's yard in Ireland to kill cattle. From Madrid we went to Malaga to stay with Irish friends who were spending their retirement in Spain.

The luxury in which we travelled on these privately organised occasions did not extend beyond the railway stations of our destinations. From that point onward we reverted to the status of tourists and to phrase books, except in France. Inadequate skill in languages detracts greatly from the value of foreign travel and organised sight-seeing tours do not fully overcome the problem. The widespread use of English helps, but we found on our trip to Istanbul that English or French was very little use to us. Mary was a very good traveller and notwithstanding language difficulties she had the ability to make conversation with fellow passengers or with shopkeepers or street traders. Her natural affability and lack of diffidence enabled us to enjoy and benefit from travelling in countries whose language we did not know.

On official visits, the usual procedure was that the hotel charges were paid by the visiting party and the host organisation took over the expenses from that point. In my early pre-war experiences of travelling on behalf of Bord na Móna I accepted the proposition, common among my circle, that travelling abroad on official engagements was a holiday at the public expense. Consequently I felt that it was wrong to mix pleasure with business and was reluctant to accept entertainment from my hosts or to avail of sight-seeing opportunities. I also felt that it was proper to save public money where possible by travelling at night and at weekends.

In this respect my attitude was a legacy from the puritanical mores of the Republican movement of which at that time Fianna Fáil was a derivative. But I soon discovered the falsity of this narrow approach and came to realise how the value of such visits, even in official terms, was diminished by failing to see as much of the country as circumstances permit. I recall an occasion when a delegation of engineers from Bord na Móna went to see the Finnish bogs. They arrived in Helsinki in the afternoon and were taken up-country to see the bogs where they spent a week. They returned to Helsinki in the afternoon and despite the pursuasion of their most hospitable hosts to stay and see something of the city they decided to go straight to the airport and home. We took steps to ensure that this example of excessive virtue was not repeated. I think Bord na Móna was something of a pioneer in sending staff abroad on a regular basis and I never found anything but good to come of it.

While I was in CIE we were invited to visit Japan as guests of the Japanese Railway Authorities. We knew enough about the Japanese railway system to realise that it was so far advanced technically and operationally that we were unlikely to find much that was applicable to our relatively modest undertaking. The outstanding item of interest was, of course, the Tokyo to Kyoto line which ranks among the wonders of the modern age and which we were anxious to see if only to put our own railway operation in perspective. Moreover both the Department of Foreign Affairs and the Japanese embassy in Dublin were strongly in favour of the visit as a means of establishing closer contact between the two countries.

Dan Herlihy, the chief engineer of CIE, and I left by air for Tokyo but the flight was diverted to Cairo owing to the India-Pakistan war. *En route* from Dublin we were introduced by Captain Vincent Horgan, a Dublin hotelier, to a senior member of the Egyptian Tourist Bureau with whom I had an interesting discussion ranging from Nasser's economic programme to the fabulous history of ancient Egypt. As a gesture of unique hospitality he made special arrangements to enable us to inspect the Tutankhamen treasure in the national museum. A rare experience and an auspicious start to our journey.

The Japanese railway authorities had set up a special section of their Foreign Affairs Department to cope with the flow of international railway executives wishing to study the working of the

famous Tokyo-Kyoto railway. It was indeed an engineering master-
piece designed to withstand the hazards of frequent earthquakes
and constructed without benefit of level crossings, tunnels or overhead bridges. The Japanese were very anxious that visitors should
form a favourable impression of the country derived less from such
things as food and drink as from the cultural features of Japanese
life. We were shown their beautiful gardens — the Japanese
Garden at Tully, County Kildare does not rate at all badly — their
Kabuki theatre which was to me unintelligible and bore no
resemblance to the version I had seen presented in Dublin. We
were present at a public performance of the traditional tea ceremony and feeling perhaps that this was in some way inadequate our
guide, in a friendly gesture, brought us to his own home where the
ceremony was repeated by his wife in the manner in which it is
carried out domestically for an honoured guest. The tea ceremony
is supposed to produce tranquillity in the participants. In my case
the public performance produced no sensation whatever but, to my
pleasant surprise, the domestic ceremony did induce a feeling of
calmness.

Every public place in Japan including, of course, the many railway offices we visited, displayed flower arrangements exquisite in
design and construction. As a dedicated gardener I had been looking forward to seeing at first-hand Japan's unique contribution to
the development of flower arrangement art form called 'Ikebana'.
The different types of flower arrangement have a special significance for the Japanese and there are several schools of teaching. In
'Ikebana' form is more important than colour so that it is possible to
produce very attractive floral designs all the year round.

Discussions with American Express in connection with the
development of CIE tour business brought me to New York. At
that time Fred Boland was Ireland's ambassador to the United
Nations and he and his wife, Frances Kelly the artist, were family
friends of ours. I stayed with them in New York and was able to
explore the city under the best possible auspices. Fred showed me
over the United Nations' headquarters where I was introduced to
many political notabilities whose names I have forgotten as surely
as they have forgotten mine. He also took me to a buffet reception
given by the United Nations on the roof of the Empire State Building. I was not unaccustomed to what was, by my standards, lavish
entertainment but this reached a level of gourmandise comparable
to that supposedly provided for Churchill by Onassis. It seemed to
include every comestible from shrimps to caviar and every drink
from tequilla to champagne.

My working life has brought me into contact with three public servants of outstanding quality — John Leydon, Fred Boland and Ken Whitaker — all men of no property. Each operated in different fields — Leydon in industry, Boland in diplomacy and Whitaker in finance. Boland was a man of middle size and ruddy complexion, dapper as became a diplomat. He had put himself through Trinity College by scholarships supplemented by what could be earned from playing the piano in a local dance band. He was awarded a Rockefeller scholarship which enabled him to travel all over the USA. No one could have had a more suitable training for diplomacy and no one could have used his training more to the advantage of Ireland. As president of the United Nations Organisation, the high point of a distinguished diplomatic career, he reflected honour on himself and on the country. The success of that career was greatly helped by Judy (as his wife, Frances, was always known) whose calculated *faux pas* amused everyone while embarrassing no one. In addition to being a talented professional painter she had the eye of a cartoonist but instead of putting her victim's absurdities on paper she articulated them with extremely comical results. She was a woman of exceptional intelligence who cultivated astronomy as a private hobby. I was never quite sure whether, in addition to being an astronomer, she was also an astrologer. A most generous woman, she painted portraits of Mary and myself and presented them to us, as well as several other treasured examples of her work.

15

At Home

Few people have been given the opportunity that I and my friends had of leaving a permanent mark on the country such as was brought about by the development of the bogs. A generation is growing up that will never have seen the Bog of Allen which from time immemorial has been the centrepiece of the topography of Ireland. Nor is the opportunity given to many to have a very free hand in the reorganisation of a national transport system.

From this it will be clear that I was well satisfied with myself when I retired. In retirement I found I had the leisure, the modest comfort and the intellectual resources to enjoy it. With my garden, my books, my family and friends I had no fear of boredom, that dread of retired public servants.

I have reason to regard myself as a very lucky man both in my working career and in my family life. Not the least part of my good luck was to have my roots in Ireland undisturbed, particularly in Dublin. My absences from the city never lasted longer than a couple of months at a time and I was always glad to return because it imparted to me a sense of friendship, security and pride. I could not imagine a better place to live and bring up a family. Dublin has every amenity that any reasonable person could want — theatres, picture galleries, beautiful public parks and gardens, good schools, two universities, facilities for all kinds of sports and hobbies, easy access to the mountains and the sea. It is moreover a capital city; no city however big can aspire to the status of a capital city however small.

I do not think I was a typical public servant. I was too closely identified with the political events of my generation. The economics of my family life, on the other hand, followed the pattern of the average public servant. Having coped with the problems of rearing and supporting a family, he retires with a gratuity which represents his life savings and enables him to clear his house mortgage and pay his debts. He also has a pension from which to meet the expenses of everyday living. He can never hope to accumulate a fortune. The only inheritance his children are likely to enjoy is a share in the proceeds of his house and its contents. But the public servant, even if he never achieves riches, has a secure job, a good credit rating with the bank and a status of sorts in the community.

This was the financial framework within which Mary and I lived. Though enriched by the experience of foreign travel and a constantly growing acquaintanceship in official, artistic and academic circles, the manner of our family and social life scarcely changed from the day we married until Mary's death nearly forty years later. We had five children, four sons and at the tail end of the family a daughter. We changed house twice to accommodate our growing family but we remained all the years in the parish of Dundrum in County Dublin. We experienced the common vicissitudes of rearing a family, some minor, some serious. One of the boys had severe eye trouble, another had to spend a year in bed with tuberculosis. Mary's interest was devoted almost totally to the children and though I supported her decisions I am sorry to have to admit that I contributed little or nothing to their upbringing. I was a poor parent in that I never attempted to teach them anything or to develop their interests. One example of my lack of parental understanding was that of banning the children from the livng room whenever we had company. Much later in life I discovered how much resentment this piece of insensitivity had caused.

Mary's brothers and sisters married. My brother, Patrick, married and settled in Dundrum parish as did my mother having sold her business in Terenure. Most of the young people with whom we grew up married and set up house at much the same time as ourselves so that between our family connections and a wide range of friends we had no shortage of social intercourse. In those days the rules of entertainment in our circle did not include formal meals: tea and sandwiches were all that hospitality demanded. As we grew older, sherry and whiskey were added to the bill of fare.

Apart from our immediate families the people with whom we were on regular visiting terms were exclusively of Republican origin. It is a reflection of the wounds of the Civil War that, though the open bitterness which caused protagonists to ignore one another in the street had disappeared by the end of the Thirties, no family with a Free State background ever visited our house or vice versa until well after the war, with the exception of some members of Mary's relatives to whom she was particularly devoted. This despite the fact that the Fourth Battalion of the Dublin Brigade of which I was a member, was the first to make a positive effort to reconcile the antagonists of the Civil War. We formed a club in Thomas Street where meetings were held from time to time. We erected a memorial to our deceased members and kept a role of honour. There was an annual remembrance service with a parade from the memorial to the church. For my part, I never lost touch with the men of the Fourth Battalion and particularly those of my own company, 'E' Company. As a senior official in the public service, I made it a rule to be available to any member of the old IRA from whatever side in the Civil War, who wished to see me — with the exception of one whom I regarded as a psychopath. With the members of 'E' Company, I maintained a lifelong personal relationship. Almost all of them are now dead.

In the households we frequented the only form of amusement was conversation and the dominant topics were Ireland in all its aspects, world politics and books. Although basically Republican not all of our friends were supporters of Fianna Fáil nor, curiously enough, were many of them interested in either economics or social issues. My sympathy with socialism and particularly the Communist movement left them mostly untouched. Religion also was rarely discussed. Most Republicans had decided to forget the Bishops' Pastoral of 1922 and were reconciled to the Church while the bishops had apparently got over their aversion to having murderers (or ex-murderers) within their fold. Apart from the common interests shared by all, some of our friends had their own special affinities such as painting, the theatre and Irish history. It has to be admitted that our intellectual range was limited because we tended to regard Ireland as the numbril of the world.

Incidents of the Civil War were relived and recounted and memories of IRA friends who had emigrated to America and elsewhere. One of the first of the Civil War exiles to return was an old friend of mine, Seán Nolan, quartermaster of the Four Courts' garrison, who had made a modest fortune in America by combining his talents as a carpenter and a musician. As a carpenter he worked on the building of film sets in Hollywood and later in New York he organised the Seán Nolan Dublin Ceilí Band, which in addition to Seán himself, consisted of a a Czech, a Jew and a priest from Offaly who acted as vocalist and collected money on behalf of his home parish.

Two days before the Wall Street crash Seán had quite fortuitously withdrawn all his money from the bank. While waiting to start the journey home, he spent his time in Greenwich Village in New York. One evening in a restaurant there he got involved in an argument with some WASP who called him an Irish pig to which Seán responded by breaking a chair over his opponent's head. When the uproar died down Seán was told by one of the waiters that a lady customer who had witnessed the scene was anxious to meet him and invited him to join her for a drink. The lady turned out to be the film actress, Elissa Landi. She was entranced by the story of Seán's life and adventures — how he aspired to be a violinist but became a carpenter on his father's insistence; how he joined the IRA, the street fighting, the siege of the Four Courts, his experiences in jail, followed by unemployment and emigration; how his carpentry skills were put to use in the Hollywood studios, the formation of the Dublin Ceilí Band and how finally he avoided being caught in the Wall Street crash.

It was quite a story and as told by Seán it reached homeric proportions. Not surprisingly, Miss Landi was keen to see more of him and readily accepted his invitation to dinner a few days later. To his dismay she selected The Lafayette, an extremely expensive and fashionable restaurant frequented by the Scott Fitzgerald set, but Seán's Irish pride (or gaucherie) compelled him to accept. Seán arrived at the appointed time with his tuxedo and a wad of dollar bills prepared to give his companion her gastronomic head. His worst fears were realised. After two cocktails she proceeded to order two dozen Blue Point oysters for each of them and, with every one she swallowed, Seán's heart missed a beat. The oysters were followed by roast pheasant and rum baba for dessert. Though by this time mentally prostrate, Seán called for the bill with a flourish, only to have it snatched from his hand by Miss Landi who laughingly asked if he really expected to be allowed to pay. 'Every dollar you have in the world is there in your wallet. I earn more in a week than you would in a lifetime. I'm taking the bill.' So great was Seán's relief that he almost talked himself into believing that he realy wanted to pay the bill and threatened to create a scene unless allowed to. 'A scene! Go ahead. I love them. That's what attracted me to you in the first place.' They took a taxi to her apartment and as they stood on the pavement she said, 'Please, Seán, don't let us behave like a washerwoman and her beau.' They said good night.

All my friends supported Fianna Fáil in the 1932-33 elections but as the years wore on disillusionment with the conservative policies set in. John Dowling, who had influenced me intellectually though not politically throughout most of my life, founded a new party, Córas na Poblachta, but it failed to get support. John returned to his special interest in Patrician studies and produced a paper which identified Avonmouth on the Severn as St Patrick's birthplace and claimed that he had not been sent from Rome but had come to Ireland in defiance of his superiors in Britain. It was a highly original thesis though not universally accepted.

In 1938, the Economic War ended with the Anglo-Irish agreement which also provided for the handing back of the Treaty ports. At this time, Jim O'Donovan, who had been director of chemicals of the pre-Truce IRA and later on a colleague of mine in the ESB, was deeply involved in preparing for the bombing campaign in England. I regarded that campaign as the most foolish and irresponsible act which bedevilled Anglo-Irish relations in my lifetime. Without its disastrous effects on political opinion in England Dev's good relationship with Neville Chamberlain might well have made some progress towards ending Partition. It was only many years afterwards that I learned of O'Donovan's connection with the bombing campaign although he and his wife, a sister of Kevin Barry, were frequent visitors to our house and we to his.

During Mary's absences in Carraroe for the summer holidays I moved in with my mother. I found it impossible to get her to accept the fact that I was a grown man with a family. She insisted on treating me as though I was still a schoolboy. 'Will you be home for dinner? What time will you be in for tea? What would you like me to get you to eat? Steak, stew, boiled mutton? Rashers and eggs or sausages and pudding?' I could not make her understand that I did not come back from school at 3 p.m. nowadays and that I would be happy to eat whatever she cooked because I knew within narrow limits the range of her menus and had no preferences between them. The last straw came when she tried to insist on polishing my shoes; I was almost impelled to leave.

My mother was born and reared in Summerhill in the very heart of the city. When she moved to suburban Terenure in her thirties she felt as if she had arrived in a frontier town and Dundrum, where she now lived, was no better. My mother-in-law, Mrs Coyle, was a regular visitor to Carraroe during the summer holidays. I thought I should suggest to my mother that she might also like to spend some time with the family. My invitation was received with a derisive laugh. To her idea of crossing the Shannon was as distasteful as if she were asked to go to the Arctic. She was never reconciled to living outside the heart of Dublin. It is a feeling I well understand because, given suitable accommodation, I would not be adverse to ending my days in the neighbourhood of Summerhill. I certainly sympathise at the distress caused to so many people forced to move out from the inner city to the new satellite towns.

During the Second World War Mary joined the local Fianna Fáil Cumann and at election time conscripted such of our children as were old enough to distribute leaflets and deliver election material. Almost from birth they were involved in politics. Mary and a very formidable village shop owner, Mrs Mulvey, who was the local chieftainess of Fine Gael, fought bitter verbal battles at different community gatherings. The Mulveys are still in the village and our families are friendly.

Over the years I played golf, first with my Coyle brothers-in-law in Delgany and later with a small group of friends in Kilcroney. We were more interested in each other's company and in enjoying the beautiful scenery of Kilcroney than in the golf. In the summer evenings and sometimes at the weekends, I fished, wet-fly, for trout in the rivers surrounding the city — the Liffey, the Stoneyford, the Deale, the Kells Blackwater, the Moynalty and the Trimlestown. One Whit Monday, while fishing on the lake at Blessington, a gust of wind blew my cast into my shoulder. The tail fly stuck there and my hand-fly swung around and caught me in the eye. I had the good sense to do nothing but wait until I attracted the attention of my companions, Ben Carty and Joe Griffin. Ben, who was our family doctor, cut away the cast leaving the hook embedded in my eye. We drove at great speed for the Eye and Ear Hospital and were fortunately able to locate Alan Mooney, Dublin's leading eye surgeon. Alan saved my eye by his superlative skill and although I had to spend three weeks in hospital the sight was undamaged.

Carty and Griffin were friends from IRA days. Before I became friendly with Mary, Carty and his brother, Gus, went regularly with me to the Drama League Sunday night performances in the Abbey where we were introduced to the European Theatre of Brecht, Toller and Pirandello. Carty was a man of unusual humility and generosity. It was difficult to persuade him to take a fee from an old IRA man.

I had known Joe Griffin when he was head of the IRA intelligence service in the Four Courts and later when, as an accountant, he looked after my father's income tax. He was appointed secretary to Comhlucht Siúicre Éireann, moved on to the position of Price Controller at the start of the Emergency and eventually became managing director of the Waterford Glass Company of which he made such a spectacular success.

Joe was a very complicated man. He had suffered from a drink problem, though by this time he had not taken a drink for years. He described freely and frighteningly his mental condition while in the throes of a drinking bout. I tried, without success, to persuade him to put the experience on paper. At a later stage he immersed himself in the philosophy of Maritain and became an intellectual adversary of Communism. Though notably hot-tempered, he was also the most generous of men, always ready to rescue lame ducks.

The pattern of our family life was altered with the Emergency. Owing to transport difficulties, it was no longer easy to exchange visits with our friends. I had a car for official business but it had to be garaged overnight at the office unless I got back to Dublin after the last bus had left town. When the children had gone to bed Mary and I 'walked the block', stopping off regularly at our local pub 'The Goat' which has now become a leading restaurant but was then no more than a country inn. There we met our neighbours and formed a new set of acquaintances.

After Sunday morning Mass, we usually congregated for drinks and discussion at the very hospitable home of the Digby family. Jim Digby was managing director of Pye Radio (Ireland). He had worked all over the world in jobs connected one way or another with the radio business. He was one of the first entrepreneurs to appreciate the advantages offered by the Fianna Fáil protectionist policy and had prospered as a result. Digby was generous in his patronage of the arts and supported *The Bell* for many years. He had a passionate interest in the development of the inland fisheries and was partly responsible for the establishment of the Inland Fisheries Trust. He wrote a book which aimed at proving that our salmon fisheries, if properly developed, could solve the national emigration problem. Clearly he was a victim of his own enthusiasm.

At the beginning of the Emergency, a parish council was formed and it in turn formed a Home Makers' Guild. The Guild consisted of some twenty women and its purpose was to provide a substantial daily meal for anyone in need of it. It was a non-denominational body and operated from the local Protestant Hall. Mary took a very active part in the Guild which served a genuine local need. Quite unexpectedly, it was intimated to the Catholic members of the Guild through the local curate that this kind of inter-denominational community work was unacceptable to John Charles McQuaid, the Archbishop of Dublin. Mary was furiously annoyed and sent a letter of protest to the archbishop to which there was no reply. She urged her fellow members to ignore the archbishop's intervention but failed to get their support and the Guild was dissolved. Later the Catholic members formed a sewing circle which met weekly in our house to make vestments for missionary priests. What effective good it did in this way I cannot say but it certainly helped to promote a community spirit in the village of Dundrum. The sewers were known, ironically, as 'the holy women'.

Housekeeping during the Emergency caused some problems but no real hardship. Essential footstuffs and fuel of all kinds were rationed but Mary did not find it difficult to cope with the situation. Tea we had in plenty because Mary had bought in a chest of tea immediately before the outbreak of war when the public was being urged to stock up with commodities likely to be in short supply. Since our children did not drink tea and I favoured coffee, which was not rationed, we had a surplus from which Mary was able to help out the older people among our friends and neighbours with gifts of tea. As to the other household items, such as butter and sugar, we simply learned to live within the ration resisting any temptation to buy in the black market. Mary had very strong anti-black market views; she once broke off social relations with friends who had treated her to bread and cakes made from what was admittedly black-market white flour. The wartime austerity did not bother me unduly apart from the nearly black bread which was to me both unpalatable and indigestible. I willingly settled for potatoes.

Our chief problem was that of fuel. As we did not use gas we were at least free of the attentions of the 'glimmer man' whose inspections ensured that the domestic gas ration was not exceeded. Our anthracite allowance was barely sufficient to keep the cooker going in the kitchen which became the family living room for the duration of the war. We had rarely enough turf to light the sitting room fire and often on winter evenings were forced to go to bed early. My association with the fuel business culminating, after Hugo Flinn's death, in my appointment as Fuel Controller, ruled out any question of supplementing our fuel supply from off-ration sources even if I had the inclination to do so.

Apart from the rationed commodities, many non-essential and semi-luxury items were scarce but the only shortage that really counted with me was that of cigarettes. It was unfortunate for the sake of my future health that I enjoyed an adequate supply through the good offices of an ex-jail friend who ran a prosperous tobacconist business.

Money, rather than things to buy with it, was our main concern at this time. The cost of living was constantly rising but my salary was frozen by government order during the Emergency so that we had to resort to borrowing from the bank. Fortunately our credit was good although it took me some time and caused much worry before I made this discovery. On one occasion I was so hard up that the family electricity bill could not be paid. Faced with this financial stringency I applied for my military service pension which, like many other old IRA men, I had refused to accept when it was instituted by the first Fianna Fáil administration.

I always had difficulty in working out my income tax liability and spent many uneasy hours wondering where the money could be found to pay it. At one time I had accumulated tax arrears of £300. I hesitated to make an approach to the bank because I could never convince myself that that banks were in business to lend money; in increasing my overdraft they seemed to be doing me a favour rather than the reverse. Joe Griffin rescued me from this particular crisis with a loan of £300, which he had not got but knew his cheque would be honoured. Being an expert on banking and income tax, he persuaded me to go to the bank and demand, if necessary, extended overdraft facilities which, as it turned out, were granted without demur.

In the 1950s, Mary became deeply involved with the Irish Housewives' Assocation. It seemed to me to be a worthy organisastion though unlikely to be effective in its main objective of resisting retail price increases. Some statement issued by the Association gave offence to the *Roscommon Herald* or one of its correspondents, and resulted in their being described as Communists. The Association, represented in this instance by Mary and Andrée Sheehy-Skeffington, took legal action for libel which was settled out of court with an apology from the newspaper.

I knew nothing of the affair until I arrived home from work one evening to find Mary triumphant because of her legal victory over the *Roscommon Herald:* all the more so because the whole proceedings had been masterminded by Mrs Sheehy Skeffington and herself without reference to me. Mary was far from being a Communist and she resented being labelled as one in those halcyon days of Catholic extremism.

All during our married life Mary and I sustained our interest in the theatre. We saw every play of any significance performed in Dublin. We were present at the first night of *The Rose Tattoo* by Tennessee Williams at the Pike and felt that the prosecution subsequently brought against Alan Simpson, the producer, was as stupid as it was futile. We attended the first production of the Gate Theatre Company — *Peer Gynt* — but partly due to the smallness of the Peacock Theatre where it was played, it rated to my mind as a very indifferent performance. We often talked of the theatrical occasions we enjoyed most. Mary plumped for *The Playboy of the Western World* with Cyril Cusack playing Christy Mahon and Bríghid Ní Loinsigh played Pegeen Mike; I chose *Hedda Gebler* in which Micheál Mac Líammóir played Lovborg and Peggy Ashcroft played Hedda.

When we made our final domiciliary move, it was to a house on Taney Road (at that time little more than a country lane) which we called 'Ardcath' from the name of the village on the Meath-Dublin border whence the Andrews family originated. The new house proved to be a bargain but one that left us without enough money to surface the drive not to mind laying out a garden. I felt obliged to make an effort at least to keep the ground tidy. In the process I found I could grow flowers and vegetables quite easily, assisted by a few gardening books and with some guidance from my friend, Tony Woods, who was an ardent gardener. I became passionately interested in the garden and gave up golf and fishing in order to concentrate on it. Apart from reading, gardening became the dominant hobby of my life. Woods, who served for many years on the board of Bord na Móna, was something of a universal man. By profession an engineer he was also a booklover, an art collector and an expert cabinet maker. We spent many enjoyable evenings in Woods' hospitable house where he and his wife, May, kept open house.

During the Emergency years, the garden provided an adequate supply of vegetables for the family. But my interest was in flower growing and after the end of the war I grew a herbaceous border of which I was very proud. Frank Aiken once said to me, 'That border is as good as the one in the Botanic Gardens.' He was a little taken aback when I asserted that it was better. Each year, in addition to maintaining and improving the border, I specialised in one particular flower. One year was devoted to rose growing, another to sweet pea, and so on. My greatest success was with delphiniums — fully up to show standard — including every shade of blue with tall and perfect spikes. For me it is the greatest tragedy of old age that I can no longer do any effective work in my garden and I would be badly at a loss if my older grandchildren did not come to the rescue. On the other hand, one of my sons has been bitten by the garden bug and expects me to be at his disposal for advice.

Mary died in 1967 but not before she had the gratification of seeing her five children suitably married and of welcoming into the world the first four of her nineteen grandchildren. We had a good and very full life together. We got more than our share of what Ireland could offer by way of personal satisfaction. We were both on the threshold of old age and so great was the depth and span of our shared experience that Mary's loss was all the more grievous. The kindness of her family and of my family helped me over a difficult time.

Being temperamentally quite incapable of enduring the loneliness of a bachelor existence, it was fortunate for me that I was able to re-marry. I married Joyce Duffy who was the daughter of Edward Duffy, the distinguished engineer and expert on peat; he had been with me on our Russian expedition in 1935. She had been my secretary for a time in CIE and had become a friend to my family. She has helped me to write this book and gently to descend into old age.

I have lived long enough to have had the satisfaction of seeing Ireland take its place among the nations of the earth. In creating this situation, 'that large and respectable class of the community — the men of no property' did not fail Tone. My great regret is that our six northern counties are still occupied by the British but it is certain that partition cannot last. While it does, there will never be peace in all Ireland.

INDEX

323